Milton Berle

An Autobiography

MILTON

AN AUTOBIOGRAPHY

BERLE

WITH HASKEL FRANKEL

DELACORTE PRESS / NEW YORK

Grateful acknowledgment is made
for permission to use the following lyrics.
"My Yiddishe Momme":
Copyright © 1925 by DeSylva, Brown & Henderson, Inc.
Copyright renewed, assigned to Chappell & Co., Inc.
Used by permission of Chappell & Co., Inc.

"Near You"
(Kermit Goell/Francis Craig):
© 1947 Supreme Music Corp.
Reprinted with the kind permission of the publisher.
All Rights Reserved.

"Take Me to the Land of Jazz"
by Edgar Leslie, Bert Kalmar and Pete Wendling:
Copyright 1919 by Mills Music, Inc.,
Copyright renewed 1946.
Used with permission.

"The Texaco Song": By permission of Texaco Inc.

Manufactured in the United States of America
DESIGNED BY JERRY TILLETT
First printing

Library of Congress Cataloging in Publication Data

Berle, Milton.
Milton Berle, an autobiography.

1. Berle, Milton. I. Frankel, Haskel.
PN2287.B436A52   791'.092'4 [B]   74-9720

ISBN: 0-440-05609-8

To the funny men
who were, who are, who will be.

Heroes
who face the world naked
but for the weapon of laughter.

ACKNOWLEDGMENTS

A book of this size, covering so many years and events, does not happen by itself. Many kind and talented people have contributed to it with their personal memories, research materials and, most of all, their time.

A special word of thanks to Marilyn Frankel for two and one-half years of making room for the book, for listening, for reading, for valuable suggestions, and especially for excellent, painstaking research.

The authors are also extremely grateful to Lewis Rachow and the Walter Hampden Memorial Library at The Players; Paul Myers and the Library of the Performing Arts at Lincoln Center; Walter Goldstein and The Friars Club of New York; William R. Behanna and the A.C. Nielsen Company; Miles Kreuger and The Institute of the American Musical, Inc.; Sharon Sampson, Al Rush, and Bob Dunn of the National Broadcasting Company; Bernice Cohen and ASCAP.

Michael Abbott; Goodman Ace; Joey Adams; Steve Allen; Buddy Arnold; James Bacon; Eileen Barton; Ella and Harry Baum; Marian Behrman; Frank Berle; Jack Berle; Philip Berle; Ruth Berle; Bobby Berse; Jay Burton; Ruth E. Clarke; Shirley Clurman; Marian Colby; Hal Collins; Jackie and Barbara Cooper; Helene Cutler; Paul Dafelmair; Stan Davis; Fred DeCordova; William Demarest; Ralph Edwards; Carl Erbe; Billy Feeder; Danny Fisher; Stan Fisher; Hy Gardner; Barry Gray; Sandy Gray; Stanley Green; Paul Grossinger; Buddy Hackett; Mickey Hayes; Buddy Howe; Lou Jackson; Eddie Jaffe; George Jessel; Irv Kupcinet; Michael

Lipton; Irving Mansfield; Guy Martin; Seymour Mayer; Jack Melvin; Florence Mills; Gilbert Millstein; Toni and Jan Murray; Vicki Nokes; Jack Oakie; Mark Plant; Irv Raskin; Saul Richman; Norma and Ken Roberts; Hubbell Robinson; Joyce Mathews Rose; Irwin R. Rosenberg; Stan Rosenfield; Maya Schaper; Toots Shor; Alfred Simon; Louis Sobol; Jacqueline Susann; Jonie Taps; Margie Taylor; Lou Walters; Daniel Welkes; Rosalind Berle Wigderson; Earl Wilson.

And last, but far from least, Nancy Andrews, who was the start of the whole thing.

1

June 14, 1955 . . . 8:54 P.M. We had just finished the "Alabama Jubilee" finale with the entire cast and guest stars Martha Raye, Steve Allen, Joan Blondell, Johnny Desmond, Alan Dale, and Art Mooney and his orchestra. I could see little Ruthie Gilbert's eyes start to fill. Arnold Stang put an arm around her shoulder.

Out of the corner of my eye I caught the downswing of the baton, and the sign-off theme began. Christ, how I had grown to hate the song. My head must have been up my ass when I decided to use it. With five hundred songs to my credit and a solid ASCAP rating to my name, instead of writing my own sign-off I fix it so that seven years of royalties go into somebody else's pocket. Only tonight, it sounded good and terribly beautiful and very sad. I guess the arrangement and tempo were the same as always, but tonight it sounded like a funeral dirge as I went into it.

> *There's just one place for me,*
> *Near you.*
> *It's like heaven for me to be*
> *Near you.*
> *Let us make a date*
> *Next Tuesday night at eight. . . .*

Next Tuesday at eight? If I were in anybody's living room, chances were that it would be my own. It wasn't just the end of my seventh season. It was the end of everything I had worked for. All gone: the *Texaco Star*

1

Theatre, Uncle Miltie, the switch to the *Buick-Berle Show*—all of it gone, over, finished. Even Mama was gone.

The cameras were dead now. Someone threw a towel around my shoulder. I pulled it up over my head like a hood. I was soaked clean through to the skin, that nervous, flop sweat that has always been with me when I work. The last of the audience was at the studio doors. Lights were being killed. Lots of kissing and handshaking and tears. People who had hated each other's guts the entire season were hugging each other and swearing that it had all been great.

I worked my way across the snarls of wires and cables toward my dressing room. Somebody kissed me. Somebody pumped my hand and said something. I don't know if I answered. The silence was growing around me, and I felt older than God. In July, I would be forty-seven, the prime for most men, but I was feeling sorry for myself.

Television was such a young industry. New techniques were being created, new "discoveries" were being made every day. There were lots I had made when I had first gone with Texaco. And now I had another one—the discovery that the public grows tired. It can crave you, love you, worship you, then suck you dry and spit you out. I was the first to discover what others after me would find out. Over-saturation comes quick through the tube. That's one even NBC didn't know back then, or I wouldn't have been leaving with a thirty-year contract in my vault.

I had made lots of money. I was very secure, but that wasn't enough for me then—not even now. Money's great—there's nothing like it—but it runs a slow second to work for me. Thinking back, I feel like I was born to work. Work is all I can remember as far back as I can go. I hear that there are people who work certain hours every day and then put it aside and go home or go out to play. That's never been me. Work is home and wife and mother and kids and love and everything else a man needs to stay alive. It's all snarled up in one big ball. Stick two teeth in the front and you can name it Milton Berlinger. If I stop working, I die. If there's another way of life, I don't know it.

And maybe if I knew it, I wouldn't want it.

I went home and ate sandwiches in the kitchen with my wife, Ruth. She didn't even make any of her usual funnies when I asked for corned beef on white. (You want to know what a Jew's doing eating corned beef on white bread with mayonnaise, you go spend your childhood moving across the country eating in diners and hash houses and railroad lunch counters and dumps you can't even imagine, and you'll find out. Catsup is hollandaise to me, and mayonnaise is mother's milk, and dead, packaged white bread is my staff of life.)

At two in the morning I gave up trying to sleep, and went into the living room to sit out the night in my chair. I didn't turn on the lights. What for? There was nothing I wanted to see. I found one of my cigars on the end table and stuck it in my mouth.

Tomorrow there would be meetings with agents and producers about future projects. So what? Right now, I felt drained, finished, washed up, and terribly tired. I used to tell people when they asked about my life that I had worked so hard that I was tired by the time I was fourteen. But tonight I was more tired than that. Seven solid years of live television when it was really live, seven years of going seven days a week trying to make each week's show better, bigger, and funnier than the week before —and for what? To end up axed, out . . . I was really working my way down to the depths.

I reached for the lighter—Ruth kept one on every table in the house —and spun the wheel. Sparks and nothing. I spun it again. It was out of fluid. I shoved myself to my feet and started across the room to find another lighter.

I don't know why, but I happened to look over at the bookshelves, and there was the row of dark brown leather scrapbooks and, at the end, one old paper scrapbook. That was the first one, the one Mama bought when the *Bronx Home News* did a paragraph on me: "LOCAL BOY AP-PEARS WITH PEARL WHITE." In my mind, I saw us, all together again, standing around the kitchen table watching Mama cut the para-graph out of the paper and paste it on the first page of the scrapbook.

And now, both Pa and Mama were gone. Time was dividing up the Berle family the way no one else could.

I reached up and took down a scrapbook from the middle of the row —it was too dark in the room to read the years stamped on the binding —and went back to my chair. I put on the lamp and started turning the pages. It was the late 1930s, when I thought I was going to set Hollywood on fire.

There were all the crazy pictures someone took of the big costume party I threw at the Beverly Hills Hotel. There I was, my hair parted down the middle, wearing sandals and a striped union suit, pretending that I was going to dive into the pool, while all three Andrews Sisters grabbed at my seat to drag me back. And Laird Cregar in a striped robe and blond wig. Buster Keaton feeding a hot dog to Joan Davis. Marie Wilson. Carole

Landis. My God, how many of them were dead or had disappeared from the screen, those beautiful faces that all of America went to see at the movies. They were the people everybody thought they wanted to be, the people who led special lives, and who couldn't grow old or sick or suffer any of the things that the people in the audience did.

There was Judy Garland holding a beach ball and laughing.

I was going to close the scrapbook—it was too depressing—and then the name hit me. I started going through all the pictures of that party, searching for Linda, who hadn't been invited but who had come anyway.

At one time or another, I had been involved with some of the most beautiful women of my time—some of them real romances, some of them just rolls in the hay—but Linda's name never showed up on any list. God, we thought we were so smart. None of the columns carried even a hint about us.

And that's why I have ended up hurt for life. If I had known what Linda was going to do to me, instead of keeping our love secret, I would have called Hedda and Louella and Fox-Movietone News and invited them into the bedroom to watch. The scandal that would have followed would have made anything that Joyce Mathews went through later on look like an event from a church picnic by comparison.

But it would have been worth it.

You can walk the entire length of Hollywood Boulevard and read every movie name on every sidewalk square, but you won't find Linda Smith's name on any of them, even though she made several pictures, a couple of which still play late-night television. The reason is that the name's a phony. I made it up to protect someone, and unless I go out of my head completely or start babbling in a fever, I will never tell Linda Smith's real name. Not that I guess she'd care now. But there's someone else who would.

I met her at that party I tossed at the Beverly Hills Hotel. It was a costume swimming party, with everybody invited to come in silent-movie outfits. The pool garden of the Beverly Hills Hotel was filled with Keystone Kops and Wampus Baby Stars and Mack Sennett Bathing Beauties. The girls wore high stockings and bandannas and bathing slippers with their bloomer suits, and the men wore handlebar mustaches and striped suits with tops. George Raft, Cesar Romero, Linda Darnell, Robert Stack, George Montgomery, the Ritz Brothers, Virginia Grey—you name 'em, they were there. And Mama was queening it up all over the place. I was picking up the tab for the bash, but Mama was carrying on like it was her private ball. And I was running around snapping orders at waiters all over the place as if I were staging some giant Busby Berkeley number.

When I first saw Linda, she was sitting by herself in a lounge chair at one end of the pool. She wore a white bathing suit, not a costume, that showed off her tan arms and legs. She had her eyes closed and head back to catch the sun. I had seen her around town on the arm of Jed Weston, a producer who was making a big name for himself at one of the major studios.

"How about joining the party?" I said.

She opened her eyes—deep, dark brown, like her hair. It was like looking into velvet. She smiled. "I wasn't invited."

"Well, you are now."

She raised her hand to shade her eyes. "I came with Jed Weston." (I changed that name too.)

"He wasn't invited either."

She shrugged. "I hope you won't throw me out. I'm just a poor little working girl who doesn't have her own pool yet."

"Where's Jed?" I asked.

She shrugged again and waved a vague hand over toward the mob scene. "Who knows? Somewhere advancing his career."

"And leaving you alone? He's crazy." I remember thinking to myself that we were speaking dialogue that would have been thrown out of a Grade Z picture. "Can I get you anything? A drink? Something to eat?"

She squirmed deeper into the lounge chair. Just before she closed her eyes again I saw her run them down the front of my old-fashioned striped bathing suit. The front of it was beginning to feel a little tight. "I have a great appetite for everything," she said. "I'll leave it up to you. I hear around town that you're a great host."

I laughed. "I've heard around town that you're a great guest to play host to."

The reason I laughed was not because I thought I was tossing off such a great line; it was because Linda was playing Linda off the screen. Her movie roles at the time were the office-wife, other-woman types. It went with her looks, which suggested a heavy-breathing fireball caught inside the body of a girl who only half knew it all but was very willing to learn the rest. The trouble with Linda on screen was that she was a second-rate actress. It was her looks that carried her. And here she was doing the same performance poolside at the Beverly Hills Hotel. Only here, I found, it was working.

"So now we've got a lot settled," she said, and stretched her head to catch the sun. "And I wouldn't be surprised if Jed came back at any minute."

"Is Jed always around?"

"No."

"Like when no?"

"Like tomorrow night, say around nine." She gave me the address of her apartment building, on Fountain Avenue.

She gave herself completely to the sun, and I walked away. When I looked back at her a few minutes later, Jed was with her. He was wearing a sport jacket and slacks, the standard Hollywood uniform, even at costume parties, for the movie executive too busy for nonsense. I don't think Jed was more than thirty-eight at the time, but he looked older. His hair was gone on top, and he had that thin, pasty look that seemed to go with high-powered ulcers. Jed had pulled his lounge chair close to Linda's and was hunched on the side of it, talking seriously to her. Linda was still paying attention to the sun, but occasionally she would nod her head.

Sometimes you know, even before you start, that you've met a woman who is going to be something major in your life. I felt it about Linda. I felt it all day on the set of *New Faces of 1937*. I was all business when the cameras were rolling, but the minute I had a break, Linda would pop into my head. In the afternoon I started watching the clock. In six hours, I would be at her apartment. In five hours; in four and a half . . .

I can remember exactly what I wore that night: dark gray flannel slacks and a blue blazer. I chose an open sport shirt and a neck scarf to go with it. The impression I wanted to make was "dashing movie star," whatever the hell I thought that was then, but I didn't want to look as if I had any plans to take her out that evening. My plans were to stay home.

When I came out of the bedroom, Mama was setting up a card table. "Game tonight?" I asked.

She nodded. "Where are you going?"

"I've got a date."

"That Wendy Barrie again?"

"I told you that was over, Mama."

"So then who?"

I grabbed my polo coat out of the closet. "Mama, I'm almost thirty. Do I have to ask permission to go out?"

Mama turned her back to me and got busy taking the cards out of the box. "What do I care? If it's *someone,* I'll see it in the columns tomorrow anyway."

I slammed out of the door.

I was at Linda's apartment house at two minutes after nine—I didn't want to look eager. I parked down the block from her building, just in case Jed Weston had a serious claim on Linda and was curious about why she couldn't see him tonight. He wasn't a producer at RKO, where I was working, but he was a pretty big producer in town, so why go out of your way for trouble?

Linda's building was a second-rate apartment house, but I was pretty sure she had plans for leaving it soon for something better. She buzzed back, and I took the stairs up to the second-floor rear. She was waiting for me in the doorway in something pink that made her look more like brown velvet. I was glad to see that she didn't look like she expected to go out.

She stepped aside as I came in. I took a quick look around. The pictures on the wall were all cheap prints, the furniture was ordinary. "This is all very temporary," she said, "and none of it's going to move with me."

There was a radio playing somewhere, soft lights, and a bar shelf with glasses and ice. Fine. It meant that what had started yesterday was still on for tonight.

"Want a drink?" she said from the bar.

"I don't drink."

She fixed a highball for herself and then sat down on the sofa. I sat down beside her. Linda took a long swallow from her glass. I put my arm around the back of the couch, behind her shoulders, the standard opening move. Linda pretended not to notice, which was also a standard move. "How's the picture going?" she said.

I let my hand touch her shoulder. "You really want to hear about that?"

She leaned forward, which got rid of my hand (also a standard move), to pick up her glass from the coffee table. "Sure I want to hear. I didn't leave Nebraska to talk about crops." She emptied her glass and got up to fill it again.

I watched her walking away from me. The movement was sensational. In my mind, I was already undressing her.

Linda made herself another stiff drink, but instead of coming back to the couch, she turned at the bar and said, "I wish you'd drink something. I don't know why, but I wish you would."

I patted the couch beside me. "And I wish you'd come back here."

She took a swallow. "So tell me about your picture."

Something was going wrong, but for the life of me I couldn't figure out what. It had been all right when I came in, with everything—including Linda—set up for what we had set up. So what was turning it sour? I decided to ignore it. "Instead of the picture, I'd rather talk about you and Jed Weston."

"What do you want to know?"

"Is Jed important to you?"

She gave a dry little laugh. "Sure. Jed's important in this industry, so Jed's important to me."

"Are you sleeping with him?"

"That's none of your business!" She turned her back to me and finished her drink.

I went over to her and put my arms around her. "What's going on here?" I asked. I could feel her trembling. "Linda?"

I turned her around, and there were tears running down her face. "Hey! What is it, what's wrong? Tell me."

"Oh, Christ!" she said, and buried her head on my shoulder, sobbing.

I get panicky around crying women. I never know what to do or say. "What is it? What? Linda?"

I led her over to the couch and sat her down with me. She stayed on my shoulder, still crying. I couldn't think of anything to say, so I waited for it to end.

Finally, she stopped. "I'm sorry, Milton, forgive me."

"Will you tell me what's going on? Is it what I asked about you and Jed Weston?"

"I must look like hell. Let me fix my face. Will you make me another drink?"

She went into the bedroom, and I went to the bar. The bedroom door was open, so I could hear when she called to me: "About Jed. Yes, I've gone to bed with him, but it doesn't mean much with us that way. Half the time he's impotent. I don't know if it's me or his business problems or what. Anyway, so now you know. Okay?"

Except for being red around the eyes, she looked as good as ever when she came out. I handed her her drink, and we sat down again. She looked at the glass, not at me. "I suppose I owe you an explanation," she said.

"Well . . ." I didn't finish it. Frankly, I was beginning to think she was a crazy. Hollywood has always been full of them.

"You didn't do anything wrong, Milton," Linda said. "It's me. I suddenly felt cheap, that's all." And that led to her life story. About what it was like to be on a Midwestern farm during the Depression, and how Linda had left for Hollywood. "I figured if I was getting grabbed in barns all over Nebraska, maybe I had something that would pay off in Hollywood. So here I am, with a couple of B movies under my belt but nothing really going for me, unless Jed Weston is the big payoff."

"Do you love him?"

Linda swirled her ice cubes. "I like him. Out here, you get so mixed up, you can't be sure you'd know what love is. It's really lousy for a woman. Half the men in this town expect you to be a whore if you want to get anywhere in pictures, and if you do screw, they treat you like a whore and that's the end of it."

I suddenly felt like a heel. I started to apologize, but Linda said, "Don't, Milton. You don't have to. I was on the make for you yesterday, the same as you were for me. You're a star, so I thought if I gave you a little something, you might be able to do something for me over at RKO. Only it turned out that in some crazy, mixed-up way of thinking, sleeping with one guy is romantic to me, maybe love. I guess that's how I explain Jed. But two guys makes you a whore. I probably am one already without knowing it—"

This time, I stopped her. "Why don't you get a coat, Linda, and we'll take a drive somewhere and stop for hamburgers?"

Her eyes filled up with tears again, but she took my face in her hands and kissed me on the mouth. "You're the greatest, Milton."

So we took a long drive to Malibu and stopped for hamburgers and malteds. We parked where we could see the ocean. And we necked like kids. Then I took Linda back to her apartment.

I kissed her good night in the doorway. But she didn't let go. "I want you to come in," she said.

I tried to untangle her arms from around my neck. "Come on, Linda, I'm only human."

She giggled. "I know you are." She pressed closer against me. "I want you to come in."

I looked into those deep brown eyes. "How come?"

She put her head on my shoulder. "I think because you bought me a hamburger, and you talked to me. I don't feel like just another Hollywood piece anymore. I feel like a girl from Nebraska again, who's out with her guy, and she's decided to go all the way with him because she wants to." She snuggled in closer. "God, isn't that corny? Go all the way! I haven't thought of that expression since I left home."

She was still in my arms as we moved through the door and across the living room, into the bedroom. "Don't turn on the lights," she whispered.

There was just a little light from the street outside. I could only just make out shapes as Linda led me over to the bed. She wasn't the wise, tough babe I'd met yesterday at the Beverly Hills Hotel pool. She seemed shy and soft and easy to hurt as she undressed with her back to me. Even in what little light there was, I could see her body, and it was fantastic.

Like a schoolgirl, she jumped into bed and pulled the covers up around her neck while she wriggled out of her panties. Maybe this will sound hokey to you, but it all became sort of special to me too. After all, what the hell did I ever know then about love or romance? My past was mostly easy sex, with sometimes some colored lights that made things look better than they really were. But with Linda suddenly caught up in some special dream of hers, I found it easy for me to go along with it. I guess maybe I was beginning to want some of the things I had missed. And for a minute the sight of Linda, looking wide-eyed, her head just sticking out over the covers, made me feel as excited as a green kid. This wasn't the usual take-it-out, stick-it-in routine I had known before. It was as if Linda hadn't known Jed Weston or anyone else before me, and there hadn't been any of the nameless pushovers before Linda for me.

As soon as I was under the covers and touching Linda, that *Reader's Digest* dream went right out the window. Miss Hometown USA turned into a tiger. She went wild with her hands, with her mouth, with every part of her.

Later, stretched out flat on my back, trying to get my breathing back to normal, it crossed my mind that there had to have been more men than Jed Weston in her life. More men? At least a regiment for her to have learned to be so terrific. But it didn't bother me. Not then. As we lay there, not talking, just holding hands and listening to each other breathe, I was damned glad for whatever had happened to Linda before me.

I turned and looked at her, that deep brown hair spread out on the pillow next to me. I leaned over and kissed her. "Honey, I think maybe you and I have something important going."

She smiled and started to turn to me, but the telephone rang. She picked it up. Her voice became warm, just like when she had said to me, "I want you to come in."

I listened to her purring into the phone. "No, no, it's quite all right, Jed. I only went to bed a little while ago. I wasn't really asleep . . . No, I was here all evening. I just had the phone shut off. Oh, you know, don't you ever need to be all by yourself sometimes? . . . I miss you too . . . All right, tomorrow at seven . . . Me too. 'Bye."

She hung up, then curled in against me. "I'm sorry, what could I do?" She whispered it into my ear, but all I felt was the tickling sensation. The rest of me had turned to ice.

Linda waited, but I couldn't think of anything to say. "Well, honestly, what could I do? For Chrissake, you knew about Jed and me before. Things don't come to an end that quickly, you know." When I still didn't say anything, she added, "And other things don't begin that quickly, either."

"I think we've begun already," I said.

Linda sat up and turned on a lamp. She reached for her cigarettes without bother about covering her breasts. She wasn't Nebraska anymore. She took a deep drag on her cigarette and shoved back against the pink satin headboard. "Maybe we have, maybe we haven't. A guy can say anything when he's in bed, but the next day is something else. We'll have to wait and see about us."

So I sat up too, and got a cigar. We must have looked crazy, two people naked to the waist and puffing away, talking without looking at each other. I said, "I like you. I really do."

Linda didn't move.

"What about you? What do you feel?"

She took her cigarette and jammed it into the ashtray as if she were killing something. Then she turned on me, furious. "What are you up to, Milton? What are you after? Do you really give a crap about what I feel? Do you? Aren't you just another movie-town stud trying to get the girl he just screwed to say he's the greatest? If that's what you want, okay! You're better than every assistant cameraman, better than every director, better than every front-office flunky who promised to help my career in return for a one-night stand!"

She was beginning to sound hysterical. I reached out for her—"Hey, Linda honey, hey, wait a minute"—but she pulled away.

Her face was red, and the tears were running. "Is there anything more you want me to say before you leave the money on the dresser and run? All right, so you've got the biggest—"

I slapped her across the face. She collapsed in sobs that shook the bed. She didn't stop me this time when I took her in my arms. "Linda, Linda, Linda," I kept saying, over and over again, until she calmed down. "Tell me what it is. What did I say so wrong?"

When she could control herself, Linda got out of bed and put on a robe. She just stood beside the bed with her back to me, her head hanging down. "I'm sorry," she said. "I'm so sorry, Milton. I guess for a minute you sounded like a lot of guys I've known. And I'm so tired of feeling like a piece of shit about myself."

"Look," I said, and I crawled across the bed to get to her. I grabbed a blanket along the way and pulled it around myself. "I probably spoke too soon. You're probably right about that, but what I said now I meant. I really did, Linda. And I really wanted to know if you felt anything for me at all."

Linda turned to me and touched my face. "Wouldn't you know I'd turn on you? You're probably the one really nice guy I ever met."

I tried to take her hand, but she pulled away. "Maybe you don't drink, Milton, but I could use one, bad. Come on in the living room."

She fixed herself a stiff Scotch and then leaned against the bar and looked at me. "What do I feel? That's a great question, and the answer is, I really don't know. Love, home, babies, I don't know. Say any of those words to me, and you want to know what I see? I'll give it to you straight, Milton. I see my mother fucked to death by my father. Eight kids is what she left behind. Eight kids and a clean house, and dead at thirty-one. That's what love is to me. And my father making more babies with another woman six months after my mother died."

"It doesn't have to be that way," I said.

Linda shrugged. "Maybe not. So far, I wouldn't know. 'Cause love out here isn't even as much as my mother had. Here, it's strictly something you do on your back for a couple of days of work in a picture. If there's a guy around who likes me with my clothes on, I haven't met him. He must work at some studio I haven't been to."

"Maybe he's not in any studio," I said. "Or does he have to be?"

Linda smiled in a tired way and brushed the hair away from her face. "That's his problem. But I'm going to make it out here, and I plan to make it big, big as I can. And when that next Depression comes along, Linda's going to be sitting so high up on her money pile, she won't even be able to see it. And maybe, just for laughs, I'll pick up the phone and have the studio send me out a boy starlet whenever I feel in the mood. Hell, if he's any good I'll get him a couple of days on my next picture. How's that for a switch?"

I looked at my watch. It was getting late. I got up and went over to Linda and took the glass out of her hand. "I don't believe you," I said. "You know what I think? I think you're scared stiff."

We kissed for a long time. Then Linda said, "I am scared. And I'm lonely, too. I'm scared of me, Milton. Sometimes I don't sound like me anymore."

I kissed her again. "I've got to go," I said. "Work tomorrow."

There was nothing tough about Linda now. She took my face in her hands and stared at me. "Will I see you again? Tell me the truth."

"I promise. I'll call you tomorrow from the set. If I can't, I'll call you as soon as I get home."

Linda nodded. "You know Jed will be here tomorrow night. You heard on the phone. Please understand. I can't just throw him out. Not yet. Sometimes he says he loves me."

"I'll call. I promise."

Linda followed me back to the bedroom and watched in silence while I got dressed. At the front door, after we had kissed good night, she said, "I do like you, Milton."

I turned in the hall. Linda said, "Try to forget tonight. I'm really not that way. Honest."

"I don't remember a thing."

But I remembered everything the next day. I think that was what made me put off calling Linda. There were plenty of breaks during the day's shooting when I could have picked up the telephone, but I didn't. I waited until after seven, when I knew Jed would be there. Linda sounded cautious when she answered. "Oh, Mr. Berle, what a surprise. It's I who should be calling you to thank you for letting us crash your party."

I said, "I know he's there. And I'm sorry I couldn't get to a phone all day. But I'm keeping my promise, and I want to see you."

Linda laughed, "Yes, we must," and I heard her turn to Jed and say, "Mr. Berle says we must all get together again soon."

"Does he stay the whole night?"

"No."

"Then I'll call you very early before I leave for the studio tomorrow."

"Nice talking to you too, Mr. Berle. And give our regards to your mother."

To have an affair nowadays in Hollywood is no big deal. Attitudes have changed, and besides, the world is not that interested in what goes on with what they call movie stars today. But in the late '30s it was something else. The most sizzling affairs (which were called romances then, no matter what was going on) were the whole world's business. Every move was reported.

It made it rough on Linda and me. We found it almost impossible to go out together. In those days there were gossip columnists hiding under the tables in diners, and kids who would phone them while working the pumps in gas stations. It's not that we didn't want publicity, but one mention of us together and it would have caused trouble for Linda with Jed. And don't forget my mother, who knew I was involved somewhere and was dying to get a line on the girl.

"What is she?" Mama asked me one day. "Is she someone so terrible you're ashamed for me to know her name?"

"Leave things the way they are, Mama."

Something was happening inside of me. Maybe it was that I had my thirtieth birthday coming up, or maybe it was that Linda mattered to me more than any woman had before, but I felt flashes of an anger at my mother that I had never let myself feel before. Suddenly, I was strangling on the silver cord that was between us. Maybe I owed Mama my life, but I was finding it harder and harder to *give* her my life.

I thought I knew my mother's every expression, but suddenly she was looking at me with a new one: hurt and confusion. "I don't understand, Milton. Secrets between you and me all of a sudden? Why? Just tell me, why?"

"You know why. You've been against every woman I've ever been involved with. You don't ever want me to get married, and you know it!"

Her hand went to her breast—Mama's favorite gesture. "Did I ever say I didn't want you to get married? Did I even once? Admit it."

"Come on, Mama!"

She shook her head. "The most I've ever said is that you've got time. Maybe I didn't like every girl, but I never said you shouldn't get married."

"Time!" Now I was furious. "In a few weeks I'm going to be thirty. Thirty! And I'm still reporting in to my mother!"

Sometimes Mama could look small and fragile. It was never out in

public. There she was a tower of strength and dignity. It happened only
when we were alone and I was going into a screaming rage that I hated
in myself but couldn't stop. Did Mama shrink herself, or was it my guilt
at what I was doing that made me see her that way?

"Milton," she said, with a sad note creeping into her voice, "don't tell
me anything ever if that's what you want. But sharing with your own
mother is not reporting. Share with me. That's all I ever asked. That's my
pleasure, my only pleasure. The hard work we did together is done now.
Let me share the cream with you."

I turned away from her. The anger was still inside, boiling away, but
now guilt was racing through me like ice water to freeze up my guts. I
just stood there, not speaking, not moving, and Mama waited quietly
behind me.

It all drained out of me, and I felt weak. "Her name is Linda Smith.
She was at the party at the Beverly Hills Hotel."

Mama thought about it. "Dark-haired? She was in_____?" Mama
named one of Linda's pictures.

"That's right."

"She's very pretty. But I thought she's Jed Weston's woman?"

"What does that mean?" I was angry again.

Mama looked surprised. "How should I know? I just saw something
about them in one of the trades. A preview, maybe a party, I don't
remember."

"Well, she's not Jed Weston's 'woman.' She dates Jed, she dates me.
Where's the crime in that? It's a free country, Mama."

Mama shrugged. "I guess so," she said sadly.

Before I could pick up on that, Mama looked at the diamond-banded
watch I had given her. "Anyway, isn't it time for your appointment?"

That ended that round.

The appointment was with the radio department of William Morris,
my agents then. *New Faces of 1937* was already in the can, and I didn't
have any illusions that it was going to make me the idol of the nation.
And the talk about my next one, *Radio City Revels,* wasn't sending me
off to my local Rolls-Royce dealer either. But what William Morris had
lined up for me sounded very exciting, a real chance to get back to radio
and make it very big.

The Buchanan Agency was handling a radio show—get this—called the *Texaco Star Theatre*. This wasn't the one on which Ed Wynn played the Fire Chief, but a live, one-hour star-studded extravaganza. If I remember right, for their opening show they had Eddie Cantor, Bette Davis, Paul Muni, Humphrey Bogart, and Ethel Barrymore signed to appear, and Jimmy Wallington for the announcer. Nobody knew exactly where I would fit in, but could I get down to CBS and do anywhere from five to fifteen minutes to warm up the studio audience, get them in a good frame of mind, and blend right into the first show's opening? A happy audience would help the stars, who were all on edge over this first show. It sounded like a great chance to show what I could do.

My warm-up went over perfectly. I was watching the show from a soundproof booth when my agent came in, beaming. He grabbed my hand and pumped it. "You're in! The sponsor, the agency, they loved you. I tell you, Milton, you're in!"

I came home that night riding high. I found Mama packing. "It's Pa. He had a heart attack."

I remember my very first thought: How could I be doing a show and having a great time while my father was having a heart attack and maybe dying? What kind of son was I?

That kind of thinking makes no sense, and I know it. But it's still part of me. Where it came from, I don't know to this day, but my life runs on guilt and adrenalin.

"I'll pack a suitcase," I said.

Mama shook her head. "Your sister Rosalind called me, and I spoke to her husband. Charles is with him, so he's in good hands. Pa's going to be all right. Your place is here, my place is there."

More guilt. As soon as I knew Pa was going to be okay, I thought of Linda. With Mama away, I could have her over to my place.

Three days later, the William Morris office heard from the Buchanan Agency. They wanted to meet with me and talk about the *Texaco Star Theatre*. I was in!

The next afternoon, my agent and I met with the account executive at Buchanan. The client loved me and definitely wanted me for the entire run of the show. I was wild inside! For about twenty seconds. They wanted to sign me for thirty-nine warm-ups!

That night, Linda came to my place for the first time. "Isn't this crazy?" she said as she pulled off the scarf that covered her hair and the big sunglasses that hid her eyes. "The way you have to sneak around in this town. I feel as if I were smuggling plans for a battleship or something."

She threw herself into my arms. We kissed, but I wasn't in the mood to put much into it. "What's the matter with you?" she asked.

So I told her about my big offer *not* to appear on radio. "Oh, Christ!" she said. "I thought we were going to celebrate your good news and mine."

"Forget mine. What's yours?"

"I got the part at Twentieth! Remember that test Jed got me over there last month? Well, they want me!"

It was a lead, and it was a comedy, and it was scheduled for a big budget, not a B feature. For once, Linda would be doing something more on the screen than threatening somebody else's marriage, which she didn't do very well. Linda had big hopes that this would be a turning point in her career. She was right. The picture made her a star.

Between her big up and my big down, our first evening in my bed wasn't too great. There came the moment when we stopped trying and just lay back. "Linda?" I asked, after a while.

"Huh?"

"What's this picture mean for us?"

"I don't follow you."

"You know. You and Jed?"

She took my hand. "Milton, please let's not start that again. This is my big chance, and Jed got it for me. What do you expect?"

There was a long silence, and then Linda said, "He asked me to marry him."

"What did you say?" I was afraid of the answer.

"I didn't say."

"What are you going to say?"

"I'm not going to think about it unless I have to." She sat up and reached for her cigarettes. "Anyway, what's it to you, Milton? Really, I mean. I haven't heard you asking me to marry you."

Now I sat up. "Is that what you want?"

It was ground we had gone over many times before. Linda sounded tired as she said, "What I want is to make this picture, and to make a bigger one after it, and a bigger one after that. If I want to marry you or Jed, I don't know. And right now I don't want to know. And neither do you, Milton, let's stop kidding ourselves. We both want exactly what we've got, and we think we have to talk about marriage or we'll lose it. Am I right?"

"Maybe."

"You know," Linda said quietly, "I don't remember you bringing me around to meet your mother."

A cigar is a great thing when you don't want to speak. It takes longer to light than a cigarette.

Linda broke the silence. "So, say something. What happens next with us?"

I slipped an arm around her. "We go on," I said. "We make pictures and we make love. And that's us for now."

Only "now" exploded in our faces two months later.

The time between the end of *New Faces* and the beginning of *Radio City Revels* meant a chance to get back to New York and see Pa, who was recovering from his heart attack. When I returned to Hollywood, I went straight into *Radio City Revels*. With both Linda and me tied up on pictures, we saw less of each other. Early studio calls and learning lines the night before got in our way. And with Linda's face becoming well-known—the publicity men on her picture were grinding out stories about her daily—we had to be twice as careful about getting to each other. Now, when she came to my place, she usually wore a blond wig with her sunglasses.

The first night we were together after I got back—it was at her place —she was hitting the Scotch pretty heavily. "You'd better lay off that stuff," I said. "It does things to the face, and the camera catches it."

"I know, I know," Linda said, "they've already told me that a hundred times." But she continued drinking.

She asked about my father, about New York, about my picture, but she didn't seem to hear the answers. "What's wrong?" I asked.

"I don't know," Linda said, "but sometimes I think being nobody was better. God knows it was easier. Somebody is always after me now, every minute, for something. A story, a picture, a supermarket opening, a handout. Christ, where's the fun that's supposed to come with being a movie star?"

I lit one of my cigars. "Who said it's fun? It's work, and it's fun if you like the work. Anyway, you're not there yet."

"Yeah? The word is I'm a cinch. Jed's seen some of the rushes, and he says they're good. And the studio thinks so, too. They're starting to talk money contracts with my agents. Even if this picture flops, I expect to be all expensively signed up before anyone gets the first whiff of it."

Linda came over to me and sat down. "Rub the back of my neck, will you, honey? It's like there's a log jammed in there."

I started rubbing. Linda purred, "Oh God, that's good."

I kept massaging the back of her neck with one hand. I slid the other one around in front, against her breasts.

Linda said, "Have you heard about Jed?"

It wasn't the reaction I had expected. "What?"

"The word is that he's going to be made head of his studio."

"Well, what's that got to do with us? Or does it?" I didn't take my hand off her breasts, but whatever special feeling I'd been getting was gone.

"Nothing, I guess," Linda said. She leaned back against me, and I stopped rubbing her neck. "Just that Jed is going to be a very powerful man out here. A real power."

"Good for him," I said. "If you're going to be a movie star, that comes with some power too."

Linda untangled herself from my hands and stood up. "Movie stars are shit to studio heads, the way I hear it. They make them and they break them." She grabbed my hand to pull me to my feet. "Tomorrow's an early day. Why don't we take a quick look and see what's going on in the bedroom?"

Two days later, the papers were full of Jed Weston. He had got the job. Two weeks later, Mama came back. Three days later, everything hit the fan.

I had a day off from shooting on *Radio City Revels*, and I wanted to sleep late. All I had planned was an afternoon at the bookie joint on Hollywood Boulevard that had become a second home to me. By the way, if you ever want to know what it feels like to be a movie star, be a big-money loser with a bookmaker. You'll get the full star treatment as long as you can cover your losses.

I was asleep when Mama came into my room and woke me. "The telephone, Milton."

I hated being awakened early. "What time is it?"

"Almost ten o'clock."

"I'll call back."

"It's that woman, Linda Smith."

That woke me up. Linda had never called me when she knew Mama was around. I sat up in bed and reached for the phone. My mother just stood there. "I'll take it in here, Mama," I said, and waited until she'd left the room. "Hello."

"No names," she said. "I'm calling from my bungalow on the lot."

I hadn't heard Mama hang up in the other room, so I said, "I understand, but I'm sure no one would listen in!"

Mama got the message. There was a click. "Okay," I said, "what's the matter?"

"I want to see you tonight. It's important."

"What is it?"

"Not on the phone. Tonight at my place. Nine okay?"

"Okay."

She clicked off.

Now what the hell was biting her, I wondered. That was one of the troubles with Linda—maybe with all of us who are unsure of ourselves inside—anything could set her off, from a hangnail to a hangover.

When I got to her place that night, Linda was drunk and doing her best to get drunker. "Oh for God's sake, Linda . . ."

She just laughed at me. "In the immortal words of one of the songs out of your past, Milton honey, I got a right to sing the blues. And so have you."

"What are you talking about?"

Linda waved her glass at me. "If you're ever going to drink, Milton, this would be a helluva good time for you to start. Anyway, you better sit down."

I took a seat and a cigar. "Shoot."

Linda nodded. "Okay. Like they say in the movies, I'm going to have a baby. I thought you should be the first to know, because it's yours."

I felt as if I had been whacked between the eyes. I couldn't think straight. Maybe that's why I said, "How do you know it's not Jed's?"

"You son of a bitch," Linda said, but she didn't sound too angry. "Because I missed my period, and I saw a doctor yesterday. Jed hasn't made it with me in a month. He's tried, but it seems that studio heads don't have hard-ons. Too much on their minds and not enough anyplace else, something like that."

Linda raised her half-empty glass. "So here's to Linda, the knocked-up movie star, having a quiet little drink with the proud daddy! Send that exclusive to Winchell." She emptied her glass in one swallow, and suddenly she crumpled up beside me, sobbing against my chest. "Oh God, Milton, I'm scared."

So we talked about what we should do. I mentioned marriage, more because I thought I was supposed to than anything else, but inside I felt trapped by the idea of a wife and a child all at once. And Linda said she didn't want that either, not yet. She was just starting to get where she wanted to be, and she didn't think the wife-mother image would help her career. So we talked about abortion, and we made a date for two weekends ahead. I'd charter a private plane and we'd fly down to Mexico on Friday night, when our sets would be closed down for the weekend. The abortion could be done on Saturday morning, and we'd both be back in plenty of time for Monday. Linda would phone in sick if she didn't think she could get through her day on the lot. With the buildup her studio was giving her, they might be sore but they'd have to accept her illness and shoot around her for a couple of days.

Up until that point, I had never set up an abortion, but I knew I would have no trouble finding out who and where. There was enough traffic in those days between Hollywood and the Mexican abortion mills to have made a fortune for an airline shuttle service.

I planned to leave straight from the studio to the airport on Friday night, so I packed on Thursday night. My mother came into my room while I was packing. I told her I was going away for the weekend. She asked where.

"Tijuana."

"By yourself?"

"No."

Mama looked hurt. "I've never been to Mexico."

I don't know why I told her, but I did. I think it was because I felt bad enough about what Linda and I were doing without also hurting Mama. I lived and worked in a world where people had abortions without suffering too much over it, but I didn't come from such a world. I was doing it, but inside I didn't approve of it.

But I expected Mama to. I knew she didn't like Linda, and I knew she didn't want me to get married yet, if ever. Mama was a realist—maybe not about herself in terms of me, because she seemed to have some picture of the two of us going on together forever with just Mama being enough for me—but she was realistic about everything else. So it was okay to tell her. Mama would understand and approve.

Mama looked stunned. "Who wants this . . ."—she couldn't seem to say the word—"this operation?"

"What do you mean? Linda and I talked it over. We both want it."

Mama couldn't seem to understand. "She wants to kill her baby?"

"Aw, come on, Mama, don't be so dramatic. It's not a baby yet. It's not anything, really."

"And you, you'd let her? You'd help her kill your child? Your flesh?"

"Mama, what are you saying?"

Suddenly, Mama moved. Before I had realized what she was going to do, she slapped me with all her might across the side of the head. I fell against the bed. "Murderer!" she screamed at me. "What kind of man are you?"

I grabbed her arms and pinned them to her side before she could hit again. "Mama! Please! Stop it!"

We stood that way, locked together, staring into each other's faces like strangers, both of us breathing hard.

When she could speak, Mama said, "You've got to marry her. It's the only thing."

"What are you saying? You don't even like Linda."

"I hate her like poison, but there's life in her, Milton. Do you hate that life? What kind of person are you, Milton? Take, push, fight, grab —anything, but not kill!"

I let go of Mama, and she backed away from me to a chair. "I don't know if Linda would marry me."

Mama nodded. "Then you didn't ask her!"

"Well, we sort of spoke about it—"

"That's not enough. You go to her, you ask, you beg. Anything, but you marry the mother of your child. You hear me?"

We went on that way for another half-hour. Of course, Mama won. She made me feel like the schmuck of the world, and I agreed to do what she wanted. She even made me think that was what I wanted.

I telephoned Linda's apartment, and got her. I was surprised at how easily she agreed to cancel our trip. Later, I knew why.

Mama was pleased again. "Now, go to her. And convince her!"

I was at the door when I said, "You know, I don't really think I love her, Mama."

"So what?" Mama said. "You're doing this for the sake of your child. Later we can divorce that tramp!"

When I got to her apartment, Linda was waiting for me in a housecoat. "I've got to talk to you, Linda."

"Sure," she said, "come on in."

She had a drink in her hand, as usual. When I think about Linda today, I see her as a woman with one hand with fingers on it and the other arm ending in a wrist attached to a highball glass.

"So what's up?" she said, making herself comfortable.

I just blurted it out. "I've been thinking about it, and I don't want the abortion."

Linda nodded. "Fine. I've decided neither do I."

I felt like a two-ton weight had dropped away. It was going to be that easy. "I think we should get married and have the baby."

Linda said, "That's funny, because I also decided I should get married and have the baby."

I reached for her hand, but she pulled it away. I still didn't see what was happening. "You name the day for us. I guess it should be a justice of the peace because of the religious differences—"

Linda interrupted. "Hold it, Milton. I said that I should get married, but I didn't say that it should be to you."

That stopped me. "What the hell do you mean? Of course to me. It's my baby. You said so."

Linda took a swallow of her booze. "But that's going to have to be our little secret for ever and ever, Milton. I'm going to marry Jed."

"What the hell are you talking about? It's my baby."

Linda nodded. "But I can convince Jed it's his. You don't love me, Milton, so what the hell? And I've decided the head of a studio is a good husband for an actress."

I was beginning to come out of shock. "You'll never do it. You told me he couldn't even get it up."

"Couldn't lately," Linda said. She was calm through the whole thing. "But that doesn't mean can't. I didn't care one way or the other when he couldn't, because I had you, so I didn't try too hard to help him. But I will now, and I imagine I can restore the old magic. At least for one night, and that will be enough. I told you Jed said he loved me, and he had asked me to marry him."

"You can't do this to me! It's my kid!"

Linda tried to take my hand, but I pulled away as if from a snake. "I'm truly sorry, Milton, but I've done it to you. No one's ever known about you and me. Jed will believe me, not you, if you want to tell him. And there's no one else to tell, unless you want a big scandal. I might come out of that looking like a slut, but just think what you'd look like." My head was spinning so that I couldn't seem to think straight. I couldn't make sense out of what Linda was saying. It was like some insane movie plot that couldn't happen in real life.

Linda didn't give me time to think. "And one more thing, Milton. If you make a stink, just remember that whatever you do to you and me, we'll survive somehow. But what about your baby? It will grow up with a scandal hung around its neck that it will never get free of. Think about that."

It was the kayo punch. I got to my feet feeling dizzy. "Look," I said, "let's not make any decisions tonight. Let's give it a day or two. I'll call you and we'll get together and talk about it again."

Linda stood up and went to the door. She shook her head. "No, Milton, we're not going to see each other again. There's no reason for me to take any more chances. I've got what I want now."

She closed the door behind me, and I heard the lock twist. I spent at least two hours in my car, which was parked in a gas station that had closed for the night. I tried to think it all through, and I couldn't make myself make any sense to myself. At first I hadn't wanted the baby; now I was ripping my guts apart because I wasn't going to have my baby. What the hell did I want? What did I really feel inside for Linda, for the kid, for anything or anyone? The next thing I knew, I was doubled up and crying so hard that I couldn't stop. And I wasn't even sure what I was really crying about. But I think it was me.

I called Linda at her apartment two nights later and told her I wanted to see her. "There's nothing to talk about," she said.

"I think there's plenty to talk about."

I could hear ice cubes in a glass, but she didn't sound drunk. "Milton, I said it all the last time. And that's it. I don't want you to call anymore. I don't believe in prolonging pain."

"Look, I don't want to go into this on the phone. But there's more than just you and me to talk about now."

There was a pause; then Linda said, and her voice was hard, "We also talked about Tijuana once, so don't start coating this thing with schmaltz,

Milton. Be the good gambler you're supposed to be and take your loss."

There was a click, and the line was dead.

I called again, and as soon as she heard my voice she hung up. When I called the next night, I was told that the number was changed and the new phone number for that party was unlisted.

Two weeks later I got the announcement, a cream-colored card under a leaf of tissue paper. It said that Linda and Jed had gotten married in Palm Springs. I showed the card to Mama. She read it and said, "Oh, that's good news . . . And they should both drop dead in the desert!"

The scrapbook was still open on my lap. My cigar was still not lighted. Ruth called from the bedroom, "Are you ever coming back to bed, Milton?"

"Soon," I said.

I began turning the pages of the scrapbook again, searching the corners of pictures, looking for Linda stretched out in a lounge chair. Then I turned one more page, and there was Mama in a portrait by Bruno of Hollywood. Only my mother would have gone to Bruno of Hollywood. His specialty was the bleached blonds pouting sexily over one naked shoulder while clutching a fur stole over their best points.

I stared at Mama's face, with the little wire-rimmed glasses and the crown of silver curls all tight in place, as if I had never seen it before. The strength that was there, the strong chin—I guess it made her look fierce to people who didn't know her, but I could see a million soft memories in that face.

A million memories of Mama and me were coming back. I started to smile. I somehow heard her laughing, that wild, crazy mounting giggle she had created and used for years to build a laugh for me. ("Don't laugh, lady, you may have children of your own some day!") It began like running water coming down a mountain stream, just flowing easy, then bouncing higher and higher as it gained momentum, until it was out of hand and breathless, carrying an audience along with it. I heard it, I guess, from inside my mind, and suddenly I was laughing along with my mother.

Crazy! In the middle of the night in a half-dark New York apartment, I'm laughing my head off with Mama across time and space, across all the years, the people, the places we shared together from way, way back when . . .

2

The beginning of Milton Berle happened long before I was born, even before Sarah Glantz met Moses Berlinger. She was a tall woman, five foot eight and statuesque, which was the popular shape of the day. With her figure and her height, and the auburn hair she had as a young girl, men would turn and look at her on the street. Mama liked the attention. In fact, she loved the limelight. Later, when she was married and had her five children, sometimes, on one of those rare nights when the whole family was together, she would talk about the past, and she would always recall the night she was taken to the ball at the Manhattan Casino in New York City. Her hair was piled high on her head and she wore a rose-colored gown, and she was asked to lead the Grand March. Head high, her back straight and proud, the corsage of pink roses her beau had given her pinned to the shoulder of her gown, she stepped out across the floor to the waltz, "The Band Played On." What the line of couples behind her looked like, Mama never knew. She was too caught up in the private excitement of her moment in the spotlight as she circled the entire floor, one gloved hand resting on her escort's arm, every eye at the tables focused on her alone. At that moment, my mother felt the pull of show business, and it was an excitement that never let go of her.

Being the properly raised daughter of a proper mother and father, the life of an actress on the wicked stage was out of the question for her, but the longing for the limelight, the fascination of applause stayed with her for life. If it had to smolder underground for a while, it exploded with me.

And I think the explosion took place on Halloween when I was five years old.

We lived at 957 Tiffany Street in the Bronx. For weeks before, I had sat on the stoop listening to other kids talk about Halloween and going trick-or-treating. I wanted to go too. Imagine getting pennies and apples —especially pennies—all over the place, just for walking around in a costume. When I asked my brothers if they would go with me, they just fluffed me off. That was kid stuff to them.

So I was on my own, which was okay by me. But the big problem was a costume. In our house, the next meal was a problem. Costumes for five-year-old kids weren't given the same priority. So I figured it out for myself.

When the great day came, I sneaked into my parents' bedroom and put on one of my father's suits—he was wearing the other one. I rolled up the sleeves and the legs so I could walk without tripping. I took his derby and stuffed it with paper to keep it from dropping down over my eyes. Then I got my mother's little kolinsky fur muff—the only piece of fur she owned—and cut out a small square to make a mustache, which I pasted under my nose. Then I took Pa's cane, and stuck a paper chrysanthemum from the vase in the parlor into the lapel, and I was all set—a midget Charlie Chaplin. I even had a Chaplin walk, which was part imitation and part from holding up Pa's pants.

I worked all the streets around our house, sometimes tagging along with other kids in costume, sometimes going on my own. I was a small sensation. Mothers nudged one another and made clucking sounds of approval, men patted me on the head, and the pennies poured in. And as the day wore on, one man started following me.

He followed me back to our door, where my mother was waiting to whale the crap out of me for cutting up her muff. Then she saw the man.

"Is this your little boy, lady?"

Mama was always dramatic. She put a hand to her chest. "What's happened? What's wrong?" Even before she knew, she whirled on me. "I told you not to do this!"

The man said, "It's all right, lady. There's nothing wrong. I just want to know, are you his mother?"

Mother got that look she used for suspected collection agents and landlords. "Yes," she said cautiously. "Why?"

The man explained that he ran a theater in Mount Vernon. "We're

having a Charlie Chaplin contest. It's just for kids, and I'd like for you
to enter him."

"Is there any money in it?"

The man said, "No, but first prize is a silver loving cup."

Silver wasn't as good as money, but this was show business. Silver
could be converted into cash money, was the way my mother must have
figured it. It took some cutting corners to get the necessary forty cents
that would take my mother and me to Mount Vernon on the day of the
contest, but Mama managed it.

To my mother's pride—she wasn't at all amazed—I walked off with
the contest and the silver loving cup. It didn't take a jeweler's eye to see
that the loving cup was nowhere near silver. Maybe, in a rising market,
it would have been worth eight cents. On top of that, Mama had figured
short on our trip costs. So there she was with the sun going down in
Mount Vernon, a five-year-old kid and a tin loving cup for company, and
no way to get home. She didn't know anybody up there, and she was too
proud to go up to a stranger and ask for carfare, so we began to walk.

With my short legs, and with my mother in the narrow skirts of the
day and her best shoes, it was slow going. We slept—or I did, with my
mother on guard—on park benches, at train depots, for fifteen minutes,
a half-hour at most, and then we began walking again. I remember crying
once because I was hungry. My mother just gave me a look, and I dried
up. We went on walking.

It took us all night and half the next day to get back to Tiffany Street.
So what if it wasn't silver? Mama put the loving cup in the middle of the
kitchen table. At least it was proof of talent in the Berlinger family. If
I still hadn't figured out where my future lay, my mother already had it
charted. Maybe she didn't know where she was going at the beginning,
but she knew she was going to go somewhere. I don't think she was afraid
of anything.

She was born on Watt Street, near the Hudson River down by Green-
wich Village. Her family came from Russ-Poland, which in the Jewish
social structure was not considered as classy as Germany. Her father,
Henry Glantz, was a cobbler. I can remember when my mother would
take all of us to see Grandpa Glantz, who was a widower. He'd always be
working in his postage-stamp-sized store. When I was very young I
thought my grandfather had tacks instead of teeth growing out of his lips.
They were always in his mouth as he hunched over the boots he was
working on. He was a striking-looking man, round-shouldered from his

work but powerful through the chest and arms. He was bald on top with a gray fringe of kinky hair by each ear, and he had a gray mustache. He would look at his daughter's four sons with love when we first came in (my sister Rosalind hadn't been born yet). But after a while, after we had poked around in the big galvanized bucket in which he soaked the leather he worked, and after we had cranked his three chairs up and down, and mixed up the boots he made for the men who worked in the slaughter-houses, he would turn to my mother and say, "It's enough, Sarah. I love them, but take them."

It was to the Glantz side of the family that we went at Passover. It was from the Glantz side that we got whatever sense of religion we had.

My mother was working in the notions department of Wanamaker's Department Store at Ninth Street and Fourth Avenue when she met my father. What he was doing at the time is hard to pin down. Pa did so many things that never went anywhere, it's difficult to keep track of his career, if you can call it that. After his father's paint store died under him, he became a house painter, and even worked his way up to contractor, with a contract for all the benches in Central Park. How that fell through, none of his children can remember, but it did. Pa had the knack. He was also a salesman in paints and varnishes, a traveling salesman in millinery, a night watchman, and much, much more.

What Grandpa Glantz thought of Moses Berlinger, one can only guess. He was a dressy young man, and all of his brothers and sisters were doing well, but young Moses seemed more charming than steady. What the Berlingers thought of Sarah Glantz is an easier guess. They already considered Moe a loser, and with a cobbler's daughter—and not even from Germany!—it was too much. Instead of closing ranks and helping their brother, they dropped him. Family contact was kept, but kept to a minimum. It wasn't much more than a telephone call after the children were born when there was a suit that wasn't being worn that might fit one of the boys, or a dress that might look nice on the little girl. The hand-me-downs were never delivered. Pa would walk to Morningside Heights, from wherever we lived at the time, to pick up the clothes. We were never rich enough to tell anybody what they could do with their rags. We needed, so we took and shut up. I can still see Pa in spats and a rich white vest with piping down the front—both hand-me-downs—looking like a slightly worn million bucks, and without two cents in his pocket.

Sarah Glantz became Sarah Berlinger in 1900. A year later she became a mother when Philip Louis was born. Three years later, they had my brother Francis, a year after that Jacob, and then me. I was the baby of the family for four years until the last child and only girl, Rosalind Marianna, came along.

I think we are one of the few large families who can look back and say they have had more addresses than children. Rent in those days for the railroad flats we used to call home was about $11 a month. When he worked, Pa earned $12 a week. I don't know what other parents talk about at breakfast, but at our house the day usually began with "Moe, we gotta have money." Pa would nod his head and give a *shush, not in front of the kids,* and soon after he'd set out on his day's business. He often came home at night with a wilted lettuce or a few tomatoes that were going soft, maybe a few pieces of candy—it depended on which storekeeper friend he had dropped in on for a visit—and maybe once in a blue moon with some money.

Mama often had to go to relatives to try to borrow the rent money. Naturally, it was to her side of the family that she went, and most often to her brother Dave, who lived nearby with his wife, Jennie, when we lived in Harlem. If my Uncle Dave hadn't been the nearest in distance, Mama would probably have tried elsewhere—and sometimes she had to—because my Aunt Jennie wasn't too wild about her. This couple became an even better touch during World War I, because of Uncle Dave's job with the telephone company. Telephones were hard to get, and what with Uncle Dave's connection and a bit of a schmeer, life improved for the David Glantzes. But I don't remember Mama telling us that the wealth had filtered down to us.

One-hundred-thirty-eighth Street and Eighth Avenue, 960 Kelly Street in the Bronx, 957 Tiffany Street (also in the Bronx), 103 West 118th Street, 181st Street and Fort Washington Avenue, 65 Wadsworth Terrace, 205 West 119th Street—you want addresses, I've got a million of them in my childhood. In my memory, the streets change but the apartments all melt into one. It was always a railroad flat—one room after another off a hall that ran from one end of the flat to the other. The only real difference between the flats was whether you walked up four or five flights of dark stairs to get to them. Four flights was better on the feet, and it was nearer to the basement, so you didn't have to bang as long on the pipes before you could hope for the hissing that meant heat was coming.

It wasn't until I was fairly grown up that I learned that moving could be done in the daytime. When I was very young, I thought it was, like sleeping, something you did at night. Moving by day was for people who didn't owe rent and could decide when they would leave. That wasn't always the Berlingers. I can still see Mama with her finger to her lips as we all tiptoed down four flights of creaky stairs, everybody carrying something. I thought it was some new game where you had to keep quiet—like hide and seek—but my folks and my older brothers didn't look as if they thought it was such a great game.

And there was the time we were evicted. A three-day notice from the landlord was nothing new to us. Mama usually found a way to beat it, but this time she didn't. Suddenly there were men in our flat, shoving, pushing, grabbing our things. Mama was all over the place, her arms flying in all directions, trying to protect what we had, while the landlord stood like a dark cloud in the doorway, watching.

An eviction is something that stays with you all of your life. It happened to us four times. I still grow cold and sick thinking about it. To suddenly find your whole life piled up in the street . . . You're torn between protecting what's yours and wanting to run away and hide in shame. Maybe everybody else in your building—on the whole block—is starving, but indoors nobody knows. No matter what goes on behind your door, you've still got your pride. But there's nothing left after everything you own in the world is vomited out onto the street.

Mama spread us boys around our possessions, so that there was one of us in every direction. "You stay here," she said. "Right here! And Moe, you stay with them, and watch until I get back."

She looked at me. "I want no crying, Milton, you hear me?"

I nodded, but I felt too scared and ashamed to look up at her.

"All right," she said, and began buttoning up her gloves. "I'll be back soon. I'm going to see about a new place." She looked up at the building, and shouted so the landlord inside would hear. "A place a lot better than this one!"

Mama marched down the street and turned the corner, her back straight and her head high, as if she were on her way to meet President Taft.

None of us boys spoke, or even looked at one another. Pa said, "Look what I found in my pocket. I didn't know I had it."

We looked, but nobody spoke.

"A good nickel. Who wants a charlotte russe?"

Nobody answered. Then Frank said, "Mama said we should wait here."

I could hear street noises from the next block, but our street was empty. No kids came out to play, no women went to the grocery store. I took a quick peek around. The curtains were closed at all the windows as far as I could see. There were no faces at any of them, just blind glass eyes watching the shame of the Berlingers.

I don't know how long we stood out there, but it seemed like forever. The sun was going down. Men coming home from work walked by us quickly, as if we carried a disease they could catch. The ones who knew us mumbled a quick hello but pretended not to see what had happened to us.

I whispered to my father that I had to make.

"One or two?"

I held up one finger. He led me to the curb, where the bureau from their bedroom stuck out, as if that guaranteed privacy. I peed in the street and then went back to my post.

I started crying, but quietly so no one would hear. We were going to be on the sidewalk forever, and the policemen would come and put us all in jail. Mama was lost, and would never come back.

The shadows were long in the street when suddenly there was a whooping "Yoo-hoo!" and the rumble of a wagon. Mama came around the corner, waving and laughing. "Moe! Boys!"

Not only had she found a new apartment—good for a month at least —but she had somehow gotten two men with a wagon to come and move us.

Suddenly, lights went on, people came to the windows, neighbors rushed into the street. There were friendly faces all around us. Someone shoved half a cake at us, a jar of soup. There was kissing and hugging and crying, and much shouting of "Luck!" and "Don't forget you should come back to see." It was safe to know the Berlingers again. Mama had cured us all of the eviction plague!

I was born on July 12, 1908, in Harlem, in a five-flight walkup at 68 West 118th Street, between Fifth and Lenox Avenues. Harlem, back then, was white—Italian, Jewish, German—and black. It wasn't Sutton Place, but it wasn't bad. What I remember most is that there were trees all down Seventh Avenue. George Jessel was born and lived next door to us, at 66 West 118th Street. Not that I was aware of Jessel back then, and I don't suppose he knew I was being born next door either.

A baby is a wonderful thing, but it's a mixed blessing when you don't know for sure how you're going to feed the kids you already have. The one really great thing about a new Berlinger coming into the world is that the other kids got to go to the Imperial Nickelodeon, while the baby was being born. Rags, which is what we used to call my oldest brother, Phil, was in charge of the money tied into a corner of his handkerchief. Admission in those days was a nickel—that's why they called them nickelodeons—and you got a rebate ticket good for a penny's worth of candy inside. Who could ask for more?

Phil was also in charge of Frank, who was in charge of Jack. A baby you could always get, but the movies was a real treat. And with Mama and Pa busy, you could stay for more than one show—that is, if one of the McKibbon brothers, who owned the Imperial, didn't spot you hiding down around the chair legs when he put the lights on between shows.

At the time I'm talking about, the Imperial, which was on 117th Street and Lenox Avenue, had two employees who were destined for bigger things. One was Lottie Jessel, Georgie Jessel's mother, who sold the tickets. The other was a young man named Harry Cohn, who later went to Hollywood and became the head of Columbia Pictures. At the Imperial Nickelodeon, he would lead the community sings between pictures, pointing to the words on the slides.

Eventually, we were all in charge of Rosalind. Her arrival wasn't such a great event, beyond another trip to the movies for my brothers (I was sent to a neighbor's house). When we all came home, Pa met us at the door, a big smile on his face. "Boys, come meet your new sister."

He took us into the bedroom, where Mama was lying. The bottom bureau drawer was pulled out, and there in a shoebox was our sister. Her name was bigger than she was. At birth, Rosalind Marianna weighed two and a half pounds.

When Grandpa Glantz came to see his new granddaughter, he took one look, tossed a penny into the shoebox, and said, "That's all she's worth." Then he kissed Mama to show her he was really pleased.

I had been born at home. Midwives were pretty common in those days, but, after talking it over with my brothers and sister, the decision is that I was delivered by a Dr. Wagner. Wagner, I've got to tell you, is a very famous name in our family.

My father knew the Wagner family from way back to his bachelor days in his father's paint store on First Avenue. Old man Wagner used to sit in the window of a small store a couple of doors up the block and roll cigars by hand all day. He was a very fat man, and he wore his pants, held up by suspenders, high up, almost under his armpits. Whenever he got the call, he headed for the outhouse in the yard behind the store. For a man of his size, buttoning a fly could be a big job. He always came back from the outhouse working on the problem, and for his own comfort usually left the buttons at the top undone.

He raised both of his sons to be doctors. The one who delivered me was Dr. Jerome Wagner, who married Norma Terris, the original Magnolia in Ziegfeld's *Show Boat*. I think Mama got him for me because either he did the job for nothing or he worked cheap because of the long connection between the two fathers.

But what makes Wagner famous in our family are those fly buttons. The name became a code for "Your fly is open." If any of us was ever open, someone would sing out, "Wagner," and we'd all turn to the nearest wall for a quick inspection.

In the 1930s, I remember, I was playing the Capitol Theatre in New York as master of ceremonies. This was back when every top Broadway movie house had a stage show along with the picture. On the bill were the Maxellos, a risley act—you know, foot jugglers. After they did their flash with the barrel and the girl, I got into the act.

You work an act a couple of times, you know pretty much where the laughs are going to come. Well, I was standing on the feet of one of the Maxellos, and suddenly I got a laugh I had never gotten before. It was a big scream, and I thought I was a smash. I was trying to figure out exactly what I'd done so that I could keep it in the act. Well, the audience was going wild, and I was grinning, happy as hell, when over the whole thing I heard my mother yelling from the balcony, "Wagner! Wagner!"

I had gone to the bathroom before the show, and I had forgotten to button my pants. While I had been juggling around with the Maxellos, a piece of my shirttail had worked its way out of the fly of my pants. Did you ever try to close your fly in front of a whole audience while standing up in the air on another man's feet? It ain't easy.

Another time, I was playing Loew's State. With my big mouth, I must have told the Wagner story to some of the show crowd I hung around with when I was in New York. At the opening matinee at Loew's State I came bouncing out on the stage. Big fanfare, lots of applause, and three guys in the front row shouted, "Wagner!" I spun around, ran a hand down my pants. Everything was fine. Then I looked over the lights and spotted the guys, who were doubled up. I wanted to kill. But I couldn't take it out on them, or on Wagner either. What the hell, he was a family tradition. And his son had brought me into the world.

When he did, I was named Milton, no middle name. To my knowledge, I did nothing that first day of my life to indicate any talent for show business except staying alive. And in this crazy business, that is a very big talent.

3

When my father was a boy on 13th Street off First Avenue, he used to chase after fire engines. It was something that stayed with him all of his life. I don't think it was the fire that attracted him, but the excitement and drama of men against impossible odds. I think in some crazy way it fit in with all the dreams that kept him going—and that got in his way, day after day, as he set out to try to make a living for his growing family.

Mama had no impossible dreams, because she was too practical to dream, and because nothing was impossible to her. Oh, maybe she dreamed a little each morning when she stood in front of the mirror and pinched her cheeks to make the color rise. But then she would pin her hat firmly in place and start out on her day. If there was a child home old enough to take care of the younger boys, or if Moe was between jobs, Mama worked. She had put the ribbon counter at Wanamaker's behind her. She became a store detective, part time or full time, depending on the home situation.

She started out in the big time of store detectives—Saks, Wanamaker's, Lord & Taylor—but as my career went up, hers went down, to Blumstein's and Koch's, the small time. Being a store detective was a tougher job back then than it is today. Mama was ready for it. She learned jiujitsu, and if she had to she could bring a truck driver in line with a twist of her wrist.

For a while she had her own business, the Sarah Glantz Detective Agency. The business cards, which she passed out wherever she went,

36

brought in mostly collection work. Mama, with only guts and jiujitsu, went into tenements and joints that I wouldn't go into in the strongest years of my life. She always came out, and usually with her client's money.

And once that I remember, she followed my father down the street like the detective she was to see that he was doing his job. He was selling paints and varnishes then, and he would start out every day with his case filled with sample chips of his products. There were too many nights, though, when he came home with no orders. Pa would grin sheepishly. "I went to see twenty-five people today. Twenty-four of them weren't in, and one told me to come back next week." We kids would roar with laughter, and press in close to him as he took off his coat. Pa always brought something home with him for us, and on the best days it was a candy bar, which we would divvy up. But Mama didn't find his jokes very funny.

So one day she decided to follow him to make certain he went into the stores he was supposed to. I was old enough to understand what she was going to do, and to sense that it was somehow wrong.

When I asked her not to go, she said, "Look, he goes out all day. Where does he go? What does he do? I've got a right to know."

"Still a detective," I said.

Mama shrugged. "I've got a right to know."

She spent the entire day following him from store to store. She stayed about half a block behind him, but he knew she was there.

That night when I crept out of bed to go to the hall toilet, I heard Mama and Pa whispering in their room.

"Why, Sarah, why? You think that I haven't any pride? Why did you do such a thing?"

Mama sounded angry. "You can have your pride. I got children to feed, and they can't eat pride."

I heard the bed groan as one of them turned over. It must have been Pa turning away, because his voice sounded muffled now. "Please, Sarah, I try."

"Moe, we got to have some money. It costs to live!"

"Sarah, I'm working on an idea right now, you'll see. Soon, soon, we're going to be okay."

"Sure." Mama sounded resigned. The bed groaned again. "Sure."

*   *   *

Poor sad, loving Pa. Life just never came through with the jackpot for him. He had more charm than ambition, more dreams than follow-through. Tomorrow was always his big day.

His name was Moses Berlinger; he was the son of an immigrant who came to this country from Wamp, Germany, in 1849. My grandfather had opened a paint store on First Avenue just three doors from 14th Street in New York City. The paint store didn't exactly make Jacob Berlinger "Our Crowd" aristocracy, but he thought he belonged on top, and he passed the attitude down to his children. Moe, my father, was born in this country, and spoke without an accent, unless you count the "dese," "dems," and "dose" of New York, which were part of his speech all his life. My father thought of himself as an American of German ancestry. That he was also a Jew was something else again. To him, there were Jews and there were Jews.

To my father, anyone not born in America was a foreigner, a foreign-born Jew was way below an American-born Jew, and Moses Berlinger was American-born. I remember that once, as a little boy, I was riding on the elevated train with him when an orthodox Jew got on with his little boy. The man had a heavy beard, and he wore a long black coat and a flat black hat. The little boy wore a *yarmulka* and *payess*, those long curls that grow down in front of the ears. No one looked at them as they came into the elevated car, but my father spotted them. "Let's go into the other car," he said to me in a tense, low voice.

I said, "Why?"

He shrugged his shoulder in the direction of the father and son, who were halfway down the car from us, talking quietly to each other.

I tugged at Pa's hand as he was starting to get up. "Why, Pa?" I whispered. "They're Jews, and so are we."

He yanked me to my feet. "Yeah, but not *that* kind!" he snapped, and we went to the next car.

Grandpa Berlinger must have given his sons and daughters the drive for success. All of them, except for my father, picked up whatever lessons on the American way he passed out. One son, my Uncle Henry, became the head of the Internal Revenue office in New York. My Uncle Phil made it big in the millinery business, and on one of his business trips to Paris fell in love with and married a French girl. He became so French that he changed his name from Berlinger to Bourlangé, with a soft "g."

I remember how he yelled and carried on when he learned that a nephew of his was going into show business. It was the worst disgrace in the world to him. What kind of business was the acting business for a respectable American family to be in? But later on, when I played the Palace, guess who was outside parading up and down in his Morris Gest, the brim turned down on the side, his black, flowing tie catching the breeze, pointing with his cane up at the name on the marquee and saying, "That's my nephew!" That was Uncle Phillip Bourlangé.

Both of my father's sisters married big in the optical world. One became Mrs. Ben Levoy, of B. M. Levoy; the other married Peter Wolfe, of Kohnstamm-Wolfe, whose store was on Fifth Avenue back then. Pa's younger brother, Milton, for whom I was named, was a vice-president of the Ex-Lax Corporation. Everybody made it in the land of opportunity but Moses Berlinger.

He stayed in the paint store until there wasn't any more paint store to stay with. When Grandpa Berlinger died, it was over. There was nothing left for my father, because it turned out there wasn't any money for anybody, not even the loyal son.

My father was a short, stocky man, with bright red hair in his youth. He was shorter than my mother. It was only one of many differences between them. My father was a gentle man, a kind man, but lost. There was gentleness in my mother, and great love, too, but she was never lost. I wonder why Mama and Pa had so many children when I think about the struggle they had to make a living. The only answer I can come up with is that they had no choice. There wasn't much that was known about birth control in those days, and what was known wasn't talked about. It wasn't nice. And anyway, Mama and Pa loved each other—even though they were soon to switch roles in the family setup—and love led to babies.

Pa's ideas were dreams that he worked on in the mornings before anyone was awake. He had a little book that he carried around with him. I don't know where he got it, but it contained instructions on how to make all sorts of things, from aspirin to taffy apples. One morning when we woke up, the whole flat smelled of chocolate.

We all ran into the kitchen, and there was Pa at the stove with his book beside him. He was learning to dip cherries. On a plate beside the stove were finished chocolate-covered cherries, little puddles of dark brown with lumps in the middle. Mama took one look and gave one of her deep sighs. "Moe, Moe."

Pa held up a hand. "There's money in hand-dipped chocolates, Sarah. It just takes a little learning. A little patience is all."

Mama drew her wrapper tight around her. "There's money in the paint-and-varnish business, too. And you don't need patience. All you got to do is get dressed and go out on the street!"

Mama turned her back on him and started bustling around the kitchen. She reached into the cupboard and got down the jar in which she kept the rice. "And everybody who is not cooking should go and get dressed!"

My brothers and I scattered.

We had rice at every meal when I was a kid. Rice was poor-people food, like potatoes, only Mama had decided rice was healthier, so we got it three times a day. With a little sugar and milk, it was breakfast cereal. It showed up in soup, mixed in with stews, and under any sauce on the stove. We could complain all we wanted to, but it was there every day. "If you don't like it, don't eat it" was all Mama ever said. So we ate it, because there was a longstanding rule in our house: You ate what you got or you didn't eat. There were no special orders. The family joke was that we ate so much rice, we got up and did our own laundry.

Another morning when we woke up, there was a strong sweet smell all through the flat, as if the place were stuffed with flowers. I thought I was in a funeral parlor.

It turned out to be Pa in the kitchen again, with his little book. There were bottles and powders all over the table.

"What are you doing, Pa?"

He looked up and smiled. "Here, smell." He picked up a saucer with a mound of white powder in the middle.

"I smell it. The whole house smells."

Pa smiled. "You like it? What does it smell like to you?"

I didn't know. It was just sweet. "Flowers?"

Pa grinned. "Roses! It's La Rose Perfume Powder. You like the name?"

He reached into a pocket and pulled out a small envelope on which he had drawn a black-and-white design. The name was printed in the center. "See."

Mama came into the kitchen. "So what's a perfume powder?"

Pa said, "You put it in a ball and you hang it in the closet. It makes everything smell nice. You could even sprinkle it in clothes drawers. Maybe on a handkerchief. It's got lots of uses. I'm still working on it. There's big money in perfumes, and it doesn't cost too much. A little of this, a little of that, and there's a fortune."

"There's also a fortune at Weiss and Klau," Mama said, talking about his new job. "Do you know what time it is?"

The perfume powder followed the chocolate-covered cherries. One day it was dreams of fortunes, and the next day it was over, put away for another new scheme that wouldn't go anywhere. Just like his job at Weiss and Klau. That came when I was already getting somewhere in show business. It was probably Pa's best job, because it lasted longest, but, like all of them, it went nowhere. Weiss and Klau were dealers in oilcloth and other kitchen materials. Their store was down on Grand Street and Broadway. Pa worked for them as a salesman on the floor. Oh, they made a big fuss over good old Moses Berlinger when he brought his son down to the store, but they never took care of him otherwise. He started as a salesman on the floor, and he stayed there. No promotions, no raises. And when they sold out, Pa was left with nothing to show for the years he'd given them.

I can go on with Pa's jobs for pages. There was the Cayuga Club in Harlem. It was a Democratic club, connected with Tammany Hall. Several times my father ran for the head of the club. He always lost.

Pa was the original hard-luck guy. His biggest dream of all was to have his own diner, where he would be the short-order cook. He was a good cook, but he never got inside anybody's diner, and, of course, he never got his own.

But if he couldn't bring success to his family, he made up for it with love. It was in the candy bars he'd shyly pull out of his coat pocket some nights when he came home. He showed it with the fruits and vegetables and the newspapers he picked up along the way during his business day. Pa didn't seem to know the right people to help him in his career, but he knew a lot of the local storekeepers, and they liked him, which explains all the free stuff he brought home.

Pa had an elegant handwriting. Every December when we were kids, he would wet a bar of soap and write "Merry Christmas" on the biggest mirror in the flat. It was typical of him that he didn't write "Happy Chanukah."

And when my sister Rosalind came along and was old enough to want things, it was just like Pa to go out on a freezing-cold Christmas Eve and wait in front of a toy store on 125th Street until they marked down the prices. There was a doll that walked—you held it by the hand, and if you walked very slowly and didn't lift it off the ground, it sort of walked beside you—that Pa had shown to Roz. She had loved it, but it cost almost three dollars. Pa bought it after a two-hour wait, when the owner marked it down to fifty cents. That was my father.

But being poor is not what I remember about my childhood. Poor is something grown-ups know about. A kid knows about being poor only if he's around rich kids. No matter what, we always had food on the table, and I didn't have anything less than any of the other kids who lived around us, so who was poor?

What I remember are things like when we lived in the Bronx and Jack got a big idea for making some money. About ten blocks away, at the Hunt's Point railroad stop, there was an open spring that flowed down the railroad embankment. It was July, and hot as hell, and Jack and a kid named McDermott, who was the janitor's son in our building, found two big jugs, like the kind they use in water coolers today. They were wrapped in cane. Jack and McDermott went around the building asking if anyone wanted fresh cold spring water. A lady said she'd take the two jugs and pay them a nickel, which seemed like pretty big money.

I was allowed to tag along when they went to fill the order. The empty jugs were heavy enough going to Hunt's Point. They were murder coming back filled. And then, because it was Saturday and McDermott was a Catholic, we had to stop by the church while he went in to confession. He said he would be only a few minutes. Jack and I sat in the grass outside with the two jugs. It was boiling hot, and there must have been a lot of people waiting inside, because it was almost an hour until McDermott came back out.

When we finally got home, McDermott took us down in the cellar, where the dumbwaiter was. They got one jug up on the bottom shelf and one on the top, and hoisted them up to the lady's apartment. They rang her bell, and the lady called down, "Wait. I wanna taste first."

We waited and waited for the nickel to come down. Finally McDermott rang again. "What?" the lady shouted down.

"Where's our nickel, lady?"

"A nickel you want? The police you could get! You call that hot stuff spring water? You filled it from the tap."

Jack shouted up, "We went all the way to the Hunt's Point spring. It's hot outside, lady."

"Get away from there, you liars, or I swear, I'll call the police. I'm counting to five!"

We ran.

Another moneymaker was waiting in the street outside the IRT subway station on rainy days with an umbrella. Jack would get there when the people were coming home from work. Jack would run after anybody without an umbrella. "Take you home, mister? Take you home, lady? Only a nickel." If he got a customer, Jack would give him or her the umbrella and walk alongside in the rain until the customer got home. Then he'd collect his nickel, take back his umbrella, and run back to find another customer. It was a small-time Hertz operation. When I got a little older, I tried it once. I got pneumonia.

All sorts of neighborhoods, all sorts of memories. There was Annette's ice cream parlor at the corner of 119th Street and Seventh Avenue. Annette was always nice to us kids. Sometimes she'd give you a second piece of candy for your penny, or she wouldn't scrape the extra from the ice cream scoop when she made you a cone . . . Stamler Furs, across the street, and even if Rose Stamler was supposed to be rich, she was always friendly if she saw you going by . . . Izzy Moses' Drugstore on 118th Street and Lenox Avenue . . . Shapiro's Delicatessen . . . Peck's, a sporting goods store at 117th Street and Seventh Avenue, where if you had a nickel you could buy a hard rubber ball called a Hi-Bouncer . . . and a little patch of grass that never seemed to be any color but dusty brown, which we called Goldberg's Park. It was at 116th between Seventh and St. Nicholas, and that's where all the kids would meet to choose up teams, plan adventures, sneak cigarettes, whatever it was that kids did in those days, when it was easier and safer to be a kid. I was a part of it all for just a little while, before everything changed. Not because we moved—which we did, of course—but because I had won a tin cup in a Charlie Chaplin contest, and that started the whole thing.

My childhood ended at the age of five.

4

Flippant, aggressive, a wise guy, a corner comedian, big city slicker with a put-down, an insult, with venom, with bitterness, with smiles, without smiles, a smart-ass—sure, I know my image. Christ, I created it. It's somebody named Milton Berle who lives in lights. It's not me. Or at least it isn't now. Looking back, I guess there were times when I fit the image. Those days way back, when other kids were going to school and having friends their own age, I was busy fighting with the drummers in pit bands all over the country.

I guess I thought my childhood was fun while I was living it. Looking back, I can feel in my gut that it was lousy. But there's no one to blame. Pa had no talent for supporting a family, and Mama had to take over. She had seven Berlingers to keep alive and together. And I guess she never recovered from her girlhood dreams and how it felt the night she led the Grand March. She had long put the dreams away. As Mrs. Moses Berlinger, Sadie—as her friends called her—didn't have time for dreams, unless they were the day-to-day nightmares of living without money.

But the dreams came to life again when I won the Charlie Chaplin contest in Mount Vernon. I guess I had a little talent then, maybe no more than any other five-year-old, but the difference was Mama. When I took the contest she saw a door opening, and she was determined to get her whole family through to where it was safe and warm.

I still can't figure out how in hell Mama managed it all. She had a newborn baby sleeping in the open bureau drawer in her room, four sons and a husband to take care of, and she was back working part time as a store detective whenever my father was between jobs. With all that going on, Mama decided that she had a maybe-talented son. Before anyone knew it, Mama had turned herself into a one-woman talent agency, and I was just about her whole client list.

Not that Mama wouldn't drop all of us like a hot potato if she heard that one of the moving-picture companies filming around New York was looking for a mature woman. Bang!—my father was suddenly in charge of feeding and changing the baby, making meals, getting kids off to school on time, seeing that anybody who had an after-school job went to it, and Mama was dressed and running.

Or if the word was that they were looking for kids, Mama rounded up her own and a few neighborhood strays and took off—$1.50 a day was nothing to sneeze at. One of her movie appearances took her up to the Bronx, where they were hiring people for a winter street scene. The director had them walking back and forth all day through the snow, which they faked by piling up ground-up rock salt. There was no such thing as costumes then, so she wore her own hat, coat, and shoes. The buck and a half she brought home at the end of the day didn't even pay for one of her specially fitted shoes (she had bad feet), both of which had been eaten away by the salt.

Once, Rosalind got lifted from the open bottom bureau drawer where all newborn Berlingers started out, and wrapped in warm blankets. Years before she knew what a movie was, she was doing a day's work in some long-forgotten picture.

Mama heard one day that the Packard Model Agency, downtown in Manhattan, was looking for Buster Brown models. Before I knew what had hit me, I was sitting in a barber chair having my hair cut Dutch-boy style with bangs across my forehead, and away we went. She even put a stiff Buster Brown collar on me, from one of the suits passed on to us by the rich relatives. I got some modeling jobs for magazine ads, clutching a dog that looked like Buster Brown's Tige. I also got the shit kicked out of me a couple of times a week.

Maybe Buster Brown was a popular style with mothers, but he was just another sissy to kids. In those days, the gangs around our way shaped up by race or religion. All it took was one tough kid to bring the other kids in line. In my neighborhood, we had Johnny the Wop, Milton Diamond, and Harvey Watkins—Italian, Jewish, and Irish. I wish I could say that Milton Diamond's gang protected me, but I can't. I was the favorite target of all the gangs, the Jews included, when I made a run for home after school with those dumb bangs flopping against my head. It was one thing if I was with Mama. Then the guys would just laugh or whistle or yell a few words, but they didn't do anything. But if I was on my own, look out! They were all over me if they could catch me, and "sissy" was the kindest thing they called me.

I guess when that sort of thing happens to a boy, he has only two choices. He either pulls back into himself and quits the rest of his life, or he learns to fight back. I decided on fighting, street style, which meant a continuous case of skinned knucks, an occasional bloody nose, and black eyes. Later on, when I grew older, I learned to handle myself better.

I'm talking now about 1913, 1914. Vaudeville was the king of entertainment, and New York was the king's heart. You had only to go downtown and take a look at Mr. Keith's brand new Palace Theatre, which opened on March 24, 1913, to know how important vaudeville was.

There was another new entertainment around, but nobody took it seriously. The movies were something for the lower classes and immigrants. Nice people didn't go to the "flickers"—which is what early film did—or the "galloping tintypes," as they called them back then. And even though the movies had improved and grown from the little one-scene quickies they showed in the nickelodeons to the point where some crazy people were building theaters just to show films, vaudeville sneered at them. Sure, they were starting to be shown as part of the vaudeville bills, but not as real entertainment. They were "chasers"—something to chase the people out of the theater to make room for the next audience.

Serious actors still looked down on movie work, and did it only if they needed money. All this is just a little background history. It had nothing to do with the Berlingers, who would go anywhere there was a job.

The movie companies were already starting to move west, to a place called Hollywood in California, where land was cheap and there was supposed to be plenty of sunshine daily, which was good for the cameras. But there were still plenty of movies being made all around New York. There was the Famous Players–Lasky Company down on the south side of 56th Street between Sixth and Seventh Avenues. And there were companies like Keystone, Vitagraph, Biograph, Eclair, Essanay, Fox, and Pathé working out of shacks and cowbarns in the Bronx, Brooklyn, Long Island, and over in the area of Fort Lee and Coytesville in New Jersey.

Where my mother got her information from, I don't know, but my first film job came when she heard that Pathé was looking for a boy my

age for a serial they were making with Pearl White, Crane Wilbur, and
Paul Panzer. Pathé's offices were at 1 Congress Street in Jersey City
Heights, but Mama found out that the film was being made in the Fort
Lee–Coytesville area. It meant my cutting school for a day, and Mama
playing sick from the department store, but she didn't think twice about
that. She had me up at the crack of dawn, and we set off for the Fort
Lee ferry at 125th Street.

To my knowledge, Mama had never been to Fort Lee or even New
Jersey before in her life, but she headed for her target like a homing
pigeon. The ferry docked at Edgewater, about three miles from Fort Lee.
Mama and I got off, and she moved with all the sureness of Queen
Victoria stepping down on native soil. Before I could look around, she had
hitched us a ride with a farmer going in the right direction. He let us off
right at Rambo's, the roadhouse where all the actors and film crews
showed up if they were working in the area. She just walked around asking
for the Pathé people until she found them, and I got my first job in *The
Perils of Pauline.*

I was so young that I really didn't know what was going on. Mama
told me to listen carefully to the man who kept talking through the
megaphone, because he was the director and he told everyone what to do.
And the man who kept cranking the machine on legs was the cameraman,
and he was very important too.

Of course, I didn't know the first thing about putting on make-up—
in those days, every actor did his own—but a nice, pretty lady came over
to me and said, "Let me help you, sonny."

All I really remember about her is that she was friendly and that she
had blond hair with a headband across her forehead. I kept looking around
hoping to see a "star." I wanted someone who really shone, and all the
time I never knew it was Pearl White who was putting my make-up on
me. I found out who she was only when we got over to the car of the
railroad train on which we would be filming. It was there that I also met
Crane Wilbur, who played the hero who was always helping Pauline, and
Paul Panzer, who played the evil secretary who pretended to help Pauline
but was always trying to get her killed. I liked them equally, and eventually
I decided all stars didn't have to shine to be okay in my book.

The director told me that I was to play a little boy who was a passenger
on the train who gets thrown from it while it is moving. I was scared
shitless, even when he went on to tell me that Pauline would save my life.
Which is exactly what happened, except that at the crucial moment they

threw a bundle of rags instead of me from the train. I bet there are a lot of comedians around today who are sorry about that.

With one picture under my belt, Mama saw no reason why there shouldn't be more. The world was going to be my oyster—though none of us had ever tasted an oyster at that time. Mama started making the rounds of the local studios with me. If she heard that they were looking for a ragamuffin, she dressed me in my worst clothes and sewed patches at the knees and elbows. If they wanted a Little Lord Fauntleroy type, out came the suit with the Buster Brown collar. Whatever they were looking for, I showed up as it.

I played kid parts in *Bunny's Little Brother*, with John Bunny and Flora Finch (I don't know who his little brother was, but it wasn't me); *Divorce Coupons*, with Corrinne Griffith; *The Maid's Night Out*, with Mabel Normand; *Tess of the Storm Country*, with Mary Pickford; *Birthright*, with Flora Finch; *Love's Penalty*, with Hope Hampton; and the other big serial, *Ruth of the Range*, with Ruth Roland.

Whatever movie I appeared in, Mama somehow managed to get the stars to pose for a picture with me. It didn't mean so much to me, but it seemed to mean a great deal to Mama. If anyone was star-struck, it was Mama, and she just couldn't believe that her son was actually working and talking with people like Mabel Normand and John Bunny.

There were even trips out to Hollywood—the studios paid—where I got parts in *Rebecca of Sunnybrook Farm*, with Mary Pickford, *The Mark of Zorro*, with Douglas Fairbanks, Sr., and *Tillie's Punctured Romance*, with Charlie Chaplin, Mabel Normand, and Marie Dressler. If you can find prints of any of these films today, look for a kid with two Bugs Bunny teeth. I don't remember much about California, except a railroad trip that seemed to go on forever until we reached a hick town with dusty dirt roads, but the thrill of being able to say I had once worked with the great Chaplin was worth it. And I saw a real orange growing on a tree! That impressed me. I thought they grew in pieces of tissue paper inside wooden boxes.

I can also remember a day off from *Tillie's Punctured Romance* because Mack Sennett, the director, was shooting scenes with Mr. Chaplin and Miss Dressler. Mama saw it as a chance to scout for more work. We went over to the Semiflex Studios on LaBrea, and then to Nestor Studios at Sunset and Gower. I say studios, because that's what the moviemakers called them, but they were just one-story buildings of wood or stucco. There were trees and open lawns and fields around Sunset and

Gower, and if somebody went by too fast in his flivver, you got dust all
over your clothes. I think Mama smelled money in Hollywood, but to a
city-born kid it was nothing special. Grass was just something that came
up in the cracks of the sidewalks, and that was about all you needed of
the stuff unless you were a cow. And the kind of trees that grew around
Hollywood—the kind that didn't give any shade from the heat—well,
who needed that?

Tillie's Punctured Romance was Hollywood, 1914. Jump cut now to
England in 1966. Charlie Chaplin had come out of Switzerland and was
working at Pinewood Studios, directing Sophia Loren and Marlon Brando
in *A Countess from Hong Kong*. I was in London too. When I heard that
Gloria Swanson had driven out to Pinewood and visited with Chaplin, I
decided the great man was in a friendly mood, so why shouldn't I try to
see him too? After all, I had worked with him once. Anyway, the worst
that could happen was that I'd get turned away.

I was taken onto the set. The first free moment in the shooting, I went
straight up to him and stuck out my hand. "How do you do, Mr. Chaplin.
I'm Milton Berle."

He shook my hand, but I could see no bells were going off in his head.

"I guess you don't remember me, but we worked together over fifty
years ago."

Now he looked interested. "Oh? Where was that?"

I told him. "In *Tillie's Punctured Romance*. Remember, there's a
scene in the picture where you're walking down the street, and there's this
little kid selling newspapers. And he's got a dog with him. You patted the
dog and bought a paper from the kid. Well, I was that newsboy."

I don't know what I expected—that Chaplin would hit his hand
against his forehead and gasp, "Oh my God!" or that he'd break into
smiles and give me a big bear hug—but it wasn't what I got. Chaplin just
looked at me for a moment, gave a little polite smile, and just said, "Oh
I see . . . exposition." A minute later, he turned away and was back
working out something with technicians on the ship's cabin set.

When I think of all the great silent-picture names I was lucky to work
with, I think mostly that I should be making some contribution to the
history of the movies. No dice. I was just a kid, and what I remember are
kid memories. Like being fascinated, on some movie set, by a man standing out of camera range playing romantic music on a violin to get the hero
and heroine in the mood for a kissing scene. The hero kept saying over
and over to the director that he had a hangover and that he was doing

the best he could. The leading lady—I can still see her, but I can't remember who she was—was picking at a fingernail all the time. Something about her standing in the sunshine in front of half a boudoir wearing an evening gown with the sun shining off the beads of the gown made her look silly. And all the while, the man with the violin kept sawing away and swaying with his eyes closed, and nobody was listening.

I remember a little girl with fat yellow curls like Mary Pickford's— all mothers who dragged their daughters around to the studios were starting to fix them up to look like Little Mary—sitting by herself in front of a mirror over by the dressing rooms at a studio. I wasn't needed on whatever picture it was, so I was just wandering around, looking at things, when I spotted her. She kept bending her thumb in at a right angle and sort of hooking it over her lower lip while she stared in the mirror and batted her eyelids.

"What are you doing?" I asked.

She couldn't have been more than ten, but she was wearing bright lipstick that came to two points under her nose. It was called "bee-stung," and I had seen grown-up actresses that way, but on this kid it just looked like her mouth had been slammed in a door. She kept on with the thumb business.

"What are you doing?" I asked again.

She tossed her curls. She really did. "Practicing acting."

"What's that?" I said, pointing to her thumb.

"It's called fig bar."

"Huh?"

"Fa heaven sake, haven't you ever seen anybody do this in the movies?" And she turned toward me, opened her eyes wide. "That's innocence," she said. Then she pouted her lips even more than they already were, on account of the lipstick. Then she bent her head a little and started batting her eyelids like two butterflies having a nervous breakdown. She made her lower lip quiver a bit as she brought up her bent thumb and hooked it in place. "Fig bar! It tells an audience that I am pure and unsullied and modest and shy. And that men should protect me."

I thought the kid was crazy.

She turned back to the mirror. "My goodness, there are all sorts of expressions you have to be able to do if you want to be in the movies."

She went back to her thumb work.

But the things I remember most about that time are the bad things, when something went wrong—and maybe that says something about me, that I can remember failures more than successes. Like the time Mama took me to the barber shop for a trim. It was in the middle of a picture, and there was nothing for me to do for a couple of hours. I had gotten into the barber's chair when Mama spotted a friend outside the shop and went out to talk to her. The barber went to work and gave me a full haircut. When he was finished, I thought I looked great. But when the director and cameraman saw me, it really hit the fan. I had forgotten about all of the completed film on the picture that showed me with longer hair. There was nothing for them to do, unless they wanted to start all over with a new boy, but wait for my hair to grow out.

Another mistake I made didn't turn out as well for me. For one of my birthdays, Mama and Pa had given me a gold—I think it was—signet ring. I was so proud of it that I wore it every day. It was the most beautiful ring I had ever seen. I wouldn't take it off even for the picture I was working in, because I was afraid that somebody might swipe it. I remember that in the middle of a scene in which I didn't have much to do, my eye caught the sunlight shining on the gold. It fascinated me, and I watched the ring as I wiggled my fingers.

The director spotted me. "Cut!" He came running over. "What the hell are you doing? We're not paying you to make shadow pictures with your hands!"

"No, sir," I said, and I moved my hand a little. I thought if he saw my great ring he'd understand.

He saw it all right. "For Chrissake, how long you been wearing that?"

Remembering the haircut business, I gave him the good news. "Oh, it's all right. I've had the ring on since the beginning of the picture."

"Marvelous! Just marvelous!" he screamed. His face was blood red. "Look at you! Dirty hands, ripped knickers, a crummy jacket! The only penniless urchin in the whole world with a gold ring. Every scene you're in is ruined!"

For that picture, they got a new boy. On the trip home, Mama said calmly, "What does he know? Nothing, that's what he knows. Tomorrow you'll get a better picture."

Whether I got another picture the next day or not, I don't remember. But I'm willing to bet that Mama and I went looking.

5

There was a war in Europe, and prices were going up. There was talk about the United States getting into the war, but most people didn't believe that would happen. Woodrow Wilson kept us out of the war, and that's why the grown-ups reelected him. The only change the war talk made around our house was that my father toned down the talk about his proud German background. After the Germans torpedoed the *Lusitania*, German popularity started shrinking fast. With sauerkraut renamed Liberty cabbage, Moses Berlinger, born in America, wasn't going around asking for trouble.

Mama was asking for everything. It was her drive that moved us, but I don't think I was too excited by working in movies. At the very beginning it seemed great to really be with the famous people other kids just talked about. But you get used to anything pretty quickly. What started out as make-believe just became what it really was—fake—to me. And the great names ceased being great and became just people who worked hard and who sweated and got pimples and were just like anybody else. Oh, it was nice when the local paper had a little paragraph about me with the headline "LOCAL BOY APPEARS WITH PEARL WHITE," but it meant more to my parents than it did to me. I remember Pa coming home with a stack of newspapers under his arm, and both he and Mama cut out the paragraph. Pa put his in his wallet and said, "Wait till the boys at the Cayuga Club see this! Then they'll know who they're dealing with."

When I wasn't working in silent movies, Mama used to take me around to the music-publishing companies, offices like Waterson, Berlin and Snyder; T. B. Harms; Witmark; Remicks; Fred Fisher; Shapiro-Bernstein; and Mills Music. It was a good place to meet musicians, performers, and agents, and who could say where the next break would come from? And besides, all of the offices gave out free copies of the new songs to professionals.

When I got rolling in vaudeville, I had to take my schooling where I could get it. If any booking anywhere was long enough for it, Mama always hired a tutor for me and, when my sister was old enough, for Rosalind too. When I was in New York, I went to the Professional Children's School, where the schedule was worked out to accommodate kids who had to be free for matinee days, and kids who disappeared for weeks at a time on an out-of-town booking. In those days, the school was located in a brownstone on 46th Street next to the old Dinty Moore's restaurant. In that school, there were kids like Ruby Keeler, Gene Raymond, Lillian Roth, Beatrice Kay, Helen Mack, Helen Chandler, Miriam Battista, and Penny Singleton.

I was also going to dancing school when I lived in Harlem. The lady who ran the school was named Mrs. Rock, and she would put on shows using her pupils. That's what interested Mama the most.

Mrs. Rock didn't charge for the shows she put on—after all, she was only showing the parents what they were getting for their money—but local bookings came out of it. With one dancing-school partner or another, I appeared at the Beaver Club, Rena Club, Anthlon–Pom Pom, Avon-Chickering, and every other social club that would have me, including the Elks, Masons, and Knights of Pythias. A mother always went along —usually mine, but sometimes the girl's—to chaperone us and to collect the money. We got between three and five dollars. You can figure out the take from a two-way split after carfare. It wasn't much, but the couple of bucks bought a lot more groceries in those days.

It was around this time that I got my first tuxedo. When I say got, of course, I mean rented. With Mama's help, Sylvia Jacobs, from my dancing school, and I had branched out to club dates. Nothing big—local clubs like Elsmere Hall and the Hunt's Point Palace in the Bronx, and the Palm Garden Terrace in Manhattan. Mama took me over to Hahn's tuxedo-rental place on 125th Street when we got our first club date. The kid's version of a tux—jacket, knickers, and long socks—rented for fifty cents. It didn't bother Mama much the first time we rented from Hahn, but when we had to go back a second, third, fourth, and fifth time, and each time shell out another fifty cents for the same used kid's tuxedo, it got to her. And when Mama was bugged, she thought and she made decisions.

One night after dinner, she was sitting in the kitchen with Pa. I was also at the table, trying to do my homework while listening. "Fifty cents again!" Mama said, looking at the suit I had worn the night before, which was now neatly folded in Hahn's box, waiting to be returned the next day. "I tell you, Moe, that Hahn has some business. The same suit over and over again, and every time fifty cents. A business like that we should all be in. And I'm supporting it!"

Pa took her hand to calm her down. "Every business has its expenses, so what can you do? This is Milton's entertaining-business expense. In the closet, do we have a black suit with a silk stripe on the knickers and silk lapels? No. So we pay. If that's what has to be, why get excited?"

"No!" Mama said firmly. "The next time I have to go to Hahn's, I'm going to make him an offer. I'm going to buy Milton a suit outright. This pay-forever business is not for me."

She made Mr. Hahn an offer of seven dollars. He asked for ten, and they settled at eight. Mama gave him four dollars with a promise to pay the other half the next time I worked. I had my first tuxedo. God, I felt proud carrying the box home.

That night, Mama steamed it over the bathtub, and brushed it down as if she were grooming a racehorse. They didn't have kid-size suspenders in those days, so Mama bought wide black elastic and sewed it to the pants. As I got taller, she substituted longer elastic so the trousers could hang farther down on my hips under the jacket. The suit sort of grew with me. She also sewed some dark buttons on an ordinary white shirt, which made it look fancy and dressy.

We also got some bookings through the kiddie shows that were staged at the Mt. Zion Temple, where I was later *bar mitzvahed*. The shows were rehearsed in the basement of the temple and put on at the Palm Garden Terrace on 52nd Street off Eighth Avenue. Every mother and father who had a kid in the show was given ten tickets to sell. You can bet on it that Mama sold her tickets.

I think I appeared in the temple show with Ruth Roaman, a very sweet little girl. (Until recently she ran a successful dress shop on Madison Avenue in New York.) We did the same song-and-dance act that I had done with Sylvia Jacobs, but to a different song. We did "How'd You Like to Spoon with Me?" with all sorts of cute gestures that I can get a little sick thinking about today. I think the reason we came to do that Jerome Kern number is because Mama and I had gotten professional copies for free when we were up at the T. B. Harms office.

I said before that I wonder what my life would have been like if Mama hadn't been guiding, steering, pushing me in show business. In a way, that's unfair. If a person can be born for something, I guess I was born for show business. All I needed was just one little push. After all, Mama had nothing to do with the shows I put on in the backyards of the buildings we lived in. I'd mooch wooden crates from the grocery stores to make a stage, and I'd borrow a bedsheet when nobody was looking. If you hung it over a clothesline and then pulled on the clothesline, you had an almost-real professional curtain. That was all I needed, plus Rosalind, who was only about three, to walk around with a hat to collect the pennies I charged for the great show. For their penny, I gave the local kids the best of Mrs. Rock's dance steps, plus whatever jokes I had heard in my travels with Mama. But instead of "How'd You Like to Spoon with Me?", which I think would have gotten me flying rocks from the backyard bunch, I gave them the hotter stuff from the song sheets I wasn't sup- posed to study, numbers like, "Since Maggie Dooley Learned the Hooley Hooley" and "They're Wearing 'Em Higher in Hawaii." I think it was while doing that last number that I learned that you can get laughs by leering.

I also did a medley of the songs that were coming over from what we thought of then as the European war—"Keep the Home Fires Burning," "Pack Up Your Troubles in Your Old Kit-Bag"—and then I switched right into "I Didn't Raise My Boy to Be a Soldier," which I thought was a real sharp transition that would bring whistles and screams. I found out the first time I tried it that the kids preferred the racier songs.

My finish was "Take Me to the Midnight Cake Walk Ball." I put a lot of kicking and strutting and hand waving into it. I can't say that it was a cakewalk I did, but since most of my audience in the backyard didn't know what a cakewalk was, I got away with it. As I took my bows, yanking the bedsheet back and forth in front of me, I could hear Roz out front, in her squeaky voice yelling, "More! More!" just the way I had taught her. I guess this was a forerunner of what Mama was to do in years to come for my performances.

That show had nothing to do with Mama. The backyard entertain- ments were my idea. Maybe Mama moved me out where the show-biz bug could infect me, but the decision to keep moving on was my own.

Sometimes I dreamed of a life like other kids', but I guess I didn't really want it hard enough or I'd have refused to go on.

Not that all my early jobs were behind footlights. One of my after-school jobs was song-plugging in the five-and-ten, standing behind the song-sheet counter on a little box so the customers could see me while a pianist played and I sang the numbers that were for sale. My voice, which hadn't changed yet, was high, but it wasn't bad if you like kid voices. Now, I wouldn't particularly call that a theatrical booking. And delivering for a delicatessen, which was another part-time job, was way out of the business, though it had some great moments for me. I'd get paid in tips, but the big payoff from the delicatessen man was raspberry soda and a piece of halvah, two favorites. I'd come home at suppertime, belching and happy.

I was working a lot, but we weren't getting anywhere. By now, the downtown agents, producers, bookers all knew who I was. Some of them had used me for small-time stuff, but most of them knew me through Mama, who made the rounds every free moment she had, always pushing for me. What seemed like a break didn't come from any of them, but from one of our trips together to the music publishers.

I don't remember what office we were in, but I was trying out a song. Mama had slipped the house pianist fifty cents to play for me, because there was an agent across the room. I kept singing while Mama kept watching the agent, who kept on talking to an actor. He never looked at us once. It seemed like wasted money, but at the end of my song, another man who looked sort of familiar came over and tipped his hat to Mama. "Hello, Mrs. Berlinger."

Mr. Schoenstein was a short, stocky, and vigorous man who lived on our block, and whose son sometimes played with me. Mr. Schoenstein was known as Taps to everyone in the music business. Among his many activities, Taps took care of rounding up the talent for the famous Thursday nights at the Mt. Morris Theatre on 116th Street at Fifth Avenue.

Mama gave her big smile and put an arm around me. "You remember Mr. Schoenstein, Milton. Say hello."

I said hello. Taps said to Mama, "The kid's got a good voice on him. I think I could use him up at the Mt. Morris. It would be a chance for him to be seen, if that interests you."

Thursday night at the Mt. Morris Theatre was songwriter's night. It was good for everybody all around. Taps would invite a top songwriter to appear on stage at the theater as a special guest on the vaudeville bill. It gave the songwriter, after playing and singing a medley of his past songs, the chance to plug his new numbers.

I appeared at the Mt. Morris Theatre, but not on the stage, thanks to the Gerry Society. They were a do-good organization under the direction of Elbridge T. Gerry, a lawyer and a founder of the New York Society for the Prevention of Cruelty to Children, who protected children from exploitation on the stages of several large cities along the East Coast. The Society had power in Boston, wasn't active at all in Philadelphia, and was very powerful in New York. They set all sorts of rules, such as what hour at night a child had to be off the legitimate stage, and how old a child had to be before he or she could appear at all.

All of what the Society was doing might have been a good thing in the case of kids whose parents were working them against their will, but that wasn't me. I wanted to work. Now, I didn't have the clout of an Eddie Foy, who somehow got the Gerry Society to give permission for all "Seven Little Foys"—even the ones under sixteen—to appear on stage, so when I went up to the Mt. Morris Theatre, I was put in the box nearest to the stage. The songwriter for that night turned out to be George M. Cohan, and I stood up in the box and sang "Over There" for him and the audience.

I went back to the Mt. Morris thanks to Irving Berlin, who had heard me sing on one of our trips to his music-publishing company. He took me with him on his Thursday night. Since it was an army song from his big show Yip, Yip, Yaphank, I wore my Boy Scout uniform (somehow I had found the time to join, and Mama had found the money for the uniform), and I was introduced from the box. I stood up and threw Mr. Berlin my snappiest three-finger Boy Scout salute. Then he went to the piano and I sang "Oh! How I Hate to Get Up in the Morning."

I guess the songwriter's nights were good exposure for me, but that's about all the good they did. Neither George M. Cohan nor Irving Berlin was banging down our door to make a star of that great kid who had helped plug their songs. The break came, but it wasn't from New York. It was from Philadelphia and a man named E. W. Wolf.

Kid acts were a big thing in vaudeville, thanks mostly to Gus Edwards, who had a knack for finding talented children by the carload and putting a pack of them together into acts like "School Boys & Girls" and "Kid Kabaret." Gus Edwards had helped Eddie Cantor, Walter Winchell,

George Jessel, Lila Lee, Georgie Price, and many others on their way to
stardom. His acts were very popular on the vaudeville circuits for many
reasons, one of which was that young kids worked cheap.

Like all things that click with the paying public, the imitators come
rushing to get on the gravy train while it's still rolling. One of those guys
was E. W. Wolf, who created and packaged acts that worked the vaudeville houses in the Philadelphia area.

When the offer came for me to join one of Wolf's acts out of Philly,
it must have been a tough decision for Mama. If she had sold her soul
to show business, her heart was still with the family. It would mean a break
longer than any of the California movie trips. Maybe we had never had
an easy row to hoe, but we had always been together. This would split the
family in two. I was still too young to be on my own, so she would have
to go with me. Moe was a lot of wonderful things, but he wasn't a tough
businessman who could hang on to money—how often had he given away
a needed dollar to someone "who needed it more than we do"?—when
up against the crooked managers, the soft soap, and the hard-luck stories
that were part of every backstage. No, Mama was the one to go, and
besides, it was the world she knew she belonged in. And if Mama went,
Rosalind would have to come too. Moe could take care of the three older
boys, but a baby girl should be with her mother.

There were other factors pushing Mama toward Philadelphia. Hollywood had definitely turned out to be the place for moviemaking, and the
growing industry had moved west. There was very little film work left in
the East. If we were to stay in New York—and who thought of leaving?
—then the stage was the place for me. But New York had the Gerry
Society protecting us right into the poorhouse. Because of them, roles on
the legitimate stage for youngsters were rare. Sometimes a kid did show
up on Broadway, but playwrights did their best to avoid putting kids in
their writing, and producers discouraged productions with kids altogether.
Who needed trouble?

So that narrowed me to vaudeville, and there the Gerry Society was
strong. Maybe the Foys could get around them and work in New York,
and Buster Keaton could work because he looked older (When he was old
enough to work without fear of the Society, he took an ad in *Variety:*
"Today I Am a Theatrical Man—Goodbye, Mr. Gerry!"), but at ten, I
looked ten, and worst of all, there was no audience demanding to see me.

Mama had felt the power of the Gerry Society once. That was when
I nearly got arrested while working a club date in a hall at 41st and

Broadway. I was doing a little act I had gotten up as "The Shimmy Kid" or "Al Jolson's Double"—I had used both those billings for shows put on by Rabbi Tintner of the Mt. Zion Temple, and you can practically figure out the act from the billing. There must have been somebody in the audience from the Gerry Society, because when I finished and came off, there was a policeman waiting for me.

Mama was there too, and, just like so many of the heroines she had loved in silent movies, she pushed herself with an arms-outspread gesture between the cop and me. "What? What is it, officer? Don't you dare touch that boy!"

"Calm down, lady." The cop raised his hand in a soothing gesture, but unfortunately he had his billy club in that hand, which only made Mama stiffen her position in front of me. "Is that your boy, lady?"

"Of course it is. And *I am* calm." One of Mama's nicknames in later days was "Queenie," based in part on the dignity she could pull together in all sorts of situations. This was one of them.

"Well, we've had a complaint from the Gerry Society that minors were working on this stage. I'm going to have to take the kid down to the station."

Mama was always a fast thinker. "What station house? Which one?"

The cop told her. Mama smiled. "I don't think you'll like it when you bring my son in. Isn't the sergeant on duty there named McCloskey?"

"Yeh." The cop was looking at her with new respect.

I was still behind Mama, but I was looking around her and watching her. Mama went on in her class voice, cool as a frozen lake. "And I think that an officer named Breen works out of that station, too?"

"Well, yeah. Look, lady, I'm only doing my job."

Mama relaxed a little, becoming the policeman's pal. "Sure you are, that is unless you didn't see any underage minor working here, like if you got here too late to catch the act. Because I sure don't think Sergeant McCloskey's going to like it when a fellow law-enforcement officer's child is arrested and put away like a common criminal."

The cop was very puzzled. "You're not on the force! We don't have women."

"I am a store detective. You just tell McCloskey you pulled in Sadie's kid and see how he likes it. And when Breen spreads the story around the locker room, I think you'll be the laugh of the force."

The poor guy was sweating. "Well, I didn't know. Look, Mrs. . . . uh . . ." He waited for Mama to fill in her name, which she didn't. "Look,

I think we can forget this whole thing, but why don't you take your son and get out of here fast, okay?"

"That's very kind of you, officer." She turned to me and snapped, "Get your coat, Milton. Quick."

But the cop wasn't too happy about being beaten by a woman. He turned in the doorway. "You're just lucky that kid isn't a Jew, lady, whoever you are, or he'd be behind bars so fast . . ."

Mama just ignored him. "Button up, Milton. You don't want to catch cold." And we sailed out for home. Mama didn't start shaking until we got on the subway. It was an experience she wasn't about to forget and had no desire to repeat again. And that meant Philadelphia.

When the time came to go, everybody went to the station. We stood in a miserable huddle waiting for the gate to open. Anyone passing by and looking at the seven Berlingers, every one of us with tears in our eyes, except baby Rosalind, who was bawling and clinging to Pa's trouser legs, would have thought we were seeing someone off to an orphanage, or maybe Siberia.

"You'll write?" Pa said.

Mama nodded and dabbed at her eyes. "Like a clock. And you'll write too?"

Then she turned to Phil, Frank, and Jack. "I don't want to hear a word from your father of trouble, you hear me?"

They nodded.

"You get up the first time he calls you, and you help with the cleaning and whatever. And I don't want to hear that Pa has to go looking for you when it's suppertime. Six o'clock I want to be able to look at a Philadelphia clock and say to myself, my family is sitting down eating a good, wholesome meal, my four men together, all right? And I want—"

But the conductor's announcement cut her short. When he said "Philadelphia," we fell into each other's arms. My brothers all punched me on the arm or patted me on the back. They all thought they were too old for kissing me. I was ten. I thought so too. But Pa took my face between his hands. "I'm going to be so proud. I know it." And he kissed me on the cheek, and his face left a wet mark against mine.

Everybody was talking at once, and nobody was listening. Rosalind had to be pried out of Pa's arms, and suddenly there were three Berlingers inside the train gate and four Berlingers outside.

We were off to fame and fortune . . . and Philadelphia.

1909-1922

The Berlinger family. Back row, from left: Moses, Phil, Sarah; middle: Frank, Rosalind, Jack; front: Milton.

Milton Berle, age 1.

Milton Berle, age 4.

Sarah Berlinger.

Moses Berlinger.

Milton Berle, age 7 (L) and 11.

A scene from The Maid's Night Out, *1916. Pete Raymond, Milton Berle, far left; Mabel Normand, seated at table.*

Tid-Bits, 1919, a vaudeville act. Milton Berle, second from right.

Kennedy & Berle in Broadway Bound, 1921.

Milton Berle, age 11.

The Florodora Sextette, 1920. Milton Berle, last boy on the right; Ben ("Bunny") Grauer, third boy from left.

Milton Berle, age 15 and 16 (R).

With Ruth Roland, 1922.

With Louise Fazenda, 1922.

Dup

Professional Children's School

Record of _Milton Berlinger_

Year 192**2** – **3**   Grade **8**

Subjects	Sept.	Oct.	Nov.	Dec.	Jan.	Feb.	Mar.	Apr.	May
Arithmetic	B–	nme B–	B–	B+	A	C	A	P	
Spelling + Composition	B–	B–	B–	B–	B–	B–	B–	B–	P
Reading	B	C	C	B	B+	A– C+	B	P	
History		B	C–	C+	B–	C+	C+	B–	P
Geography		C+	C	C+	D	D	B–	C–	P
Science		–	B–	B–	B–	B	B–	B	P
French			C	C	–	–	C	C	incomple.
Thorndyke	Reading	test							

Average			C+						
Days Late	in the road –	in the road	in the road	in the road	0	1	in the road	in the road all but 7 days	in the road
Days Absent					0	9			
Deportment					B	C			

6

Vaudeville kid acts were a lot coy, a lot cute, and plenty brash. The way the precocious kids were presented, I don't think they came across as talented children so much as midget grown-ups. They didn't do kid stuff well, but showed off at how well they could imitate grown-ups.

The acts that E. W. Wolf dreamed up and packaged were all variations on the same act with different names. I worked in five of them: "Playmates," "The Melody of Youth," "The Rising Generation," "Ting-a-Ling," "Tid-Bits." We played houses around Philadelphia like the Alhambra, Nixon's Grand, the Allegheny, the Cross Keys, and the William Penn—strictly regular vaudeville, nothing big time. And the acts would tour after they were played out in Philly. Then back for a new act by Wolf that was like the old act with different songs and different set pieces.

The acts consisted of three boys and three girls. The girls were in fluffy skirts with lots of bows and lots of curls. The boys wore knickerbocker tuxedos. We did an opening song, and then each kid had a solo spot for his specialty. I did an imitation of Eddie Cantor. I can't say it was the greatest imitation of Eddie Cantor ever done, but it got a hand every show (I think it was my mother's). All I had to do was hop around a lot, roll my eyes and pat my hands together as I hopped, and I was halfway to Eddie Cantor.

The kid singers did the popular songs of the day, songs like "Till We Meet Again," which made everyone in the house who had a boy in service fill up with tears, and "I'm Forever Blowing Bubbles." The way Wolf staged the acts, everyone stayed on stage throughout, sometimes just standing there while others did their turn, sometimes becoming chorus. It made the six-shrimp act look like a big flash.

When everyone had had his solo, we went into the big finish. In "Tid-Bits" we did a number called "Take Me to the Land of Jazz." It was fast and peppy with lots of finger-snapping on stage and with one trumpet player in the pit:

> *Take me to the Land of Jazz.*
> *Let me hear the kind of blues that Memphis has.*
> *I want to step to a tune that's full of ginger and pep.*
> *Pick 'em up and lay 'em down,*
> *Learn to do the razzmatazz.*
> *Let me give you a warning,*
> *We won't get home until morning.*
> *Everything is full of jazzbo*
> *In the loving Land of . . .*
> *Said the loving Land of . . .*
> *In the loving Land of Jazz!*

For that number we all got straw hats and canes and big glittery bow ties—the girls too—so that without going into blackface we became a sort of minstrel show for the finish.

I remember that almost always after a show, when we came out the stage door with our mothers, there would be parents with their kids waiting to take a look at us. The kids just stared at us, as if we came from another planet, some special dreamland that they would never get to see. They were lucky, only they didn't know it.

I don't think we had anything going for us as kids. You'd think that a six-kid act would mean that each child had five playmates. It never worked out that way, because six kids on stage meant six mothers waiting backstage, each protecting her own. Feelings ran high. "If your Norma steps in front of Imogene once more, I'm going to tell Imogene to push her right into the orchestra pit!" "You just tell your kid to wait for his cue. If he cuts Herbie's last note again, I'm going straight to Mr. Wolf!" "Albert, don't let her do that. I don't care if she is a girl, the audience wants to see you!" By the time the mothers got through with us and with one another, there was no chance of playing together, much less even talking. We all distrusted one another.

I would have liked to have had another boy to play with in what little free time I had, but I was lucky that at least I had Rosalind. She was always backstage with Mama. Where else could she be left safely when I was working?

Once, on the way to the theater, I found a baseball and stuck it in my pocket. Between shows, another boy in the show, Herbie Barris (who's now a burlesque comic in Las Vegas), and I went out into the alley for a game of catch. We were just tossing the ball back and forth, pretending we were rival pitchers on opposite teams. I accidentally tossed a wild pitch that just grazed his shoulder. I know I didn't hurt him, because he turned and started to run after the ball that was bouncing down the stage alley. The stage door slammed, and his mother came out. She was burning mad. "I saw that! You deliberately threw the ball at my son's head. Herbie, you come back here this minute! Just let that ball go out in the gutter. It will serve him right."

Herbie stopped and turned around. He looked at me sheepishly and started toward his mother.

Mama came out. "What's going on here?"

Herbie's mother said, "Your Milton tried to kill my son."

Mama looked at me. "Milton?"

"We were just playing catch, that's all. Herbie's not hurt, are you?"

Herbie's mother had him hugged against her skirt. He shook his head. "No, Mother, honestly. We were just—"

"Enough," his mother said. "Thank God he's all right, but your Milton tried to kill him. He's always been jealous of the way the audience loves Herbie."

Mama just looked at her. "They don't exactly hate Milton," she said very calmly. "Go get your ball, Milton, before someone takes it."

Mama turned away from the other mother and waited for me at the stage door. When I came back with my ball, Mama turned in the doorway for one last shot. "I wish I could have a picture of you just like that. You look so at home standing in the alley." And then "Queenie" Berlinger sailed into the theater.

That night, as we were coming off stage, Herbie whispered to me, "My mother says I'm not allowed to play with you anymore. I'm sorry."

"Sure," I said. "I understand."

The next day I played catch in the alley with Rosalind, which wasn't half as much fun.

* * *

Wherever we stayed when we were on the road, the landlady's rules were always the same: No visitors in your room, and no cooking in the room. We always ignored the no-cooking rule. Everyone in vaudeville did, except maybe the star acts, who could afford to pay for breakfast at the house or eat in a restaurant. We couldn't.

The first thing that Mama always unpacked after the landlady left the room was her small cooking heater. If there was no good hiding place in the room, Mama carried the little stove in her big purse. On our way to the theater she'd stop at a grocery store and pick up the next day's breakfast. Every day she bought one egg and one orange. She bought bread by the loaf and kept it wrapped in a petticoat at the bottom of our trunk.

Mama would let us sleep in the morning until the water boiled and the egg was ready. Then she divided the orange into three parts and cut the egg in half—she always said she didn't feel like an egg that morning —and we'd eat. This was back before the days of instant coffee, and making real coffee was out, because it would have meant carrying a coffee pot, and the smell of coffee boiling was risky. What we got instead was hot water with evaporated milk in it. After breakfast, Mama carefully picked up all the pieces of eggshell and orange rind, so the landlady wouldn't catch on, and we'd throw them away on the way to the first show at whatever theater we were playing.

Once a week, on payday, Mama sent a letter home with money in it. We'd hear from Pa about once a week, too, with the neighborhood news and the latest doings of Phil, Frank, and Jack.

Between letters, Mama would work up a head of steam worrying about the missing members of her family. Judging from Pa's letters, always asking, "How is the baby? Is she growing? How is Milton? Tell him to do his homework," he was worrying and wondering, too. But when you're living on every cent, even penny postcards run into money. Even though we knew we'd hear only once a week from Pa, we checked in at the post office every day in whatever town we were playing. It was something to do. And even though we were show folk, the man in the post office talked to us. There were other people who didn't. I still remember seeing signs in boardinghouse windows that said, "No theatricals!" and "No dogs or actors."

That was the worst part of touring: loneliness. We were in Philadelphia when the armistice was declared. That day everybody loved everybody else. Mama took us to see the dancing in the streets. People ran around hugging and kissing strangers. It made us feel good, like the whole city was our friend. Only, the next day everything was back to normal, and we were alone again. All of those new friends I had imagined were as fake as the armistice turned out to be. When the real armistice came, I didn't feel so excited about all of those happy smiling faces.

And when I wasn't working, there was schoolwork. When you went on the road, you took assignments with you from the Professional Children's School. I had schoolwork to do every day, and papers and homework to mail in.

Our first home was one room in a boardinghouse in Germantown. The lady who ran it was a huge fat woman with iron-colored hair tied in a knot on top of her head. She never smiled, not even when she got her rent. Though she catered to vaudeville people, she didn't seem to like them much. She even bragged that she had never been to see a vaudeville show. Rosalind was scared stiff of her.

But Roz got scared of everything when she learned that the name of where we were living was Germantown. The war stories of the Huns bouncing Belgian babies on their bayonets had filtered down to her, and Roz kept looking around, when we were outside, for men with bayonets who might think she was bounceable. "Nobody wants you," I told her. "You're too skinny to bounce."

Working for E. W. Wolf didn't make for fat kids. He paid the least he could get away with, and Mama had to cut corners wherever she could, since three of us had to live on what I made and there had to be enough left over to send something home each week to Pa and the boys.

When we traveled for Wolf, the three of us would sleep in one upper berth on the train, Mama and Rosalind with their heads at one end, me with my head at the other end. In all the places we stayed, it was also one bed, unless you wanted to pay extra for a cot, which we didn't. Mama and Roz slept the way the bed went, and I slept across the bottom. My whole childhood seems to have been spent sleeping with feet in my face.

One morning in Scranton, we woke up to a heavy snowfall. The landlady's son was the world's slowest shoveler. He had the walk only halfway cleared when it was time to leave for the theater. It was impossible for Mama to make it to the sidewalk in her long skirt. Mama said I should go on alone and she would follow after with Rosalind. "Go straight," she called after me, "and watch both ways when you cross the streets."

There was traffic moving, but less than the usual number of cars and horses. Some people were out shopping, but most of them were still clearing away the snow. I remember thinking as I ran to the theater, taking slides on the ice patches, that we wouldn't be playing to much of a house that afternoon. As I turned in to the alley leading to the stage door, I noticed three or four boys hanging around out front. I didn't think twice about it until I got an iceball smack on the side of my head.

I spun around. "Who did that?"

"Me. What are you going to do about it?" the biggest boy said. He looked heavy and tough, and he was a good couple of inches taller than I. I hesitated, and he laughed. "Maybe you want to sing a song for us, huh?"

His friends laughed. "Watch out, Fred, he might kick you with his toe shoes."

That did it. I rushed straight at the guy. Before I knew what was happening, I was flat on my ass in a snowbank, and Fred was over me. "Well, you had enough, sissy, or you want some more?"

"More," I shouted, and got up swinging. I think I tapped him once before he sent me back into the snow.

I was struggling to get up again when Pat Anderson, who minded the stagedoor, came out. "Stop that! I told you kids to stay the hell away from this theater, and this is the last time I'm telling you. Next time I'll have the police on you!" He came toward me. "And you, kid, get inside where you belong. You can't fight for shit, anyway."

The kids scattered, and I went into the theater. I checked my face in a mirror to see if there were any marks that would show on stage. Luckily, there was nothing. Mr. Anderson was right behind me. "You all right, sonny?"

I nodded. "I hit him one good one."

He put his arm around me. "Sure you did. I saw the whole thing. Didn't nobody ever teach you how to fight?"

I shook my head.

He looked at the backstage clock. "You gotta little time yet. Come over here. You better learn a thing or two before you get yourself killed."

He took me behind some flats where no one coming in would see us. "First thing, if you're going to fight, don't get mad. A little mad's okay, but real mad gets in your way so you don't know what you're doing. You gotta be able to think so you can send those signals out from your brain to your fists. Now, make fists and put 'em up so I can see how you stand."

It was the beginning of my fight training. From that time on, I started practicing throwing punches in front of the mirror, jabbing at imaginary enemies. If Mama and Roz were out of our room, I would wad up our dirty laundry to make a punching bag. I shadow-boxed all the way to the toilet, dancing and sparring down the hall. Nobody was going to push me around anymore.

If I got any spare change, I would buy a copy of *Ring* magazine and study the stances of professional fighters like Jess Willard and Benny Leonard. I'd practice in front of the mirror in our room, imitating their angry scowls. I didn't know it then, but I was building toward a day when I'd actually step into a professional prizefight ring.

But all I was thinking about at the time was that kid named Fred who had belted me into the snowbank, and the kids back home in Harlem who thought I was a pushover. Well, they all had a surprise coming to them if they took me on. Of course, I never did run into Fred again, and when we did get back to New York I was too busy to hang around the streets waiting for a chance to test my new skills—if I really had any.

The only thing I was really aware of when I grunted and jabbed and threw my imaginary haymakers was a lightness inside myself, as if someone had lifted a load of bricks off my chest. It was still a good few years before I learned words like *tension* and *resentment* and *hostility*, but I guess it was building up inside me even then. You don't take on grown-up responsibilities while living inside a kid's body without paying a price for it.

That same year, I became interested in cards, but I don't mean gambling. It started with a magician who appeared on the bill with our kiddie act. His name was Nate Leipzig, and he was the first man I ever saw do magical things with a deck of cards. He was a fine gentleman, and his act fascinated me. I'd watch from the wings every chance I got as he went through his routine. He worked with a deck of cards doing fancy shuffles, riffling cards so they fell like a waterfall, pulling aces out all over the place. I was hooked.

One day he spotted me and came over after he finished his act. In his German-American accent, he said, "Do you want to be a magician, sonny?"

I felt shy. Nate Leipzig seemed like a great celebrity to me because he could do the impossible. "I dunno."

"Would you like me to teach you a trick with cards?"

I was floored. "Would you?"

Leipzig laughed. "I will show you how to do a magic shuffle with the cards."

He gave me a deck he no longer used, and he showed me a simple shuffle. I learned it easily, just the mechanics. I couldn't do it with the style and smoothness he did, but he told me that if I practiced every chance I got, the shuffle would get smoother and smoother. I practiced. Hell, I slept with that deck of cards under my pillow at night for fear that someone would come into the room and take them. I was going to impress people with anything I had going for me: boxing, cards, everything I could learn.

7

In the year 1900—thank God, at last a year that *was* before my time—the smash hit of the theatrical season in both New York and London was a musical called *Florodora*. I've got to tell you a bit of the story, because you won't believe anybody could ever have gotten away with it.

Florodora is an island in the Philippines. Its chief industry is perfume manufacturing. The owner of the perfume business dies, and his business is taken over by a rich American. Meanwhile, the real owner's daughter is poor, working on a Philippine farm. A Scotland Yard detective, disguised as a phrenologist and a hypnotist (so help me!), comes to the island searching for the girl. There's also the American's daughter, in love with the Scotland Yard man; the American's business manager, who's really a titled lord; and an English lady searching for a new husband. From Act One in the Philippines, the plot jumps to the lord's castle in Wales, where the detective tells a ghost story which scares the dishonest American so he confesses the perfume takeover and is forgiven in time for all the right boys to pair off with all the right girls.

As you can see, it didn't make any sense at all, but it was a fast hit, especially the Florodora Sextette, which was six pretty typewriters (girls who could type on that new machine) and six clerks singing "Tell Me, Pretty Maiden." Nobody cared much about the six guys, but the six girls had the town on its ear. Everyone of them ended up with a millionaire, and one replacement cutie named Evelyn Nesbit made headlines when her husband, Harry Thaw, shot Standford White over her.

So that's 1900. For some crazy reason, J. J. Shubert decided to revive *Florodora* in 1920. Now, 1920 was in no way 1900. Those "pretty maidens" were bobbing their hair and showing their legs and turning into vamps and flappers and drinking bootleg hootch because of Prohibition. Worst of all, that shocking music called "jazz" was coming in. Who'd go for all that old-fashioned innocence?

The Shuberts must have decided a lot of people would go for it, or they wouldn't have brought it back. Mr. Jake and Mr. Lee Shubert were accused of a lot of things in their day, but never of tossing away their money. This show was to be Mr. Jake's baby, and he backed up his revival with such box-office names as Walter Woolf, Eleanor Painter, George Hassel, Harry Fender, John T. Murray and Christie MacDonald.

I got with *Florodora* because of an idea Mr. Jake had for the revival. The big number, as in the original, was to be the second-act double sextette, "Tell Me, Pretty Maiden." It would be staged first with the girls in costumes right for 1920. Then, as a topper, there'd be a second sextette which would re-create the original number as it was first seen in 1900. Then, for the killer, he decided to do the number with six little girls and six little boys who would be the "Florodora Sextette of 1940"! (Between you and me, I don't care if you don't think it was such a great idea. It got me out of Philadelphia!) I was chosen as one of the six boys. Another one who joined us later on was Bunny Grauer, who became Ben when he grew up. Some other kids who appeared in the number at one time or another during the run were Junior Durkin, Miriam Battista, Marguerite Churchill, and Helen Chandler.

The show was set for the Century Theater, a big musical house on 61st Street and Central Park West. I remember coming down with my mother from Harlem for rehearsal one cold winter day. Mama had made some stops along the way. She had to get Pa's glasses fixed, and there was another stop at a drugstore to pick up something—Mama believed that druggists could cure most things over the counter, and besides, they were cheaper than getting a prescription from a doctor. Then we caught the trolley down Broadway. When we were outside the theater, Mama opened her purse and started poking around. "I'm just going to run down the block a minute to the—" She let out a scream and started rummaging like crazy.

"My change purse. It's gone."

She searched the pockets of her coat, and she made me search mine. Nothing. "Mama, how much was in it?"

There were tears in her eyes. "I had more than four dollars. Oh my God, I must have dropped it along the way. Milton, you go in to the rehearsal, and behave. And wait for me until I come. I'm going to find that money."

She started up Seventh Avenue, dabbing at her eyes with her handkerchief and walking along the gutter, her head going back and forth as she searched.

She didn't show up again until late that afternoon, her eyes still red. Mama had walked all the way back up to Harlem searching for the missing money. She never found it.

Florodora went into rehearsal right after New Year's, 1920. We opened our out-of-town tryout in Atlantic City on a bitter-cold winter night. The ocean wind seeped in backstage, where we kids huddled in our thin costumes. The boys wore top hats and cutaway suits. The girls wore pretty summer dresses gathered up at one side and pinned by flowers, and hats with plumes.

The first sextette strolled off to big applause, but the second sextette, dressed in copies of the 1900 costumes (one New York critic, when we opened on Broadway, called them cheap copies of the original—that was the Shuberts for you) brought down the house. I was in a panic as the orchestra went into the vamp for the Baby Sextette's entrance. At that moment, I couldn't remember one line or step. I was sweating, my mouth was dry, and I wanted to go to the bathroom. And suddenly I was on, strolling along the stage, which was supposed to be somewhere high up along the walls of the castle in Wales, tipping my hat to my girl partner, and singing, "Tell me, pretty maiden, are there any more at home like you?"

I was in a fog throughout the number. I didn't hear the big explosion of applause that greeted us, or all the oohing and aahing from the ladies in the audience throughout the number. Mama told me about it after I came off and calmed down.

From Atlantic City, the show moved to Philadelphia—a better theater than any I had worked in the last time around—and then to Baltimore and Washington, D.C. Opening night in New York was set for the Century Theater on April 5, 1920. Suddenly it was a whole new ball game. I had gotten used to the number and the show on the road. The sweats and nervousness had stopped after the opening in Atlantic City, and I settled down to feeling as cocky as a seasoned Broadway pro—which, I might add, is something a pro never should feel if he plans to stay on top.

But suddenly it was opening night on Broadway, and if I thought I had been nervous before, I was terrified now.

The first blow fell when we saw the program. I wasn't even listed in it. None of the Baby Sextette was. Out of town, we had been listed, but New York was Gerry Society headquarters, and the feeling was not to rub their noses in the fact that twelve underage kids were working on stage late in the second act. They'd hear about it right away, but why shove it at them? And the other reason was that the Shuberts wanted us to be a big surprise to the opening-night audience. So I was going to make my Broadway debut, get my big break, as one unidentified kid among twelve. Some break.

The tension mounted backstage as the audience started filing in, dressed to the hilt. The word drifted backstage of who was out front. There were major opera stars in the boxes, and there were women who had gone to all sorts of trouble and expense to come up with opening-night dresses based on the gowns the ladies of the original production had worn. There were three members of the original Sextette out front. And, of course, all of the critics.

The first act went like a house on fire. The jazz-age audience was loving it. When Walter Woolf sang the love ballad, "Dolores," the show stopped cold. He had to repeat it six times.

Intermission was wild backstage. The stage manager had to keep telling people to keep their voices down. The entire cast was laughing and carrying on and hugging one another. Opening-night jitters were easing away in the excitement of the audience reception. The only tense pocket was where us twelve kids, who hadn't gone on yet, waited together.

A few minutes before the beginning of the second act, Mama pulled me off to the side, where no one could hear us. "When you start the number," she whispered to me, "what foot do you step out on?"

"My right one."

She put her hands on my shoulders and looked me straight in the eyes. "Tonight, start on the other foot."

"Huh?" I thought I hadn't heard her correctly.

"Start on your left foot!"

I shook my head, which made my top hat fall off. I had been afraid to hold it because my hands were sweating so badly. "Mama, I can't. I'd be out of step through the whole number. It would wreck it!"

Mama's face was turning red. "Listen to me, Milton. Do I ever give you bad advice?"

I shook my head. "No, Mama."

"Do I ever tell you wrong things to do?"

"No, Mama." I could feel my stomach going into bigger knots than it already was in. I was being caught between Mama and the Shuberts.

"Would your own mother tell you to do something that was bad for you? Answer me, Milton."

"No, Mama."

"Then *do* what I tell you. Start on the other foot—on your left. You understand?"

I nodded.

Mama shook me. "I didn't hear you."

"I said yes, Mama."

They were calling places for the second-act opening. Mama was still holding me. "And if somebody asks why you did that, you'll tell them that you were so scared and nervous because it is the first opening night in New York you ever had that you got all mixed up. You understand? You were scared and it was an accident. Yes? Let me hear."

"Yes, Mama."

She gave me a hug. "Now, go get in line." She gave me a little push. "And be marvelous!"

I was the last boy to come on in the Baby Sextette, so I fell in behind the other five boys. The girls had moved to the other side of the stage, from which they would make their entrance. What I felt in Atlantic City on that first night was nothing compared to what I felt now as the second act was moving closer and closer to that moment when I would saunter out on the stage on the wrong foot and screw up a Shubert production number. I wanted to run out of the theater, I wanted to puke up my guts, I wanted to pee so bad I thought I would explode, and at the same time all of me was clamped to the floor, totally paralyzed. Stage fright wondering if you are going to do it right is bad enough, but when you know you are going to do it wrong, that's a whole new nightmare.

The second sextette came off, and the orchestra swung into the vamp for our entrance. The tiniest girl strolled out from stage left as the shortest boy started from stage right. Two at a time we came out, boys lining up behind the girls. There was wild applause followed by the oohing and aahing from the mothers in the audience. The boy in front of me heard his note and started out, like the others, on his right foot. And then it was my turn. I took a deep breath and stepped off on my left foot.

At first the audience didn't spot it, but then there were a few giggles.

And then pandemonium. As far out into the audience as the lights would let me see, there were laughing faces and people nudging one another and pointing at me. When we came to the part where the girls sang "What would you say if I said I liked you well?" and the boys answered "I'd vow to you on bended knee," they were beginning to quiet down a little. But when the boys all kneeled, and there was a gap in the line between my left knee and the next boy's right knee, they started howling all over again. We came off to wild applause.

I couldn't have been offstage two minutes after our last bow when the stage manager and the director descended on me, boiling mad. "Do you know what you've done? What the hell happened to you out there?"

I saw my mother's face beyond them. She was glaring at me, reminding me of what I was to say.

I didn't get a chance, because there was sudden silence as J. J. Shubert came running backstage. "Where is he? Where is that boy? Get him here immediately!"

Like a public enemy, they hustled me off to a corner where our voices wouldn't carry out to the stage. Mr. Jake looked like he was going to have a heart attack. "You're the little boy who was out of step all through the number! Do you know that?"

"Yes, sir, but—"

"Do you know what you've done? Did you hear them laughing out there?"

"Yes, sir, but—"

"Were you with this show in Atlantic City?"

"Yes, sir. But you see—"

"Then you did it the right way there. And Philadelphia? And Washington? And Baltimore?"

"Yes, Mr. Shubert. It's just—"

"But tonight of all nights you do it wrong. I want to know why a little *momser* wrecks a Shubert opening night!"

I burst into tears, and it wasn't acting. I was scared shitless. J. J. Shubert wasn't much taller than I, but he was ready to kill. "I was scared, Mr. Shubert. I've never been in a Broadway show before, and I got scared and I started out on the wrong foot and I couldn't get straightened out."

Mr. Shubert was shaking his head up and down. "And from that a beautiful multi-million-dollar Shubert production number is turned into a laugh riot! From one little *pisher* who can't keep in step."

"Please, Mr. Shubert, it won't happen again. I promise. I'll be all right tomorrow. It was just tonight. I got all nervous—"

Shubert waved me to be quiet. "Never mind excuses!" He turned and threw his arms into the air. "Through the whole number they laughed!" Then he turned back to me, and his voice dropped. "Can you do it again tomorrow night?"

Before I could say anything, he was out the stage door and heading around front to catch the end of the show. Mama ran over and pulled me to her in a big bear hug. "You see! You see! You're discovered!"

Discovered? Maybe, but the most the audience could talk about would be the kid on the wrong foot. Without a program credit, they wouldn't know my name, and the Shuberts paid the same amount for boys who start on their left foot as for boys who start on the right.

The reviews the next day were great. One paper called *Florodora* historic because its "tunes marked the transitional stage between Gilbert and Sullivan operettas and present jazz revues." Alan Dale of the *New York American* began his review with: "The joy of jazz and the shock of the shimmy ceased for three delightful hours last night," and ended with: "The young generation can go hang, or better still go to the Century Theater. Between you and me and the bedpost, I haven't had such a good time in many moons."

Every critic singled out the Baby Sextette for special mention. *New York Evening Sun:* "But the biggest hit of the evening was scored by the double sextette of little tots, and the tiniest girl and her partner were the 'sextette' stars of the evening." And Henry T. Finck in the *New York Evening Post:* ". . . one tot who sang, danced and acted as if she liked it. She was certainly having the time of her young life." How do you like that? I risk my job by going out on my left foot and some little girl plays it straight and gets all the notices!

Mama just read the notices and shrugged. "Big deal, her! She can have it. Mr. J. J. Shubert himself knows who *you* are!"

Florodora ran for nineteen weeks in New York. It closed during the mid-August dog days, when the pre–air-conditioning theaters boiled hotter than they did in June and July. The show moved to Boston and New Haven and such other places some maniac decided were cooler than New York, and returned to Broadway on November 29, 1920, to finish out its run. As I said, it was my first Broadway appearance. There's another first connected with *Florodora* for me—maybe even more important.

I turned twelve that July. Not quite a man, maybe, but there were masculine things happening physically. In fact, the problem had been coming up for about six months. At first I didn't know what to do, but, like almost every other boy, I figured it out in the standard, secret way. Women were out of the question. I liked peeking at them when they didn't think I was looking, but I didn't think of going beyond that. To tell the truth, I had heard stories, but I really wasn't too sure exactly what you did with what and where. I found out that summer.

It was one Saturday afternoon after the matinee. The Baby Sextette dressed on the top floor of the Century. The climb wasn't bad, seeing as how we were kids, and we had to make it only twice, once to get into costume and once to change back to street clothes. There was always lots of horsing around in the boys' dressing room—kids will be kids—and that afternoon I was the last to leave, because some wise guy had tied my shoelaces up in knots. Below me I could hear people saying, "See you later," and the theater quieting down. It was a murderously hot day, and Mama was late in coming to pick me up.

Finally I got the laces untangled and my shoes on. I started down. The grown-up sextettes and some small-part players dressed on the next floor. The empty dressing rooms were open. I looked in as I went by. One of the Florodora women was sitting by the open window, wearing just a dressing gown. Her legs were bare and showing pretty far up, because she had her feet propped on the windowsill. And her loosely tied gown showed more bosom than I had ever seen before. I took a quick look as I went by, and my eyes popped.

I kept moving until I got past the open door. Then I stopped, and after listening a minute inched my way back for another peek. I slowly stuck my head out past the door frame, and I froze. I was staring straight into the lady's boobs. She laughed. "I heard you going by, and then the footsteps stopped. Naughty, naughty."

She wiggled a finger at me, and that made everything jiggle. I must have blushed. "Honest, I wasn't . . . that is, I . . ."

She smiled. "That's quite all right. In fact, that's very flattering to a lady, didn't you know that?"

I think I said something brilliant like "I . . . I . . . I . . ." I felt as if I were burning up, and to make things worse, something was happening below my belt buckle that made me want to die of shame.

"Come on in," she said, and took me by the arm so I couldn't run —she didn't know I would have had trouble walking at that point. "It's all right. Everybody's gone."

She closed the door behind me. "You're Milton, aren't you? The last boy in the sextette?"

I nodded dumbly.

She smiled and ran her hand down my cheek. "I've been watching you every night, did you know that?"

I shook my head. I was starting to go crazy on her perfume, and I kept sneaking peeks at the great deep valley between those lovely mountains.

"Well, I have. I kept wondering what that handsome young man— that's how I see you—was doing with all those little boys."

I cleared my throat. "Well, I'm only . . ."

She stepped closer. "Don't tell me, sweetie, let me guess."

She put her hand on my knickers. Her eyes widened. "Well, for heaven sake!" She laughed. "Why, you're very well endowed." I wasn't sure of what she meant.

I think the whole thing took two seconds. One second her hand was undoing my buttons, the next she had me inside her—and from what I know now, there was room in there for the entire Sextette, all three Sextettes—and it was over.

She laughed as I rushed to hide myself back in my pants. "Take your time, honey, I've seen them before."

All I wanted to do was get out of that room. I knew I was supposed to say something, but for the life of me I couldn't think what. And I couldn't look at her.

When I was at the door, I turned, and with my best dancing-school manners I said, "Thank you very much."

She roared with laughter while I stood there turning red all over again, trying to figure out what the hell I had said wrong. She ended. "It was my pleasure, I'm sure. And I hope you'll drop by again some time. There's a few things you can still learn."

As I dashed out the door, she called after me. "Sonny, come again any time!" That broke her up completely, but I didn't know why.

Mama was just starting up the stairs. She was annoyed. "What took you so long? Do I have to climb stairs in this heat?"

I couldn't look at her. If she had ever come upstairs! "I had trouble with my shoelaces."

8

Phil was working for Perlberg and Greenberg, a children's dress house; Frank had a job with a cotton-goods firm, and on Saturday afternoons he sold shoes at A. S. Beck's, which brought in an extra $4 a week; Jack earned $10 a week as a runner on Wall Street; and I was earning $20 a week in *Florodora*. We were a family again that spring and summer of 1920, while the show was in New York. It seemed great to wake up every day in the same place, to eat breakfast and not worry about every chip of eggshell.

It seemed great, but now I wonder, was it? When I'm with my brothers and sister today, we talk love, but there are tensions underneath that we don't talk about. What did Phil and Frank and Jack really feel way back then when they came home on Saturday after a full work week and turned in their $8 and $10 paychecks, only to have their baby brother bring in almost as much as their combined salaries for maybe a quarter of their working hours? Sure, they understood that Mama had to spend most of her time with me, but did that make them, still kids themselves, understand not having a mother around? And how did Pa really feel as he tried and failed while his baby boy brought home more in a week than he made in a good month? How did he feel? How did Mama feel when she went out where the papas were and he stayed home where the mamas were? I think underneath all the love we felt for one another there was anger, maybe a little hate; underneath all the pride in their brother, there were a little jealousy and hurt, and underneath the understanding were resentment and guilt.

Mama was with me for almost every performance I did during her lifetime, and there was so much written about her with me that people who have never met her think of her as all the stage mothers in the world wrapped into one. Maybe she was, but I don't think so. To me she was just Mama. Sure, she could be tough. The world had taught her how before I was born, and if she hadn't been we'd have all drifted into the poorhouse with my father. But there was also a softness about her, a lovingness about her, that all her children remember.

I say, looking back, that there's no one to blame, and yet harm was done. Not just to me, but to my brothers and my sister. I think all the time that was spent on me and my career hurt the others. They don't say so, but I wonder how they could have felt doubling up all the time so that their little brother could have his own bed. Or being told to be quiet because "Milton is sleeping. He has to work tonight." Or having the last slice of bread being taken away from them with "That's not for you. I'm saving that for Milton." There must have been a time when they hated my guts. If I'd been one of them, I'd have hated me.

I'm no psychiatrist, and I've never been to one, but I think the fuss over me hurt them all for life. Maybe made them a little unsure of themselves, I don't know. I know it hurt me. Somewhere in the back of my mind is always the question "Did anybody really love me?" Was I loved or needed? Were they proud of their kid brother, or was it just that vaudeville paid better than paint and varnish? What if Milton Berlinger had never become Milton Berle? What if he had flopped? What if he flops tomorrow and it all ends? Maybe that's why I'm soaked with sweat every time I come off a stage, and I have to change right down to the skin before I go back out. As cocky and as sure as I might look out there in the lights, that's how unsure I am.

If we could all go back and start over, I still don't see how it could have been different. My brothers and sister never say it, but I think they must sometimes wonder what their lives might have been if Mama had had time to give to them and make them feel as important as she made me feel. Then maybe I wouldn't feel so guilty about each of them.

*   *   *

The Sunday Night Concerts at the Winter Garden were very popular around 1920, especially when Al Jolson appeared. Those Sunday nights weren't concerts any more than the shows at the Palace were. But Broadway was dark on Sundays in those days, and concerts were considered respectable enough for the Lord's Day, so Sunday vaudeville at the Winter Garden became a concert.

Audiences loved Jolson. He was a spellbinder, a superstar of his day, and he gave his audiences their money's worth. It was almost a tradition that an audience at a Jolson musical never found out how the plot line finished. Somewhere in the second act, he would come down to the footlights and say, "You want to hear the rest of this or you want to hear Jolie sing?" They always wanted to hear Jolie. They loved him, almost as much as he loved himself. He was less popular with his fellow performers, a rough customer backstage with anyone who tried to move into his spotlight.

Now, Mama was a woman who made friends wherever she went. If her son was on Broadway, Mama became friendly with people all over the street. That's how we got backstage at the Winter Garden one Sunday night when Jolson was doing a concert. Mama knew the doorman. She just wanted to watch, was what she said, and the concert was a sell-out. He waved his buddy Sadie and her little boy in.

We worked our way to the wings, staying close to the wall in case Jolson looked off stage. It sounded like there was a riot in the theater. People were whistling and shouting and applauding, and Jolson was standing there alone on stage in the lights with the sweat running down his burnt-cork-covered face, grinning from ear to ear, lapping it up. He kept waving his hands for silence, but the house was wild. He gave them a two-finger whistle. "I got more! I got more. Folks, you ain't heard nothing yet!"

And he signaled his conductor, Al Goodman, and they went into "Swanee," which Jolson had introduced the year before in *Sinbad*. Every mimic on every vaudeville circuit and every precocious kid—myself included—did a Jolson imitation, down on one knee (Blossom Seeley was the first to sing on one knee, not Jolson), but it was something all new and electric to see Jolson himself doing it. He sent chills up and down you.

When he finished, it sounded like the house was being torn down brick by brick. Mama waited until the applause started to drop. "Now, run out there," she whispered to me.

I had agreed to her scheme at home—I think Mama could have

convinced elephants to fly—but here at the Winter Garden the idea of
me going out on that stage with the great Al Jolson seemed impossible,
insane—and frightening. I remember when she dragged me backstage to
Eddie Cantor's dressing room and made me show my imitation of him.
Cantor had looked as if two nuts had broken in, but he listened through
the whole imitation before he cut short the visit with "That's very nice,
kid. Thank you for coming by."

Now, Cantor could be rough—which, thank God, he wasn't when we
saw him—but the word around Broadway was that he was nothing compared to Jolson.

"Now!" Mama said, and gave me a shove in the back that put me out
on the Winter Garden stage.

Jolson looked around for the reason why the applause stopped so
suddenly. He spotted this little kid in short pants—Mama's idea, because
it made me look younger—and his stage smile widened to cover for the
audience, but his eyes looked like shotgun barrels drilling in on me. "Well,
well. Looks like we have a visitor tonight, how about that, folks?"

He played it big and gracious for the audience, and he got a warm
laugh, but I wouldn't have wanted to be alone with him at that moment.
He was boiling. "What brings you out here, sonny? Tell Jolie."

"I do an imitation of you," I said.

Jolson shrugged. "Everybody does. So what?"

I think that was supposed to send me off the stage, but Mama was
waiting for me there. I didn't move. Jolson was stuck with me. "Okay,
sonny, what song do you do?"

" 'April Showers.' "

Jolson turned to the audience. "I think the band knows it." That got
him another laugh. "Maestro Goodman, a little 'April Showers' for the
kid, if you please."

I did my Jolson—the one knee, the whistling, the throb in the voice,
the whole schtick—and it wasn't bad, but it wasn't good. Under less
frightening circumstances even I had done it better. I got a big hand,
more for my chutzpah, I think, than for my talent.

Jolson put a heavy hand on my shoulder. "Well, that was just great,
sonny, just great." His hand grew heavier. "Now, if you don't mind, kid,
I've got a few more things to do out here for this great audience."

I got a shove that the audience couldn't spot, and I went off fast. Mama was right there, and so were the stage manager and the assistant stage
manager. They were burning mad. "How the hell did you get in here?"

Mama put an arm around me, and we started for the stage door. "Mr. Jolson told us to drop back," she said, completely calm. "Jolie said that if Milton ever had a night off from his show—he's with *Florodora* at the Century, as I'm sure you know—he should come by if Jolie was working."

The stage manager wasn't buying it. He got in between us and the stage door. "We'll see about that when Mr. Jolson comes off stage."

"Are you holding us against our will?" Mama said.

"We're going to wait for Mr. Jolson."

Mama put up a hand to brush him aside. "I want you to know that I am a New York detective, so I know the law. It is a serious crime to hold people against their wills. Are you making charges?"

The stage manager looked a little shaken. Mama always had a cool about her in tight spots that gave her an edge. "Look, lady—"

"If we had time," Mama said, "we would wait for Mr. Jolson and then let the law take its course. But this boy has his own show and he needs his rest. So you better step aside, young man, or I'll scream the house down. They'll hear me in the balcony, and we'll see how much Mr. Jolson likes that."

Mama took a deep breath. The stage manager quickly opened the door, and we strolled out onto Seventh Avenue. "You were good, Milton," she said, "but I've heard you do him better."

It was about the time that *Florodora* was nearing the end of its run. Mama and I were walking on 45th Street when we ran into a friend named Harry Baum, to whom I owe a big debt of gratitude. Harry Baum was in the printing business, and he shared offices with Hocky and Green. It was he who said to Mama, "Hocky and Green are looking for a boy to do an act of theirs with Elizabeth Kennedy. I think Milton would be very good. If you want, I'll set up a meeting for him."

The team of Milton Hocky and Howard J. Green was in the same business as E. W. Wolf, the guy in Philadelphia with the kiddie acts, but that's like comparing a pushcart to Macy's. Hocky and Green wrote and produced and owned acts—like "Stars of Yesterday" and "Stars of the Future" (with Helen Kane, before she became famous as the Boop-a-Doop girl)—that played the big time in vaudeville.

Thanks to Harry Baum, I read for Hocky and Green, and I got the job opposite Elizabeth Kennedy, a pretty little Brooklyn Irish girl. Originally Bunny Grauer was supposed to be the boy in the act, but his mother turned it down because she didn't want her son touring in vaudeville. That was a break for the Berlingers, who were ready, able, and anxious for the chance.

It was with this act that my name changed. "Berlinger and Kennedy" made for a mouthful of letters, and it might have been easier for a theater manager to leave the act off the marquee than spell it out. So Milton Berlinger became Milton Berle, a name I still don't own legally. (Alan King said, "His name was Berlinger, but they shortened it to Berle. When you're Jewish, there is a tradition of shortening things.")

Shortening a stage name is a pretty standard change in this business. The surprise was Mama. When Milton Berlinger became Milton Berle, suddenly it was good-bye Sarah Berlinger, hello Sandra Berle. That was Mama, and I love her for it. My three brothers and sister also changed their names to Berle, and you can make of that whatever you want. Legally, we're all still Berlinger.

The act was an eighteen-minute sketch which they named "Broadway Bound." The set was the office of David Belasco. It was a full set, so the act played "in three," as they say in this business. (If an act plays in one, it means it uses only the front of the stage down by the foots and in front of the curtain. Our act used the full stage.)

I was a kid actor looking for work. I came into the Belasco office and said, "Is this the office of David Belasco?"

The office was empty; everybody was out to lunch. I looked around and went into my soliloquy. "Come in." "I think I will." I walked behind the desk and sat down and said, "Mr. Belasco is not here, so I think I'll take over."

I was sitting there like I owned the place when there was a knock on the door and Elizabeth came in. She was a kid actress looking for work. "Is this the office of David Belasco?" That was a repeat for the audience, in case they'd missed the setup on the act the first time around.

I told her it was, and she said, "Is anyone in?"

I did a take and said, "Yeh, I'm here in the office."

She said, "What are you, his office boy?"

"Very funny. What do you do?"

So she started telling me, as if I were interviewing her for a job. It looked ridiculous, because we were only two kids in a grown-up office, and that's what made the act funny. It was both ridiculous and cute at the same time.

I said, "I can't lie to you. I'm here for the same reason you are."

And that was the bridge into the heart of the act and the reason for us showing each other what we could do.

Elizabeth would say, "I can do an imitation of Ruth Terry as Topsy in *The Gold Diggers.*"

I would sit down on the side and the lights would go down on me while she did her scene. Then she said, "Maybe he wants something by Shakespeare. Do you know *Romeo and Juliet?*"

"No, they haven't written anything lately." (Laugh?) "I know Romeo."

"I know Juliet."

"Let's rehearse it, and then we can show him when he comes in."

The set was designed so that we used all the props on it. I took the plume from the pen on a desk set and stuck it in my hat brim, and I took the letter opener to use as a dagger. Elizabeth climbed up on the desk for a balcony and flung her cape around her shoulders.

I went into the opening speech. "But soft, what light through yonder window breaks? It is the east and Juliet is the sun—"

Elizabeth cut in with, "The sun? Methinks you got me wrong, Romeo. I'm not the sun. I'm the daughter."

It went on that way until I said, "Good night, good night, a thousand times good night."

Elizabeth just looked at me and said a flat, "Good night." She jumped from the desk and made her exit with, "I can't say good night a thousand times, let's finish it here."

After the applause (and it was mostly hers, because I was playing straight man), I would say, "Maybe he wants something from the musical-comedy world."

"Well, I do an imitation of Fanny Brice."

"I do an imitation of Eddie Cantor." I would get a straw hat from the coat rack by the door. There was a pair of glasses with white rims on the desk. I would push out the lenses and put on the frames and go into "I'm Hungry for Beautiful Girls."

Our act also included the courtroom scene from Frank Bacon's hit, *Lightnin'.* The finish was a dramatic scene from *The Two Orphans.* We were a brother and a sister about to be separated, never to see each other again. I cried and Elizabeth cried, and if we did it well the audience cried too. But the curtain didn't come down on that. After the applause, we would sit there for a few beats, and then the phone would ring.

I picked it up and said, "Office of David Belasco."

You heard a voice saying, "Who is this speaking?"

"This is Milton Berle."

The voice would say, "Who is Milton Berle?"

I'd say, "Who are you?"

The curtain line was, "David Belasco. Tell my secretary I won't be in today."

Milton Hocky and Howard Green had once produced an act for Ada Jaffe, which is how Hocky became good friends with her son, Sam Jaffe. A nice guy and a great actor today, at the time he didn't know whether he wanted to continue trying to make it in show business or be in the candy business with the candy he had concocted and named "Snowflake." Anyway, as a favor to his friend Milton Hocky, he agreed to coach us to get the act ready. He took us over to the Lyceum Theatre, and we worked every day just outside the lounge bathrooms. He taught me how to do the Romeo speech, and blocked out the whole routine.

The billing read:

The Twinkling Stars

ELIZABETH KENNEDY
and
MILTON BERLE
in
BROADWAY BOUND

BY MILTON HOCKY AND HOWARD GREEN

Our work was affected by the Gerry Society. Because of our age, we weren't allowed to work more than two shows a day, and we had to be off the stage no later than 9:15 at night. The time meant we worked no later than the beginning of the second half of the bill. The two-show rule didn't cause any trouble, because our act was booked for the big time, and that was two shows a day. (In grind houses, you worked as many as five and six shows a day.)

We opened at Fox's Ridgewood Theatre, which was out in Brooklyn, just to break in the act. We played a split week between there and Fox's Bay Ridge. The act went like gangbusters. Believe it or not, we played "Broadway Bound" just one week, and our next move was straight into the dream of every vaudeville performer: the Palace!

We opened on May 2, 1921. The bill for that week at the Palace was:

1. Fink's Mules, *animal act*
2. Miller and Capman, *singers and dancers*
3. Georgia Campbell and Co. *in "Gone Are the Days"*
4. Toney and Norman, *songs and talk*
5. Dorothy Jardon, *prima donna*

INTERMISSION

6. Kennedy and Berle, *youthful entertainers*
7. Ford Sisters, *dancers*
8. Watson Sisters, *singing comediennes*
9. Robbie Gordone, *posing act*

All the Berlingers were out front at the first matinee. I thought Pa would bust his vest, and he kept taking off his glasses and wiping his eyes when he came backstage to see us.

The papers were good. The *New York Star* used to publish a box called the "Star's Weekly Vaudeville Laugh Bulletin (Giggles, Ripples, Snickers and Smiles Not Counted)." This is what they said about us:

"Kennedy and Berle. Youthful entertainers. Reception, none. Applause, good. Laughs, 10. Finish, excellent. 18 minutes." (That "Reception, none" means we didn't get a hand on our entrance. How could we? Who knew us except the family in the audience?)

A review in the *New York Clipper* written by Jerry Hoffman said: "Two youngsters on the bill, Elizabeth Kennedy and Milton Berle, proved a surprise hit in 'Broadway Bound,' a bright sketch by Milton Hocky and Howard Green, in which they did imitations, songs and dances and almost drew as many tears as Vera Gordon could have uncorked in a pathetic scene. They stamped themselves among the most clever juveniles on the stage, without once straining their voices."

The Kennedy & Berle act was priced, I think, at $800 a week. Our take was $110 each for Elizabeth and me, and Mama got $20 extra for handling the act, telling them how to hang the scenery, and taking care of any problems along the tour. It was pretty good money when we were playing near enough to live at home, but when we went on tour we were still living tight. We were given transportation money only. We had to pay for our own food and costumes, which were street clothes. That $130 a week had to take care of Mama, Rosalind, and me on the road, plus Pa and the boys back home. It was a lot better than the Philadelphia days, but we were a long way from rolling in mink.

Hocky and Green would give us three half fares and one full fare when we traveled. The half fare was fine for Elizabeth and Rosalind, but it was murder on me. I was starting to grow taller, and the taller I grew, the more I had to hunch down to look like a half fare, and, take it from me, the conductors were tougher than any audience we played to. We would take two berths when we traveled. Elizabeth and Rosalind shared one, and I split the other one with Mama, sleeping head to toe. Often I had the berth to myself, because Mama would make some excuse about not being tired and go to the ladies' lounge and sit up all night. Or, if she was lucky, she'd find herself a card game.

It was her years backstage that turned her on to cards. She loved poker and gin rummy, and she'd always have a game going backstage. What Mama liked about cards, I can't really say, because she was a lousy player. It must have been the company. I would say that Mama was the one stranger that anyone could meet on a train and play cards with.

When you played the vaudeville circuits you kept moving, week in and week out, living out of your H & M trunk. (Remember them, with the drawers on one side and the hanger space on the other?) I think it's the reason why geography was one of my favorite school subjects. I knew just a-bout every place on the map of the United States, because I had played it.

On the Orpheum Circuit, one of the best, you did two shows a day, seven days a week. You finished one theater on Sunday and you packed and traveled to get to the next theater in time for the Monday opening.

A typical Orpheum route would be Minneapolis to Winnipeg to Calgary to Vancouver. From there you went down to Seattle and Portland and then to San Francisco, where you played two dates. First you played the Orpheum, which was the big-time house, and then you moved to the Golden Gate, which was murder because you did continuous performances. After that came Los Angeles, but that was an expensive trip, and rather than lose working money along the way, every act would "break the jump" and play the Bert Levey Circuit, which was San Luis Obispo and Bakersfield. In Los Angeles you were back on the Orpheum Circuit. First you played the Orpheum for a week and then the Hill Street Theatre, another continuous-performance house. Then there was a tremendous jump from Los Angeles to Denver, then Omaha and Chicago, which was the end of a twenty-eight-week route.

They also had something called the Junior Orpheum Circuit, which was Sioux City, Davenport, Des Moines, and a lot of smaller Midwestern towns. They usually tagged that on to your circuit, which gave you thirty-eight weeks of work altogether. I suppose I've forgotten some cities —for instance, I know I played Memphis on the Orpheum Circuit—but the only thing I know for certain is that, great as working in vaudeville was, it was also exhausting. Even kids came home worn out, sick of living out of trunks, sick of meals in diners and hash houses. Maybe there was big money to be made by some in vaudeville, but everybody earned every backbreaking cent.

The first summer of our time on the Orpheum Circuit, I turned thirteen. This is a big moment in a Jewish boy's life. According to the Jewish religion, a boy goes through the ceremony of *bar mitzvah* on this thirteenth birthday and is declared a man. It was the one ritual my mother insisted on. My three older brothers had all been *bar mitzvahed*, and now it was my turn. Only, it would have to wait until we got back to New York. I'd have to stay a Jewish boy a while longer. Meanwhile, Mama wrote to Rabbi Benjamin Tintner at the Mt. Zion synagogue, sending him the date when I could be *bar mitzvahed* and asking that he send by return mail whatever I should study for the great day. It was added to my other homework.

Mama also took charge of Elizabeth's religious life, as she had promised Elizabeth's father she would do when we left New York. Once she got us settled in our room in whatever city we were playing, Mama would immediately find out where the nearest Catholic church was, so that Elizabeth could attend mass. Every Sunday matinee, Elizabeth would come straight to the theater from church, and Mama was always waiting for her with the make-up box and a damp cloth. While Elizabeth worked on her face, Mama would scrub her knees with the cloth to remove the smudges she always got from kneeling during the service.

The trips to the post office were still part of our daily routine. Pa had a copy of our route with the dates on it, so he knew where to write to us. And no matter what the emergency, no one ever thought of the telephone. It was too rich for us. When the big explosion occurred on Wall Street in September of 1920, Mama and I worried about Jack, who worked down there as a runner, but we waited and hoped and sweated until finally a penny postcard came from him to say he was all right.

We still have one letter from those days. It's dated August 2, 1922, and it's from Pa. Where I know what he's talking about, I'll interrupt and explain. The letter is on stationery that makes me smile with a lump in my throat. Printed on top is "Milton Berle" and under it "205 West 119th Street." To the left and below it says on two lines, "Kennedy & Berle/Orpheum Circuit."

Dear Ma and children,

I received your letter this morning after I sent my one away. Also recd the Theatre News. That was some wonderful write up they gave the children. Did you or the Stars (that was Pa's joke, meaning us) talk to Mr. Belasco, I hope they've done their best. You write asking how Frank is. He is fine and certainly looks good. As for Jack he is not working as yet. I just got finished supper. I made Sauce Louie because I had to come home early as I had to send my pants to the tailor (poor Pa, he had only one pair) they were torn so I could not walk in the street. Now tell me how are you and the children. I do not like the picture of Milton taken up in the country, his mouth is too large. What do you think of the people that were poisoned in the Restaurant on Bway 125th St? 6 of them died so far, some one put poison in the Dough that they make the pies of. How does Milton feel now, is he OK? You say you must get Milton a suit. By all means get him one but a very snappy one that will look good on him. How is my little darling girl Rosalind, my friend and pal? How is Eliza-

beth how is she feeling and did she put on any weight, and has she grown? How are you? Have you grown any yourself and of course you miss me! I miss you all very much. Shall I get a suit and shoes on Sat as they are on the bum, I can't go out on Sunday so I stay at home they looked awful last Sunday or shall I pay Dr. Morris as he asked me for the bill, and I told him I would take care of it in a few days? That Barber shop at 118 and 7th Ave is out and it is now a Reeves store. Now I think this is long enough so I will close with lots of love & Kisses to you all from

your Loving Pa

That was Pa. All love and worry, his shaky ego battered to the point that he wanted Mama's okay to buy himself a suit. Chances are that Pa didn't get the suit and shoes, and Dr. Morris didn't get paid. There was always a hard-luck story somewhere, and Pa always came through. Once he had to write Mama that the electric lights were being turned off because he had lent out the money she had sent home for the bill.

We traveled by boat from Canada to the United States on the West Coast. It was Prohibition at home, and Grandpa Glantz liked his schnapps when he played cards with his cronies. Mama bought several large bottles of liquor before we got on the boat, and lots of empty pint bottles from a Canadian five-and-ten. The day we were to dock and go through Customs, Mama opened the large bottles and poured the booze into the five-and-ten bottles. Then she cut up some rope to make yokes to go around Elizabeth's and Rosalind's necks, with a bottle hanging from each end of the rope. With luck, the girls could hold the two bottles under their armpits beneath their dresses and capes. If a bottle got loose, suddenly they had larger busts. Mama had an extra-large corset for herself that she stuffed with bottles all around her waist, and I carried bottles inside my long pants, taped to my legs. For a decoy, Mama would take a medicine bottle and fill it with liquor and plant it in the center of our luggage under some laundry, where the Customs inspector was bound to find it. Mama became embarrassed when he found it. She'd look shocked when she found out it was illegal. "For medicinal purposes," she'd say. "I never dreamed . . ."

The inspector would cluck a little as he confiscated the medicine bottle, and we would get through, praying to God that no glass clanked as we walked away.

Mama could handle anything. I remember a train trip from Vancouver, where we had just closed, to Seattle, where we were to open next. It was late at night when we got in, and the train had run about two hours behind schedule. We were all bone-tired when we got to the hotel to which Mama had wired for reservations. She left the three of us beside the trunk in the lobby while she woke up the night clerk. "I'm Mrs. Berle of Kennedy and Berle. You're holding a room for us."

The clerk checked his records. "Sorry, lady, but we held it till midnight, and when you didn't show we gave it away."

"I've got three tots here who have to sleep. We open tomorrow, what do you mean you gave the room away?"

"Lady, it's two in the morning—"

"The train was late!"

"Well, I'm sorry, lady. Look, there's another hotel about two blocks down and . . ."

Mama had spotted his Masonic ring. Now, her brother Joe was also a Mason, and through him Mama had become an Eastern Star. She wasn't a very active member, but whenever she traveled she wore the Eastern Star pin on her dress, over her heart. You never knew.

She threw open her cape and leaned forward as if she were pleading. "Oh, what am I to do? A woman alone in a strange city with three little infants!" She practically shoved the pin in his eye.

We got a room.

So many crazy things from my childhood are still with me today. I guess I got all these things from Mama, maybe even my hammertoes. A lot of people ask me if I really have six toes on one foot. No, it's hammertoes. The little toe on my left foot is curved right over the top of the toe next to it. Mama had bad feet all her life. Even when we didn't have much money, she had to make trips to Coward's, which was a big deal in those days, to buy special shoes for her feet. So it could have been heredity for me, but I think it was the result of wearing hand-me-downs. Frank wore Phil's shoes, Jack wore Frank's shoes, and I wore Jack's shoes. Rosalind—I don't know.

When I was six or seven, I went to the grocery store one day with my mother. I pointed to a pile of long green things. "What are those, Mama?"

"Don't eat them, they're no good for you."

I figured she was right; she was my mother. So I never eat cucumbers. Maybe they just didn't sit well with her.

Radishes are another thing. "You can eat radishes, but always put butter on them." Why? I don't know. Maybe it helps digest them better. And maybe not, but to this day I put butter on radishes.

And I won't drink from somebody else's glass, and I won't touch ice water, or anything with ice in it. And I live in terror of a draft. Keep the windows closed at night, there might be a draft, it could turn cold. Don't sit by a window, don't sit too close to a door. Turn down the air conditioner, don't put a fan on the floor. All from Mama.

Maybe it was that cucumbers and radishes produced gas and you might belch on stage in the middle of a number, and you could catch a cold from a draft. And a cold meant no show, and no show, no pay. I don't know. I don't think Mama was a hypochondriac. She just had a lot of old wives' tales and superstitions that she carried around with her. And I suppose I inherited them.

I've also got a pillow she made for me. It's one of three pillows I carry with me wherever I go. Mama's pillow is the middle one when I go to bed; just before I fall asleep—if I fall asleep—I discard the top pillow and sleep on Mama's. You can call it a security blanket or whatever you want, or say a grown man shouldn't need such a thing. Frankly, I don't care what anyone thinks. I have enough trouble sleeping without trying to upset a routine that works for me. On the road or at home, it's the same now as it was then.

But sometimes that pillow bit can get a little embarrassing. It was maybe ten years ago that I was booked to play a Saturday night at the Concord Hotel in upper New York State. I flew in from the Coast on Friday night, unpacked, and went down to check over the room I'd be working in and to talk over the show with Phil Greenwald, the entertainment director. It was late when I went back to my room and got undressed to go to bed. I climbed in and discovered the pillow was missing. My secretary, Paul Dafelmair, and I tore the room apart. No pillow.

If I was sleepy when I went upstairs, here it was the middle of the night and I'm wide awake. I called for the maid. She said she didn't know a thing about the missing pillow. The woman who had turned down my bed was off shift now.

Little by little, I was turning into a maniac. I had Paul searching, the night maid searching, the desk clerk calling all over the place, and then I got Phil Greenwald out of bed, and I was screaming over the phone: "This is my special pillow, Phil. I can't sleep without it. And if I don't sleep, I can't go on tomorrow night!"

By four in the morning, believe it or not, the airport I'd come into had been checked, the baggage room had been searched, and I had the entire Concord in an uproar. I guess I wasn't thinking straight at that point. I was carrying on as if we were searching for missing snakebite serum or a pacemaker that had fallen out. Somewhere along the line it hit me that we were after an old pillow, and I fell apart laughing. That happened at about the same time that the chambermaid came in with the missing pillow. The other girl had noticed it wasn't the regulation size used at the Concord and had it taken away and stuck it in a corner of the linen closet.

They say travel is broadening. Maybe so. But if there were museums or famous landmarks in all the cities I played on the Orpheum and Keith Circuits with Kennedy & Berle, I don't remember seeing them. The things I learned were different, like in which town it was easiest to get bootleg hootch (I learned that from a drunk traveling on the same route with us—I didn't drink then, I don't drink now); which rooming houses it wasn't safe to leave anything valuable in while you were at the theater; where the best cheap meal in a town was—stuff like that, and more.

The routes and the jumps were all-important once. Now, time has blurred them a little, and Keith and Orpheum sort of run together in mind. I do remember special things about cities and theaters we played: not how well the act went there or how many curtain calls we got, but incidents connected with the place.

THE COLISEUM THEATER ON 181ST STREET AND BROADWAY, NEW YORK —The stage door was at the top of a hill. It was winter, and they hadn't cleaned the ice off the sidewalk by the time the matinee let out. The weather was rotten and I had a slight cold, so it was decided I would stay in between shows. I was just running out to pick up a sandwich down the block—I had changed clothes because Mama had a strict rule that you never wore your stage suit off stage, but I still had my make-up on—when I heard, "Hey, get a load of that sissy with the paint on his face just like a girl!"

I took a look, and it was a kid maybe a year older than me. He was with another kid and they were pointing at me, but I kept moving. I had heard that crap before. But this kid wouldn't let it go. "Hey, sissy, what's your rush? Gotta buy a new lipstick?"

His friend laughed, and that did it for me. I turned around and gave him a shot on the jaw. The guy just went over sideways and rolled all the way down the hill. I think I was as surprised as he was. It was a lucky punch, but I felt great for days. All that jabbing and shadow-boxing backstage seemed to be paying off.

DAYTON, OHIO—Kennedy & Berle were on the bill with a lady I liked immensely. She had been part of the husband-and-wife comedy team of Allen and Montrose, but now Belle Montrose was going it alone as a comedienne and monologist after losing her husband, Billy Allen. As funny as Belle was on a stage, that's how warm and kind she was off. Maybe that's why I was willing to stay in her dressing room while she was doing her act and take care of her infant son in his playpen. I figure that at a minimum of 35 cents an hour baby-sitting fees, Steve Allen owes me a good couple of bucks today.

THE KEITH THEATRE, WASHINGTON, D.C.—First we heard that he was sick and wasn't coming, and then we heard that he was out front. Then there were people rushing around backstage, and then there he was, in a wheelchair. Mama was pushing on our shoulders as the chair approached, whispering, "Bow. Curtsey. Oh my God," and we were looking at President Woodrow Wilson, who had come back especially to meet us. He shook my hand and said something, but I don't know what. I was too stunned. It was like shaking hands with history! The President of the United States and Milton Berlinger!

THE ALHAMBRA THEATRE, 126TH STREET AND SEVENTH AVENUE, NEW YORK—Finally, at the beginning of October 1921, Kennedy & Berle were playing New York again. On Saturday morning, October 1, I had my *bar mitzvah* at the Mt. Zion Temple on 119th Street between Fifth and Lenox, a good location, because I had a matinee to do that afternoon. For a while, while writing my "today I am a man" speech, I thought of putting in a plug for the show at the Alhambra, but I took it out at the last minute. Mt. Zion was a reform temple, but I didn't think it was so reformed that you could work a commercial into the proceedings. To my amazement, when I finished my speech Rabbi Benjamin Tintner said to the congregation, "You think that's something? You want to go over to the Alhambra Theatre before tomorrow night, when he closes, and you'll see what this young man can do!"

Little did I know that Mama had gotten to him before the service to give me the plug. Boy, was I embarrassed—but not too much.

PRINCESS THEATRE, MONTREAL—Eddie Clark, of Clark and Verdi, two guys who did Italian-dialect comedy, was on the bill with us.

Eddie was a big fight fan, and he knew of my interest in the ring. Morry Hirschkovitch was scheduled to fight Dave Shade of Omaha in Montreal, and I wanted to see it. We were both on early in the bill, third and fourth, and it was about 9:15 when we were through for the night. The main event was scheduled for 10 o'clock. Eddie asked Mama if he could take me to the fight. She said okay.

After the fight, I said I had to get back to the hotel—it must have been about a quarter to eleven, and Mama would be there with the girls. But Eddie said, "Come on with me, kid. You'll see something you've never seen before."

He gave me a wink to indicate what I was going to see. "Hey, how old are you, anyway?"

I told him. "Fourteen, but I've been around." I was stretching the incident at *Florodora* as far as it would go.

He looked at me. "Well, you're pretty tall for your age. I think it'll be okay."

He took me to a place in downtown Montreal called the Argyle House. It was run by a French-Canadian who called himself Count Amy. You could get drinks and girls at the Argyle House, but the specialty was Count Amy's kick for orgies. He would run a circus on the living-room floor—just the Count and as many girls as there were in the house at the time. He liked to have guys standing around watching. This night there were also some girls from the Mollie Williams Beef Trust show, which was playing the burlesque house in town.

I was shocked by what was going on, but I couldn't take my eyes off it. The Count and the girls were doing things I hadn't even heard about yet. And it was easy for anyone to see that what I was watching was exciting me.

Eddie went over to one of the girls from the Mollie Williams show and started whispering to her. I saw him look over at me a couple of times. Then she nodded, and he came over to me. "Go ahead upstairs with her, Milton." He pointed to the brunette he had been talking to.

I looked at her, shocked, but she just smiled and started for the stairs. Eddie put a hand on my arm. He reached into his pocket. "And use this before you do anything."

It was a prophylactic, but it wasn't rolled up. I said, "But it's too big," which is a line he kidded me about for years.

I wasn't that girl's first, even if she was my second. I don't think I was her hundredth, either. It was like a green pea going into the Holland Tunnel. The whole thing lasted maybe twelve seconds, but I thought it was great.

When we got downstairs, the Count and his act were still going on. I couldn't figure out what he was doing wrong that it took him so long.

A few weeks later, in some other town, I got Eddie to buy me my own tin of prophylactics. I was hoping for my chance to use them. I carried them everywhere with me, true to my Boy Scout motto, "Be Prepared."

One afternoon backstage I sneezed, and while reaching for my handkerchief I accidentally pulled the little tin can out. It clattered to the floor of the dressing room, and Mama saw it. She had a card game going on, so she didn't say anything in front of the other people, but I think she suspected what I had dropped from the way I turned red and dived to pick it up and shoved it in my pocket. I was so embarrassed, I ran out of the theater. I just walked around outdoors until fifteen minutes before show time, trying to think of something to tell Mama.

She was waiting for me in the dressing room, and she got right to the point. "What was that you dropped before, Milton?"

I turned red all over again. "When, Mama?"

"Don't *when Mama* me. You know when."

I hemmed and hawed and finally told her. She said, "How long have you been using them?"

"Since Montreal."

Mama looked at me hard. "You've been *using* them?"

God, I was squirming. "Well, not exactly, but I've been carrying them."

"I see. But you plan to use them?"

"I'm growing up, Mama!"

She gave me a smack. "Don't get smart with me, Milton. I'll tell you when you're grown up. Now, tell me, you plan to use them?"

"Well," I said, "I don't want to get a girl into trouble. And I don't want to get a disease."

Maybe my whole life would have been different if Mama had handled the matter a different way than she did. She thought about what I had just said, and then she gave a deep sigh of resignation. Mama was always a woman who faced facts. She said, "Okay, so you know what they're for. Every time you go out, make sure you use them."

That's one thing I can thank Mama for. She didn't scare me away from sex. She could have ruined me for life.

I was around five feet, eight inches tall, and I was growing round-shouldered from hunching down to look enough of a kid for the "Broadway Bound" material. If only Elizabeth had done a little growing at the same time, we might have been able to work out something, but she didn't. The act was beginning to look ridiculous. It was time to call it quits, after two full seasons.

❦ 10 ❧

Show business is no business, let me tell you if you didn't already know. A plumber without a job is still a plumber, but a guy between jobs in this racket has nothing to show. And in the days of vaudeville you were nothing but a memory if you didn't have an act. I was a headliner when I was half of Kennedy & Berle. After we called it quits I was just another scrawny kid with a little greasepaint in the bloodstream in search of an act. I was too old for kiddie stuff now, and too young for grown-up stuff. I had to find something right for me.

In between searching, I would sneak down to Grupp's or Stillman's gyms to work out. There was something in me that felt good when I had the gloves on and was pounding away at the bag. I still remembered the thrill of being at ringside in 1923 at the Polo Grounds for the Dempsey-Firpo fight. I even helped push Dempsey back in the ring during the fight. The sweat, the lights, the screams all got into me and felt good—almost the same thrill I got from working to an audience.

I met and was proud as hell of my friendship with Benny Leonard, who at the time was lightweight champion of the world. He meant more to me than most of the vaudeville stars I met. Of course, I kept my trips to the gyms a secret at home. I knew how Mama would react if she learned what I was up to.

As a performer I was floundering, looking for my place, for my style. I already knew comedy was where I belonged. *Florodora* had given me the clue, and though I did some dramatic stuff when I worked with

Elizabeth Kennedy, I felt most comfortable in the sections where the laughs were. But there are all kinds and styles of comedy.

I didn't know who I was yet, what was right for me. I tried out all sorts of material. I did acts with titles like "Milton Berle, Established 1908"; "Milton Berle, Good to the Last Drop"; "Milton Berle, Informal —But Funny"; "Milton Berle, Not Funny But Fast." There was even one time when Mama didn't want me to risk my name—my *name?*—with an act I wanted to break in, so we invented one for the tryout. I was Bobby Baker. It's a good thing I didn't meet Billy Sol Estes, or I'd have gotten myself a permanent booking!

The stand-ups I was doing were a potpourri of nothing, jokes I had cut out of magazines like *Capt. Billy's Whiz-Bang* and *College Humor* and strung together into a monologue that was hit and miss. I broke it up with my impressions of Eddie Cantor and Al Jolson. The Cantor got better and better, to the point where, when I corked up and went into one of his numbers, I got a big hand. Then it was back to the magazine cut-out jokes, and I died.

I didn't know it, but I was learning even as I bombed. The timing was tightening up, and I was learning about material, why a joke works one time and not another, why some jokes I used that were not as good as others in my act got a bigger laugh. It was because they went with the personality that was beginning to go across the footlights. There was a nice but a little-bit-wise kid starting to emerge, and starting to push certain jokes.

In my search for what would work for me with an audience, I even tried drag. I think I got the idea from the annual drag balls they used to have at a place called the Rockland Palace on 155th Street by the Polo Grounds. The gay guys would work for months on the fancy dresses they showed up in. It was a wild evening, and people would come from all over the city, not to take part, but to watch. My brothers and I would go to watch too. I remember one black queen who called himself Gloria Swanson. He was hilarious. I think this was where I first realized there was humor, if you played it right, in playing gay. But if you played it wrong, it could be very, very sad.

Also, while with Kennedy & Berle, we once appeared on the bill with Karyl Norman, who billed himself as "The Creole Fashion Plate." Transvestite entertainers were very big in those days. Aside from Norman, there were Bert Savoy, Francis Renault, and the brilliant Julian Eltinge, who was the first, and maybe the only, female impersonator to have a theater named for him. And there was even Wallace Beery—yeah, Wallace Beery!—who appeared in drag in early Mack Sennett comedies.

Standing in the wings and watching the moment when the female impersonator whipped off his wig to reveal the man beneath was always electric. Even though the audience knew in advance, it was always a shock that brought wild applause, and that appealed to me, because, as I've told you, applause and love were, and are, one in my mind.

So I tried it, but I think I was too young for it to work for me then. I've worked in drag since, as everyone knows, but never seriously. It's always been a wild low-comedy put-on. Who can take a line like "I swear I'll kiwl you, a milwyun times" seriously? For me, drag is another way to get laughs. My drag is too gay to be gay.

I think I've spent too much time on this, but I get tired of people always asking, "Is Milton or isn't he?" To the best of my knowledge, Milton isn't. And so what? To me, gay is just another way of life, not better, not worse. Just different. You go to your church, I'll go to mine, okay?

Another act. This one had my mother planted up in a stage box. At one point I was supposed to grab a baseball bat and step over the footlights and swing at the trumpet player, and my mother would scream. She screamed all right on the opening day, because I slipped and went right into the pit. The audience howled, and I finished the act down there, because I gashed my leg—I had to have eight stitches. When I got backstage with my pants leg ripped and the blood running down, the manager said to me, "That's the funniest bit I've ever seen. You ought to keep it in."

I learned about anti-Semitism, too, in those years. Oh, I had run into a little of it here and there before, but somehow I thought it didn't exist with top people in show business. Then I met Frank Fay.

He was a headliner I had always admired. He was a great-looking guy, a monologist with style, who worked easy and relaxed. Off stage, he was rated a heavy drinker. Supposedly a non-practicing Catholic, when he really tied one on he'd weave over to St. Patrick's for confession.

There's a story that used to make the rounds that should give you a clue to Frank Fay. He was being sued for something, and when his attorney first put him on the stand he asked Fay to state his name.

"Frank Fay."

"Profession?"

Without a pause, Fay said, "World's greatest comedian."

At the next recess, Fay's attorney said to him, "Frank, when you first took the stand, why did you say that you were the world's greatest comedian?"

Fay looked his attorney right in the eye and answered, "I was under oath, wasn't I?"

Anyway, I was on the bill at B. F. Keith's Bushwick Theatre in Brooklyn in 1925. I was doing twelve minutes of something, including my Eddie Cantor. I don't think I was too good, but at least I was energetic. Headlining the bill was Frank Fay.

It was about the third day of the booking, and I had finished my spot and was standing in the wings watching Fay work.

There were certain top stars, such as Eddie Leonard, Sophie Tucker, Ted Lewis, Velaska Suratt, Van and Schenck, who would let the stage manager know that they didn't want anyone standing in the wings watching the act. Frank Fay felt the same way. There was also a rule that performers weren't allowed to go out into the audience to catch the other acts. These were meant to prevent a performer from stealing a song or a joke or a bit of business from another performer.

There was big applause when Fay came off for his first bow. I couldn't be certain, but I thought I heard him say to the stage manager, "Get that little Jew bastard out of the wings. I don't want him standing there."

But I wasn't sure. So I waited a few days, and then I went back into the wings again when he was on stage. He spotted me right away, and when he came off I heard him say something about "that little kike." That did it for me.

I waited until he had finished for the night, and I was ready for him as he cut around behind some flats on the way to his dressing room. I had picked up a stage brace—they're made of wood and metal, and they're used to hold the scenery together—and as he went by me, I reached out and spun him around. Before he knew what was happening, I hit him right across the face with the brace. It ripped his nose apart. He tried to get at me, but he was too dazed. They took him to Brooklyn Hospital.

Maybe that sounds brutal, but I can't even take credit for being the only one to do that to Fay. I have to split honors with Lou Clayton, of Clayton, Jackson and Durante.

Fay was so well known for his bigotry and so disliked by many people in the business that the big inside joke on both coasts when he married a certain female movie star was "Who's got the biggest prick in Hollywood?" The answer was, "Mrs. Frank Fay."

* * *

I could also fight clean. I was on the Professional Children's School boxing team with guys like Ashley Buck, Howard Oppenheim, and Jerry Devine. At 135 pounds, I fought lightweight. My style was light-footed with what I thought was lots of razzle-dazzle. I kept moving around so much, jabbing and hooking, that they used to stop my fights in one round. But my style impressed some of the guys at school. They went around to the boxing promoters and talked me up for amateur fights.

I got one at St. Nicholas Arena and another at the Star Casino on 107th Street. They were only three-rounders. I won one and I lost one. I didn't make boxing history in either case.

My last fight—in a ring—was when my school team challenged a team the New York Athletic Club sponsored for kids. This black guy I was up against gave me a shot in the stomach that dropped me to my knees. I vomited right in the ring, and they threw in the towel.

I must have sat in the locker room for a half-hour before I felt well enough to get dressed and go home. My stomach hurt me, but I was more afraid of what Mama would say about the cut over my eye. It wasn't that much of a cut—a small piece of tape covered it—but Mama couldn't miss seeing it.

I wasn't in the house two minutes when Mama was on me. "What happened to your face?"

"I fell."

"What do you mean you fell? How do you fall on your eye but you don't hit your nose?"

"I don't know, Mama. I must have fallen funny. There was some slippery garbage in the street, and—"

Mama had been reading the newspaper when I came in. She rolled it up and gave it to me—whack!—across the back of my head. "Don't tell me about garbage, Milton! You were prizefighting!"

I decided to bluff it, which was always a mistake with Mama. "What prizefighting?"

I got the rolled-up paper again. "Don't lie to me. I know."

"Okay, okay, so what?"

"And do you know why I hit you on the back of the head? Because I care about your face, that's why. The question is, do *you* care about your face? Do you want to be an actor or do you want to be a prizefighter? You better make up your mind right now. If you're an actor, you need a face. If you're a prizefighter, you don't."

That finished my career in the prize ring. I still worked out whenever I could, but I permanently put away any dreams I had of winning the heavyweight title.

And I also said good-bye to school.

There had been too many nights when I had dragged my school books along on a club date or a smoker only to fall asleep coming home on the subway with a book in my lap and wake up at the ass end of nowhere; too many nights sitting up at a table in Pomerantz's Restaurant between 119th and 120th on Lenox trying to do the next day's homework. The decision had to be made. I could work or be educated, and my working was more needed at home. And the way I saw it, a kid in the spotlight was a lot better than a flop in a schoolroom.

When I was about fifteen and a half, I was home for a couple of days with a cold that turned into the flu. One day, while I was in bed, Uncle Mickey, my mother's brother-in-law, came by for a visit. I was bored stiff with lying in bed, so when he came into the room with what looked like a newspaper sticking out of his back pocket, I asked if I could see it. He gave me a quick look at it. "It's a scratch sheet for picking the horses. It wouldn't interest you, Milton."

I don't know how he happened to drop it, but after he left I found it in the bathroom. Even back then, if you told me something wouldn't interest me, I was interested. I took the scratch sheet back to bed and studied it. What interested me most was where some expert had picked the winners in the races. The next day when Pa came home with a newspaper, I checked out the winning horses against the selections in the scratch sheet.

In one race, the guy had picked the win, place, and show horses correctly. I didn't know it, but he had had a hell of a day, with winners in six out of seven races. I thought it was that way every day. My God, playing the horses was like picking money off the ground.

I started following the race results in the papers, making paper bets. I was making a fortune in scraps of paper. I was starting to burn up inside to really make a bet and get some of that easy money.

It was two or three months later when I was doing a single in Baltimore—naturally, Mama was traveling with me—and I saw the stagehands huddled backstage over their scratch sheets. I could hear them talking about their one-dollar bets. I think Mama had gone ahead to the dressing room. It was the chance I had been waiting for. I had been following the horses, so I knew who was running where. I went over to one of the stagehands. I pulled two bucks out of my pocket and asked him to place it on the horse I had chosen to win.

I thought he would turn me down. But he just said, "Sure, kid."

The horse won, and I got back four for my two. It was a cinch. I began placing bets through the stagehands at every theater I played. And from them I learned all the stuff that every broke horseplayer knows. I learned about handicapping, parlays, and round robins. And I started increasing my bets from two to three, four, and five dollars. Unfortunately, I made money that first year. It would have been a lot cheaper for me if I had lost. Maybe I wouldn't have gotten hooked.

It wasn't long before Mama got suspicious and asked me what I was doing, always hanging around the stagehands. I told her I was just learning about horses.

"Are you betting money?"

"Yes."

"That's gambling, and it's not good for you."

"Mama, I made ten dollars today."

"So you'll lose twenty dollars tomorrow."

"Mama, you don't know anything about it."

"Don't tell me what I don't know, Milton. I know. Do I have a brother-in-law, Mickey? Then I know from horses and horse racing and from gambling. It's an illegal crime!"

Now, I was getting impatient. I was growing up, and she was still treating me like a kid. "Aw, Mama, everybody does it."

"When the President of the United States says okay, everybody bet on the horses, then it's okay by me. Until then it's an illegal crime. And I am asking you not to do it."

There was no point in going on with it. "Sure, Mama."

"Good, I'm glad."

But I was really hooked. Fascinated by more money than I had ever had before. Nothing big, but more folding money in my kick than Mama gave me at the end of every week. And I liked the excitement.

Only once was I ashamed. That was when I wanted to place some bets and I was temporarily broke. I lied to my mother and said I wanted to go to a trick shop—I was still fooling around with cards—and maybe buy some things. She turned away and fished inside her dress, where she kept our money hooked to her brassiere with a safety pin. She handed me ten dollars, which was a big piece of change for Mama to give away. But she regarded my interest in card tricks as an investment in the future. Who knows what I could work into an act?

I took it straight to a bookie joint somebody backstage had told me about.

It was in between the matinee and the evening show, and the place was crowded. At first, the guy who looked through the door didn't want to let me in, but I said the magic words "Benny sent me," and the door flew open—Benny must have been a big loser. It was the first bookmakers' place I had ever been in. I thought it was great. My luck, the police raided it my first afternoon there, and before I knew what was going on, I was in a paddy wagon and on my way to the precinct house.

I was torn between missing the evening show and calling my mother to come and get me. Staying in jail seemed a better deal than facing my mother. But I called, and she came right down and bailed me out.

When we were outside, I braced for her hollering. But Mama, being Mama, was always unexpected. She said, "So you didn't go to the trick shop at all?"

I shook my head.

"Did you lose the whole ten dollars?"

"I guess so. The race I bet it on wasn't over when the cops came."

Mama took it quietly. "I hope you learned from this. Your business is on a stage, Milton, not with a horse."

And that was all she said.

It didn't stop. Because, after the thrill of winning and the greed to win more comes the losing and the betting to get it back. The horses were with me, and they were going to stay with me for years.

When Mama and I met Sam Bergen in 1924, we thought we had stumbled into heaven. Here was a man who believed in my talent, knew how to handle an act for the big time, and was willing to put up the money for the proper material for me. Working with him at the time was Harry Delmar, who later went out on his own and made a name for himself with his *Revels*. Harry was a friend then; he is a friend now.

The man who was to write the new act for me was Al Boasberg, a jewelry salesman from Buffalo, who had a flair for comedy and a big desire to change his life style, which he did. He later became one of Jack Benny's top writers.

The act he wrote for me was called "Guilty!" and I worked it first with my brother Phil and then with Frank. The set was a jail cell. Phil or Frank would play the jailer. The way it went, I'd do my imitation of Eddie Cantor, Al Jolson, or Ed Wynn. The audience would be asked to decide if I was guilty or not of stealing. The answer was always guilty, because that led to comedy bits about putting me in the jail cell. I'd get out on one excuse or another, and I'd say to the audience, "As long as I'm guilty, let me try this one!" And I'd go into another routine, and back into the cell again.

We tried the act out in Brooklyn (I was Bobby Baker), and afterward the manager of the theater said to Mama, "Mrs. Berle, I saw your son at the Palace with that kid Kennedy, so I know how clever he is. But if I didn't know he had talent, I'd cancel this act right now."

There was a thing in vaudeville of those days called the first rehearsal check. If you had a song in your act, and another act showed up first with the same song, they got it and you had to cut it out of your act for the week. It paid an act to rise early and get first check; it also meant you could rehearse first with the orchestra instead of hanging around waiting for the other acts to finish. Whenever I played around New York, Pa would take it on himself to get up early and get to the theater so I could have first rehearsal check. He used to show up at stage doors at 6:30 in the morning, about three hours before the pit band started dragging in and long before any of the other acts.

The longer I stuck with "Guilty!" the less it worked, but from it I learned what was working for me. It was the brash, pushy gags that went over. I began to see me as I thought the audience saw me. Or maybe I should say, saw through me.

I hadn't had a normal childhood. Watching Mama fight for the breaks, fighting for the spotlight myself, I had learned that maybe the meek inherited the earth, but that was after the takers got through with it. I had learned that you had to fight for everything you wanted or chances were somebody else would get it. Between my kid years in vaudeville and my secret sessions at the gym, I had learned to fight for attention on a stage and fight with my fists off stage. I had all the confidence of poverty—nothing to lose and everything to gain by fighting. I guess I wasn't growing up to be the nicest guy in the world. Mind you, underneath the brash, pushy outside there was still a scared kid inside. Somehow an audience saw it all, and responded to it.

I went out on the road as a stand-up single, hoping to polish whatever I was doing through trial and error. The big gimmick of the act was my Eddie Cantor imitation. Everybody was still doing Cantor, but what made mine different was the little trick of blacking up in front of the audience while talking to it, and then going into the routine.

Vaudeville was family entertainment, and almost always no matter where you played on the circuits there would be a sign backstage saying, "No Hell No Damn." Enforcement was up to the manager at each theater. (Another sign said, "Don't send out your laundry until we see your act.") I did a joke at the time in which I said: "Gee, these times we're living in, it's going so fast, the words even have to be said fast. You go into a restaurant and you want bread, you say 'Bread me.' If you want coffee, you say, 'Coffee me.' I was embarrassed because I went in for milk!"

It got a big laugh, but some managers told me to cut it. I can't remember the theater, but I sure can remember the manager's name. It was Dominic Baracci, and he told me to cut out the milk gag. I protested. "It's the biggest laugh I've got, Mr. Baracci."

He just said, "It's out," and walked off. His attitude didn't upset me too much. I had met worse than him. I remember one guy who ran his theater from a wheelchair. He'd sit in the wings during the first show, and if he didn't like an act, he'd just hand them their pictures from the billboard in front of the theater as they came off, and they were through without his saying a word.

It's one thing to agree to a cut, but it's another to do it. You work an act long enough, and even if you're on your toes throughout, one line feeds into another and you can find yourself going into cut material without even knowing you're doing it. At this particular theater, I was doing three shows a day. I cut the milk gag on the second show, but on the night show, the audience was great and the laughs were coming in big, and I was sailing high. Before I knew it I was into the milk line. It was too late to stop, and the audience roared at it. I did my Eddie Cantor finish, blacking up and going off to "You've Got to Have It in Hollywood." I hadn't even stopped the dance step that took me into the wings when a fist caught me hard in the mouth.

It was Dominic Baracci. I had to take my curtain call with my head spinning and the taste of blood building in my mouth. Baracci had no right to do it. He had it in his power to chew me out, to dock my salary, to fire me, but not to do what he did.

I didn't see it—I was sitting in the dressing room with a chunk of ice against my mouth—but one of the other acts told me that Mama took out after Baracci and gave him a few words that would have closed the circuit and a few shots with her pocket book that evened the score.

But if you think I had a rough time, I've got to tell you about the team of Demarest and Collette and what happened to them out on the circuit. That's William Demarest and his late wife, Estelle Collette. They did a knockabout comedy act—low stuff with lots of falls, and Estelle playing straight woman to Bill. The act was so strong that they were always on next to closing, the choice spot on the bill. They were on the Orpheum Circuit, playing one week ahead of me, for thirty solid weeks.

They opened at the Hennepin-Orpheum in Minneapolis. As soon as Demarest and Collette were on, the stagehands started setting up the closing act behind the front drop. The act was Lady Lottie's Pets, which was made up of one woman and all kinds of talking birds, mostly mynahs. All through Demarest and Collette's act, they could hear the chattering and cheeping behind them as the birds were warming up. It threw Demarest, so that his act bombed.

Right after the first show, he went straight to the manager's office and told him to wire the New York office that he wanted either to be changed to another show or to get a different spot on the bill. The answer came back, "Play or Pay." And the act had an iron-clad contract that he couldn't get out of. So he was stuck with thirty weeks of working against chirping birds.

Bill Demarest got a big idea. In every theater, the routine was the same. When the afternoon show was over, which timed out at about a quarter to five, the stagehands would put the work light up and everyone would clear out for dinner before the evening show. Demarest made it a point of coming back an hour ahead of everyone else. He would sneak over to the bird cages and lift the covers, and he'd say to the birds, over and over, "Fuck you! Fuck you! Fuck you!" Then he'd put the covers back on and go to his dressing room.

The act moved from Calgary to Vancouver, to Seattle to Portland, and all the way Demarest was saying, "Fuck you! Fuck you!" to the birds.

The unit I was with had a layoff, so I was in San Francisco a week ahead of schedule, and I caught the first matinee. Demarest and Collette bombed out again because of the birds behind the drop.

Then the pit band went into a syrupy arrangement of "The Dance of the Sugar Plum Fairy," and the curtain opened on the birds on their

perches. Lady Lottie came out, looking very square and small-time in a paste tiara and evening gown with long white gloves that were gray at the fingertips. She went down the line of perches, chatting with the birds.
"Hello, Petey."
"Hello, Lady Lottie."
"Don't you look pretty today, Loulou?"
"Yes I do, Lady Lottie."
She got to the fifth bird and gave it another one of her cutesy greetings, and, clear as a bell, the bird sang out, "Fuck you!"
Like a shot all the birds took it up. The stage was ringing with "fuck yous" as they quickly closed the curtains. The audience was helpless in its seat with laughter.
Punch line: They canceled Bill Demarest.

My act was tightening up, getting better, getting stronger. There were still soft spots in it, but as I grew more and more comfortable working as a single, I started trying things. Like when I opened at B. S. Moss's Jefferson on 14th Street in New York. On the first matinee, the orchestra leader missed one of my cues and I tossed an ad lib at him about it. It got a laugh from the house, but, better yet, he laughed too, which led to our friendship. So I started throwing more lines at him, and one day I reached over the foots and took the baton out of his hand and started conducting the pit band in my own crazy way. That got big screams from the audience, so I did it at the next performance. It became a part of my act.

Even though the act was getting better, something not so good was happening to me. To this day I'm not certain what it was all about. If it all ties together, I have to mark the beginning as when I was about fourteen. I started having trouble sleeping. At first it didn't mean anything to me. So if I couldn't sleep one night, I'd catch up the next. But sometimes that didn't happen. I'd drag myself back to the room after the evening show, certain I would go straight to sleep, and I'd find myself staring at the dark ceiling half the night. Just about when I decided something was really wrong and I should tell Mama about it, it seemed to go away. So I forgot about it, and maybe two weeks later I was staring at the ceiling again.

Then it was constipation or the runs. That was damn annoying, but I didn't worry about it. I thought I understood. The counter joints, hash houses, diners, flea bags we stayed in, the boardinghouses and all the other second-rate places we ate in on the road were responsible. I'd just have to try to be more careful about what I ate and try to skip the junk fried in stale grease. I sure as hell didn't tell Mama about it. She'd be off and running to the drugstore, and then shoving laxatives down my throat or terrible chalky stuff to bind me, or, worse, trying to get me to have an enema.

I was about sixteen, and though I can't remember the theater, I can remember everything else. I was on stage doing my monologue. The audience was with me, and I was going over big. The lights seemed to change. The foots went from even spots of light in front of my feet to a widening smear of light. I broke out into a sweat, and it seemed that the proscenium arch was beginning to melt and shift to one side. I was still talking, but I couldn't hear what I was saying. I could hear the audience laughing, but they seemed to be getting farther away. Then the whole theater started moving, and I staggered. I reached out for something to grab hold of, but there was nothing there. I tried to brace my feet against the movement of the floor.

From far, far away I heard my mother's scream. Then she was up the stage steps and coming toward me. She grabbed my arm, and the spinning stopped. Mama helped me off stage, and a stagehand shoved a chair under me. Somebody gave me some water, and after a minute I felt as good as ever.

Mama's face was dead white. She kept dabbing nervously at my face with her handkerchief. "What is it, Milton, tell me."

"I don't know," I said, "I just got dizzy for a minute. I'm all right now, honest."

"You swear? You're sure?"

"Honest, Mama. I could go back out there and do my finish, I feel so good."

Mama ignored that. "Has this ever happened before?"

I shook my head.

But it did happen again. In fact, two or three times. I noticed that it never happened when I was moving around on stage, but only when I was standing still doing my monologue. And then one night, in front of an audience, I blacked out completely. I had no warning, no feeling of illness, no dizziness. One minute I was there yakking it up, and the next I was out.

That happened a couple of times too. The blackouts went as quickly as they came. None of them lasted for more than maybe thirty seconds. What was odd was that if I got dizzy I knew I wasn't going to black out. When that happened, there was no dizziness, no warning at all. It just happened, and the next thing I knew, there was Mama hovering over me with a glass of tap water at my lips. She said it had to be medium temperature, not ice water. Whether she got that from a doctor, one of her druggists, or one of her card-playing buddies, I don't know, but she believed in it, and I went along with it.

We had shrugged off the dizziness as growing pains, but the blackouts frightened us both. Mama took me to doctors, who took blood tests, peered into my ears, and examined my eyes. They discovered nothing. When we got back to New York, Mama came up with Miss Fitzpatrick as the solution.

Miss Fitzpatrick was a wiry woman, all bone and muscles. She dressed completely in very starched white, which made her look medical, but I don't think that she was even a nurse's aide. Miss Fitzpatrick's specialty was the high colonic, and from somewhere Mama got the idea that this was the solution to the blackouts.

I still remember Miss Fitzpatrick leading me into the back room of her apartment on 54th Street and Seventh Avenue, which she had fitted out to look like a hospital room—very antiseptic. She put an arm around my shoulder—and I was a little old for that from a woman—as she walked me back. She was very hearty about it all. "We'll just wash out the bad to make room for the good!"

She washed several times. I don't think it helped much. The blackouts and dizziness continued on and off into the 1930s, and then, amazingly, faded out of my life. We didn't know much about Freud back in those days—Pa once read an article about him and gave him the stamp of approval as a Viennese Jew, which was second best to a German Jew—but I assumed whatever it was all about was mental. But now I don't know. I sort of suspect that it was my mind making some kind of protest against the life I was leading. But frankly, I don't think about it much. I don't want to go back and find the answer. Even if I had found it back then, it was already too late. I was getting ahead in show business. It was the only life I knew, even then. And it was the only life I wanted.

I think Mama's worry about the dizziness and blackouts explains something that started happening as I moved into my late teens.

Mama was always out front for every show I did, laughing it up for every gag, applauding like crazy. One night—I think it was in Omaha—

she came back after the show with a pretty girl in her mid-twenties. I was just finishing taking off the last of my make-up. All I was wearing was a bathrobe, with a towel around my neck. "Come in, come in," Mama said in her most friendly voice. "Don't be shy."

And the girl came in. I stood up and pulled the belt tight on my robe. "Milton, this is Mary Anne, and she's a big fan of yours. Say hello."

I gave her my big professional smile as I took a quick look up and down, thinking I wouldn't mind being a big fan of Mary Anne's for a while.

"Well, hello, Mary Anne, how very nice of you to come backstage. Please take a seat."

Mary Anne just smiled shyly and sat down, carefully tucking her skirt in around her legs.

"Can you imagine, Milton?" Mama said in that same strange, happy voice. "Mary Anne was sitting right next to me during the show and we happened to get talking. When I found out she liked you—I mean on the stage, of course—I just had to bring her back. Mary Anne said she thought you were cute, didn't you, dear?"

Mary Anne blushed and giggled. "Please . . . I don't know what to say."

Mama laughed. "Anyway, I done what I promised. There he is. And now, while you young people have a nice talk, I'm going out for a bite. I'll faint if I don't eat soon."

Before I could stop her, Mama was out the door. She couldn't have been up to what I was thinking. But if not, why did Mama leave us alone? She and I had had dinner together just before the show.

I really wanted some answers from Mama, but the way the evening went with Mary Anne, who turned out not to be shy at all, I wasn't going to ask the questions when I got back to our room. Mama was awake, as usual. She always waited up for me.

Neither of us said anything on the subject until I came back from the john down the hall, where I had changed into my pajamas. Just as I was getting into bed—I was too big to sleep across the foot of Mama's bed now—she said, "Did you have a nice evening?"

"Very nice," was all I said.

"That's nice," Mama said. "It always pays to be nice to your fans."

I looked at her across the room, but she turned away from me. I put out the light, but I didn't think I'd sleep. I was still trying to figure out if Mama had picked up that girl for me.

Mama spoke in the dark. "You know, growing up is very difficult. The body and the bones are stretching and pushing in a lot of ways. They need a lot of things at such a time, and you got to get them. Vitamins and good food and who knows what else? And who can say what can go wrong if the body doesn't get what it wants? Good night, Milton."

I had my answer. I suppose what she did for me sounds terrible and wrong. But I know Mama. She was, above all things, a realist. She had known about me and girls since the day the tin of Trojans fell out of my pocket, so bringing Mary Anne backstage wasn't exactly corrupting me. And God knows Mama loved me, and she was scared stiff about the blackouts. How she put it all together and decided that sex would cure the blackouts, I don't know, but I liked her solution.

There were several other Mary Annes that Mama brought backstage in other cities. I found out that when Mama took her seat for the show, she always picked it next to an attractive girl, always about five or six years older than myself. She'd strike up a conversation with the girl during the show. If the girl said anything during or after my act to show she found me attractive, Mama offered to bring her back to meet me. What happened after that, Mama never wanted to know. The only comment she ever made was if the girl was back in my dressing room more than twice. That's when she'd turn on the ice. "You back again?" she'd say, or, "I didn't think you'd come around again, the way everybody in the theater is talking."

The girl usually disappeared.

"What did you do that for, Mama?"

"Do what? Anyway, that girl was too old for you. At least a good ten years." Which was an exaggeration, but it did explain why Mama never brought anybody back who was the right age for me.

⚞ 11 ⚟

Finally, finally, I thought I was ready as a single. And finally I got to New York. I opened at Loew's State on December 29, 1924, on the bill with Janet of France, who sang in several languages and was more French than France; the McGushen Twins, a hoofing flash act; and the Belleclaire Brothers, hand-balancers. The *New York Star* said I was the "comedy hit of the bill," which was pretty good considering the team of Bragdon and Morrisey, who did a burlesque routine, were also on the bill.

I knew I was in when *Billboard*, the trade paper that could make or break an act, came out with:

Milton Berle

REVIEWED MONDAY MATINEE, DECEMBER 29, AT LOEW'S STATE THE-ATER, NEW YORK. STYLE—SONGS AND CHATTER. SETTING—IN ONE. TIME—TWELVE MINUTES.

Berle puts over his single in great style. Possessing a big voice, he can be heard easily from any part of the house. His opening number, "Put Away a Little Ray of Sunshine," is sung a bit too hastily to make any kind of impression. According to his own lights, he bubbles over with pep and ambition, and to prove that he is sincere in what he says, Berle follows with "Swanee." This number affords him ample opportunity for pathos and emotion, which he punctuates with frequent gestures.

He makes a reference to other singles who work with piano and
stage decorations. He can have all these things for the asking, where-
upon the curtain is momentarily raised, disclosing piano, etc. Berle
then does a hokum card trick which he admits he appropriated from
Houdini. After a few gags about married life, crossword puzzles and
the income tax, he goes into a soft-shoe dance. With all sincerity
Berle informs the audience that Mr. Loew offered him $1,000 a week
if he would black up, which he does. This leads into an impersona-
tion of Eddie Cantor. Berle's versatility is worth a showing on the
big time.

In case you didn't recognize it, that line about Mr. Loew offering me
$1,000 a week was one of the laughs in my act. At least that's what it
seemed like to Mama and me—a big, bitter laugh. How could you get
notices like the one in *Billboard* and still be making peanuts? Sure, we
had spoken, shouted, pleaded with good old Silent Sam Bergen for more
money for me, but what could he do? Did he do the booking? Did he run
the circuits? Sure, he agreed, I was worth more, and he was fighting for
me all the time. But I was still a kid, and while I definitely was getting
hot, I wasn't that hot yet. You had to understand.

So we understood, and I got $275 a week for my appearance at Loew's
State. That's what I got until I found out what I was *really* getting. It
was a fat $600 a week. The money was paid directly to my manager, Sam
Bergen, who had somehow gotten a little confused about who got the ten
per cent.

Besides that, he wouldn't pay the extra $1.94 so Mama could also have
a lower berth when we were on the road.

So long, Sam. It was nice knowing you.

In 1925, I played B. S. Moss's Regent Theater in New York. It was
a top vaudeville house on the corner of 116th Street and Seventh Avenue.
Across the street was P.S. 10, so we got lots of teen-agers at the afternoon
shows. I was doing a single, and it went over, maybe even better than it
should have, because of the kids in the audience. I was seventeen, near
to their own ages, and I think they liked me more than they would have
if I'd been older.

One day after the three o'clock show let out, I went down to 115th
Street to an ice cream parlor for a soda. There was a bunch of kids in there,

and from the way they looked at me when I came in with my make-up on, I knew they had been at the show. I walked slowly over to the fountain pretending not to notice or to hear the girls giggling, but secretly I was lapping it up. I ordered a soda, and while I waited I pretended to be very busy studying the syrup jars and the glasses behind the fountain.

In a few minutes four or five of the girls came over for autographs. I made a point of asking each girl her name and signing personally to her. One girl interested me in particular. It wasn't that she was so much prettier than the others. She wasn't. She was cute and a little on the plump side, and inside her middy blouse there was a lot of woman developing. She seemed quite sure of herself. I was sort of interested until I asked her age and she told me she was fourteen. I decided not to be interested.

I didn't think of her again until 1926, when the *New York Evening Graphic* had a field day with the breakup of the three-month marriage of fifteen-year-old Peaches Browning and her fifty-one-year-old millionaire husband, Edward "Daddy" Browning. Day after day the *Graphic* carried Peaches's byline over her version of what had happened to her sacred love. It was pretty hot stuff for its day, with Peaches telling the world things like: "I would have given up every nice dress I ever had to have been spared the moment of torture when Mr. Browning would come lumbering into our bedroom and growl, 'Woof! Woof!' like a bear in my ear. I was so frightened I went into a sort of swoon."

Daddy Browning's statements about his manhood made good copy, too. "I am willing to submit to examination by any reputable group of physicians and they will prove that I am as virile and potent as a youth of 20."

Peaches! Peaches! The name drove me crazy until I finally remembered the girl at the soda fountain asking for the autograph. "Sign it please to Frances Heenan."

I knew how to spell Frances, but I said, "Is that Frances with an 'e'?" It gave me a chance to take another squint at her bust.

She nodded. She knew where I was looking, but she didn't even blush. "Everybody calls me Peaches."

I gave them another look. "Peaches, huh? I would have said a *pear* suited you better."

She smiled, and then I asked her age, and that was that.

The public, in case you haven't heard, is fickle. While the Browning divorce was in the courts all you heard all over was "Peaches this" and

"Peaches that." After the divorce she made a brief splash in vaudeville as a freak attraction, someone the public wanted to take a closer look at, like Evelyn Nesbit after Harry Thaw shot Standford White. After they got their look, it was not too fuzzy for Peaches.

In 1936, I was starring at the Chez Paree in Chicago. There was a great gal there named Dorothy Gulman who handled publicity for the nightclub. I was talking with her one day in the lobby of the Sherman Hotel when she spotted a friend and waved her over. It was Peaches Browning, a little older, a little heavier than when she was making newspaper headlines, but still sort of bubbly and full of fun.

"I bet you don't remember me," I said.

She laughed, and it made the little swell of flesh under her chin shake. "Wanna bet? Regent Theater, 1925. The ice cream parlor afterwards. Am I right?"

"Right."

She put her hands on her hips and did a playful half-turn. "And I'm all grown up now."

It was my turn to laugh. "So I read in the papers."

She brushed it aside. "Oh, that! That's old stuff. In fact, it's getting so old"—and she laughed again—"that the name Peaches Browning is beginning not to ring bells. Soon I'm going to have to have talent to bring in the customers."

"What are you doing now?" I asked. I hadn't seen her name in the papers in a long time.

The question didn't seem to bother or to hurt her. The Peaches I knew was a pretty down-to-earth woman. Maybe she had once kidded the world, but she didn't kid herself. "Oh, I'm still in the business, but I'm a long way from the Chez Paree league. I've been working the small clubs and burlesque houses. If you've got some time between shows some night, drop over to a theater called the Troc—Dorothy knows the way—and take a look."

I did. The theater was typically burlesque, with a comic, straight man, juvenile, main stripper, and Peaches as the extra added attraction. Peaches wasn't great, but she was younger and fresher than the Troc. She sang a few songs and talked her way through a couple of others with some special material that cashed in on her brief life as Daddy Browning's wife, if anybody still cared. If it hadn't been for him and the publicity surrounding the divorce, Peaches would probably never have been in show business. Her voice was okay but nothing special. The one thing good about her act was Peaches herself. She sent something likable out into the audience, and even if you didn't give a damn for what she was doing, you sort of liked her. I did.

Then she dropped over and caught me at the Chez Paree, and when I finished there for the night we made the town and closed up the joints on Rush Street. She was fun and easy to be with. I don't think she took me any more seriously than I took her. We just enjoyed each other every way a man and a woman can.

What we had together continued as her work took her to Detroit, St. Louis, and Cleveland. I followed her. How I managed to keep Mama in the dark, I'll never know. Peaches had certainly learned what it was all about somewhere along the way, and I was lucky enough to share what she had learned for three or four months.

It was nice, it was fun—and then it was over. There was a nightclub waiting for me in one direction, and a burlesque house waiting for Peaches in another. And that was it. I have only good memories of Peaches.

During those early years, I dated several beautiful girls. Although Mama, in her own way, was looking out for my welfare in this area, I can't say the same for my sister, Rosalind.

There was a lovely brunette showgirl I was involved with when I was in New York. She's been happily married a long time now, so let's call her "Myra." She and I had a good time together in a lot of ways. She was also a good friend of Roz's, and the two of them often used to go roller-skating together in Central Park, which wasn't one of the ways Myra and I had good times together.

Anyway, one afternoon I was at home wheeling and dealing with the scratch sheets when the phone rang. It was Myra. "Hi, darlin', what you doin'?"

I told her, a little of this, a little of that.

Myra made her voice low and sort of kittenish. "I'm not doing anything. And I'm all alone and lonely over here."

It was like syrup running down my body. I said I'd be right over.

When I got there, Myra was waiting for me in some sort of sheer negligee that made the trip totally worthwhile. I grabbed her right in the doorway and kissed her. She pushed away.

"Not here. We don't want the neighbors to see, do we?"

She closed the door and took me by the hand and led me into the bedroom. The shades were down, and it was sort of dim and very cozy-looking. I grabbed her again, and this time she didn't try to stop. Things progressed very nicely until . . . I remember the exact moment. I was kneeling by the bed, stark naked, my back to the closet behind me. Suddenly the door flew open and Roz came roller-skating out with a flashlight shining on me. "Surprise! Surprise!" she said. She skated through the room and out the front door before I knew what hit me.

"My God, my God, my God," I kept saying over and over, still on my knees. Myra collapsed on the bed, helpless with laughter. The matinee party was out the window. At first, all I wanted to do was get my hands on my kid sister and kill her. I would have killed Myra, too, but she wouldn't stop laughing long enough for me to stay mad at her. Finally I saw the humor in the situation. I fell on the bed beside her, laughing. At last, we stopped and got back to Plan A.

The end of the '20s, the beginning of the '30s—the movies talked, Lindbergh went up, Wall Street went down. Business wasn't jumping, but people were.

The country was still dry, and still everybody drank. Vaudeville as we knew it was dead, but it didn't know it yet. If you wanted to argue the point, you only had to walk down Broadway to 47th Street and look at the once great Palace, turned into a grind picture house. What we called vaudeville was just a stage show between pictures at those houses that could still afford the luxury of live entertainment. The movies, which once were the "chasers" between vaudeville shows, were now the main attraction, and we were the "extra added," and even that was fading out.

For me, it was a time of working as a single and serving as master of ceremonies for the whole bill—exactly what I would be doing twenty years later on television, and somehow audiences would think it was something new.

Things were happening on the home front, too, to the Berlingers-turned-Berles. My brother Phil, who had been the first of us to get married—in 1923—was now the first to get divorced. We thought that was terribly important and sad, but something much more important happened—and even more sad—and nobody really knew it.

Pa had been down around 155th Street, and, in his usual, impractical way, he decided to buy a piece of candy to bring home to Roz. He got one of those honeycomb squares covered in chocolate, which used to come in yellow boxes, that all of us loved. Only, after he bought it Pa discovered that he didn't have enough money left for carfare home, which was now in Washington Heights. That didn't bother him too much. He had often walked miles on the hard streets of New York.

The police found Pa sitting on the curb at 173rd Street. He was gasping for breath so hard he could barely tell them his address. They brought him home. Roz was scared stiff and wanted to run for a doctor, but Pa wouldn't let her. Doctors cost money. Whatever it was seemed to pass and was forgotten.

Now we know that we should have gotten the doctor. It wasn't just the too-many cigarettes that Pa smoked or the constant worry about making a living. And it wasn't just the walk uptown. It was probably the warning of the heart attacks to come, and, hard-luck guy that Pa was, nobody realized it. We were all too busy leading our own lives to pay attention to Pa, who had no life but us.

Things were happening for me—and Mama, of course—that were moving me up. I appeared on Rudy Vallee's coast-to-coast radio show. I made my first talkie for Warner Brothers Vitaphone, something called *Gags to Riches*, and I did a short in New York called *Poppin' the Cork* for Education Pictures.

In vaudeville, I became "Milton Berle, the Wayward Youth." It was another act, and that meant going back to the small time again—Pottsville, and Steubenville, and rundown vaudeville theaters to work in, and rat traps to live in—while I polished the act.

I thought we were rolling again when I got my first big-time booking with the new act at B. F. Keith's Riverside, a two-a-day house in New York at 96th Street and Broadway. The rehearsal before the first show was called for 9 on Monday morning. Mama and I got down there at 8:30. As usual, the first thing Mama did was check the display in front of the theater for my billing. I was on second, a poor spot on the bill. The type on my name was very small. Mama, who knew the words but rarely used them, was so angry she said, "You're so far down, dogs can piss on your billing!"

She fished in her purse and gave me a nickel.

"What's that for?" I asked.

"To go home because you don't feel well. Maybe Bobby Baker would work such a spot on the bill, but Milton Berle doesn't. I'll take care of everything."

So I went home, and Mama went to the manager of the theater and told him that I had a very bad sore throat and couldn't work. They believed her, of course. Mama was one of the better unknown actresses of her day. And my billing value, which only Mama seemed to recognize at the time, was protected.

The next place I played, the billing was better, the type larger, and the good notices started coming in. I began to draw attention as "the youngest master of ceremonies in vaudeville," and it pleased audiences when, besides introducing the acts, I started getting a little bit involved in them, swapping a few lines or doing a bit of business. It got laughs and made both the act and me look good. The audience thought it was all ad lib and that I was pretty pushy for horning in, but the acts always knew what was going to happen, because they had rehearsed the "ad libs" with me. It was the beginning of what I was to do years later on the *Texaco Star Theatre*.

For the record, I made my television debut in Chicago in 1929. Trixie Friganza and I had been asked to appear by F. A. Sanabria, who owned the United States Television Corporation. It was one of the early closed-circuit experiments. Things like writers didn't exist then. My instructions were to do eight minutes and keep it clean, and don't move around too much. Of the actual broadcast, all I can remember is a small room and fierce heat from the lights and the heavy make-up we had to wear. We were part of history, but I don't think either of us made history. The broadcast was sent out to maybe twelve people in Sanabria's company who had sets.

The way I work today—the timing, the push, the brashness—often makes people think I've worked in burlesque. And that's funny to me, because I think I've worked every phase of show business except burlesque, which explains why I hold cards with every theatrical union. (Once I picketed the Roxy in New York with the stagehands when I should have been on stage as a performer there.) But I did appear on a burlesque stage once. This was back about the end of 1929 or the beginning of '30, when I was doing a single, as usual, traveling with my mother. When you got your booking route on the Keith Circuit, the route always included the Old Howard, the famous burlesque house in Boston. They ran a burlesque show with the strippers and comics the first half, but the second half was three vaudeville acts. If you wanted the other thirty-five or thirty-six weeks on the route, you had to play the Howard or no dice.

So we showed up for rehearsal before the first show. I was out on stage and Mama was backstage taking care of our H & M trunk. Now, Mama was quite young-looking at that time, so it wasn't surprising that this stagehand who was carrying our trunk up to the dressing room said, "What is Berle? A comic? You two do a double stand-up act?"

Mama didn't like his approach, so she became dignified. "How far up is Mr. Berle's dressing room?"

The grip ignored that. "You two with the burlesque show?"

"No, we're with the vaudeville show." Mama always referred to us as "we," as if I were doing a double act instead of a single.

The guy said, "Oh Jesus, I feel for you. We had an act in here last week, a guy and his wife named Dave Vine and Harriet Temple—you know them?—and they died the death of a dog. I don't know what kind of an act you two do, but whatever it is, you're going to die."

Mama didn't understand. "Why?"

She shouldn't have asked, because the guy said, "Well, when these broads get through shakin' their friggin' tits, nobody's going to give a shit about you two."

He dumped the suitcase in the middle of the dressing-room floor, gave her a wink and the standard show-business wish for success, "Break a leg, honey," and left.

When I came upstairs, expecting to find Mama busy as usual unpacking my stage suit and setting out the make-up, I knew something was wrong right away. Mama was just sitting in a chair, her face chalk white. I ran to her and kneeled beside her chair. "Mama? What is it? Are you all right?"

"Nothing, nothing" was all she'd say.

"For God's sake, Mama, tell me what it is."

"A man said something, but I can't tell you what."

"What man, Mama?"

"The stagehand who brought up our trunk."

"Mama, I'm not a baby anymore. What did he say?"

The color started creeping up her face. "Well, first he said we were going to flop here. And when I asked him why—Milton, I don't like to say such words."

"Mama!"

She patted her face with her handkerchief. "Well, he said nobody would care about us after the girls got through shaking their chests. Only he used different words."

I got up, and I was seeing red. "I'm going to kill him. I swear I'm going to kill him!"

I ran for the door. Mama shouted after me. "Milton, please, no trouble!"

I found the guy right away. "I'm Milton Berle. You the guy who took my trunk upstairs?"

The stagehand nodded, "Yeah."

"And did you say to Mrs. Berle . . ." and I told him what Mama had told me, only I put back what I was certain were his words.

The guy didn't see what was eating me. "Yeah, sure. I thought somebody ought to fill you two in."

"Yeah. Well, I'm going to bust you one in the mouth. That lady upstairs is my mother."

The guy's mouth flopped open, and it was his turn to blush. "Oh Jeez, fella. I didn't know. I swear it. I thought she was your partner. Oh Christ, I'm sorry. I'll apologize to her. I mean it."

The man couldn't have been nicer to us during the rest of that week. He even had us to his home for dinner. But he was right. I was no sensation at the Old Howard. In my only appearance at a burlesque house, I bombed.

In 1930, I took "Chasin' the Blues," a girl-studded flash act, out on the Orpheum Circuit. I was at the RKO Hill Street in Los Angeles the week there was a big charity show at the Shrine Auditorium. Every name act in town was asked to appear along with every movie star who gave a damn about something beside him or herself. The huge auditorium was filled, and backstage was like a sardine can packed with the world's most expensive sardines.

Only one person stood alone, a woman well into her forties who wasn't half as beautiful as most of the movie names backstage. But there was something special about her. I felt it, and I didn't even know who she was, though her face looked familiar. It wasn't her dyed blond hair—there were lots of dyed blonds around—and it wasn't her dress, which didn't compare with some of the gowns the stars were wearing. It was something in the calm, sure way she stood—head up, back straight—waiting to go on.

I pointed to her, and whispered to somebody standing next to me, "Who is that?"

The guy looked at me as if I were a hermit who had just come out of the hills. "Aimee Semple McPherson." *Aimee Semple McPherson!*

Who hadn't read about the evangelist's disappearance in 1926, when she went swimming at Ocean Park, California, and vanished in the waves, only to walk out of the Arizona desert a month later in a clean dress and shiny shoes and tell the world she had been kidnapped and held for ransom? Add a couple of husbands, a wife who threatened to name Aimee as corespondent in a divorce suit, plus a lot of ugly rumors, none of which seemed to hurt the lady's reputation or cut her power as a religious leader, and that was one hell of a woman over there. Like I said, she was a woman, and I was both impressed and very curious.

12

Aimee Semple McPherson was big news in the '20s and early '30s, an
evangelist who drew crowds by the hundreds of thousands wherever she
went. I suppose if you were religious, just looking at her would give you
a charge, as if you were near the Pope; and if you weren't, well maybe
you felt like *Vanity Fair*, the magazine that listed her as an actress on a
par only with Duse and Bernhardt, a woman who "made Billy Sunday look
like a piker."

I went on before her and did a couple of minutes of my material, and
then I hung around backstage waiting to get a look at Mrs. McPherson
in action. She was all dignity and class when it came her turn. The house
went wild when she walked out into the lights. She didn't bow or anything; she just accepted the applause with a slight smile and waited for
them to quiet down. When she spoke, she didn't say anything so original
or brilliant about the charity we were all there for. It was her husky voice
and the sincerity she put into it that made her seem electric. I was
fascinated . . . and I was more curious than ever about her.

She spotted me as she came off stage, and she headed straight for me.
Another woman might see a man she wanted to talk to, but she'd play
it casual—sort of walk by and then be surprised when she bumped into
him. But that wasn't Aimee Semple McPherson. She was direct. No
nonsense. "How do you do, Mr. Berle," she said, and stuck out her hand.

I took her hand, but I was startled. I never even knew what to say to
rabbis, so what could I say to the great Sister Aimee? But she didn't wait

to find out. "I watched you out there. You're a very funny young man. I admired your energy."

"Why . . . uh . . . thank you . . . uh . . . uh Mrs. . . . uh . . ."

She smiled. "Aimee."

"Aimee." She put me at ease. "And I liked watching you out there. I've read so much about you in the papers." I could have bitten off my tongue for saying that.

It didn't bother her. She just laughed. "Don't believe everything you read. Are you appearing here in town?"

I nodded. "The Hill Street. I'm only there for three more days."

"Oh, and then where do you go?"

"We're laying over here for a week before working our way back east."

"We?"

"My mother's traveling with me." Aimee took a look around. I said, "Mama's out front watching the show."

She smiled. "And have you been over to visit us at the Four Square Gospel Temple?" That was the big shrine—it looked something like the Capitol, dome and all—that Aimee's followers had built for her with their contributions.

I shook my head. "I haven't done much sightseeing. Three shows a day and all."

"I'd be pleased to show it to you when you are finished at your theater."

I wasn't sure if she was making a pitch for conversion or what. "Well, I'd like to see it, but I wouldn't want to join."

She just laughed at that. "Don't worry, Milton. I'm on my own time now. Tell me at what hotel you're staying, and I'll have my secretary call and arrange things."

I got the call four days later, but it wasn't a secretary. It was Aimee herself. "Has your engagement ended?"

"Last night."

"Then I trust you have time for a little sightseeing. I promised to show you the Temple. Are you free today?"

I was.

"Good. I'll pick you up in, say, an hour in front of your hotel. I have a dark blue Packard."

And she clicked off.

I went down to Mama's room. The daily card game had already started, and the air was blue with cigarette smoke. I waved to the players, people who had been on the bill with us at the Hill Street, and I signaled my mother that I wanted to speak to her.

"I just wanted to tell you that I'm going out."

Mama was curious. "Where?"

"I'm going to temple."

The gag worked. Mama looked startled. "Temple? You? Since when? It's not even Friday."

"Wait, wait. Hold it, Mama. It's Aimee Semple McPherson's temple."

"Why are you going there?"

"Because Mrs. McPherson offered to show it to me. She's picking me up at the hotel."

"Aimee Semple McPherson is coming for you herself?"

I nodded, and Mama swelled with pride. She nodded her head toward the cardplayers. "Wait till they hear that!"

The chauffeur was standing by the car waiting to open the door for me. Aimee was seated inside, wearing something light and summery, her face hidden by sunglasses and her braided hair under a wide-brimmed hat. She gave me her hand—and I thought she held it a beat too long—as I sat down beside her. "Now let's show you some of the sights of Los Angeles."

The car started moving. I didn't know Los Angeles that well, but I was pretty certain as time went by that we were heading away from downtown. I was sure of it when we passed a sign that said "Santa Monica," but I didn't say anything. I wasn't sure, but I wasn't taking any chances. If there were any moves to be made, they were all going to be hers until I was certain.

She kept chatting with me, asking about my career, my childhood. Things like that. She never gave any instructions to the chauffeur, so wherever the hell we were going had all been planned before I left the hotel.

The car slid to a stop in front of a sea-shack restaurant. I was comfortable enough with her now to kid around. "This is your temple?"

She laughed. "Not quite. I thought we might have lunch first, and give you a look at the Pacific Ocean at the same time."

So we had lunch, and more talk that didn't give me any clues as to which way the wind was blowing. As for the Pacific Ocean, it looked pretty much like the Atlantic Ocean.

Then back into the car again. As we pulled away, she said, "I have a little apartment I keep nearby. If you don't mind, I'd like to stop a moment and change into something cooler. It's turned a little warmer than I expected."

It was warm, but it wasn't that warm. I was wearing a suit and tie. Aimee's dress, which looked like chiffon to me, seemed okay for a tropical heat wave.

Something told me I was never going to see the Four Square Gospel Temple. I didn't mind a bit.

The car stopped in front of one of those semi-Spanish-looking cream-colored stucco apartment buildings that are standard equipment in Los Angeles. Aimee, as I said before, was a direct woman. The minute the chauffeur opened the door, she got out and headed straight for the building, expecting me to follow. I was pretty certain now where the afternoon was heading. Another woman might have made a big routine out of the heat and the need to change to cover the moment of arrival before the big game began. But not Aimee. She had made the excuse once to set things up, and that was enough. Out of the car and into the building. I followed.

It was a small apartment—living room, kitchen, and bedroom. I figured Aimee Semple McPherson rated something bigger and grander than this, so this place must be a little hideaway. She left me in the living room. "I'll be right back." She went into the bedroom. I saw the light go on in there before she closed the door most of the way.

"Do sit down," she called out. "I don't keep any liquor, but I think there are some juices in the icebox."

"No, I'm okay," I said.

I wasn't. I was nervous. It wasn't Aimee the woman that made me feel shaky, it was Sister Aimee the Evangelist that bothered me. I kept seeing those newspaper pictures of her in the flowing white robes, her arms outstretched and holding a Bible. And once I had heard a radio broadcast from the Temple. For days after I had laughed, thinking of a whole mob singing "Yes, Sir, He's My Jesus" to the tune of "Yes, Sir, That's My Baby." It didn't seem funny now.

I looked around the room. It was done very simply. Lots of what I decided were good Early American antiques, and very little else. No pictures on the walls, very little on the tables besides lamps.

Aimee was still in the bedroom. "You're not a very religious man, are you, Milton?"

It was the first time she had ever gotten near her field of work while talking to me.

I didn't know how to answer her. "Well, not the way you are."

"I know what you mean," she said, "but I don't quite see myself that way. I work in the area of religion, but I think of myself more as a scientist and a crusader."

"Why did you ask about me?"

"I was just thinking," she said, and the light went out in the bedroom, "that unless you were really interested, perhaps a visit to my Temple could wait for a cooler day."

The door opened, and there was Sister Aimee in a very thin, pale blue negligee, her braid undone and her blond hair hanging down around her shoulders. There was a soft flickering light somewhere behind her in the bedroom—candles, I guessed—and it was enough to show me that she wasn't wearing anything underneath. "Come in" was all she said.

It was candles all right. Two of them on the night table by the bed, which she had already turned down. They were burning in front of a silver crucifix that stood before a triptych panel of the scene on Calvary. That started my nerves going again, but I solved the problem. I decided not to face that way when we got into bed.

We never got to the Four Square Gospel Temple.

And we didn't get there two days later, when she called again. This time, she just sent the chauffeur for me to bring me straight to the apartment. We didn't even bother with lunch.

When I was dressing to leave, she stuck out her hand. "Good luck with your show, Milton."

What the hell. I couldn't resist it. "Good luck with yours, Aimee."

I never saw or heard from Aimee Semple McPherson again. But whenever I hear "Yes, Sir, That's My Baby," I remember her.

In 1931, I appeared at the Capitol Theatre in New York. On the bill with me were Bing Crosby and Eddy Duchin. I used to drag friends over to see the marquee at the Capitol, not because it had my name on it, but because it said in big letters:

BERLE   DUCHIN   CROSBY

Later on in the year I came back to New York to play Loew's State. One day, after I'd finished the first show, I started walking toward Sixth Avenue. I was on one of the side streets in the Forties, and I came to this little print shop with a sign in the window, "We Do Comedy Cards"— the same sort of one-line gags that they print as newspaper headlines today —and I wanted some, so I went in. The guy running the printing machine was tall and thin, a couple of years older than I was. He said he was a great fan of mine, and we started talking. He said his name was Henry Youngman, but people called him Henny. "I play the violin," he told me. "I work weekends up in the mountains with a combination, a couple of other guys, and sometimes I introduce the other acts."

He was a naturally funny guy, and I enjoyed talking with him. I invited him to come back with me to Loew's State and watch the next show from the wings. He turned the shop over to an assistant, and we took off. Henny was there every afternoon and most evenings. He even gave me a couple of jokes, and I talked to him about timing, delivery, doing a monologue. I didn't go near his natural style of delivery, which was fast but easy. That was Henny from the beginning. He once said he was the king of one-liners, but I told him that was because he couldn't remember two.

I was held over for a second week, so it gave the friendship—which has lasted to this day—time to grow. Later on in the year, through some guys I knew, I got Henny a job at a club called Gallagher's, which was on 47th Street at Seventh Avenue, next to the Columbia Theatre. It was a basement joint, and Henny did seven shows a night, a real grind. He soon discovered that he got hold-over business from show to show, so he rotated his two routines so that he did routine A the first and third shows, and B the second and fourth.

Then I really did Henny a favor—and, thank God, he lived through it. I knew a lot of the mobsters around town, and they had just opened a new place on the first floor of a brownstone. The speakeasy was called Club Abbey. It caught on fast and attracted everyone from Beatrice Lillie to Dutch Schultz. Talking to some of the guys one day, I said, "You ought to book this guy Henny Youngman. He's new and he's funny."

They did, and Henny went over big. I would show up between and after my own shows and work with him to help out. Henny's engagement was cut short despite his success. He was in the middle of his act in front of a packed room when two rival gang chiefs, Chink Sherman and Dutch Schultz, both showed up. Bullets started flying, and knives flashed. Both men got stab wounds and Chink got two bullets in him, while Henny and I and the rest of the audience got the hell out of the Abbey as fast as we could. Sherman and Schultz both survived that night—though not too much longer—and Henny, God bless him, is still going strong.

At this point, 1931–32, I was being handled by Charlie Morrison, a hell of a nice guy. It was his idea to get Jack Osterman to write my next act. I wasn't in the lucky position of some classic acts that worked the vaudeville circuits. They were able to do the same material year after year —acts like the Avon Comedy Four, starring Smith and Dale doing "Dr. Kronkhite"; Roger Imhoff and Corrine in "The Pest House"; Victor Moore and Emma Littlefield in "Change Your Act or Back to the Woods." Their audiences expected it. But most of us would have to come in after a season and begin the search for new material for the next season.

Jack Osterman was a brash, funny comic in his own right, and I worked a little like him—fast one-liners, throwaways—so he was a good choice for me. The only thing wrong about Jack Osterman was that he liked to booze it up, which killed him a few years later. Anyway, he asked for a thousand in advance, and Charlie Morrison gave it to him. Osterman said he would have the act for me in six weeks.

At the end of the six weeks we went around to see Osterman to get the material. Osterman was a little smashed. There were no papers in sight anywhere. "Where's the material?" Charlie asked. We could smell where the thousand had gone.

"Here's what we're going to do," Osterman said. "You open with a big joke, and then you do a little shit. Then you do another big joke, and some more shit. Then another big joke. You see?"

For a thousand bucks, all we got were three jokes and a lot of shit.

In 1931, I played my first nightclub, the Vanity Fair. It was a small but expensive place over a store across from the old Roxy Theatre in New York. The place only held 125 to 140 people, but Benny Clinton, who owned it, booked me in as comedian and m.c. at $1,500 a week, so you can imagine the prices he was clipping the customers for. In the show with me was a dynamic singer, Gertrude Niesen. At the time she was seeing a lot of Marty Crompier, who was tied in with "the boys" in some way. (The word around town in '31 was that it was Dutch Schultz who was behind the shooting at Spinrad's barber shop, at 47th and Seventh, that had nearly cost Marty his life.) Marty hung around the Vanity Fair a lot, waiting for Gertrude, and for that I am grateful to this day.

I was a pushy kid, coming up fast, and I thought I could handle anything. I didn't have any real material for nightclubs, but I knew a string of one-liners and I was fast with the ad lib and I knew how to handle hecklers, so what the hell? When I got out on the floor I looked for hecklers to work against. I would find my marks and ride them so that they had to answer back. So, one night I was out on the floor and I spotted this table with three guys and a very flashy blonde trying hard to look like Jean Harlow. I settled on the youngest of the three guys for my target— he looked about twenty-five—and I started in with the stock lines:

"No drinks on the table. Tourists, huh?"

I got a laugh from that part of the audience that hadn't heard the line before, but no laughs from the table I was working on. Usually, the guy you're needling blushes at being the center of attention while the others at his table roar. But not this night. There was no reaction at all from the four of them. So I tried another. "Novelty night. You're out with your wife!"

Nothing again. I tried a few more and finally switched away from them. It was like working a fish-store window. Just glazed eyes.

When the show ended I went straight to my dressing room. I don't think I was in there a minute when the captain knocked. "Table twelve wants to see you."

I was surprised. I must have been a bigger hit with them than I thought. I went back out front. "How do you do, sir?" I said.

The twenty-five-year-old hardly noticed me. "Take a chair," he said. His voice was cold, and I got the first hint that maybe I wasn't meeting with a fan club.

Nobody at the table nodded or said hello or even smiled at me. The kid seemed to be in charge. When I sat down, he said, "What are you drinkin'?"

I told him that I didn't drink. He smacked me on the shoulder and said, "Take a drink."

When the waiter came over I said, "Give me an orange blossom," and I winked with the eye I thought my host couldn't see to tell the waiter I didn't want any liquor in it. The waiter knew the signal because there were B-girls working the Vanity Fair. They always asked for the same drink and gave the same signal.

But the kid caught it. "Whatcha wink for, pal?"

"I didn't wink. There's something in my eye."

"Yeh, yeh," he said, and turned to the waiter. "Cancel his orange blossom and bring him a double Scotch."

When the waiter left, no one spoke. I was getting very nervous, so I said, "Did you like the show?"

"No. It stunk."

He turned to me and reached out and grabbed my necktie. He began pulling the thin underneath end so that the tie tightened around my neck, and I started gagging. Then he yanked my face close to his—it was like a bad scene from a Cagney movie. "Listen, you little wise prick, the next time I come in here, don't even look at me. There may not be a next time, but just in case, don't look at me. I don't like what you said about me."

He released my tie maybe half an inch so I could talk. "I was only kidding around."

"*I'm* not. And I could kill you right this minute, you little rat bastard."

He had been eating a steak before I came over. Before I realized what was happening, he had picked up his fork, but not the way you do when you are going to eat something. He grabbed it in his fist and raised it the way you grab an ice pick you're going to use.

He jabbed the fork straight up into my chin. Marty Crompier stepped in and grabbed his wrist and forced his hand open. The fork fell to the floor. Marty said softly, "Easy, Pretty. Take it easy, Pretty."

I grabbed a napkin and pushed it against my chin. Then I realized whom I had been needling. It was Pretty Amberg, one of the toughest of the hoods in the rackets. I broke out into a cold sweat.

Pretty looked up at Marty and just laughed. Then he signaled to the waiter. "Hey, bring me a clean fork."

I got the hell away from that table as fast as I could. Crompier rushed me into the street, pushed me into a cab, and gave the driver the name of a doctor the local boys had on call. I got two stitches for each prong of the fork: eight stitches in all. I was afraid to go back to the Vanity Fair again, so I closed. (Amberg ended his career in a block of cement, his penis in his mouth—the mobster's tribute to a squealer.)

It was back to vaudeville. I was headlining now in the Loew's Presentation Houses, as they called them, places like the Valencia out in Jamaica on Long Island and the Paradise up in the Bronx. They were great spots, and I got a lot of notice and did good business, but I wasn't getting what I wanted. I wanted to play the Palace, but it was no dice, so I went out on the road again.

I was at the Loew's Syracuse in upstate New York when the break came. The Palace had started using teams of comedians as masters of ceremonies. Eddie Cantor and Georgie Jessel were one pair, William Gaxton and Lou Holtz another. For the week of January 18, 1932, they had signed Benny Rubin and Jack Haley to m.c. a bill that starred Beatrice Lillie; Fifi D'Orsay; Al Siegel at the piano accompanying his new protégée, Lillian Shade, who had much of the pow and power of his previous discoveries, Ethel Merman and Bee Palmer; the Mills Brothers; and George Olsen's band with Ethel Shutta. Benny Rubin got an attack of appendicitis two days before the opening, which killed off the tandem-m.c. idea for the bill, because the material the two had planned together didn't work anymore.

There was panic among the big brass at the Palace to find an m.c. comedian for the bill. God bless Arthur Willi, who was one of the top bookers of acts for the Palace. He had followed my career since the days of Kennedy & Berle. He's the one who said to Albee and his top booker, Eddie Darling, "There's a kid up at Loew's Syracuse, name of Milton Berle, and I think he'd be great here at the Palace for the m.c. spot." I got the job.

Nervous! Boy, was I nervous. All through the Sunday night run-through I was riffling slips of paper, shuffling gags around, trying to figure out what would work best where. The more nervous I got, the more nervous the Palace brass became about me, but Arthur Willi kept assuring them I'd be fine.

And, God, I was nervy in those days! I knew that Beatrice Lillie was a big star, but I didn't really know too much about what she did until that rehearsal. She broke the usual Palace tradition of the top star appearing only in the second half. She appeared in both. In the first half she did "The Late Comer," a skit she had done on Broadway in the *Third Little Show*, a pantomime about a woman in a movie theater eating popcorn and wearing a big picture hat that blocks the view of the people behind her. In the second half she did several of the songs that she had made famous. I watched her in the first-half sketch, but without an audience there didn't seem to be anything to the number. I am ashamed to say that

I turned to Arthur Willi and said, "This dame is going to slow up my show." Thank God, it didn't get back to her.

At two in the morning, I was pacing out front of the Palace, still riffling my papers and staring at my name on the marquee. Ted Healey, who was one of my idols—his walk, talk, speed, flippancy were what I secretly had sort of patterned myself after—came by. He slapped me on the back. "You look a little shaky, kid."

"I feel as shaky as Gilda Gray."

Healey shrugged it off. "Listen, I've got a great gag for you if you want it."

"Sure."

"Well, you know that in private life Beatrice Lillie is Lady Peel. So you do this joke with her."

The next day at noon before the opening matinee, I knocked on the door of her dressing room. She told me to come in.

I got straight to the point. "I got a great gag I want to do with you." Before she could say anything, I told it to her.

She smiled politely and said, "I'm sorry, young man. You're very sweet. I'm sure your joke might be very funny. In fact, it is quite a funny joke, but I don't work with anyone."

"You don't understand, Miss Lillie. This would be after you get through with your act."

She was still polite, but she spaced out the words to make the point. "I—do—not—work—with—anyone, Mr. Berle."

Now just who in hell did she think she was? No one had ever talked like that to me before. (Now that I think about it, just who in hell did I think I was?) "Do you mean you won't do this one gag with me? Are you too big?"

Miss Lillie turned back to her dressing-table mirror. "Good day, Mr. Berle."

I found out, after I got dressed and ran down to the wings, just how tight a ship Beatrice Lillie ran in connection with her work. I got strict instructions from the stage manager that Miss Lillie didn't want me coming on stage after her exit to milk applause for her. I was to stay in the wings—even if I had to be held there by force—until she gave the signal from the other side of the stage that I could come on.

I was steaming until I saw her work in front of an audience. That sketch I thought would slow down the show was the sensation of the first half. Whatever I felt before just faded away in complete admiration for a top pro who knew exactly what she was doing every minute she was on stage. It didn't hurt me one bit to stick to the script in the second half and say only, "Ladies and gentlemen, the incomparable Beatrice Lillie!"

She was scheduled to do about thirty-five minutes of her songs, which included a camp impression of Libby Holman singing "I Apologize." Every number brought down the house, and I kept thinking she couldn't top herself so she must be coming off. But each time I took a step toward the stage, I got a firm hand on my shoulder.

After fifty-four minutes she ran out of her repertoire, and she exited on the opposite side of the stage with the house still screaming for more. She signaled for me to go out there. I did, but I was afraid to do any of the usual stuff like "Let's hear it out there!" or whistling the performer back on. So I just stood there, grinning at the audience to show that they should go on with the racket they were making.

Finally, she came back on. As she bowed, she whispered to me through clenched teeth, "Let's do that joke."

With her out on stage, the applause started dropping in the hope that she would do another number or something.

I said to her, "Miss Lillie, aren't you Lady Peel?"

And she said, "You're goddamned right I am!" and walked off stage to the biggest laugh I have ever heard in a theater. And she stopped the show all over again.

That night, when I came back at eight for the eight thirty show, I was told that Miss Lillie wanted to see me in her dressing room.

"Come in, Mr. Berle," she said.

And I said, "What is it, Bea?" I told you I was brash.

"Mr. Berle, I want to explain about our conversation before the matinee. I hope you didn't take offense at what I said. I certainly didn't mean to be offensive, but I was just telling the truth. I don't work with people. I just didn't want you to think my saying that to you was directed at you in particular. I don't work with anyone."

"Sure, I understand, but you know, that joke did get a big laugh . . ."

I got a terrible feeling. It's out; she was going to kill the joke.

"Yes, and that's the reason I asked to see you. At tonight's show, I think we should do that joke earlier in my act. After the second encore, not after the fourth."

Her stock, which was very high with me after watching her at the matinee, went up another few points. Figuring the gag was surefire, and show biz being what it was, a number that had gone great at one show might not go as great at another show, so she'd have the gag to hypo things up before she went into her big final encores.

By the end of eight weeks, which is how long our show ran at the Palace, Bea and I were good friends—for that matter, so were Fifi D'Orsay and I, but that's another story.

There's a bit of pantomime I've been doing for years in front of audiences. It's when I move my lips to form the words."I love you." That began back at the Palace toward the end of our run, when I was doing more and more bits with her. I would walk her off stage while telling the audience how wonderful she was. She'd say thank you, and I'd mouth the "I love you" at her, and then she'd mouth it back.

In this crazy business you might not see a friend for years because you're not working the same places at the same times. And that's what happened with Lady Peel and me. I didn't see her again until the night of November 4, 1953, when Norman Krasna's comedy Kind Sir opened at the Alvin Theatre in New York. It was a whale of a dressy house because of Mary Martin and Charles Boyer in the leads. Suddenly I spotted Bea Lillie coming down the right aisle as I was going up the left. She didn't wave or anything, just moved those lips in a silent "I love you."

One Sunday night during the run at the Palace, the Mills Brothers invited me up to Harlem with them after the show. The hot spot up there was Connie's Inn, at 133rd Street and Seventh Avenue. One of the stars of the show was Louise Cook.

She was known as one of the greatest belly dancers in the world, and her act was sensational, with everything going like a flag in a hurricane. She was one of those rare women that men had only to look at to want. And that was even standing still. She was slender, and light-skinned like the color of coffee with too much cream in it, and she had her hair in an Afro, which wasn't standard gear then. When she worked, she covered her body with oil that made it shiny and sexy-looking.

Louise and I got to talking after the show when she came over to our table. I thought she was terrific, but she was involved with another guy. I didn't see her for a while after that night, but I didn't forget her. And when I heard that she was free, I called her up and asked to see her. She agreed. But getting together was no easy thing. In those days, it was bad enough for a white man and a black woman to see each other—nobody approved on either side of the color line—but for us it had the added

problem that we were both known to the public and to the gossip columnists.

In order for us to see each other, we'd set a meeting spot, like a street
corner a block or so from Connie's Inn. Louise would show up with all
of her hair stuffed under a hat and wearing sunglasses. I usually wore
sunglasses too, and a slouch hat. One night, we were parked in my car
up along the Hudson, and she took out a little brown cigarette and lit it.
It smelled funny. I asked what it was, and Louise smiled and said, "Take
a puff."

I did, and it made me cough so hard I nearly vomited. That was the
first and last time I ever tried marijuana.

Somewhere along the way during the six months I knew Louise, I
found out I wasn't the only man in her life. Harry Richman was also
meeting her *a few blocks away*. He would wait there for her in his white
Cord, which was a pretty ridiculous way of being inconspicuous.

Louise and I called it quits when Lee Mortimer got wind of us and
was planning to run an item about it in his syndicated column in the New
York *Mirror*. It took a lot of talking to his editor, Jack Lait, to kill the
story.

I didn't hear of Louise again until sometime in the middle 1950s,
when a friend told me that she was very, very sick and in jail in Chicago.
She had gone the Billie Holiday route with booze and God knows what
else. I went down and bailed her out, and about three months later I saw
to it that poor Louise Cook had a decent funeral.

There was a cute little redhead about this time, but I can't even
remember how I met her. All I can remember is that her first name was
Bobbi and she had come North from Galveston, Texas, hoping to become
a fashion model. Her mother had brought her up to be a good girl—and
Bobbi wasn't too interested in that—and made her promise to go straight
to the Barbizon for Women, where men weren't allowed above the lobby
floor, and live there while she sought fame and fortune in the wicked city.

Which is just what Bobbi did, but after our third date, Bobbi found
the place just as frustrating as I did. At the time, I was still living at home,
which left us both with the urge and no place to release it. Why we didn't
go to another hotel for a night, or borrow a friend's apartment I don't
remember, but I do remember the crazy solution I came up with.

I went to Brooks Costume Company, which did most of the theatrical work around town, and rented a dress and high-heeled shoes, and everything else I needed to turn me into a woman. I topped it off with a black wig and heavy veil. I changed right there, and told them I'd pick up my suit the next morning. I used a lipstick I had bought at a drugstore to complete my transformation into a very tall, strange-looking woman. But I wasn't too strange to make it inside and up the elevator of the Barbizon for Women for a night with Bobbi.

What I didn't count on was the next morning. My beard had grown —Bobbi toned it down with her makeup—and my feet had swollen so that I couldn't get back into the shoes. I insisted that Bobbi come down the elevator with me and stand between me and the female elevator operator, who did her best all the way down to get a good look at the very tall bare-footed lady.

It seemed like years, standing on a busy New York street at the height of the morning rush hour with everyone staring, until Bobbi got me a cab back to Brooks.

I wish I could say that Bobbi was worth it. As I remember it, she wasn't.

Some time after Bea Lillie, I appeared in New York with another headliner, and that was pretty interesting too. (For my appearance at one of the top picture houses along Broadway, I hired a guy at fifty cents a show to laugh it up and lead the applause for me. His name was Jack E. Leonard.) The movies were talking steadily now, and the day of the silent-screen vamp was over, but the public was still curious enough about those sultry women who drove men mad to pay money at the box office to see them in person. The one I worked with was as big in her day as Vilma Banby, Nita Naldi, Pola Negri, and Nazimova.

At the dress rehearsal, I thought her act was sort of square. It was a big production, beginning with lots of smoky lighting and throbbing jungle drums. The curtains opened on a staircase and deep blood-red velvet drapes. Chorus boys, dressed like muscle-bound savages, were swaying around the staircase. The drum throbbing got intense and suddenly cut off as the siren came on, wearing black, of course, and lots of heavy snakelike eye make-up. She paused for a moment on the top stair, and then slowly came down. Each of the guys collapsed as she walked by. At the bottom step, she looked around at the flesh fallout and shrugged. "Vot can I do?" she asked the audience. It led into a sexy sketch and a couple of songs, all sung in a heavy European accent I've never heard the likes of since. Maybe the country she came from was disbanded after she left.

Anyway, I was wrong again. The matinee audience loved her. I didn't meet her until after the last evening show, when she sent for me. I thought I was going to get chewed out for some of the gags I pulled on stage using my version of her accent.

There were vases of long-stemmed red roses—obviously, her flower—all over the place, and a bottle of champagne—a press release said she was "a champagne fiend"—in a cooler by her dressing table. She dismissed her maid when I came in. "You may go, Marta. I vish to talk to Meestair Bairle alunn."

The dressing room was softly lighted, and heavy with the smell of French cigarettes. She was wearing a black velvet dressing gown, cut low enough to give her a head cold in the navel. She stood up. "Ahhhhh," she said, as if she were going into an asthma attack.

I didn't know what the hell she was up to. I thought that vamping was an act, but it still seemed to be going on. "I heard you wanted to see me? If it's about the gags I've been doing . . ."

She looked puzzled. "Geggs?"

"Jokes. Laughs, you know."

She brushed it aside. "Dat is your beezness. I dunt interfere. I juss tought it vood be good idee to meet. Alvays, I like to meet pipple I vork vit. It mekks for better, no? Vot you tink?"

That was a relief. "Sure, you bet."

She smiled. "Gud. Gud. Den come in. Ve be friends."

She took the champagne from the cooler and poured two glasses. She handed one to me. "A tust to new frainds."

"Gee, I don't drink."

"A seep to be pullite."

"To friendship," I said, taking a good look at the long triangle down from the neck of her gown. I took a sip of the drink she gave me. "Nice," I said and put the glass down. I hated the stuff.

She put her glass down and came over close to me. "Yes. I ulso tink you are nice, and I am never wrung bout pipple."

I was nervous. Maybe she was just nearsighted, but she was right on top of me. I didn't mind mixing a little business with pleasure, but I wasn't sure about this woman. A wrong move with the star could mean trouble. "Well," I said, and made a move for the door.

She put her hand on my shoulder. "Pliss, must you go? New Yawk is a lunly place for me."

She let the hand trail from my shoulder down to the chest buttons of my jacket.

The message was coming in clear now. "I'm in no rush," I said.

She smiled. "You are vairy yung."

"Oh, well, I'm over—"

She touched a fingertip to my lips. "Pliss. Dat is a vairy nice ting to be. I tink yung men are vairy, vairy nice."

The hand started down my jacket front again. "And you are vairy tull." She pressed her fingers against my chest. "And very strung, I fill."

The hand continued moving down toward the bottom of my jacket. I think you could have heard my breathing across the river in Jersey. The hand slipped up under the bottom of my jacket. "And vairy beeg, I tink. And I tink dat is vairy, vairy nice ting to be."

"I tink we ought to lock your dressing-room door," was the last thing I said.

The one thing I can say for certain about that screen siren is her accent wasn't a phony. She never dropped it once under any circumstance, and we had plenty of circumstances during the remainder of our time together.

I was still young enough to be impressed by the woman I had been to bed with. Somehow, to my kid's mind, the fact that she was a world-famous sex symbol every man was supposed to want, and she wanted me, made me think of myself as one hell of a guy. Special! Later on, I found out that she was always on the prowl for young men who were well-endowed, and to her I was just the lay of the week.

There's really no polite way of getting this story into the book, but the punch line is just too good to leave out. About fifteen years ago, I was in the locker room at the Luxor Baths in New York with two other guys. One guy was a friend, the other was his friend. The one who was a stranger to me said, "Hey, Berle, I hear you got a big one."

It caught me by surprise. "Whaaaa? Go 'way."

But he didn't. "You heard me. Well, I'm willing to bet cash money that mine is bigger than yours."

"Will you knock it off? You drunk or something?"

But he wouldn't stop. "I hear you're a gambler, so I'm making you a bet. A hundred bucks says mine is bigger than yours."

"I don't want to bet," I told him. "Let's drop the subject."

"I'm serious. A hundred bucks mine is bigger than yours."

I was starting to get annoyed, when my friend said, "Go ahead, Milton, just take out enough to win."

The last two appearances in New York did it for me. My personal notices were great, a long way from the first time at the Palace with Elizabeth Kennedy, when *Variety* said, "The boy borders on the precocious."

Suddenly everybody knew me, and I saw the years ahead as one big ball with laughs all the way. I don't know where the hell I got that idea from. I think the top is tougher than the climb to it. Maybe it's great for the kid who's sitting on a drugstore stool one day and is a sensation the next. But that wasn't me.

I was only twenty-four, and I had been working for nineteen years. I had a young face and body, but there was a tired man inside. Never sure if anybody loved me, suddenly I was surrounded with everybody loving me. It was great and it was terrible. At least when you're climbing up, you know where you want to get, you know what you're gouging and kicking and punching for. There seems to be a goal and a purpose to things. But suddenly you're there, and it's more frightening than anything you knew before. Everybody seems to like you, yet you know they're all waiting and watching for you to fall on your face. You find yourself working twice as hard, fighting twice as hard—and just to stay in the same place.

ᘰ 13 ᘰ

I'll never forget Mama's face when I gave her the mink stole right after I signed to appear in the *Earl Carroll Vanities* at $1,500 a week. I handed her the box one night after dinner when just Mama and Pa and I were home.

"Oh my God," was all she said when the last piece of tissue paper was folded back. It was like a sigh from inside her soul, and then she burst into tears.

There were tears in my eyes, too. I pulled her to me. Always with the gags in tender moments—somehow those are rougher on me than anything else—I said, "This makes us even now, Mama, for the fur muff I cut up for my Charlie Chaplin costume."

She rubbed at her eyes. "Go 'way. Milton, every time I see you on the stage you pay me back."

It was that easy to please Mama. Maybe she wanted too much from me, but she wanted what I had to give. Pa was tougher. The big event in Pa's life was to come downtown every day and stand on "the beach" in front of the Palace Theatre. There he would run into other fathers in the business—Jack Benny's, Jack Pearl's—and they would compare clippings, talk about times gone by. I suppose it was nothing, but it was something for Pa. He was in his late fifties, but he looked much older. Years of chasing dreams that he never caught up with had worn him out. Mama, of course, was blooming. She had caught her dream early, and she had never let go. The things Pa still dreamed about no one could give him.

He was getting too old now for that diner he had always wanted. I couldn't finish his inventions for him, and I couldn't roll back the years to give him another shot at the brass ring.

Mama knew I was going to talk to him that night, so she got very busy in the kitchen. I put my arm around his shoulder and steered him toward the parlor. "Pa, I want to talk to you."

"Sure," he said.

As soon as he sat down in his chair, he reached for his cigarettes. "Pa, you smoke too much. You know what the doctor told you."

Pa brushed it aside. "He said I could have a smoke after dinner. It's after dinner, isn't it?"

"I guess so."

He took a puff and looked at me. "So go ahead and talk."

I took a deep breath and plunged in. "Pa, did you ever think about retiring from business?"

It was a crazy question, considering Pa's career. But Pa didn't see the irony in it. "I don't know, I've thought about it. But, Milton, the truth. How can I? To retire is to retire *from*, and what have I got to retire from? What have I got to retire with?"

It broke my heart. Pa had never spoken like this in all his life to anyone. Sometimes I wondered if he knew the truth about himself. And now that I knew he did, I wished he didn't.

"Look, Pa—"

"Of course, I've still got some good years ahead of me, and a lot can happen yet. I was downtown just yesterday and I was talking with a man who—"

"Pa, I'm starting to do very well, and I think you should retire. You've worked long enough. It's time to enjoy now."

He shook his head. "Don't think I don't appreciate what you are saying, Milton, I do. Honest. But how could I face people when they ask what I do? What could I say to them?"

"Why say anything? Just point to my name up there, and say you helped put it there, and now that's what I want for you. What's wrong with that?"

Pa puffed on his second cigarette. "Well, I'll think about it."

With a loophole for his pride, Pa went into retirement.

* * *

I signed for the tenth edition of the *Earl Carroll Vanities*. I was set to co-star with Will Fyffe and Helen Broderick. The company also included André Randall, Edwin Styles, Lillian Shade, Harriet Hoctor, and lovely Beryl Wallace, who died in 1947 in a plane crash with Carroll. The show had songs by Harold Arlen, among others, and sets designed by a nineteen-year-old kid named Vincente Minnelli who was making his Broadway debut.

And, of course, there were the Earl Carroll girls, all hand-picked by the master himself, and picking wasn't that easy back then, with Ziegfeld and George White working the same long-stemmed garden. But Earl Carroll found them, girls like Anya Taranda, who married Harold Arlen; Gay Orlova, who was a close friend of Lucky Luciano's; and Evelyn Crowell, who was to become a close friend of mine.

His audiences at a *Vanities* had come to expect spectacular girl displays from Carroll, and even though the Depression had made money as tight as a pair of two-dollar shoes, Carroll had them. There was a number in which the girls paraded on a darkened stage carrying glass tubes that lighted in assorted colors and designs when passed through an electromagnetic field. In other numbers the girls were in a garden of gardenias, a railroad locomotive, around a maypole that lighted up. It seemed like I was set for one hell of a hit as we sweated through rehearsals in the New York heat of August and September, 1932.

Watching Earl Carroll work in rehearsal and after the show was running, I learned a way of working that has stuck with me to this day. I can't say that when I have directed I have worked as quietly or have been as much of a gentleman as Mr. Carroll, but I sure learned a lot about perfection from him. Carroll watched and took notes on every detail connected with the productions that carried his name.

My first beef with him came when he announced that on the opening number the stars would come out in evening clothes, which meant top hat, white tie, and tails for the men. I had always worked in a business suit and a hat with the brim turned up in front. I protested. "That's funny? What's funny about white tie and tails? I'll tell you," I said. "Nothing!"

Mr. Carroll wasn't even ruffled by me. "This is not a nightclub, nor is it vaudeville, Mr. Berle. This is Broadway, and it draws a more sophisticated audience. They do not need funny clothes to know you are a comedian. They already know who you are, which is one reason for your billing out front. They expect a certain amount of class from a *Vanities*, and I expect to give it them. Considering the price they pay for their tickets—and in times like these—I think they are entitled to a cast that exudes a similar amount of class. You will wear tails, Mr. Berle."

I liked Earl Carroll a lot. And I respected him, too. He never let down his standards on his shows so long as there was one more performance to go. Either he'd be there in person or he'd have a stage manager watching throughout. And there'd be the note sessions afterwards, with Carroll sitting out front, speaking quietly. "Miss Orlova? Where are you, please? What color make-up did you have on tonight? Too dark." He turned to me. "Mr. Berle, were you wearing garters tonight?"

"What does that mean, Mr. Carroll?"

"One of your socks was falling. It spoiled the look of the scene. Is the electrician there?"

"Here, sir."

"The cue on number forty-three. You dimmed down too swiftly. And may I once again remind all of the ladies of the ensemble that if I see one bit of sunburn or tan on your skin, you are automatically out of the show."

Carroll believed the sign he had put up over the stage-door entrance: "Through These Portals Pass the Most Beautiful Girls in the World." His girls had to be pale pink without a mark or blemish, like some perfect ripe peach that no one had ever picked.

But this *Vanities* was not a hit. It opened on September 27, 1932, at the Broadway Theater, and ran for only eighty-seven performances. It was followed by a cut version that Carroll sent out on the road, so I got several months of work out of it. On the opening, the critics raved about the girls and said some kind things about me that didn't hurt. What surprises me today is that most of the notices never mentioned the one song from the show that became a standard: Harold Arlen's great "I Gotta Right to Sing the Blues," which Lillian Shade introduced and I reprised in the second act.

In November, there were some cast replacements. One call was for an English straight man. Since I would have to work with the guy who got the part, I showed up to read opposite the candidates. The guy who got the part was tall and slim with dark curly hair. He said his name was Brice Hutchins, which was such an English-sounding name that it sounded phony to me. In fact, the guy was so British I decided he was phony. But he gave a good reading and he got the part. Naturally, I didn't say anything to him about my suspicions until after he was signed. But then I cornered him backstage. "Listen, Brice Hutchins, or whatever the hell your name is—"

"What is that supposed to mean, Mr. Berle?" he asked in a veddy English accent.

"It means I'm on to you. You son of a bitch, you're no more English than I am."

He smiled slightly. "I don't know what you're talking about. Mr. Carroll was looking for an Englishman, and since I got the part it stands to reason—"

"That you must be English. Bullshit! If Carroll was looking for a Chinaman, you'd probably be Brice Wong. Level with me, pal, I just gotta know. I didn't queer your act when you were auditioning, and I won't queer it now. I just want to know."

He stuck out his hand. "Shake hands with Robert Cummings."

Working the *Vanities* was like a feast for a bachelor. Backstage was crawling with beautiful women, only you had to be careful because an awful lot of their stage-door johns packed rods. Before you made a play —and both Bob Cummings and I were heavily on the make in those days —it could save you a lot of grief to find out if the girl was anybody's special property. It was an ordinary occurrence to have guys like Lucky Luciano and Frankie Carbo showing up backstage.

The girl that attracted me the most was named Evelyn Crowell, a twenty-year-old blond who looked like melted honey when she walked. I tried to get near her several times, but no dice. And finally I found out why. She was secretly married to Larry Fay, who owned the El Fay fleet of cabs—yellow with a swastika, before that symbol took on a more frightening meaning. Larry Fay was one of the top men in the Syndicate. When I found that out, I decided to look but not touch, since I planned on being an old comedian some day.

And then in 1933, while the tab version of the *Vanities* was playing at the Brooklyn Paramount, everything changed. Larry Fay was in his office at the Casablanca, his nightclub on 56th Street, when Eddie Maloney, the doorman, came in and demanded $100 owed him in salary. He pulled out a gun, cut loose with the bullets, and killed Fay. Whatever I had felt before for Evelyn changed now. I'd see her on stage smiling and looking radiant, and then she'd come off and her eyes would fill up and she grew silent. I wanted to help her and comfort her, but what can you say to someone mourning a secret?

I started taking her out, trying to console her, and as time passed and she could begin to smile again, I think we fell a little in love with each other.

Mama began what I now realize was her attack, with little one-liners. Like: "You're seeing a lot of Evelyn Crowell, aren't you?" and, "I suppose by now you know she's not a natural blonde?" or, "A girl wants to get out of the chorus, it's very smart of her to date the star."

It annoyed me at first to have Mama pouring the sour grapes on us. I honestly liked—maybe even loved—Evelyn, and I was sure she liked me for myself, too. But Mama kept nagging at it, making me ask myself questions that hadn't even crossed my mind before. I knew Evelyn had no great show-business ambitions, and I was pretty certain that she went out with me only because she liked me. But Mama kept tossing the needles, and it got to me a little, so sometimes I'd find myself wondering if just maybe there wasn't something to it.

And then Mama moved in with the heavy ammunition. "What do you need this for? You're just beginning to get all the things we worked for all these years, so now you want to tie yourself down? Does that make sense to you? You're a young man, and you should enjoy while you can. There's time enough later on for responsibilities."

"Mama, did I say one word about marriage? Did I?"

Mama looked amazed. "Did *I?* I ask you, did you hear me say the word even once?"

"Aw, come on, Mama, what else are you talking about?"

Mama moved in. "I suppose she's talking about getting married, then?"

We were in my dressing room, and I turned away, afraid of losing my temper, but there was Mama in the mirror. "Look, Mama, nobody's talking about marriage."

Mama shook her head with bitter wisdom. "A woman goes with a man, she wants to get married. And if a woman goes with a man—and I know you, Milton—and she isn't thinking about marriage, then she's not a lady."

"Mama, for God's sake, what do you want from me?"

Mama put a finger to her lips. "First, lower your voice. These walls aren't concrete."

I took a deep breath, and spoke more softly. "Tell me what you really want. Do you want me ever to get married? The truth."

Mama brushed it away. "Marriage is your problem. When the right one comes along, you won't ask me, you'll tell me. What I want is what every mother wants. The best for her son."

I threw my make-up towel on the table and started for the door. I'd heard that routine before. "I'm going out, Mama!"

"Give my regards!" She watched me go to the door. As I opened it, she said, "One thing more. Remember, it takes more than one man to make a gangster. And a gangster's widow still has a lot of friends from when she wasn't a widow. It's possible, you know. Think of all that while you are out with the bereaved!"

I must have shaken all of my wardrobe off the hangers, I slammed the door so hard.

I knew what Mama was up to. She didn't want to lose me to anyone. She had spent more of her married life with me than she had with Pa. I was her entrance ticket to all the fun places of the world, the places that Pa had never heard of. I was the man, not Pa, who could open backstage doors, get the ringside tables, the good seats, and she didn't want to lose it all. I couldn't blame her. I'd give her everything I could, but I couldn't give her the rest of my life.

The romance broke up—Evelyn changed her name and married a man who had waited six years for her—but what was most important about it for me was my mother. Her actions were a sign of what was to come during a more important time in my life. I began to worry a little. Would I be strong enough to stand up to Mama when the time came?

There was a tailor in New York, on Sixth Avenue in the low Forties, who through word of mouth had built up a big show-business clientele. Sam's shop became a place you dropped into, even when you didn't want a new suit, because chances were you'd run into friends. When Sam announced he was getting married, a bunch of us decided to throw him a stag dinner at the McAlpin Hotel. For the occasion, Fred Whitehouse and I decided to write something special. We took the hit song by Sam M. Lewis and Victor Young, "Lord, You Made the Night Too Long," and put new words to it, in honor of my pal Sam. Our version, called "Sam, You Made the Pants Too Long," got a lot of laughs when I sang it at the stag. But the next day I forgot about it. It had been written for a special occasion, so that was that. I forgot about it until an actor friend, Paul Small, said he was looking for some parodies. What the hell, I wasn't doing anything with "Sam," so I gave it to him.

The next thing I knew, I had a hit song—only the credit for it was given to Joe E. Lewis. He had gotten it from Paul Small and had used it in his act. Don't get me wrong. Joe E. Lewis wasn't trying to pull anything. He was just doing a piece of material that worked for him, not knowing that I had written it. And thanks to an honest publisher, Shapiro, Bernstein, and its head of the music department, Jonie Taps, the parody is back under the credit of myself and Fred Whitehouse.

A tailor figured about the same time in another important moment in my life.

One day in 1932, I bought a suit at a place called Ben Rocke, on 50th Street and Seventh Avenue. I paid a lot for it, and I thought I had something special.

About two days after I got the suit, I wore it over to Dave's Blue Room in the Broadway area. Dave Kleckner's place was the big hangout for people in this business, and also the Syndicate boys and the detective squad, before we all switched over to Lindy's. Anyway, I walked in and looked around to see who was there I could chew the rag with, and right off I spotted Richy Craig, Jr., sitting with some mutual friends. I had always liked Richy. He was a very bright clever young comic who worked sort of like Dick Cavett does today.

He spotted me and stood up to wave me over, and then we both did a take. We were wearing the same suit. I said, "Where did you get yours?"

Richy said, "Ben Rocke."

I said, "That bastard said this was an original and there's not another one like it."

And Richy said, "You're wearing my material, Berle. Next thing I know, you'll be doing it."

That gave me an idea. I dragged Richy away from the mob to a quiet back table. "What do you think about this feud between Walter Winchell and Ben Bernie?" This was back before the Jack Benny–Fred Allen feud.

Richy looked at me like I was a nut. "What are you talking about? It's a phony."

"Schmuck, I know that, but look at the publicity they're getting."

Richy still didn't see where I was driving. "So what? That's what the feud's for. It makes good copy."

"Exactly. So what are you and I, shy? Let's get some of it for ourselves. Why don't you send that crack of yours about our suits to a columnist. And I'll send Winchell a wire and say that you're doing my best joke at the Palace."

Richy liked it, and we went to work, taking swipes at each other from stages, nightclub floors, over radio mikes. And the columnists ate it up as good copy. By 1933, the feud was rolling so good that Richy and I were talking about doing an act together.

Richy was a very funny guy with a wild sense of humor. I don't know if the gag that was played on me in 1934 was Richy's or Bob Hope's, but it was a good one. Bob was on Broadway making a big name for himself in *Roberta* at the time. Richy and I were working all over town, but not together. In those days, aside from vaudeville or nightclub appearances, I did an average of five benefits a week, very often three or four of them in the same night.

Now, Richy Craig and Bob Hope were buddies. They even wrote a parody together of "Let's Put Out the Lights and Go to Sleep" that began:

> He steals everybody's act,
> Comics say that that's a fact.
> What's to do about it?
> Let's put out the lights and murder Berle.

Well, one night I had agreed to appear at four benefits. I got to the first one, which was at a place called the Level Club, and went into the routine I had for benefits. I didn't get one laugh. I bombed all the way. I was shaking my head, sort of stunned as I came off the stage. What the hell had gone wrong?

I grabbed a taxi across town to the Waldorf for the second benefit, and I bombed out completely again. I thought I was going out of my mind. Luckily, there was a friend of mine backstage, and he set me wise. "Hope and Craig were here ahead of you, and they did all your jokes, and then they said to the audience, 'Don't tell Berle we were here. Let him bomb!' "

Well, I could play that game too. I don't know where the hell they got the word on which benefits I would be playing and in what order, but I switched the third and fourth, figuring they were just finishing doing my act at the third place. I raced uptown to a club called the Nordacs, which was running a benefit for retarded children. I did my whole act, plus Hope's and Craig's, and this time I went over. Then it was my turn to tell the audience, "When Hope and Craig show up, don't tell them I was here."

I stayed out of sight when they arrived and watched them die on stage. At the end I came out, "I finally caught you, you sons of bitches!"

The audience got an extra as the three of us started tossing the ad libs around. And out of the audience came Jack Osterman—the guy who wrote the act for me that was three jokes and a lot of shit strung together —and there was four of us working for free.

Jack Osterman took one look at Richy, whose skin looked like old candle wax, and ad libbed a line that you've heard comics take down hecklers with for years: "What did you do before you died?"

We all broke up on that one, only it didn't turn out to be very funny.

Richy was keeping it quiet, but he had tuberculosis, and it was bad. A few months after the benefit, Richy was playing the Palace, and I dropped back to his dressing room as he was getting ready to go on. He looked like hell, with deep hollows in his cheeks which he was trying to hide with heavy make-up. We were talking one minute, and the next Richy was doubled up and falling off the chair. He couldn't go on. I took his place for the show without telling the audience what had happened, and an ambulance rushed Richy to the hospital. He died that night.

Richy should have made it big, and he would have if he had been given a little more time. As things stood, Bob Hope and I ran a benefit in his memory.

Walter Winchell labeled me "The Thief of Bad Gags." The image of joke-stealer is fine by me. Most of the time. I've capitalized on it ("God, I wish I'd said that, and don't worry, I will"; "I laughed so hard I nearly dropped my pencil and paper") the same way that Jack Benny has built on his being cheap. It's when somebody in the business takes it seriously —and they should know better—that it hurts.

I don't really know when the idea of myself as a joke-stealer really began. I suppose it was there subconsciously way back when I worked the act "Guilty!" with one of my brothers. The act was based on the idea of me being guilty of stealing material. And sure, while I was pushing and punching on the way up, I floundered about looking for what would work for me. Like every other comedian, if I heard a joke that I thought would work, I used it. Kate Smith summed up my style at the time when she passed me on the street and gave me her famous line, "Hello, everybody!"

When I started to hit it big, the hate started pouring out of the other comedians. They didn't seem to mind me on the way up, but when I started to arrive, they suddenly didn't like me. I got hate letters from Ed Wynn, Eddie Cantor, Lou Holtz, Al Jolson, and many other biggies, accusing me of stealing from them.

Receiving a letter from Jolson about stealing a joke was a joke in itself. Jolson's trick when he was in a show like *Honeymoon Express, Sinbad,* or *Bombo* was to go to a top vaudeville house for a matinee, hear the comic's best joke, and put it in his own show that night. Then he would have his attorney write a letter to the vaudeville comic and tell him that he was doing a joke that was written especially for Jolson's current legitimate show, and that the comic would be sued if he didn't take the joke out of his act.

It's crazy the way you find out that you've made it. I found out that I was bigtime in a terrible way. It was in a headline on the *New York World Telegram* of Wednesday, December 14, 1932:

BANDITS KILL COP, SHOOT 2, KIDNAP MOTHER, SISTER OF MILTON BERLE

On that day, my mother and sister were thankful to be alive. They had gone through something right out of a Bogart movie and somehow lived, but to the headline writers at the papers they didn't even have names. They rated space because they were related to me.

This is what happened. On the night of December 13, 1932, Mama and Rosalind had gone down to the Empire Theatre to see the play, *Firebird.* I had a date that night with Ann Teleman, who was appearing with Paul Muni in *Counsellor-at-Law,* so I arranged with them to meet us afterward at Dave's Blue Room for a bite to eat.

They left the restaurant long before we did, so I didn't find out the hell they went through until much later. They left Dave's Blue Room and caught a taxi to take them home to Walton Avenue in the Bronx (another new address). Meanwhile, two young punks had robbed a store uptown on Amsterdam Avenue and killed the policeman who tried to stop them. Two other cops also got shot (but lived) in the running gun battle that followed. While this was going on, Mama's and Roz's cab was moving uptown along Central Park West. Their cab was stopped by a traffic light at 91st Street and Central Park West. And that's where they met up with one of the punks, who had already been shot in the stomach . . . but I've got to let Roz tell it, the way she told it to James Meade of the *World Telegram:*

A bullet thumped into the back of the car, just over our heads. I saw a hole suddenly appear in the windshield. It all happened at one and the same time. Then the boy walked up and yanked the driver out of his seat by a leg, and climbed in and took the wheel.

Mother was hysterical and began screaming, "He's taking us for a ride! He's taking us for a ride!" She kept screaming it over and over and clung to me. The boy started up the car and it leaped away and he turned around with his revolver in his hand. He pointed it at us and said, "Shut your mouth or I'll shut it for you." That was all.

But if ever I was scared in my life that was it. I thought, "He means it, he means it." I dragged mother off the seat. Somehow I managed to struggle out of my mink coat. I threw it over her. I wanted to muffle her screams.

Then we turned west toward Amsterdam Avenue. It was awful. The boy at the wheel—what a cold little demon! I thought, "He's a devil. He's full of cocaine. His heart is glass and he'll kill us if he happens to think of it."

And those bullets! There seemed to be a million streaming through the car, thudding the car, thudding through the back window, through the body, through the back seat. The squad car behind us couldn't have known there were two defenseless women huddled on the floor of the cab.

It didn't faze that cold little devil at the wheel, either. When he'd look back and fire, I could glimpse his face. It was fixed, staring, unchanging. And cold! Not cool, just cold!

I thought, "He mustn't think of us or he'll shoot." And I pressed the coat tighter over mother. I even put my hand over her mouth. Poor mother. If it hadn't been for having her need me, I don't know what I'd have done. I guess I'd have gone to pieces.

Anyway, the taxi was stopped at 110th Street and Central Park West, and the punk ran down the subway stairs. A cop shot him in the leg and captured him. By some miracle, neither Mama nor Roz was hurt. Looking back, the only thing funny about the nightmare ride was the news pictures taken afterward. One showed Roz staring at a policeman's bloody finger —fat lot of good that did him. Another one clearly shows that Roz didn't have a mink coat to throw over Mama, but a cloth coat with some other kind of fur collar.

They were taken to the West 68th Street police station for their statement and first aid, and then home, where I found them. I burst in the door expecting God knows what—anything but what I did find, which was Mama in bed posing for the photographer from the *Daily Mirror*. Roz had changed into something frilly and innocent and was seated by the bed, holding Mama's limp hand. Mama was flat on her back with the look of a Jewish St. Joan on her face and a wide white bandage across her forehead—the kind they used to put on the star's head in Hollywood movies for everything from warts to prostate trouble.

For a moment I believed that bandage (there wasn't anything under it but Mama's unhurt head), and I moved to throw out the photographer. Mama stopped me with a look and then slipped back into her sainthood pose for the camera. I shut up. I knew Mama. If she had to go through what she did, at least she liked the publicity that followed. For once she had her own spotlight.

Once I knew my family was safe, I can't say that I minded the publicity either. It's always important to an entertainer. It keeps your name in front of the public, it helps get jobs, it makes the price go up. And I needed the money then, more than ever, and not just to help my family to live better.

Ask any bookmaker about that. Horseplayers die broke. After my first year's winning streak, the inevitable had started happening. I was as hooked on the ponies as any junkie with his brand of drugs. And, like the junkie's habit, mine was beginning to cost more and more. I began with a buck here, a buck there, placed through stagehands. Then it was five- and ten-dollar bills at the local horse parlors of whatever town I was in. When my name and face became known through my work, I suddenly found I could start calling in bets on credit to New Jersey, or placing them through people who were "in" in the rackets and hung around the clubs I was working.

My bets mounted. In the morning, I couldn't wait to get to the scratch sheets and the phones, and to get to the bookmakers' joints. If I was playing one of the big movie houses and the first show was 11:30

or noon, I'd be over at some bookie joint before that. I was such a sucker, I'd be pleased that they brought me breakfast free while I ran my finger down the columns in the papers, picking my bets. And I was backing up my win bets with show bets in the same race. I believed I had a better chance to win, without thinking I also had more of a chance to lose. It wasn't long before I was betting not to win more money, but to cut down my losses.

Through the bookmakers I met the shylocks, and when my debts got too high and the threats started coming, I turned to them for quick money, which put me in even worse trouble than I was in before. The interest was incredible, and the longer you owed it, the more it compounded. There were times when I was paying 35 and 40 per cent and more on shylock money. And I still didn't learn.

I remember one week having $77,000 in cash delivered to me. I felt like a king, out of hock and ten feet tall. I swore that I was through with it all.

I think the decision lasted at least one full day. By the end of the following week I had given back $40,000 of my winnings.

In 1933, I got booked into Chicago, maybe the last city in the country a wise kid who thought he knew all the answers should have been in.

1930-1940

Milton in 1930. Portrait by Baron Missakian.

Mama and Milton in Chicago in 1936. Portrait by Maurice Seymour.

Milton in 1932 at his CBS microphone on the Fred Waring Radio Show.

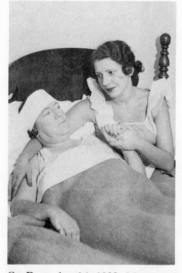

On December 14, 1932, Mama and Rosalind posed for a publicity shot after being "taken for a ride" by a New York thug. (UPI)

With Baby Rose Marie at the Steel Pier, Atlantic City, 1935/36.

Mama and Milton, Hollywood bound in 1937.

Relaxing on the set of New Faces of 1937.

With the Andrews Sisters (L) and Ann Miller (R).

Joan Davis and Buster Keaton (L) and Mama with Milton (R).
The party at the Beverly Hills Hotel in 1937 where Milton met "Linda Smith."

From left: Linda Darnell, Robert Stack, Lynn Bari, and Milton.

With Sophie Tucker in 1938.

Milton dressed as Greta Garbo, getting off the train in New York in 1938.

Mama's portrait by Bruno of Hollywood.

⚔ 14 ⚔

Nineteen thirty-three was a lousy year for everybody but me and Sally Rand—and maybe the former governor of New York, Franklin Delano Roosevelt, who became the president of the country at the beginning of the year. Prohibition was still keeping the country dry—on the surface; underneath it was very damp—and the Depression was getting more depressing every day.

The big bright spot of the year was the Century of Progress Exposition. It was opened in Chicago on May 27, 1933, when a beam of light from the star Arcturus somehow flipped the switches that turned on the lights of the new World's Fair. It was a fantastic success, with more than twenty million paid admissions—you could hardly tell that everybody was starving to death. The fair had everything from all the newest wonders of science to a whole Mayan temple reconstructed, a midget village, and rickshaw boys all over the fairgrounds pulling limping mamas and papas around. There were fortunes spent on pavilions and exhibits, but the biggest hit of all was a little blond, barely five feet tall, whose costume cost her next to nothing, because that's about what she wore over her open work sandals. Sally Rand, with her two huge fans that always seemed about to part and show all but never quite did, was a sensation. She had them on line across the fair grounds for a peek through the plumes, and when they got used to that she switched to a huge balloon and was a sensation all over again.

If she was the hit of the Chicago Fair, I turned out to be the hit of

Chicago. I was set to open on July 21, 1933, at the Palace on Randolph near La Salle. The Palace was the top presentation house in town, and I was headlining at the height of the tourist business for the fair. I hadn't played Chicago since the kid days of Kennedy & Berle, but word had come west from New York that I was supposed to be hot stuff, so I knew all the local critics would be out front waiting to be shown. And Chicago wasn't Scranton or Syracuse. It was second only to New York. Chicago audiences had seen the best, so there was no palming anything less off on them.

I arrived four days early to get set up. Except for Roz, who would be doing some bits with me, and Mama, I didn't know a soul in town. But before I left New York, I had called Tony Canzoneri, the prizefighter, of whom I was a big fan, and he had given me some addresses and some names to call—guys who knew their way around town.

The first thing I did after getting Mama and Roz to our hotel was take a look at where I'd be working. Scheduled to appear with me at the Palace were Irene Bordoni, the French songstress; Chilton & Thomas, dancers; Owen McGiveney, a quick-change artist; and "12—Virginia O'Brien Girls—12," who would back me up in the show they were calling *World's Fair Frolics*. I told the Palace my idea for a small runway out over the orchestra pit so I could work closer to the audience, and they agreed to put it in for Friday.

My next stop was the address on Randolph that Tony Canzoneri had given me. It was just another office building, and the room I went to looked like any other second-rate business reception room. But when I gave the girl at the desk the names Charlie Baron and Dave Halpern, which Tony had given me, I found out what the score was. She pressed a button that let me through the door behind her. It was a horse parlor with sheets up on the walls, phones going, and guys making bets. The air was blue with smoke. Now I felt at home in Chicago.

Charlie and Dave were the top men there. They told me that Tony had called to say I would be coming around. "That's good enough for me," Charlie said. "Dave and I will do everything we can for you. You name it."

Looking around at some of the guys in the big hats and the suits with the heavy shoulders made me wonder what Charlie's offer meant. It could have meant broads, or a good table at a club, or it could have meant a little muscle if I needed it, because Chicago was that kind of town back then. If you've seen any of the old Cagney–Warner Brothers pictures about the way it was during Prohibition in Chicago, you know what I mean. But at the time I didn't need any special favors.

Hooked as I was on the ponies, I started dropping by every day. The day before I was to open, I said to Charlie Baron, "I like to work out. You know, punch the bag, skip some rope, keep in trim. You know a place?"

Charlie said, "Sure. Trafton's Gym. Right upstairs in this building. Wait a minute, I'll take you up and introduce you to Jim Mullen, who runs the place."

It was at Trafton's that I met Max Baer and Joe Louis. Trafton's was Chicago's version of Stillman's and Grupp's in New York, only it had that special look that was Chicago during Prohibition. The guys with the suits and the cigars in their faces and the white-on-white ties were all over the place, silently watching the boys they owned a piece of working out.

Jim Mullen tossed me a pair of trunks and the headgear and the shoes and I went to work. I worked out a little with the bag and the rope. It felt good to get the sweat up. I could feel the tension of the coming show work out of my shoulders and neck as I jabbed away at the big sandbag.

A guy in a wide-brimmed hat drifted over in my direction. He had his hands folded behind his back, and he was watching me. I've always reacted to an audience, even an audience of one. I pretended not to notice him, but I started jabbing around, flashing my fancy footwork. I caught him out of the corner of my eye. No reaction.

When Jim Mullen put me in the ring with another guy, the same man was at the ropes, watching. I got in a couple of easy shots to the other guy's ribs.

Suddenly the stranger said, "What do you do for a living?"

Considering he saw me in the ring, I took his question as an insult. "Is that supposed to be funny, buddy?"

The man didn't notice my tone. "No, I just asked you."

"I'm a comedian."

He nodded, matter-of-factly. "Well, you sure as hell aren't a fighter. You shouldn't ever get in the ring with a real pro or you'll get your friggin' brains knocked out."

Who the hell did he think he was? "Listen, pal, I'm just working out . . ."

He nodded his head. "You could work yourself out to the graveyard the way you go about it."

I was beginning to get angry. "Look, pal, if you want to review my work, come down to the Palace tomorrow."

I turned back to the guy in the ring with me. I was steaming mad, which got me one on the jaw. If you're going to fight in a ring, you use your head and your muscles. If you bring your emotions in, it throws you, and you can get killed.

Later, when I was in the dressing room on the rubbing table, I looked up, and there was the same guy again. "Hey, kid," he said, "I wasn't trying to be fresh with you, I was just trying to help you."

"Sure," I said, still feeling a little sour.

"No, I mean it. I train fighters. I'm a trainer like Izzy Klein and Arty Wench, all those guys. I'm Lou Jackson."

Any anger I had felt vanished. In fact, I felt like the smart-ass punk I had been acting like. If you followed the fights in those days, you knew Lou's name. It kept turning up in the boxing news. He had been chief second for Sam Langford and other big-money fighters, as well as a trainer of up-and-coming kids. Lou was also mixed up in other things around Chicago, but you didn't ask questions about that.

I stuck out my hand. "Gee, I didn't know."

"Forget it. Get your clothes on, kid. I'll buy you a cup of coffee."

He took me over to a coffee shop by the Bismarck Hotel. When we were perched on the counter stools, he said, "You say you're opening at the Palace tomorrow? What's your name?"

I told him.

"Berlee, huh?" he said to himself, trying it out and adding on another syllable.

"Berle," I said. "Milton Berle."

It hit him. "Oh sure, I think I heard you once on the radio with Rudy Vallee. You're a funny guy. Listen, Berlee, you got nothing to worry about tomorrow. You're gonna be a great hit. It's a cinch."

"I'm glad you're so sure."

"I tell you, you're in. It's a cinch."

I said thank you. What the hell can you say to something like that? And I figured, what does Lou Jackson know about show business? Maybe in the fight racket, with a little finagling, you can guarantee a winner, but how do you fix an audience?

But Lou was off on another topic. "Only you shouldn't fight, Berlee. For two reasons. One, you don't know what the hell you're doing. And two, you're an actor, and you'll get your face all cut up. You see some of those mugs over at the gym? You want a face like that?"

"What do you mean, I don't know what I'm doing?"

Lou put an arm on my shoulder. "What's with all that footwork, Berlee? Huh? You go into that dance of yours, and before you even get your mitts up you'll be flat on your ass. Forget the dancing. You need your right up and ready, and you got to have leverage. Look, you come around to Trafton's when you got the chance between shows and I'll teach you a few things, maybe you'll come out of an alley alive some day."

By the time we finished coffee I liked Lou Jackson. I thought of him as a guy I'd like to see more of whenever I came through Chicago. I didn't know that I was going to see a lot more of him this trip, and that I'd be damn glad to have him for a friend.

Lou was a man with friends and connections all over Chicago, not only in the fight game. Exactly what the "not only" was all about, I never asked and Lou never told me, but whatever else he was into, he must have been important enough, because of what nearly happened to him. I didn't hear the story from Lou—he could be pretty closemouthed—and I never got all the names, but when I asked Lou about it, he told me it was true. In the late 1920s, Al Capone was the racket king of Chicago, with all of the city's ten thousand speakeasies under his control. If anyone tried to muscle in, Capone sent his men out to get rid of the competition. Early in 1929, the thorn in Capone's side was the Dion O'Banion gang, under the leadership of Bugs Moran since O'Banion's death. They had a piece of the beer racket and a flower business that made a fortune on wreaths and other displays at gangland funerals. But their big crime in Capone's eyes was that they were still going around taking revenge for O'Banion's death.

Well, on the night of February 13, 1929, Lou Jackson was shacked up with his woman at the Sherman Hotel. Sometime during the evening, he got a call from a supposed friend asking him to meet the friend at a certain garage the next morning. Lou didn't think much about it, except that the time was too early, considering the night he had ahead of him.

"Come on, Lou," the guy said at the other end of the phone, "you know who'll be there, and they want to see you."

And Lou said, "It can wait, can't it? It's too early."

The other man said, "I'll tell you what. I'll come by in the morning and pick you up. I'll call you from the lobby."

The call came while Lou and his girl were still asleep. He was starting to get up when the girl said, "Aw, what do you want to go for? Stay here with me, Lou. Please."

So Lou told the guy to go ahead if he wanted. "I'll see you later."

Only there was no later. On Valentine's Day, 1929, Machine Gun

Jack McGurn, who worked for Capone, sent a group of his men dressed in police uniforms to the garage, where seven of the O'Banion men were waiting for a delivery of stolen liquor. A few minutes later, the McGurn men made their getaway in a Cadillac and there were seven dead men and a dog on the floor of the garage. Lou must have been doing something important enough to get him an invite for the number eight spot at the St. Valentine's Day massacre.

On the day that I opened at the Palace, I found out why Lou Jackson told me I was a cinch to be a hit. It's typical of Lou that I didn't find out from him, but I discovered later he bought about two hundred tickets out of his own pocket—so what if they only cost fifteen or twenty cents apiece?—and papered the house with all of his buddies from the west side of Chicago. Of course, that couldn't make the critics laugh if they didn't find me funny, but it was a hell of a nice try on Lou's part. (The picture the week I opened was *Double Harness*, with Ann Harding and William Powell. How's that one, trivia fans?)

Waiting for the final celluloid clinch, I did what I always do backstage before a show. I sweated, feeling my clothes grow damp and begin to stick to my body.

I didn't relax until the first laughs started coming at me. I started breathing again after the reviews came in. The dean of Chicago critics headlined his column, "Ashton Stevens Becomes Justly Sore with Indignation and Laughter," and went on to say: "The most amazing thing about Mr. Berle is his energy. He is as energetic as ten Cantors and Jessels. He is almost as energetic as one Eva Tanguay in her prime. And his ego seems even bigger and better than Miss Tanguay's; and it is a versatile ego that can laugh even at itself."

Stevens's indignation came over my horsing around with the great Irene Bordoni, who knew and approved in advance that I was going to do bits with her. Stevens wrote: "But the summit of Mr. Berle's freshness is achieved in his scene with Miss Bordoni. He mercifully goes away while she sings a trio of songs as only Irene Bordoni can sing them. But he jokes her upon her return. Indeed, he jokes her upon her repertoire. He jokes her verbally, anatomically and symbolically. This hurt me—for I am a Bordoni man—even more than it appeared to hurt her. It hurt me especially in the ribs. I was sore with indignation and laughter."

There were a few squawks here and there about some of my material being a bit strong, and a little outrage that I would dare to horse around with a star like Irene Bordoni, but all the rest were raves. The next morning when I arrived at the Palace for the first show there was a line around the corner. The line continued all day. The following morning the bosses told me that they wanted to hold me over for a second week—the first time in years that the Palace had ever done that for anyone.

Chicago was suddenly my town. To quote the *Chicago Daily News*, "To say that Berle is a Chicago sensation is putting it mildly." I was just twenty-five, and I was still young enough to go a little crazy with the fuss being made. It was as if I could do no wrong. The audiences loved me. I ran wild on the stage, and almost everything got a big laugh. I was doing four and five shows a day to packed houses, starting at ten in the morning, and I was running around half the night between the Century of Progress and the in-town cafés. In between shows I got extra publicity, by running out front to do the doorman's spiel, or to leap into the glass booth and sell tickets. I even helped the local newsboys peddle their papers. And the crowds grew larger.

One evening, I was on stage doing my act. I was standing out on the runway ripping through my one-liners. I always got a big laugh on the line "My idea of moving fast is to see Hitler running down Maxwell Street," which was in the Jewish section of Chicago. I got the laugh, which Mama built by adding her high-pitched giggle, but just as it was dying down I heard someone say, "Kike!"

Maybe I heard wrong, maybe I didn't. I went on, and a moment later I got "Jew bastard." I spotted the guy, an ox with a bald head and a neck like a wrestler. He was in the first row, which was maybe a foot away from me because of the runway I was on, and his face was red with anger. I looked at him. He looked right back and muttered, "Hitler's right."

I started steaming, but I tried to go on with the show. A minute later, I heard "Kike!" again. Danny Russo, the pit-band leader, also heard it. He signaled me to ignore it, but I couldn't. I took a flying leap from the front ramp over to the aisle and grabbed for the guy, who was in the second seat off the center aisle. I dragged him out into the aisle. "Leave me alone, you dirty Jew!" he screamed, and the theater suddenly went dead quiet. Now, everyone had heard him.

I tried to make it a big joke to keep the audience in line. I started waltzing the guy, as if we were doing a routine together. I was in close to him and I spun him so his back was to most of the audience. "Shall we dance?" I shouted, and there was some laughter. It covered the groan as I kneed him in the groin. As he sagged, I gave him a short chop in his belly. I don't know where that guy got his strength from, but he managed to stay up long enough to get in one good punch at me. It sent me into a blind rage. The last thing I saw was the guy falling into the aisle. I wanted to kill him. I slammed my foot into his face and then I fell on him, punching away. I could hear screaming all around me, and over it my mother's scream, louder than all the rest. Then there were hands all over me, pulling me off him. The next thing I really knew, we were both in the manager's office, with at least three ushers still hanging on to me. The guy's face was a mess, and I could feel my own blood running down my chin. Then the police were there and I was arrested. I missed the last show that night, but I was out in time for the first show the next day. So were the newspapers, with headlines that read: "Berle Flattens Nazi Sympathizer."

I hadn't done it for publicity, but I got plenty, and the lines outside the Palace were longer than ever. I got a lot of mail, most of it good, but there were a couple of letters that made the hair stand up. They called me every rotten thing that was ever said to a Jew, and one letter threatened my life. Lou Jackson was in my dressing room when the letter came. I showed it to him, and he read it in silence. When he finished, all he said was, "Don't worry, Berlee." From that day on, Lou took to hanging around backstage at the theater as my unofficial bodyguard.

I mentioned that my mother used to sit through every show I did, but she'd skip the picture. What she'd do was find somebody hanging around the front of the theater—it could be a kid or a bum, anybody who had nothing much to do—and she'd take him inside and pay him a dollar to hold her seat until the stage show began. This story about her took place in the early 1930s at Loew's Metropolitan in Brooklyn. I was acting as m.c. for the stage show and doing my own routine as well. The show timed out at fifty minutes exactly. And, of course, Mama was out front for every show.

She found her place in my act by working out her own private cue sheet for her laughs. She'd decide which joke of mine to give a little laugh on and which ones to really cut loose on just as the spontaneous audience laughter was starting to die down. Mama, who had great timing of her own, knew how to turn a good laugh of mine into a show stopper.

It was a late-afternoon show, and I remember I was down near the foots, going into the close of the show, when suddenly I heard a commotion in the audience. It came from about the ninth row on the side aisle. I could just make out a man standing and trying to protect his face while a lady was swinging a purse at him. I heard her shout, "You dirty, dirty man! You dirty son of a bitch! How dare you!"

It was my mother! Then I saw her grab the man's arm and twist it behind his back. She started stiff-arming him up the aisle—training left over from her days as a store detective—still swinging her purse at his head with her other arm. She also got in a couple of kicks.

I cut whatever bit I was doing and went into a quick thank you, which I don't think anyone heard, because everybody was watching Mama. I raced off stage and grabbed a towel to mop up my sweat and ran through the exit that led to the front of the theater.

The scene in the lobby was wild. A crowd was peering through the glass doors. A policeman was already there, and two ushers were holding the man. Mama was pacing back and forth like a tiger. Whenever she got near the man, she took another swing at his face, which was already cut and bleeding from the corners of her patent-leather purse.

I grabbed Mama. I had to hug her to my chest to keep her from breaking free and going after the guy again. "Mama, tell me what happened. Mama, calm yourself."

"What happened! What happened!" She was wild-eyed, and her face was dead white.

I shook her. "Mama, it's me, Milton. Tell me what happened."

I held her until her breathing slowed a little. "All right, you can let go now. I was sitting next to that guy, and I felt a hand on my knee. I push his hand away, and it's right back. Then he starts to feel the side of my leg and he tried to put his hands under my dress! No matter what I did, he was there with the hands, right from the beginning of the show all the way through!"

It didn't make sense to me. "Mama, I'm on for fifty minutes. When did this happen?"

"When you first came on—while you were doing your opening monologue."

I asked, "Why did you wait for forty-five minutes?"

Mama said the classic line: "I didn't want to miss a cue!"

For my second week at the Palace, the management came up with another film favorite we all know and remember, *Don't Bet on Love*

starring Lew Ayres and Ginger Rogers ("Fast Women and Slow Horses
—and a pair of daring young sweethearts"). The star on stage opposite
me was Peggy Hopkins Joyce, "The Orchid Lady of Stage and Screen,"
a blond who worked the diamond mines before the Gabors decided to do
their shopping outside of Hungary. Peggy was played up as a glamorous
movie star, but her screen reputation was slight, and nothing to compare
with her off-stage doings. The day after she opened at the Palace, she was
clobbered in the press. Bob Reel, writing in *The Chicago American*, said:
"Miss Joyce is rawther ultra. For some reason she has suddenly become
conscious that she is a moom pitcher star . . . Anyway, she makes a typical
nonsensical stellar personal appearance. She does nothing but come out
and bow and wave her hand—the same lily-white one wot has snatched
so many diamonds from admirers—at her pooblic. . . . Aw, Peggy, be
yourself! Get down off that stepladder. We remember when you once
came here and did a skit. Let Milton clown with you, and you'll make a
much better impression."

I had a new opening for the second week. It was a hodgepodge of
newsreel clips with a new soundtrack. I played all the voices. One minute,
the audience was looking at George Bernard Shaw and hearing him (me)
congratulate Chicago for holding me over, the next there was Hitler
addressing a Nazi rally and raving about me. It got big laughs. And this
was a good couple of years before Olsen and Johnson used the same
newsreel idea for *Hellzapoppin!*, a show I was offered and turned down,
because I didn't think there was any market for that sort of knockabout
slapstick.

In 1933, I did such good business at the Palace that not even the
pasting Peggy Hopkins Joyce took in the press cut the lines outside the
theater. The management asked me to stay on for another two weeks.
Great! If Chicago loved me, I loved it. It was a wild, wide-open town that
offered plenty of everything a twenty-five-year-old kid could want. And,
with the exception of booze, which never interested me, I wanted it all.

I was making good money, but I wasn't hanging on to my share, after
Mama took out the family money. The horse joints and the bookies were
too easy to find, and I was hooked too deep. There was always some
bookmaker I owed, some shylock who had my signature on a loan. I was
always going to quit, but every day there were new races scheduled in the
scratch sheets, and all I ever needed was just one good race, one killing,
to square everything. But that race never seemed to come, or if it did,
there was always a filly running in the next race that was such a cinch

to win, it would be a crime not to have a little something on her nose.

The movie for my third great week at the Palace was *Headline Shooter* ("He Lived and Loved Daringly . . . this devil-may-care newsreel camera-man!"). Will you ever forget that all-star cast: William Gargan, Frances Dee, Ralph Bellamy, Wallace Ford, Jack La Rue, and Gregory Ratoff? On stage with me for my third week were those great comedians Willie and Eugene Howard doing their burlesque quartet from *Rigoletto* which had stopped the show in George White's *Scandals* in New York. The woman on the bill was Eleanor Holm, still famous as an Olympic swimmer, but starting to make it as a singer and movie personality. She was a nice kid then, with a Brooklyn accent she still hadn't got rid of. She was fun to work with on stage, a good gal off. She was seeing a lot of Art Jarrett, the musician, back then.

Eleanor hadn't met Billy Rose yet, and I hadn't met Joyce Mathews. Neither of us had a clue that one day our names would be tied up together again, not just in Chicago, but in every headline in every newspaper across the country. And this time, none of us would be happy with the publicity.

One afternoon, Lou Jackson came into my dressing room. He looked sort of uncomfortable, like a kid caught with his hand in the cookie jar. I waited for him to speak, but he kept shuffling around the room, as if he'd never seen it before. "So what's new, Lou?" I asked.

Lou shrugged. "Nothing much, Milton"—he had finally dropped the Berlee—"I was just wondering what you were doing tonight?"

"I don't know. Maybe do a little cabareting."

Lou shook his head. "I don't mean then. Like around nine, ten o'clock."

"Lou, you crazy or something? You know I do my last show here at ten."

Lou shoved his hands deep in his jacket pockets. "I'll level with you, Milton. I got this very important call from a friend today who said he would really appreciate it if you could drop out to Cicero tonight—you pick the time—and do some of your act for this party he's giving."

"What!" I hit the roof. "I'm doing five shows today here, and some jerk thinks I got time to play a private party? Who the hell does he think he is?"

Lou put a hand on my shoulder. He spoke quietly. "Look, Milton, they're running a big night for the mayor out in Cicero—"

"I don't care if it's for F.D.R.—"

Lou's hand came down heavier on my shoulder. "Milton, I think you should do this thing. The party's at the Cotton Club in Cicero, if you follow me."

That stopped me. The Cotton Club was Al Capone's joint, and from the way Lou was talking, the invitation came straight from the owner. "Well, look, even if I wanted to do the show, I don't get through here until around eleven, and until I get cleaned up and out there . . ."

"Nah, that's too late. They'd really like you a lot earlier. The mayor's a busy man. He can't stay out late at night."

"Lou, it's impossible. The times don't work out."

Lou smiled, more relaxed now. "Sure, they do. Look, tonight when you come off the stage—about a quarter after eight, right?—just come straight out to the alley with your make-up on and everything. There'll be a car waiting for you."

I tried to be patient. "Lou, you don't understand. And your friend in Cicero doesn't either. I've got to be on stage here at ten o'clock—I got a contract with the Palace—and it's at least twenty miles each way right through Chicago to the Cotton Club. It can't be done."

Lou just smiled and slapped me on the back. "No sweat. No sweat at all. You just come straight out after the show."

When I told Mama, she said she was coming along. She got very dramatic about it. "I don't want to argue about it. You can't go out there alone. Who can say what could happen?"

"So what are you going to do? Twist Capone's arm behind his back?"

Mama ignored that. "With a mother along, things don't happen!" she said. Later, she admitted to me that she hadn't thought anything was going to happen. She just wanted to get a look at Al Capone.

I came off stage that night about 8:20, and I headed straight for the stage door, where Mama was waiting for me. We went out into the alley. The car was there, a big heavy job without side windows, and bulletproof glass up front. The two guys lounging against the side didn't say a word. One of them opened the back door for us—Lou was already inside—and the other one climbed up front with the driver. The door slamming behind us didn't sound regulation but like a steel bank-vault door closing.

We had a light on in the back to make up for the lack of windows, but nobody spoke all the way out. I don't know how fast the driver was going, but I know we never stopped for one traffic light.

I don't think I was in the Cotton Club for more than two minutes before I was introduced and on. It was something new for me to get my first look at a club I was working in when I stepped on stage to do my show. I made a nervous start while I tried to case the room. The lights were down, so all I got was the impression of a lot of tables, all of them packed. Where Capone was, where the mayor was seated, who else was there, I couldn't tell. After a couple of minutes of no laughs, I said what the hell to myself. An audience is an audience, even when it's a command performance, so I cut loose with my stuff, and the laughs started coming in, warming me up.

When I finally came off, I was introduced to a heavy-set man with thick lips. "I really want to thank you for making time for us in your busy schedule, Mr. Berle."

He stuck out his hand, and we shook. I felt paper in his hand transfer to mine. That's when I realized the polite, soft-spoken man was Al Capone. I looked at my hand, and there were hundred-dollar bills there, maybe twenty of them.

I stuck them out at Al. "No thanks, Mr. Capone. I don't need this."

"Keep it," he said. "I don't need it either. And you did a great job. The mayor really got a boot out of you."

I shook my head. "No. I was asked to come out here. I wasn't hired. And besides, I might need a favor from you some day."

Capone smiled and stuck the bills back in his pocket. "Just say the word and you got it."

Maybe the only time I was in danger was when I started to leave the club without introducing Mama to Al Capone. I think Mama would have killed me. As we were getting back into the car, I looked at my watch. I turned to Lou, furious. "Jesus, it's twenty to ten. I'll never make the show in time."

"Get in," Lou said, and then whispered a couple of words to the driver before getting in himself.

We couldn't see anything, but what we felt scared the life out of us. The driver was going like a bat out of hell. We were constantly being slammed against each other on every curve, and the tires screamed as if they were going to explode. Once there was an ear-splitting shriek of brakes and we were all thrown forward against the partition. We felt the car swerve and go up on two wheels. We were going to either crash or turn completely over. Then, with a spine-cracking jolt, the car dropped back onto all fours, and we were racing forward again. Mama kept moaning to herself all the way.

Suddenly, there was another slam of brakes, and the side door opened. "Okay, here we are, folks," one of the men said.

I looked out. We were parked right by the alley to the stage door. I checked my watch. It said five of ten. We had done the twenty miles, most of it through heavy city traffic, in fifteen minutes.

My feet were wobbly as I got out of the car. I reached to help Mama out. Her face was dead white, and she had her eyes closed. Her hand felt like ice, but somehow she managed to lift herself from the car. I started to turn toward the alley, when I heard the sound of water hitting the pavement.

I looked at Mama, and now her face was bright red. A puddle was forming by her feet. "I'm sorry, Milton," she said in a very small voice, "I couldn't help it."

The papers carried the announcement that I would play a fourth week at the Palace, and on the same bill would be Ethel Barrymore doing Sir James M. Barrie's one-act play *The Twelve-Pound Look*. The critics started blasting at me days before the great Barrymore was scheduled to open.

Ashton Stevens summed up the entire defense in his column in *The Chicago American:*

> Those old adorers of Ethel Barrymore, the drama critics, will be all over the house when she comes to the Palace with The Twelve-Pound Look, *ready to avenge her should fresh young Milton Berle attempt to cast berles before Barrymore, as he recently did before Bordoni.*
>
> *I am informed that the knightly Lloyd Lewis will occupy a stage box, armed with a couple of pistols manufactured by a family whose scion was the father of Miss Barrymore's gifted children. In shooting circles it is said that Mr. Lewis can wing a master of ceremonies at forty paces.*
>
> *Charles Collins, I am told, will occupy his habitual chair in the second row, carrying as usual, a perfectly balanced knife, at the throwing of which he is second to none in his profession.*
>
> *Gail Borden, I hear, will appear in the first row, bearing an innocent-looking walking stick containing a deadly stiletto. For this is an occasion when Mr. Borden does not believe that the pen is mightier than the sword cane. And your Mr. Stevens, who once pitched four innings for San Luis Obispo against Santa Barbara, will*

most likely take his stance in the balcony with a bomb, the flavor of
which will not be vanilla.

It was great publicity, and what with the promise of another wonderful motion picture (*The Secret of the Blue Room*, starring Lionel Atwill, Paul Lukas, and Gloria Stuart), business was sure to be good. Only all that What-will-Berle-do-to-Barrymore What-will-Barrymore-do-to-Berle stuff in the press didn't help either of us. Miss Barrymore was edgy enough about making her first appearance in a movie house without the added pressure from the theater critics. She caught my show the day before she was to open, and then came straight backstage. She was not in a good mood.

For that matter, neither was I. I was thinking just who the hell did Ethel Barrymore think she was, which wasn't fair to her, because she hadn't said one word to me yet. But the papers had steamed me up. For three weeks they had loved me, and now suddenly they had turned. They treated me like some bum who might offend the great goddess.

At our first meeting, there was ice in the air. She came to my dressing room. At fifty-four, she still looked great and walked like a queen with her head held high, but it set my teeth on edge.

"Mr. Berle?"

"Miss Barrymore." We didn't shake hands.

"I have just attended your performance."

"I hope you liked it."

She ignored that. "What I have come to speak with you about is my engagement beginning tomorrow."

The peak of Ethel Barrymore's beauty was already past, but she was still a damned handsome woman. And that deep voice really riveted you. "Sure," I said, "be glad to do anything I can to help."

That got a very thin smile. "That is exactly what I have come to see you about, Mr. Berle. Having seen your performance, and having read of what you did with Miss Bordoni, I request that you do nothing to help. Merely introduce me and my company, and clear the stage. Sir James Barrie's play is, I think, complete within itself, and needs no outside assistance."

I started steaming. "Just what did you think I was going to do?"

"I was implying nothing, insinuating nothing, Mr. Berle," she said, completely calm. "I saw how you work, and obviously it is correct for you. But I cannot work that way, and I thought it important to point that out to you before tomorrow. That is really all I came to say."

I opened my mouth, but before I could get out a sound, Miss Barrymore said, "Good day, Mr. Berle," and left.

I was jumpy that night, as if the next day were my opening at the Palace instead of the start of my fourth week. I didn't need anything more for my nerves, but I got it.

I had just come off stage after the first show of the evening, when the guy on the desk by the stage door called me over. "Telephone call for you, Mr. Berle."

I picked up the phone and said hello. A voice I'd never heard before said, "Milton Berle?"

"Yeah. Who's this?"

"I got some bad news for you. Vinnie Larocco died tonight."

"What? I don't know anybody named Vinnie Larocco."

The guy at the other end said, "You do now. And we know that you'd like Vinnie to have a really terrific funeral, so we got you down for ten thousand dollars. You understand?"

I hit the roof. "You're goddamn right I understand. This is a shakedown!"

The guy ignored me. "Friday night, that's tomorrow, you bring the money after the last show to the corner of Wabash and Lake. You know where that is? Say eleven thirty tomorrow night—"

"The hell I will!"

"—and bring it in unmarked bills."

"Where do you think I'm going to get ten thousand in one day?"

The guy chuckled. "A hot-shot horseplayer like you tosses that much away in one hour at the track."

"I won't pay any shakedown!" I was still coming on strong, but underneath I was beginning to feel sick.

"Wabash and Lake. Eleven thirty tomorrow night, unless you want to keep Vinnie company." The line clicked dead.

Lou came around about an hour later. I asked him who Vinnie Larocco was, and how he died.

Lou shook his head. "I never heard the name before."

So I told him the whole story. Lou didn't seem very upset by it. "Wabash and Lake's no place for you, Milton. You could knock a guy off there at eleven thirty in the morning and nobody'd pay attention."

My nerves were really snapping. "Thanks a lot, Lou! That makes me feel a whole lot better!"

Lou looked at me like I was off my head. "What's the matter with you, Milton? You're not going down there. I'll take care of the whole thing."

"What are you going to do?"

Now it was Lou's turn to get annoyed. "Do I ever ask you what you're gonna do on the stage? Then don't ask me how I handle my business." He walked out of the dressing room.

The critics were all out front for the first matinee the next day. I watched from a peephole backstage during the last reel of the picture as they came to the seats reserved for them. They weren't carrying any bombs or sword canes that I could see, but I knew they were there to protect Ethel Barrymore, and it made me burning mad. What kind of slob did they think I was? They hadn't seen me ruin anybody's act before. Maybe I had horsed around with Irene Bordoni, but couldn't they figure out that she knew about it and had agreed to it? So what would I do to Ethel Barrymore? Did they think she had come straight down from heaven to Chicago to bless the crowds? For Chrissake, she was appearing on the Palace stage for the same reason I was—to please an audience and make a buck.

I wasn't at my best at that first show, because I was tense, but I got my laughs even if I slipped now and then, and threw in a line or two that was a little bluer than I had planned to work. You could feel the tension in the house and the division in the audience. There were silent spots where I guess the Barrymore fans sat. My sections were laughing harder than ever and, led on by Mama, louder than some of the jokes were worth.

Finally, it was time for the next-to-closing spot, Ethel Barrymore and Company. Maybe there was a lot I could have said, a lot I would have liked to have said, but I decided not to bother. I worked differently than Barrymore did in front of an audience, but in my private life I had just as much dignity. Chicago had given me three solid weeks of love. I had nothing to gain by horsing around with Ethel Barrymore now, even if some of the audience out front was waiting for it. "Ladies and gentlemen," I said, without any hoke, "it gives me great pleasure to present Miss Ethel Barrymore and Company in Sir James Barrie's *The Twelve-Pound Look.*" I bowed and left the stage.

Now, who could object to that? Ethel Barrymore did. I'll tell you why in a couple of minutes.

The play ran only about ten minutes. Her applause was heavy with respect, which means not hysterical. I did what m.c.s always do. I ran out on stage whistling and waving my hands. "Come on, folks, let's hear it out there! Ethel Barrymore!"

She came out and took a dignified bow. Somehow, I thought after my very proper announcement of her act that the war was over between us, and I relaxed. When I was milking the applause for her, it was like I was helping any other star turn, and without thinking I patted her on her rear end. "Great, Ethel, just great." I swear it wasn't planned. I just wasn't thinking.

I felt her shudder and stiffen, and there was murder in her face. I got my hand away from her behind as quick as I could. She took a very stiff little bow and walked off, and I went into my closing monologue and thank-you song.

She was waiting in the wings for me. "How dare you! How dare you touch me!"

She stormed off to her dressing room, and a minute later her maid went rushing out to get Frank Smith, the manager of the Palace.

I was prepared to apologize to her before the next show for patting her on the fanny. That was an accident, but after Frank came to my dressing room to tell me about what she said and demanded, I decided the hell with it. Miss Barrymore told him that she would not work the next-to-closing spot, but would close the show instead. I was not to come out on her curtain with any of the "Let's hear it out there" stuff. She and her fellow players would respond to their applause without my help.

It was going to look strange not to have the m.c. who had been pacing the entire show appear at the close, but I could see what Ethel Barrymore was up to. She was protecting her flanks. But what burned me was what she said about my introducing her. "Just who does that man think he is? 'It gives me great pleasure to present'! Mr. Smith, you are immediately to inform Mr. Berle that he is not presenting Ethel Barrymore, now or ever! My contract is with the Palace, and no one else. Either Mr. Berle says 'It gives the Palace great pleasure to present,' et cetera, et cetera, or I walk off the show and take the next train to New York."

"I'm sorry about this," Frank Smith said to me, "but I hope you understand."

I played it nice for Frank. "Forget it. Big deal over nothing. That's the way the lady wants it, that's how she'll get it." But inside I wanted to kill.

So I changed my announcement of Ethel Barrymore for the next show. I also changed the running order of my material, and put my funniest bit on last. I couldn't help it if the audience laughed right through my introduction of *The Twelve-Pound Look*. And if Ethel Barrymore and Company had to wait to begin their play until the laughter for me died down, and had to fight to calm the audience in the first minutes of their play, no one could blame me. I was nowhere near the Palace stage.

Ethel Barrymore and I didn't speak to each other for the rest of the week.

After the last show that Friday night, I went to the B/G coffee shop, across from the Bismarck Hotel. It was the place that Lou and I had gone that first day. Lou had told me to wait there for him, but not to sit with my back to the plate-glass window. "That's just in case something should go wrong, which you don't have to worry about because it won't" was the way he'd put it.

I drank coffee till it was coming out of my ears, and I went through my entire night's supply of cigars while I waited for Lou to show up. What if something went wrong and he didn't connect with the guys? It was midnight. What if something had happened to Lou for butting in? Twelve thirty. What if they were out looking for me now? I was sweating worse than when I came off stage.

Finally, around one in the morning Lou came strolling into the B/G as casual as anything. "Hi, Milton," he said and swung onto the stool next to me. "A cup of coffee, and one of them white-icing crullers," he said to the waitress.

"What happened? What happened?" I said under my breath.

Lou brushed it away. "It's all okay, Milton. Just like I told you it would be."

"But what happened?" I thought I would explode waiting for him to finish stuffing the cruller into his face.

"It was sort of funny in a way. I just go walking down Wabash at eleven thirty, just casual, like I'm lookin' for a little action in the neighborhood, and there's these two guys hanging around and lookin' busy doin' nothing. Naturally, I know both of them, and they know me. 'Hey, Dominic! Hey, Antony!' I say, and they say, 'Hey, Lou.' So I drift over and we start talkin'. Then I say, 'What you boys doin' here?'

"One of them said, 'We got a guy down for ten grand. He's gonna meet us here.'

"That's when I told them, 'That's why I'm here. The guy you got down for the ten is a personal friend of mine.'

"Dominic was very embarrassed. 'We didn't know that, Lou.' And Antony said, 'You tell that friend he's lucky to have a friend like you, Lou.'

"And Dominic slaps me on the back and says, 'You son of a gun, Lou, we can't make a buck with you, can we?'

"So we shake hands all around, and I say, 'Maybe next time,' And that's the whole megilla. So now, what do you want to do tonight, Milton, huh?"

"For openers, stop shaking."

Ethel Barrymore finished her week in silence, as far as I was concerned, and I went into my fifth and final week at the Palace in what was billed as my "Radio Revue." The big radio name was Arthur Tracy, "The Street Singer." Also on the bill was Venita Gould, doing "Impressions of Radio and Screen Stars," and Lillian Miles, a torch singer, who along with Mary Brian, Leo Carillo, and Roger Pryor was starring on the giant screen that week (Moonlight and Pretzels—"It Tops Even Gold Diggers and 42nd Street for Speed . . . Tunes . . . Girls . . . And Fun!").

Lou did me another favor that week, one I didn't even expect. I just happened to mention to him that I had heard there was a husband-and-wife team who were doing some of my material at one of the theaters on the South Side. "How do you like that? And they say I steal! I wish I had time to go over and check them out."

Lou said, "How do you know about them?"

I told him, "One of the girls in the line here has a sister who works over there, and she told her."

Lou just grunted.

A day later the kid in our chorus told me that her sister was in the dressing room with the husband and wife when Lou came in. "Hey," he said to the man, "I want to talk with you."

Lou seemed to have a cold, because he was carrying a large white handkerchief in his right hand.

The man stood up. "Who are you?"

Lou brought the handkerchief up to his face as if he were going to blow his nose, and for a second there was a flash of blue steel underneath that looked an awful lot like a pistol muzzle. "I just want to talk with you," Lou said.

The man saw what Lou had meant him to see. He sat back down like a sack of potatoes being dropped. "Sure. Sure."

"Come on outside," Lou said, very friendly.

The man shook his head. "This is my wife. And she's a friend. We can talk right here, okay?"

"Sure," Lou said. "I just wanted to tell you that I hear you're using Milton Berle's material. You shouldn't do that, because he pays an awful lot of money for it."

"Well . . . well, I mean . . ."

"You understand what I'm saying, don't you?" Lou said, and flashed the handkerchief so the gun showed again.

"Sure. Sure," the guy said, "listen, you tell Mr. Berle that he doesn't—"

"Wait a minute, pal," Lou said. "Mr. Berle didn't send me. He don't even know I'm here."

"Sure, sure," the guy said. "Anyway, I won't go near his stuff from now on. You can count on that. Come around any time and check if you want. You'll see."

Lou slapped the guy on the back. "Gee, that's good news. I was hoping you'd see it my way."

When I told Lou that I had heard about his visit, he just shrugged. "That's show business, huh, Milton?"

✦ 15 ✦

If Chicago set me high up in the clouds in '33, Broadway brought me smack down to earth with a thud in '34.

I was hot as a pistol after Chicago. I played the top presentation houses across the country, headlining all the way. I thought I could do no wrong. I was getting offers for nightclubs, guest spots on radio; there was talk of Hollywood. The big payoff was on. I was going to laugh my way into a gold mine (and if the right couple of horses ever came in, I even planned to hang on to the gold mine). I decided that what I was ready for, what I wanted most to do, was to star in a Broadway show.

And along came Will Morrissey, a bright guy and a Broadway con man if there ever was one. Will could find backers the way other people found cockroaches in their kitchens. When he came to me, he had both a show and a backer all lined up. The backer was Arthur Lipper, Jr., a Wall Street man who dabbled in Broadway under the name R. A. Reppil, which fooled only those people who couldn't read backward.

The show, on which Morrissey worked on book and lyrics, was titled *Saluta.* The plot—Forest Lawn variety—was about a gang of Italian-American hoods who force the hero to go to Italy to stage an opera in competition with Mussolini's state opera. There's a love story and some complications which I can't remember. One of the complications I *can* remember is a number called "Chill in the Air" (a pretty good song) that had the chorus girls dancing in penguin costumes—and if you don't think penguins in an Italian setting aren't a complication, you don't know what a complication is. Anyway, the show ended with Mussolini breaking up the mob and saving the hero's life.

Saluta was set to open at the Imperial Theatre on August 28, 1934. One night before, on August 27, *Life Begins at 8:40* came into the Winter Garden. It starred Ray Bolger, Bert Lahr, Luella Gear, Brian Donleavy, and Frances Williams. It had lyrics by Ira Gershwin and E. Y. Harburg, music by Harold Arlen. If that wasn't enough, the sketches were funny and topical, the songs were singable ("You're a Builder-Upper," "Let's Take a Walk around the Block"), Robert Alton's and Charles Weidman's dances were eye-catching—in other words, the revue was a smash hit.

This was no great help to *Saluta*, which, if you believed the critics— and the audiences did, because we lasted a fat thirty-nine performances —needed all the help it could get. John Anderson said the show was "so feeble as to be virtually bedridden" and that "its eleven scenes laid end to end reach easily from hither to yawn." Burns Mantle called the show "formless and dull." There were some fair notices, too, and some pretty good ones for me, but fair and pretty good have never been good enough for Broadway, and *Saluta* gave Mr. Reppil a $60,000 bath. At least he took his bath under an assumed name. Everyone on the street knew I had bombed.

But it got me an offer. And it got me an enemy. The offer was to take *Life Begins at 8:40* on the road. The enemy was Bert Lahr, who was starring in the show on Broadway.

Bert Lahr was a great comedian. We all know that. But he was a nervous, moody man, a comedian who gave up on an audience too quickly. If he didn't get a laugh in the first twenty seconds, that was it. I think Bert started his case against me as far back as *Life Begins at 8:40*. Naturally, I was doing the same songs, the same sketches on the road that he was doing on Broadway. This wasn't stealing material. This was doing the material that was the show. But I certainly wasn't doing the material the way Bert did. He had his way, his schtick, his timing; I have mine.

We were a success on the road. Aside from good business, there was also Lita Grey Chaplin, already divorced from Charlie, in our cast. She helped make the tour pleasant for me.

One of the numbers in the show that worked well for me was a sketch called "A Day at the Broker's," by David Freedman, a top comedy writer of the day. The sketch has a man being wiped out at his broker's. Each stock he buys—always when it is at twenty-nine—automatically plunges, until the guy has only ten cents left. The broker comes up with a punch-board for ten cents a punch, on which the even numbers win. The man takes one punch. He gets number twenty-nine. Blackout.

I did the scene exactly as written by David Freedman, but in my style, not Bert Lahr's. Three years later, when I went to Hollywood to make the picture *New Faces*, I asked Edward Small, the producer, to get the film rights to the Freedman sketch and work it into the movie. Once again, I said words that Bert Lahr had first said on a stage, but they were David Freedman's words, and their use had been paid for. Yet I heard grumblings and lousy remarks that Bert Lahr was making about me for stealing the sketch from him.

Jump to 1949. The *Texaco Star Theatre* had been on television for a year and I was really hot. I was approached by Jerry Wald at Warner Brothers to do a picture. It was to be called *Always Leave Them Laughing*, from a story by Max Shulman. I had every kind of star approval you could have on a picture. I even wrote the music and lyrics for it, with Sammy Cahn, and I owned 25 per cent of the picture. The story line was about a brash, hotshot young comedian on the climb, a joke-stealer—you can see it was tailored for me. And there was an older comedian in it, and this young comedian I was to play steals both the older guy's material and his wife.

Ruth Roman and Virginia Mayo were already set for the picture the night that I went into El Morocco and spotted Bert Lahr at another table. He was sitting with his wife, Mildred. It seemed like a great break, running into Bert that way. I had been thinking about him: the perfect actor for the older-comedian role. I stopped at his table. "Bert, can I speak to you a minute?"

I told him about the picture and his role in it. Bert said he was interested. I went to the top brass on the picture and asked them to get Bert. I gave him everything in the picture, and he turned out great. Yet in the book *Notes on a Cowardly Lion*, by his very talented son John Lahr, Bert talked about how he had to fight to keep anything of his in the picture. (I don't hold any of this against his son. He only reported what his father told him. If my son, Billy, ever wrote a book about me, I'm sure he'd believe my side of everything too.)

Bert's big scene in the picture took place in the older comic's hospital room where he talks to the younger comedian before he dies. This is what Bert told his son: "We shot all morning. I came in early to see what I was going to do. I look out by the camera, and there is Berle. He stayed there all morning watching my scene. I was so upset I blew my lines. The only way it got into the picture was that I convinced him there were no laughs in the scene. I don't think he knew the difference at that time. . . ."

At the age of forty-one, I had been working thirty-six years, so I sure as hell could spot a laugh, and I could tell the difference between comedy and sentiment. And there was no question of Bert's scene staying in, because it was crucial to the plot.

Now, as the star of the picture I could have had the closeups. You would have seen my face reacting to Bert's voice. I assure you, Bert got more than his fair share of the closeups. I wasn't going to ruin my picture by hogging the camera.

Actually, I had been there watching the scene all morning—and Bert Lahr knew this—because I was taking over the direction of the picture from Roy Del Ruth, who had taken sick.

The picture came out in 1950. In 1951, I leased for use on *Texaco* a sketch from some show that Bert Lahr had done on Broadway. I remembered the sketch, and I remembered that Bert had been great in it. Once again, it may have been material that Bert first created on a stage, but it was material written by someone else—and that's what I bought the rights to. I was a fan of Bert's, but, as I've said before, I don't—and I can't—work like him. I did the sketch my way, in my style of working. The next day, I got a telegram:

THANKS FOR DOING ME.

LAHR

My last experience with Bert Lahr occurred—well, it had been going on for years, but the truth came out around 1956. I had been (I still am) a member of the Friars for years, and somewhere along the way I decided that I would like to become a member of the Lambs too. I knew a lot of the members, and I had been taken to their clubhouse in New York for several great evenings. They seemed to want me, and I wanted them. So I was put up for membership. I had some great guys behind me—men like William Gaxton and Jack Waldron, and even Bert Lytel, who was the Shepherd of the Lambs. To everyone's surprise, I was blackballed.

It takes only one blackball to keep you out of the Lambs, and the man who drops it in does not have to identify himself. I was depressed when it happened. Sure, you know there are people who don't like you—that's part of making it in show business—but you don't think about it. But here it was, sort of right out in the open, except that I didn't know who had done it. At first I thought it was Frank Fay, but I wasn't certain. It could have been one or two other guys.

I was put up for membership about once a year, and each time I was blackballed. I was also blackballed the year after Frank Fay died. And finally the story came out. I don't know how the Lambs found out, but it was Bert Lahr who had been blackballing me all along. When they called him on it and told him that they wanted me in the Lambs, Bert gave them an ultimatum. "If you take Berle, I'll resign."

Bert was told, "We'll accept your resignation."

And that was the Bert Lahr I knew. A brilliant comedian, but . . .

As for the road tour of *Life Begins at 8:40*, the only reason I ever agreed to it in the first place was because the Shuberts had promised me a *Ziegfeld Follies* when I came back. So I went out, and when I came back I heard talk about the Shuberts and Ziegfeld's widow, Billie Burke, readying a new *Follies* for the beginning of 1936. But I wasn't even asked if I was still interested. They hired Bob Hope for the male comic. The show opened at the end of January, 1936, ran for 115 performances, and took to the road. It came back in September, but without Hope. But those wonderful brothers Shubert didn't remember their promise then either. Bobby Clark took over the Bob Hope spot. The closest I came to the *Follies* in the 1930s was filling in one night when Fanny Brice was sick.

After I came back from the road tour of *Life Begins at 8:40*, I went into the Casino de Paree, which was a big booking for me. The Casino was one of the first theater restaurants in New York, smart and expensive, and it packed them in even during the Depression. It was located on 54th Street between Seventh and Eighth Avenues. Originally it was called Billy Rose's Casino de Paree, but by the time I played it Billy had walked out and Lew Brown, the songwriter, had taken it over. But he was only running it, he wasn't the owner.

The owner was Tommy Lucchese, who struck me as sort of naive, a nice quiet gentleman who must have been in an accident—I thought—because he only had three fingers on one hand. It took me weeks before I put it together and realized that my new friend, Tommy Lucchese, was Three-Fingers Brown, and that while I was working at the Casino de Paree, I was working for a Syndicate family. And though, thank God, I never saw it, Mr. Brown could turn into something more than a quiet gentleman, something that made the torpedoes around town shake and step aside when he walked into a room.

I don't know if we'd have been friends if I hadn't done good business at the Casino, but I did, and he started inviting me out with him—parties, and dinners at a little Italian restaurant he liked up at 117th Street and Second Avenue. Through him I met people like Joey Rao, Johnny Dio, and many others from the outfit. I never heard an angry word, never saw anything more than a suspicious bulge in a jacket. *Now* I remember how Joe E. Lewis got himself hacked up in Chicago, and how Janice Drake got killed for being with Little Augie when his contract caught up with him. But I was so dumb back then and so sure of myself that I didn't know I was taking chances. But Mr. Brown—nobody ever called him Three-Fingers—was always on guard. He always smoked La Corona cigars, and I remember offering him one a couple of times. He would never take a cigar from anyone. Instead, when he wanted cigars he would hop a cab and go to some cigar store where no one knew him and buy them. I think he was afraid that someone might give him one that had been fixed in some way to kill him.

On June 16th, 1935, my baby sister, Rosalind, married Dr. Charles Wigderson, an internist. I wanted to give her a nice wedding, but, as with most things I did in those days, I got carried away. The first plans were for just the family and a few close friends. By the time the day came, there were 1,200 people packed into Temple B'nai Jeshurun on West 89th Street. Sophie Tucker, the Ritz Brothers, Hal Leroy, just about any act or performer working in the New York area was there. Some of them came running in between shows in costume and full stage make-up. It was a blast, and if ever Mama deserved her nickname of Queenie, that was the day. It may have been Roz's wedding, but Mama was the star as she worked her way through the crowd, shaking hands and exchanging kisses all over the place. Pa just sat quietly at a table and smiled his joy. He was happy, but you didn't have to be a doctor to look at him—older-looking than his years, his skin very pale—and know that he was fading. And me, I cried like a baby all through the ceremony.

One break I got in 1935 was to be invited by the New York *Daily News* to be master of ceremonies at the Harvest Moon Ball, a circulation gimmick they dreamed up. It was a big dance contest with prizes in all categories from waltz to jitterbug, with the finals held at Madison Square Garden and the winners to appear on stage at Loew's State. The *News* played the whole thing up big, which meant big publicity for me. I did the finals at the Garden, maybe did a waltz turn or a couple of crazy steps with the jitterbuggers, and there it was the next day in the center spread of the *News*. Then I took the winners and presented them as part of my show at Loew's State. It was my show for the first three years, and then right out of left field I got the word that I wouldn't be doing it anymore. Ed Sullivan was taking over. Well, he had the column with the *News* and he had the juice, so I was cut out. Funny, in a life like mine lots of things happen that burn you up, but for some reason, of all of them, whenever I hear someone say, "Oh sure, the Harvest Moon Ball, that was Ed Sullivan," that burns me the most. I got it going and ran it for three years, maybe four, but all anybody seems to remember is Ed Sullivan.

You never know where you're going to find talent. In 1934, I was appearing at Loew's Willard in Jamaica, and between shows I went to a nearby drugstore for an ice cream soda. The guy behind the counter told me he did impressions and asked if he could audition for me. I told him to come over to the Willard when he was off duty. He turned out to be raw but good, and his imitations of people like Hugh Herbert and Charlie Butterworth showed definite talent. The only thing I didn't like about the kid with the sad eyes was his name. I don't know why, but I didn't think Jack Gellman was right. I convinced him to change it to one I had thought up.

Two weeks later, he quit the drugstore, and for the next four years when I worked clubs and vaudeville he worked with me. At the beginning, we just did a couple of stand-up bits together, and then I turned the stage over to him for his impressions. As Jack grew and learned, he did cross-overs and characters in sketches. In time, of course, he left me, and he left the impressions behind and went on to become a dramatic and comedy star in his own right as Jack Gilford.

There's another guy whose talent I spotted early on, but I can't say I was able to give him any help at the time, only encouragement. I forget who it was, but somebody one night came back to my dressing room at a Chicago club where I was appearing and mentioned that there was a pretty funny guy working the walkathon over at one of the armories. Remember walkathons? They were like dance marathons, and just as grueling, only the contestants walked. But in the Depression anything that might bring in a buck was worth it, and there were always people desperate enough to enter. Anyway, I went over and there was this red-headed kid working the master-of-ceremonies spot, trying to hold the crowd's interest with jokes as the miserable contestants tried to stay awake and limp another lap around the track. The m.c. was named Richard Skelton—Red to you today.

I spent most of 1936—forty-one weeks of it—playing Nicky Blair's Paradise Restaurant, which used to be at 49th Street and Broadway. I spent most of my free time that year with a brunette dancer in the show at the Carnival. Her name was Judy Malcolm, and she was as sweet and warm and fine as she was beautiful. Judy wanted nothing from me, except to be with me and give me her love. But that was more than I could handle back then. I don't think I really understood that love wasn't something dangerous. Today, thanks to my wife Ruth, I know that love means giving, but back then I saw love as a way of taking, and I didn't trust it. I never gave all of myself to Judy, and in time, what we had, which could have been very beautiful, just shriveled up and died.

One night as I was doing my act at the Paradise, I spotted a guy sitting at a table with another guy. The guy I noticed wore glasses and was neatly dressed, not a hood type at all, and he was laughing his head off. The next night I spotted him again, only he had a different friend with him. Okay, I thought, so I got a fan. But there he was again the third night, and I started getting curious about him. I started watching for him.

He came in every night for two weeks straight. I thought I was pretty good—Nicky Blair wasn't holding me over week after week for nothing —but nobody is that good. I called over Albert Berryman, who was maître d', and I said, "Listen, how can a guy come back and see this show so many times? Do you know him?"

Albert said he didn't.

"He's got to be here for some reason. Could you go over and ask him to come back to my dressing room after the show?"

The man came back right after the show. He was sort of average-looking, hair getting a little thin on top. "I didn't think you spotted me," he said. "You must think I'm quite insane, coming here every night to watch you."

"Well, you've answered one question already. I was betting backstage that you didn't speak English and were coming here to learn."

"Not exactly," he said. "I've been studying your work."

I took a good look at him. He looked familiar, but if he was a comic

I couldn't place him. "Hey, watch it," I said. "People don't come to steal from me. That's my line of work."

"I'm afraid I haven't made myself clear. I'm doing research for a play called *Idiot's Delight*. It's by Robert Sherwood, and my wife and I are going to appear in it. Oh, forgive me, my name is Alfred Lunt."

Alfred Lunt! I thought I had a fan? *He* had a fan! We shook hands, and Alfred continued. "I'm to play the part of a vaudevillian named Harry Van, a typically brash master of ceremonies—not of your quality, I assure you, Mr. Berle. So I've been studying you, how you work with an audience, how you move, timing, bits, everything I can learn."

"Well, you don't have to sit out there every night running up tabs just for that. I'd be pleased as hell to help you, Mr. Lunt. Really."

So we made an appointment to meet the next day at Nola Rehearsal Studios, and I worked with him for several weeks, teaching him movements and touches. I was out front when he opened in *Idiot's Delight*, and when he went into his nightclub number with the chorus girls I felt like a proud father watching his kid win the World Series.

At the opening-night party, I spotted a familiar face I hadn't seen since Atlantic City. I'd met Carole there a year or two before, and I'd spent every minute of my week's vacation there with her. She was a cool, lovely woman, poised and intelligent.

We were sunning ourselves on the beach when a guy I knew came along. He took a look at Carole and signaled me that he wanted to talk. I walked away from our chairs to where he stood. "What the hell are you doing with Carole?" he asked.

"What do you mean? Why shouldn't I be with her?"

"What are you giving me, Milton? You know damn well why. She's a whore, that's why."

I didn't even think about it, just swung and knocked him flat in the sand.

When I got back to our chairs, Carole asked, "What happened?"

I sprawled in the chair beside her. "Forget it. Some guy who I thought was a friend insulted my act."

I lost track of Carole after Atlantic City.

When I had a night off from the Paradise, John Garfield, who was a good friend, and I went over to Polly Adler's for dinner. Sure, the world knew Polly as a madam, but her friends knew her as an intelligent woman, fun to be with, and a good cook.

After dinner, Polly excused herself because she had to make some telephone calls to arrange for girls for her clients. John and I were talking when I said, "I don't know about you, Julie [his real name was Jules], but I feel sort of horny."

John thought he might feel that way himself, so we spoke to Polly about it, and she said she could get us two of her $100 girls—Polly handled only the best—and send them around to wherever we said.

John and I went our separate ways to await our deliveries. When the doorbell rang at my place, there was Carole. I think my mouth flopped open. Carole smiled. "You shouldn't have hit that man in Atlantic City, Milton. He was telling you the truth."

Jump to El Morocco, New York's poshest nightclub in the 1950s. I was sitting with some friends, and there was Carole again, coming in on the arm of a very distinguished-looking man. Carole was beautifully dressed, with a healthy spattering of diamonds and a floor-length mink coat. She looked great, but since she was too old to be turning tricks anymore, I wondered who the guy was that she was with. I asked the headwaiter.

"That is Mr. and Mrs. _____ _____," he told me, naming one of the top men on Wall Street.

Sometime during the evening, I caught Carole's eye. She paused just a moment before she turned away, but she made no sign of recognition.

Myron Kirk was a good-looking guy with a reputation around town as a lover. He was a Madison Avenue type, in charge of radio for Ruthrauff and Ryan, a top ad agency. Mike Kirk was also a man who had a big effect on my career, and he was a guy who at the end of our association left a very sour taste that is still with me.

He was brought backstage one night at the Paradise by Irving Mills, who was my personal manager in those days. Kirk told me that he thought I was very funny, and maybe just the man he was looking for to act as master of ceremonies for a new radio show he was putting together for the Gillette Company. They were going to try it out in Boston before going national with it. If I was interested, why didn't Irving Mills and I drop around to his agency to talk it over?

The three of us met the next day, and put the deal in the works. The radio show was called the *Gillette Original Community Sing*. The program was a success and ran for over a year. We began it in Boston, broadcasting over the Yankee Network. Later, when we went nationwid .

we came out of CBS in New York from a studio that seated an audience of fifteen hundred. The show went on Sunday nights at 10 o'clock. I can't explain it, and I've never heard of another show since that ran this way, but we were on forty-five minutes, from 10 to 10:45.

I did my usual straight for the other performers, as well as playing my brash self, with the help of a very bright writer named Irving Brecher, who later created *The Life of Riley.* The community-sing part of the program was handled by Wendell Hall. He led the studio audience with slides of the lyrics. Remember him singing "It Ain't Gonna Rain No Mo, No Mo," "Show Me the Way to Go Home"? The theme song of the show was "Let's All Sing Like the Birdies Sing," and the audience would chirp back, "Tweet, tweet-tweet, tweet, tweet."

It was a good cast that did the show. We also had Billy Jones & Ernie Hare, "The Happiness Boys"; Andy Sannella and his orchestra; Bert Gordon, who was still known as Mischa Moody, but who was already starting to use those lines I wrote for him that were to become his signature as the Mad Russian; Tommy Mack, who got laughs out of a harelipped tag line, "Ektited? Who's ektited? I'm not ektited! I'm as tool as a tootumber" (his name on the show was Judge Hugo Straight); and Betty Garde, always to be remembered as Aunt Eller in *Oklahoma!*

And we had a little girl on the show whom I had known since her diaper days. She was the daughter of Benny and Elsie Barton, who had a big flash act in the heyday of vaudeville. He had a band called the Californians, and she played the violin and sang.

Their little girl was still under ten when she came to the *Gillette Original Community Sing,* to be renamed "Jolly Gillette." The gag was that she was a brat, but she was also the sponsor's daughter. She'd always want to sing, and we'd trade insults when I tried to keep her off the air. ("That's one of my father's jokes." "Yeah, what are you, one of your mother's?") Naturally, she always sang, and she was terrific. She was such a little kid, with dark brown bangs and sausage curls, that she had to stand on a box to reach the microphone. But even though she was little, her voice was big, as everyone found out years later when she took back her own name, Eileen Barton, and had the whole country singing, "If I Knew You Were Comin' I'd Have Baked a Cake."

With a going national radio program, I got tons of publicity, and Mama got caught in the fallout, which didn't exactly displease her. My mother may not have been a performer, but she handled herself with all the sureness of one. On Friday, October 23, 1936, there was a big, beaming picture of Mama in a silver-fox boa, a smart slouch hat, and her pince-nez glasses, under a newspaper headline reading: "IT'S NOT A GREAT STORY, THIS STORY, IF MOTHER LOVE AND SACRIFICE CAN BE CALLED ORDINARY."

What followed was the standard story of how I got up there, only this time the focus was on Mama. A couple of paragraphs stopped me:

" 'I'm not a stage mother. Those are funny words—stage mother. To most people they mean a pest in the theatre. I am not a pest.' "

I chewed that one over. I couldn't decide if Mama was right or if she was kidding herself.

"But when she started Milton on his way she had to go outside her home to earn money, for there are four other children and a husband who has been a semi-invalid almost since their marriage."

I flinched at that one. What would Pa think when he read that? His whole life had turned out to be one big hurt. Why did Mama have to stick the knife in and twist? I felt a flash of anger at her. But then I thought, what should she have said? Would the truth—that Pa could never support his family—make him feel better?

"For all the time she spent with Milton here and on the road, Mrs. Berle says she never neglected the rest of her family."

That one got a sour smile from me. Maybe Mama had no choice when I was too young to travel by myself, but I wouldn't want to ask Phil, Frank, Jack, and Rosalind if they ever felt neglected. And I hoped Mama never did. I don't think she'd have liked the answer.

What interested me the most was this statement by Mama: " 'Of course, some nights he goes out with the ladies. Am I jealous? Oh, no. I would be worrying if he didn't go out with the ladies sometimes, wouldn't I?

" 'Would I be jealous if he gets married? Not jealous, glad; but I would want him to pick out a proper wife. And I know my Milton would do that.' "

I read that part a couple of times, and it made me feel sad inside. Was Mama just giving a reporter the right answers, or was she just putting up a brave front?

Though the *Gillette Original Community Sing* was a big success, I didn't think I was too great on radio. I got my biggest laughs when I did the warm-up before the show. Then I could work on the studio audience without a script, doing material I had tested out on stages and in nightclubs. But reading from a script didn't feel as good for me. I was too used to winging it in front of a live audience, feeling them out, working them. A script ties you down, and radio, being a medium for the ears, not the eyes, was not the best exposure for a visual comedian. I did okay, but I never felt I was getting across at my best.

But I had big hopes for Hollywood. The offer I had dreamed of finally came through in 1937. Irving Mills got me a two-year term contract at $3,000 a week with RKO Pictures. I thought I was a natural for movies. They were visual, and with the right script, how could I miss?

I saw Hollywood as the answer to everything. I'd make it big in movies. Picture would follow picture, so I'd always be in one place. And that would mean a real home for once, not racing from city to city, living out of trunks, checking in and out of hotels that all started looking the same.

I was amazed to find myself thinking that way. I had loved the crazy life I had been leading, or I thought I had. But now suddenly, with the possibility of a new life, I allowed myself to think about my past and to know that it wasn't a life that other people led. And there were so many of them leading lives that came with rooms that meant something to them, and windows they could look out of every day and see the same thing and the same people—it had to be good. If it was, I wanted it.

I remember the last thing I did before I left for Hollywood was to stop at the mirror in the hall and stare at my face. How would it photograph? I checked those two front teeth that had shown up in every caricature of me. Would they have to be capped? Hell, no. I was a comedian. They were a part of me.

But my nose worried me. I thought it turned down a bit when I smiled. I pushed the tip up, and I thought I looked better. Well, maybe something could be done about it.

I wasted my time in front of the mirror. Hollywood didn't turn out at all the way I expected.

The film I wanted to make in Hollywood was *Having a Wonderful Time*. It was a smash-hit Broadway comedy about life and love in the Catskills, or, as I've heard them called, "The Yiddish Alps." I was a natural for the part of the Social Director, Itchy, at the summer resort in which the story took place. So who got it? Red Skelton—one of America's best-known Jewish comedians, right? Well, that was Hollywood thinking in those days. Get a hit property and then play it safe. And safe back then was nice Protestant boys and girls to play nice people. You saved the Jews and the Italians for the not-so-nice people.

They also put Ginger Rogers, Lee Bowman, and Douglas Fairbanks, Jr., in the picture to round out their all-WASP Catskills. So it didn't turn out to be such a great picture. Anyway, I wouldn't have gotten the picture if my name had been Milton Berlington. Pandro S. Berman, the new head of RKO, didn't think I was funny. Even so, it was a better picture than the two I did make. Maybe you've seen them if your local TV station has a really late, late, late show—*New Faces of 1937* and *Radio City Revels.* Neither of those pictures guaranteed me a long happy life in California.

But it was still a fun city after working hours. It was crammed with beautiful and interesting women, and I did my best to meet as many of them as possible. One of them was a bright, warm, funny redhead named Lucille Ball, a contract player on the RKO lot while I was there. We liked to laugh it up together when we ran into each other at the studio, and it led to our going out around town. And once we dated in New York. I took her to the Broadway opening of Dante, a magician from Sweden, making his New York bow. I had seats right down front, which probably explains how he came to call me up on the stage to stooge for him in one of his tricks. He didn't know who I was, so he had no idea why the audience was screaming with laughter. Every couple of seconds I caught the poor guy glancing down to check his fly to make sure it wasn't open. There was no other explanation he could figure out. I guess he got it the next day when the papers mentioned the expensive stooge he had working his opening.

To this day, whenever we get together Lucy tells my wife, Ruth, "There was nothing there with Milton and me . . . because Mama was around all the time."

Funny thing, the RKO lot on which Lucy was a contract player, working her way to the big time, was the same one she later bought with her then-husband, Desi Arnaz, and turned into Desilu.

Wendy Barrie was also important in my life for about three or four months. I met her at a Hollywood party, and we started going around together. I shared my first earthquake with her. We were at her place, I think, and we were sitting on the couch. I had my arm around her, sort of stroking her shoulder. She turned toward me, and I kissed her. We were in the middle of it when the tremor began. It lasted for maybe thirty seconds. Nothing broke, but it threw us to the floor. Maybe I was the comedian in the crowd, but Wendy was a bright, funny lady in her own right. "Wow, that was some kiss!" she said.

Even Mama, who, of course, came with me to Hollywood, had to admit that Wendy was someone special. "She's a wonderful girl," she said, "but don't you think it's getting too serious?"

"Too serious for who?" I said, and walked out of the room.

Pa was sick. Mama had gone back to New York the night Roz called to tell us he'd had a heart attack, but I couldn't make the trip until I'd finished filming *New Faces of 1937*.

I spoke with Mama and Charlie Wigderson regularly by phone. Pa was recovering from the attack, but there had been damage. I was told he could go on for years, or there could be another heart attack at any time. It was news that was no news. I was anxious as hell to get back to New York as soon as possible.

What with Pa on my mind, it doesn't sound like a very happy trip across country, and it wasn't. But my arrival in New York was something else. *New Faces of 1937* was scheduled to play the Radio City Music Hall, so RKO was giving me the star buildup, which meant an arranged mob at the station to greet me. Now, if you know anything about comedians, you know that a comedian is always a comedian no matter what's going on inside.

So the train pulled in, and the mob was gathered for the star's arrival, with the newsmen and the RKO representatives right up front, cameras ready. The passengers came off, looked around to try to figure out who the hell the mob was for, and drifted off. There was nothing for a minute —could it be that Berle was not on the train? Then something came out of the railroad car and paused at the head of the stairs. It wore a polo coat and scarf over bare, hairy legs ending in men's socks and shoes. The face was hidden by big sunglasses. The long blond hair and the beret suggested the great Garbo, but the cigar in the right hand suggested a maniac. "I vant to be alunn," he-she said. There was pandemonium, and fat coverage in papers all across the country.

Seeing Pa was a shock. He was sitting in a chair by the living-room window, wearing the maroon silk robe I had sent to him. When I came in, he was, as I had remembered him so often through the years, sitting and reading. Only, Pa was suddenly an old man. It wasn't just the heart attack, it was more than sixty years of trying to climb a glass wall that had turned him into a man who looked much older than his years.

He took my face between his hands when I knelt down in front of his chair, and his eyes grew wet behind his glasses. "Milton. My Milton." His fingers felt like cold wax.

"How are you, Pa?"

Pa smiled. "I'm alive, so that's something. And Charles says I'm coming along fine, so who knows? If only he would let me have a cigarette, then I could give you better news. So now tell me about you and the moving pictures."

I told him all about *New Faces of 1937* with lots of stories about Parkyakarkus, and Joe Penner and Harriet Hilliard, who were in it with me. I made it sound as if I was in the greatest picture ever made.

Pa patted my face when I finished. "Imagine, my boy a moving-picture star! Maybe I wasn't such a flop after all."

I said, "When the picture comes out we'll see if I smell better than La Rose powder."

"Don't kid about that," Pa said. "That was good stuff. I could have made a fortune with it."

Mama was waiting for me in the kitchen. "He doesn't look good, does he?" she said.

I shook my head.

"When are you going back to Hollywood?" she asked.

"I don't know. Tomorrow, maybe. Or the day after."

As it turned out, I stayed a week. I found an apartment at 101 Central Park West that seemed like a great idea to me. It was a duplex with enough room so that Rosalind and Charlie Wigderson could live there too, which gave Pa a doctor right on the premises.

But it didn't change the downward course of Pa's health. I got word back in California of Pa's second, but minor, heart attack. The first day that he felt strong enough to go outside, he was sitting on a bench in the park when a friend came along. He stopped and said, "Moe, I haven't seen you in a long time," and slapped him on the back. It sent Pa into another heart attack.

❧ 16 ❧

I saw Linda Smith only once more before I left Hollywood. From *New Faces of 1937* I went into *Radio City Revels,* and then there was nothing to keep me in California. The item that appeared in several columns about my going into a picture with Fred Astaire and Ginger Rogers turned out to be nothing but talk. RKO had nothing much planned for me, and I was anxious to get as far away from Hollywood and Linda as possible.

But there she was at one of those big Hollywood parties where everybody comes whether they're invited or not. She was wearing a wedding band and a diamond ring big enough to make her lopsided, but she balanced herself by keeping one arm looped through Jed Weston's. This wasn't the Linda Smith who'd been off by herself at my costume party at the Beverly Hills Hotel. Here she was the center of attention, which was proof positive that the advance word on her picture was good. In Hollywood, the rats leave the ship even before the ship knows it's sinking.

I studied her from a distance, looking for a change in her. Inside, I knew I had no reason to doubt her condition. She wouldn't have agreed to go to Tijuana with me if she had been bluffing, but now I hoped she was. The idea that there was going to be a child of mine that I might never see was a continuous ache in my heart. But if Linda was pregnant, nothing showed. She was as slim as ever.

I elbowed through the crowd. Linda saw me coming. She stiffened and turned to move away, but her arm was linked through Jed's, and he was deep in conversation with another man. She was trapped.

"Linda," I said. "You're looking very well."

"Thank you," she said. Before I could say anything else, she yanked at Jed. "Honey, you remember Milton Berle."

Jed and I shook hands. I said, "I just wanted to congratulate you both on your marriage and wish you all the luck in the world."

They said all the standard things back at me. I looked straight at Linda and said, "And may all your troubles be little ones."

She grew red under her make-up. Jed laughed, with that cocksure male sound of the great stud Linda must have convinced him he was. "Well, you never know."

In 1938, much as I was glad to get away from Hollywood, I was also scared. I was going back to nightclubs, to live audiences. What if there was no more audience for me? What if I had lost my timing and nobody thought I was funny anymore? Now, looking back, I guess I always was one of those people who can stand anything but happiness. Tell me everything is great and I'll worry about it.

Anyway, I went back and it was fine. The people who had come to see me the last time at the Chez Paree in Chicago all came around again and packed the house. Lou Jackson came back into my life, and this time I took him with me. He's been with me ever since. Lou's in his eighties today, and he tells me he's as tough as ever. I think he's even ready to protect me again when I need it, only I don't tell him that I don't need it.

The only other thing I remember from that time in Chicago was being told about a bright young comic-entertainer over at the 5100 Club. I dropped in one night and liked the guy. He didn't work at all like me. His approach was warm and intimate, nothing brash. I met him after his show, talked with him, encouraged him, and a couple of years later, when he came to New York and I was appearing in the *Ziegfeld Follies*, I introduced him from the stage. Danny Thomas and I have been friends ever since.

I cut short out-of-town bookings in March of 1938 after talking with Charles Wigderson one night. Pa had had another heart attack. Each one had left him a little weaker, a little nearer to the end. Now, it was only a matter of time.

I came home to find Pa, an oxygen tank beside his bed, looking like a man made out of tissue paper. He had a male nurse taking care of him. When I came into the room, the nurse was propping Pa up with pillows for the twice-daily shot of whiskey that Charlie had prescribed. Pa never drank, and he hated alcohol. (I think my brother inherited his reaction to liquor from Pa. Just run the cork past Phil's nose and he's crocked.)

"Here," I said to the nurse, "let me give it to him."

I sat down on the edge of Pa's bed and took the shot glass. Pa turned his head and saw me then. "Milton, you've come home."

"Just to see you," I said, and inside I was crying already. I could look in Pa's face and know that the time had come for good-bye. "And to buy you a drink!" (The comedian's curse: The worse you feel, the harder you try for a laugh.)

Pa wrinkled his face in disgust. "Poison. I hate it. It's like a terrible medicine."

I raised the glass to his lips. "That's what it is, medicine for you."

I watched as he forced it down. How could he be going to die, when he had never really lived?

His whole body shuddered as he swallowed the whiskey. "Terrible, terrible," he said; then he looked straight at me. "Why did you come home?"

"What do you mean, Pa?" But I knew exactly what he meant. "I had some free time between bookings. Where else would I come?"

Pa gave a little smile. "You lie pretty good, Milton, but I'm glad you're here."

"Pa, I don't know what you're—"

He took my hand. "I'm very proud of you, Milton. Remember that."

"I'm very proud of you, Pa."

He looked at me sadly. "Proud? Of what? Maybe, if there was a little more time . . ." He turned his head away. "I'm tired now. I want to sleep."

I nodded to the nurse and left the room. In the kitchen, Mama was sitting by the window, just staring out at nothing. Roz and Charlie were with her. Roz was in the early months of her second pregnancy. In her arms was her five-month-old son, my nephew, Michael. I touched his hair, and the kid stirred in his sleep, but he didn't wake up.

Mama said, "Are you hungry, Milton?"

"I'm okay, Mama."

She turned back to the window. I said to Charlie, "So tell me about Pa."

Charlie just shrugged. "There's nothing we can do, Milton. He's older than his years. His heart is worn out. It's just a question of when, now."

Later in the day, Frank, Phil and Jack came over. Frank brought his daughter, Helene, Pa's first grandchild, with him. We would tiptoe in and out of Pa's room to look at him, afraid of waking him, and also afraid if it was too quiet in there for too long.

Mama made dinner, and except for Pa's empty place at the kitchen table it was like old times once again, the whole family together. But it was sad even beyond Pa. It took pain to bring us all together. The good times never did.

After dinner, Mama went to her room. When she returned she was dressed to go out, her jewels, which I had given her, sparkling at her throat and on her fingers. She put her apron on over her dress and went into Pa's room. She leaned over the bed and kissed him. "I want you to rest good, Moe. No worrying, no thinking. Only think about good sleep."

Pa touched her face with his thin hand. "Always the boss, my Sarah."

"What can I do?" Mama said. "I was a manager even before I had anything to manage."

"My Sarah," Pa said.

Watching them from the bedroom door, I saw for just a moment the love between them I was never sure of, that I never really understood. They were both what they were, and even if it didn't fit the rest of the world's idea of what a man and a woman were supposed to be in a marriage, it worked for them.

When Mama came out of the bedroom, her jaw was clenched. She didn't look at any of us, but went straight into the kitchen and took off her apron. She went and got her fur coat.

"Where are you going?" I asked.

Mama glared at me. "I've got a card game over at Len DeGoff's." The other woman was considerably younger than Mama, but she was her best friend.

I was going to say something, but Mama's expression stopped me cold.

"Roz and Charlie have the telephone number," she said, and closed the door behind her.

If I hadn't seen that moment in the bedroom, I think I would have hated Mama for leaving. But seeing it, I thought I understood. Mama wasn't any better at showing her emotions than I am, only Mama didn't have the jokes to cover her pain. Maybe for her, losing at cards—it was a miracle if she ever won—was her way of hiding her insides.

I sat around the kitchen night after night, talking with Roz, Charlie,

Frank, Phil, or Jack, whoever was there. We talked about the years gone by. We swapped memories. At times, it must have sounded like strangers talking together and filling each other in on their backgrounds. There were moments when we all shared common memories, but most of the time they could remember home and jobs that let them come home at the end of their work days. What I could remember were cities and rooms all over the country that ran together in my mind. There were lots of big names in my memories, but if you had lived the life, as I had, the names didn't mean so much. The people who sound great and glamorous turn out to be just people, good or bad, when you know them.

Pa died on March 21, 1938. The nurse had wanted him to get some sleep, but Pa insisted on seeing all of us. The last person he asked for was Rosalind's son, Michael. She brought the baby to Pa's bed. Little Mike must have been wet or cranky or something, because he cried and twisted in Roz's arms the whole time. She tried to quiet him. Pa stopped her.

He ran his fingers along the chubby little cheek and along the squirming body. "Fight, Michael," Pa whispered. "Fight all the time."

Then he closed his eyes, and Roz took the baby out of the room. We went with her. A few minutes later, the nurse came out of the room and told us that Pa was gone.

And little Michael Wigderson grew up to die before he could make his big fight for his place in the world. He grew up in Florida, where Roz and Charlie settled (they're divorced now), and became a police officer. He and his wife moved to California, where Mike became a salesman with a trailer-truck outfit. Because he liked guns and because he had been a policeman, he decided to join the sheriff's department as sort of a weekend auxiliary. It meant a six-week refresher course, and unfortunately Wiggy—that's what they called him—was at the head of his class. It was on a Monday night, and all the trainees had blanks in their guns. The topic was how to pursue a bandit, and the instructor, a ballistics expert, called Michael out. "Come here, Wiggy. Let's show them how it's done." My nephew began to run, and the ballistics expert raised his pistol, which somehow wasn't loaded with blanks. Before anyone knew it Michael Wigderson was dead with five bullets in him. Today Roz has a grandson, Joshua Michael, some newspaper clippings to remind her of the horror, and a ring which I gave Michael for his *bar mitzvah*.

* * *

In 1939 Europe was getting revved up for war again, but most of us in America didn't believe it could happen again—or we didn't want to believe it. How could the world be going to war when sixty countries got together for the New York World's Fair that year?

'Thirty-nine was a big year for me, one of the biggest I've ever had, but it began sour. You know the way it is with the big moments in life? You can remember everything about the moment, like you know exactly where you were and what you were doing that Sunday when the word came over the radio about Pearl Harbor, or when you first heard about President Kennedy being shot. That's the way it was for me on that morning in 1939—I don't want to tell the exact date—when I picked up the New York *Daily News*. I remember there was a little snow on the windowsill outside the apartment on Central Park West. Mama was humming to herself in the kitchen, and I was sitting on the sofa in my pajamas and robe, having coffee and trying to wake up. It was about 10:30 in the morning. The paper was on the end table by the sofa. It was folded in half, and it didn't look like anyone had read it. I remember I was thinking about a horse that was running at Hialeah that I wanted to get a bet down on that day. I picked up the paper. There was a headline about Hitler, and two pictures side by side. I never saw the second one.

The caption underneath was headlined "Future Star?" and there was Jed Weston smiling over Linda's shoulder, looking down at the yawning baby she was holding. It said his name was Laurence Joseph Weston and that he weighed six pounds, eight ounces at birth, even though he had arrived a few weeks ahead of schedule.

I can't tell you what it's like to stare at a picture of your own son and know that's all you are ever going to have of him—a crappy newspaper picture that breaks up into dots when you stare at it too long. My own son. I even touched the picture a couple of times.

I don't know how long I sat there staring. Finally Mama came into the room. "So what's the matter with you today? You just going to sit your life away?"

I shoved the paper at her. "Linda had her baby. It's a boy."

Mama backed away. "I saw. It doesn't look at all like you. She was lying. I know it now for sure."

I got up and walked out of the room. When I got to my room, I cut out the picture of the baby, trimming out Linda and Jed. I stuck it in my wallet. Then I lay down on top of my bed and stared at the ceiling. Mama

looked in a couple of times, once to ask me if I wanted lunch. I shook
my head, and she went away. I never got out to bet my horse.

I didn't get up until the sun was going down. Then I got dressed and
went out and started walking downtown. Somewhere along Broadway, I
went into a movie. I don't know what the picture was, but when a scene
came along that looked sort of familiar, I left.

The birth of the baby made me look at myself. I was pushing thirty-
one, and what did I have to show for it? Sure, I was riding high at the
top, where I had always wanted to be, and sure I was making the money,
but for whom, for what? To help my family, to put furs and jewels on
Mama, to make a lot of bookmakers and shylocks happy. Great, but what
about me? And I didn't mean the funny man. Everybody wanted to be
in his corner, to sit at his table, laugh at his jokes, run up his bill. But
Milton Berle was an invention. What about Milton Berlinger? Didn't
anybody want him?

Sure, there were women—Betty Hutton and Dorothy Kilgallen
paused for a while with me before moving on—but there wasn't a woman.
There was only Mama. The papers still wrote feature articles on us as the
great mother-son team, love and sacrifice and all that crap, but, tied to
a thirty-one-year-old man, the stories didn't read so touchingly anymore.
While nobody said it to my face, I think we were beginning to turn into
a bad joke. Or maybe I was beginning to take a hard look at us and see
that the silver cord was turning into a silver noose that was strangling me
with love and guilt. But had I asked her to leave Pa and my brothers and
sister to concentrate on me? Was she really sacrificing herself for me, the
way we told it to the papers, or was she really making her own dreams
come true through me? And anyway, did it matter what the truth was
between Mama and me if I couldn't do anything about the situation?

I did what too many people do when they find the truth of their lives
closing in on them. I ran. I went to work like a maniac so there was no
time to think or feel sorry for myself. In 1939 I did a nightclub show, a
Broadway show, and a weekly radio program—all at the same time.

The International Casino in New York was across the street from the
Hotel Astor. It was a huge room in the shape of a giant half circle that
could seat 1,700 people. Harry Richman and I packed it twice a night with
World's Fair tourists who wanted something more exciting to remember
when they got back home than the Trylon and Perisphere, or the General
Motors Futurama. America was coming out of the Depression and getting
ready for a wartime boom, but you could still have drinks and dinner at

the International Casino and catch Georgie Hale's spectacular floorshow, "Hello Beautiful," including one hundred chorus girls in a drumbeating finale called "The American Sway," for under six bucks. I was paid a fat —for those days—$6,000 a week.

I got another $2,500 a week from Quaker Oats for hosting a Sunday-night radio program over the NBC Blue Network, called "Stop-Me-If-You've-Heard-This-One." The show was a forerunner of "Can You Top This?" with listeners sending in jokes for a panel to try to top.

I should have been too busy to get into any trouble, but I guess you can always make time for that. The late-night hangout in 1939 for night-club people, and mobsters, and police brass, was still Dave's Blue Room. I used to drift over there after the second show at the International Casino.

We were at a big table, cops and hoods and show people all mixed together, talking about anything to kill the night. Somebody started talking about what was going on in Germany, which led to somebody saying they knew of a Nazi Bund rally that was going to take place the next Thursday night at the Yorkville Casino on 86th Street. It was going to be a big rally, with Fritz Kuhn speaking.

Suddenly, it didn't matter what side of the law any guy at the table was on. We were all Americans, and we were against the Bund, and something had to be done. The guys decided to break up the rally, which was set for 9:30. The plan was to get cars to take about twenty guys up there with sticks, clubs, anything but guns, and take the place apart.

"I want to go too," I said. They were going to leave from Dave's around ten so they'd get to the Yorkville Casino when the rally was in full swing.

"Hey, actor," one of the guys said, "just go do your show. Let us handle this."

I talked my way in. "Listen, I'm an American and a Jew, so I have two good reasons . . ."

My mother was in my dressing room that Thursday night as I raced around taking off make-up and changing clothes. "What's the big rush?" she asked.

I lied. "I've got a guy waiting for me over at the Friars who thinks he's a hotshot pool player. I'm going to show him a couple of things."

I slipped on my coat and fumbled in a pocket to feel the old silk stocking of Mama's I had swiped. I gave her a quick kiss and ran for the exit, where I had left a baseball bat I had bought in a sporting-goods store.

I ran all the way to 52nd Street, near Dave's, where there were four black cars someone had borrowed from an undertaker friend. We all piled in and took off.

We parked right out in front of the Yorkville Casino, and everybody put on their stocking masks and grabbed whatever they planned to use —planks, brass knucks, billy clubs, bats.

We went straight in the front door and charged down the center aisle, cops and hoods—and one comic—in a fighting-mad American army. At first no one moved. There were three hundred or four hundred people there, all frozen in their seats, and then all hell broke loose, with punching and kicking and screaming and the sickening sound of wood smashing into skin and bone.

Maybe the whole thing took six or seven minutes, until we ran out again, helping our wounded and leaving a shambles behind. Somebody helped me to the car I had come in. I had gotten hit across my right eyebrow with what felt like a hunk of lead pipe. Blood was soaking into my stocking mask and running into my eye. The guys I was with stopped at a drugstore downtown, and the druggist stopped the bleeding and fixed me with a hunk of gauze and a fat strip of tape.

I was white as a sheet when I came into the dressing room. Mama's eyes popped. "My God! What happened to you?"

I told her some crazy story about the revolving door at the Friars jamming as I was going through. I don't think she believed me, but she saw I was in no shape for questions.

I have no memory of how I did at the second show at the International Casino that night. All I can really remember is my entrance, when I said, "Good evening, ladies and gentlemen, a very funny thing happened to me on the way to the club tonight."

You'd think that the International Casino and the Quaker Oats radio show would be enough. I guess it wasn't, because one day while I was up at the William Morris Agency, which handled me then, I picked a script up off a desk. It was a play called *See My Lawyer*, by Richard Maibaum and Harry Clork. I flipped through the first twenty pages and thought it was funny. I asked if I could take it home and read the rest of it. That's when I found out that George Abbott was set to do it on Broadway in early fall, 1939. That interested me a lot. George Abbott, with *Three Men on a Horse* and *Room Service* behind him, was the hot director of comedy on Broadway, and I wanted to work with him. I still remembered my wounds from *Saluta*, and I wanted another crack at Broadway.

I thought it was a very funny farce, and one of the three shyster lawyers in the script seemed right for me. The next morning, I called George Abbott directly.

"Hello, Mr. Abbott, this is Milton Berle. I'd like to speak to you about something. Can I come over to see you?"

He said okay, and I was in his office in half an hour. I got right to the point. "You're doing a play called *See My Lawyer*. Nothing would please me more than to be in it under your direction." And I told him the character I thought I could play.

Mr. Abbott—that's what everybody calls him to this day—looked startled. "Do you realize that no one will be starred over the title?"

"That's okay with me." Between the International Casino and my radio program, I had star billing seven nights a week—why be greedy?

Abbott leaned over his desk at me. "Do you have any idea what the part pays?"

I brushed that aside. "Whatever it pays will be fine by me." I was already pulling down $8,500 a week. Now what I really wanted was a chance to show I could do something straight rather than just stand-up clowning. So I went into the show, with Teddy Hart, Millard Mitchell, Gary Merrill, and Eddie Nugent, for $200 a week. Only I didn't get George Abbott as my director. He produced, and turned the direction over to a kid still in his twenties, Ezra Stone. We came into New York in September of 1939 at the Biltmore Theatre. Another hit for George Abbott.

While I was in *See My Lawyer*, I only appeared in the late show at the International Casino. Between the two shows and the radio broadcast on Sundays, I was working seven nights a week, with two matinees plus rehearsals and radio script conferences during the days. There were always bookmakers and scratch sheets to fill up any free time I had during the days, and you could always pick up hangers-on, freeloaders, and stray broads to round out the nights after the last show at the Casino. I was leading the big, busy life, only it wasn't full. Once in a while I'd catch a look at my face in a men's-room mirror of some late-night joint and stare at skin that was rounding out from too much of everything wrong and turning pasty from too little of anything right, and I'd wonder what the hell I was doing it all for. Why couldn't I leave the stage after the last show, like other people? Why did I have to collect a crowd of people I didn't give a goddamn about, and pick up their tabs and work to make them laugh so I could be the star of a delicatessen or an all-night drugstore? The trouble is, I only asked myself the questions. I ran from the mirrors because I didn't want to think about the answers.

If I couldn't face the man I saw in the mirror, I did something about the face. When I finished with *See My Lawyer* and the International Casino, I went to Dr. Joseph Safian, one of the best plastic surgeons in New York, and had my nose bobbed. It wasn't much of an operation, but I thought it made a big difference in my face. After the operation, when I smiled the end didn't turn down. I liked the new look so much, I decided it would make all the difference when—and if—the next shot at the movies came.

Naturally, with the outsized ego I had then, I didn't keep the nose job quiet. I worked all sorts of nose jokes into my act ("I cut off my nose to spite my race"; "A thing of beauty and a goy forever"), and once, several years later, I went too far. It was backstage at Madison Square Garden at some big benefit, and there was Christine Jorgensen, who had just returned from her sex-change operation in Denmark. I've apologized since for what I said when we were introduced, and I apologize again here. At the time I was still brash enough to think anything I said was funny. Anyway, after we were introduced, I said, "I'll show you my new nose if you show me your old cock."

Christine Jorgensen may not have been a lady for very long, but she was a lady. With true dignity, she topped me with "Very funny, *Miss* Berle," and walked away.

In 1940 it was back to the nightclubs across the country, back to the hotel rooms, my life filled with Mama and the local so-called friends who crowd in on any entertainer in any town because they think it makes them important if they have a picture to show with their arm around the shoulder of a public face. In other words, I was still running, still lonely.

Wherever we were, my day began the same way, with me barely talking, trying to pull myself together with coffee and all the local papers in front of me. I used to turn to the race results first, but now I found myself flipping all the pages, glancing at every picture, hoping for another look at my son, Larry—I had already shortened his name—but nothing showed up. I read all the gossip columns, and they were full of Linda, who had scored big with her first two pictures and was at work on the third, with a fourth in the planning stage. Reading between the lines, I got the impression—or was I really hoping for bad news?—that everything wasn't perfect in that phony paradise Linda had built for herself. "Linda Smith looked like a true movie queen at the New York premiere of her new film, _____. She arrived on the arm of handsome _____, who was filling in for her husband, movie-exec Jed Weston, who couldn't make it east for the preem." "Table-hopping at Chicago's posh Pump Room we spotted Linda Smith, the star everyone is talking about, talking only to Man-About-Town _____, before heading back to Hollywood, hubby Jed Weston, and their baby son."

It was the boy, my boy, that kept me following the papers as my act moved west. I wanted him. I wanted to see him. He would have been a reason for my life. I felt nothing about Jed Weston. I couldn't hate him; I felt sorry for him. The poor guy didn't know what was going on. Maybe he was catching on that the little mommy he had married was running a little wild, but he couldn't have had any idea that the child wasn't his.

But I hated Linda for what she had done to me (even as I could still see myself packing to take her to Tijuana). I hated her because she had me trapped.

All I could do was continue to search the papers in every city I played, looking for pictures of my little boy, hoping for some impossible piece of news about Linda and Jed that would give my son to me.

I never forgot the boy. But when I opened my act at a club called The Bowery in Detroit, something happened that drove everything else out of my mind.

I met Joyce Mathews.

✺ 17 ✻

Hold On to Your Hats opened at the Cass Theatre while I was appearing at The Bowery. The musical was to mark Al Jolson's return to Broadway, and he hoped it would somehow save what was left of his marriage to Ruby Keeler, who was his leading lady. (It didn't work, and Ruby left the show, to be replaced by Eunice Healy.) For their out-of-town opening, a telegram was sent to be posted backstage at the Cass inviting the *Hold On to Your Hats* company to the last show of the night at The Bowery. They all came, except Jolson and Keeler.

Everyone in show business knew about Louis Shurr's white ermine coat. The agent kept it in his closet, to be worn by his date of the night. I was in the middle of my act when Louis came in. I was doing a bit I used to do, ad libbing comments about the audience and anything that came to mind to the tune of "Tea for Two," stuff like:

> *The Bowery is*
> *a classy dump.*
> *Eat the food,*
> *you'll need a stomach pump.*

And there was Louis Shurr coming down the aisle to a front table. On his arm was an absolutely gorgeous blond wearing a white ermine coat. Every head in the club turned to look at her. She was that breathtaking, like some sensational dessert made of vanilla and honey.

206

For a minute, I didn't hear the band behind me, because I was too busy staring at the woman. Then I started singing:

> *It's Louis Shurr*
> *And that same white fur.*
> *I envy him;*
> *I gotta meet her.*

As soon as I finished my act, I headed straight for Louis's table. After we shook hands and I was invited to sit down, he said, "You want to meet this girl? Okay. Milton Berle, this is Joyce Mathews."

I said, "Hello, Miss Mathews, how are you?" But I couldn't leave it at that. "That's a really beautiful coat."

"I know," she said, "it's *mine*."

I did a big comic gulp. "Sorry. Forgive me."

What happened after that, I can't remember. I couldn't even remember when I got back to my room at the Detroit Leland. I just know we sat at that table until The Bowery closed, and we talked and talked, and laughed and smiled. But about what, I don't know. Louis Shurr must have been at the table through the whole thing, but I don't remember him at all. All I could see was this gorgeous woman.

I walked by the theater the next day and studied the pictures out front. Joyce was one of two featured showgirls in the cast. The other, whose brunette beauty contrasted with Joyce's creamy look, was Jinx Falkenberg. I asked and found out that the *Hold On to Your Hats* company was also staying at the Detroit Leland.

That night, after the last show at The Bowery I dressed as quickly as I could, ducked Mama and the hangers-on I usually wasted the night with, and headed for the hotel. I took with me—like a kid bringing an apple to school for the teacher—a battery-operated portable radio I had just gotten. They were something brand-new on the market, and I hoped Joyce hadn't seen them yet.

The coffee shop at the Detroit Leland stayed open all night, so it was a meeting place for all the show people in town. I walked in with my heart thumping, hoping that she'd be there. I spotted her right away, at a table with five other girls from the show. I went over. "Hello. How are you tonight?"

She smiled. "Fine. And you? I wanted to tell you how much I enjoyed the show last night. You were so funny."

"And I wanted to say again that I didn't know that was your coat. I'm really sorry about that."

She said, "That's okay."

Then neither of us could think of anything to say, and I just stood there with six women watching me, waiting. I thought of the radio, and I showed it to Joyce. Everybody looked at it, turned the knobs. "That's remarkable," Joyce said.

The radio passed from hand to hand around the table. When it got back to Joyce, I said, "If you want it, you can have it."

Joyce said, "Oh, I couldn't do that."

"Well," I said, "if you can't just take it, how about earning it? Why don't you keep me company while I have something to eat. I'll pay you the radio for that."

A couple of the girls raised their eyebrows at that approach. Joyce, who always had a remarkable innocence about her despite everything that happened to her, said, "I guess that makes a difference."

She stood up, and I guided her to a booth far across the room. I wasn't at all hungry, but I ordered a lot of food, whatever would take the longest time.

Again, we talked way into the night, and we told each other all about ourselves. She was from Miami and had been Miss Florida at one time. She came from a wealthy family, and her parents were divorced. Though she was just twenty-one, Joyce already had a marriage and a divorce behind her. She had been married to General Gonzalo Gomez, the son of the former Venezuelan dictator. He had slapped her around, and the marriage had ended after ten days.

And by the end of the evening we were talking a little about the future. "Where do you go from here?" I asked.

"We go to Chicago next," she said. "And then New York."

"That's funny," I said, "I'm going to Chicago too." I think I'd have gone anyway—Joyce was getting to me fast—but I really was going to Chicago, to play the Chez Paree again. "I'm going to see somebody there I like very much."

Joyce didn't get it. She said, "Oh, will I see you there, too?"

"Well, this person I like very much in Chicago is a girl."

Joyce's smile faded. "Oh, well . . ."

I reached across the table and took her hand. "This girl I like very much isn't in Chicago, but I hear she's going to be there when I am. And I know I'm going to like her very much in Chicago."

I know it sounded corny, but, maybe aside from Shakespeare, who ever said anything brilliant to a girl they were falling for?

"I think she's going to like it too," Joyce said.

In Chicago, Joyce would come over to the Chez Paree after her show. Mama was there, of course. At first she welcomed Joyce, but when she showed up too often I could sense Mama tensing up. The chill was setting in. But Joyce didn't seem to notice it at first. She was pleased, at the beginning, to be with my mother. Joyce was the sort of girl to whom the mother of the man she was dating meant something. But one night, when her show was dark and Joyce could join me between my shows, we went out for dinner and Mama came along. For the first time I saw the confused look that I was going to see a lot of in the future on Joyce's face.

I had to leave Joyce after dinner to do the next show at the Chez Paree. Mama came with me. Joyce begged off, saying she was tired. I got one taxi for her and another for Mama and me. We didn't talk all the way to the club—anyway, I didn't. All Mama said about Joyce was "Such a pretty girl," and then she changed the subject to the business I was doing at the Chez Paree. I didn't listen. I was beginning to burn inside, seeing the old pattern being repeated: Me and a girl, and Mama chipping away at the setup until it fell apart.

And with the anger came guilt and doubt. Had Mama ever broken up anything serious for me? Had she said one word against Joyce? Done anything to cause trouble? Wasn't I jumping the gun? Who could say that Mama would be against it if I ever wanted to marry Joyce? Hadn't Mama wanted me to marry Linda?

I had a splitting headache by the time we reached the club.

There wasn't any party after the New York opening of *Hold On to Your Hats*, because Jolson wasn't the kind of guy to give one, so the cast went their separate ways. Joyce, dripping with orchids, which I had sent to her, and I made it a night on the town with Jimmy Ritz, of the Ritz Brothers, and his wife, Ruthie. We started out at the Stork Club and made the rounds from there. Wherever we went, heads turned. I suppose a couple of turns were because my face and Jimmy's were known, but most of the stares were for Joyce. She was that beautiful, and what made her even more so was that she acted as if she didn't know it. There was nothing hard about her. Instead, she was sweet, and very often quiet—I guess sort of shy—in a crowd. I liked being with her, and, being a guy with a shaky ego beneath a slick, hard crust, I liked being seen with her, knowing every man in the room was jealous of me.

Our nightly trips on the town started making the columns, linking us as a couple, which was okay by me. I used to head over to the Shubert stage door at 11:10 (which was supposed to be curtain time) to pick up Joyce. Now, in 1940 I wasn't somebody you could push around. I had worked my way up, and I had wised up plenty, but Jolson was still Jolson. Every night, after every other show in town had gone dark, Jolson was still holding the stage at the Shubert. Time and union Golden Hours—which can cripple a producer—didn't mean a thing to Jolson. Eleven twenty, 11:30, 11:40 would go by, and Jolson would still be out there, center stage, giving everything to the audience while he kept the entire cast on stage behind him in their finale costumes.

After hanging around a couple of nights waiting for Jolson to call it quits so I could pick up Joyce, I got sick of the whole thing.

I was standing at the back of the theater with the orange-drink sellers, and there on stage in her cowgirl costume was Joyce, the girl I wanted to be with. She didn't have a thing to do but stand there and smile and applaud while Jolson was proving to himself and to the audience that he was still the king and as great as ever. And, to be fair about it, he was. But I was kind of fed up with waiting and waiting. Look, if the boss feels like working late, that's his business, but the rest of his staff doesn't have to hang around the office.

I waited until he finished a number—it was going on midnight!—and I walked straight down the center aisle. I put two fingers in my mouth and whistled. "Hold it, Jolie!" I called out, and started up the stage steps.

The audience recognized me. They laughed and gave me a hand. I guess they thought I was an added attraction, but everyone on stage froze. I just walked over to Joyce and took her by the hand and led her back down the stairs. I turned in the aisle. "I'm going home, Jolie. You lock up!"

That line made all the columns the next day. When Joyce showed up for work at the Shubert the next night, Jolson was waiting for her. He was burning mad. "That phony fuckin' Jew comic, if I get at him I'll kill him!" He was so mad he was anti-Semitic, which is pretty mad for a Jew to get.

He went on, using every word in the book, but the topper was "I remember that little prick from the Winter Garden, when his name was Berlinger!"

More times than not, Mama came along with Joyce and me whenever
we went out together. She was always polite to Joyce, always friendly, but
I knew Mama didn't like what was happening. I could hear it in what she
said. She treated Joyce either like a child ("Don't leave that part on your
plate, Joyce dear. Eat it. It's very good for you.") or like a challenger ("I
don't see how you do it. First your show, then going out night after night.
I should think you would want to go straight home sometimes and get
a good night's sleep. Listen, it's important in your business to keep your
looks.").

The most Joyce would ever say to me was a careful, "Why don't we
just do something simple tonight, just the two of us?" She never pushed
it beyond that, but I got the hint. The rest of the time Joyce just looked
polite but confused. She told me later that she had been raised to respect
parents, so that included my mother.

As for me, I felt trapped. I wanted to be alone with Joyce, but I
couldn't seem to find the strength to stand up to my mother. I'd plan an
evening alone with Joyce, and just as I was getting set to head over to the
Shubert Theatre and pick her up, suddenly there was Mama, all dressed
up in her best. "So where are we going tonight?"

I felt my insides tighten. "I thought you had a card game on?"

Mama checked herself in the mirror and fixed the catch on her
diamond brooch. "Mary Feldman didn't feel good. And another one got
a call she just became a grandmother, so we decided to skip it."

"That's great," I said.

The way I said it made Mama look at me. "If you don't want me to
come along, I can go right home. Just say the word."

I know I should have, but I couldn't.

It was about this time that I met a man I consider a friend for life
—Frank Sinatra. He was already known, but still a few years away from
the time the bobby-soxers would be tearing down the Paramount Theatre
to get close to him. When I first met him, he was singing with the Tommy
Dorsey band. He was a skinny kid with a damp lock of curly hair hanging
down on his forehead.

The years have put a little weight on him and thinned out his hair,
but otherwise he's the same guy he was then, ready to fight anybody at
any weight if the situation calls for it, a generous guy with a buck if a
friend needs it.

Anyway, back in '40, Tommy Dorsey was a friend of mine, and I had
just written a song called "Copy Cat," which, now that I think about it,

was a piece of shit. But I believed in it then, and I asked Tommy if he would orchestrate it and make it. And that's how I met Frank. I asked him if he would sing it. He ran through it once and handed it back to me. "It's not my type of song."

I can't say that made me happy, but I respected Frank. There's no bull about him. He says what he thinks. If he likes, he likes, and if he dislikes, he dislikes. The only trouble with my hanging around with Frank is that I always seemed to end up in fights. Thank God, we're both getting older, so there are less of them, but back in the 1940s and '50s his popularity and his size seemed to make him a moving target for every would-be tough guy. There was the night that Jackie Gleason opened with his big orchestra at a place called La Vie en Rose, and some gorilla came over to our table and said something insulting to Frank. I belted the guy while Frank was getting ready to. There was another incident like that at the Rio Bomba in New York in 1943. Also Palm Springs, California, and down in Miami. Then there was the night out in front of the Moulin Rouge in Hollywood when words were exchanged between John Wayne and Frank. John said he didn't want to touch Frank because he might hurt him, and Frank said, "Yeah?" and somebody started swinging, and guess who got belted while breaking it up. Me.

I remember when Don Rickles was just coming up. I made it a point of being at his opening at the Slate Brothers, a good California club, so I could give him a boost by introducing him. I was at a front table with Frank, Louella Parsons, Marilyn Maxwell, and Richard Conte. Frank said he had to go to the john, and I gave him that line, "I don't have to go, but I'll take out with you."

We were both in this small john when the door opened and in came a supposedly tough guy, big and tall. He pointed at Sinatra and said, "I read a lot about you, and I don't think you're so tough."

Frank said, "Get away from me, pal."

The guy was more my size than Frank's, and, knowing Frank's temper, I stepped in quickly. "Would you please leave Mr. Sinatra alone."

The guy glared at me. "What are you, his bodyguard, Berle?"

I was still trying to save the situation—"No, but please . . ."—and wondering how I always got into the middle of these hassles, when the guy shoved me. In my mind that made what happened next self-defense. I feinted with my left, turned as if I were going to walk away, and then hit him a shot in the stomach, which is one of the worst places to hit anybody when he's not expecting it. The guy crashed right through the john door and into the arms of Art Aragon, another man who knows his way around with his fists. I don't know what happened after that, but the last I saw of the guy was Art Aragon taking him out of the club the back way.

Thinking back, I could wish my head worked as fast as my fists. Frank never needed my help in a tight spot, and I would have ended up with a couple less bumps and bruises. But I don't regret one of them. Frank's friendship is worth it to me.

Hold On to Your Hats closed before its time. It was in its fifth month and doing good business when Jolson caught pneumonia and was rushed to the hospital. He recovered, but the show stayed shut until he revived it in July of 1941 in Atlantic City.

Maybe that wasn't good for Joyce's career, but it was good for us as a couple, which was how I was beginning to think of us. I wanted to be with her more and more. It seemed like a gift from heaven to me that I was booked into Art Childers's club, the Royal Palm in Miami (not Miami Beach), right out on Biscayne Bay. Joyce could come down and be with me, and no one would make cracks. After all, she had her father living down there, and it was her home town.

I was booked into the Royal Palm for three weeks, along with Abe Lyman and his orchestra and a singing male sextet called "Tommy Gleason and the Royal Guards" who came out dressed as brigadiers with swords and shakos. We did three shows a night to capacity business, and one night, just for the hell of it, I put on one of the brigadier costumes and got into the act for the last show. It was all crazy ad lib but it went over so well that the act and I talked it over and we all decided to keep the bit in every night for their encore. That turned out to be the beginning of an act that became Ben Yost's Vikings, who worked with me for years in cafés, movie theaters, and the *Ziegfeld Follies*.

The whole show was such a success that the three weeks stretched out to ten. Martha Raye had been booked to follow me. She didn't. She just joined up—she and I have always worked terrifically together—and added to the pandemonium. Everybody was wild about the show—we were doing turn-away business—except Joe Adonis and his Syndicate associates, who owned the Colonial Inn out in Hallandale, a Miami suburb. To buck our show, they brought in their show, which included Ted Lewis, Sophie Tucker, Joe E. Lewis, and Paul Whiteman's orchestra. We still topped them.

Mama and I never mentioned Joyce's name once on the trip down to Florida. But I knew Mama was thinking about her. I could see her start to relax as our train pulled out of New York, and she was her old jolly self by the time we reached Florida. But I grew more tense.

I hated Mama's happiness, because I knew what it meant. She thought she had gotten rid of another woman who would take me away from her and the life she wanted from me. I had crazy fantasies in which I saw myself, like a silent-movie character, raising an arm and pointing out into the dark night, ordering Mama to get out of my life. I saw myself getting her a terrific apartment in New York, and her eyes filling with tears of gratitude as she walked from room to room. This is what she had always wanted, and she was so grateful not to have to travel with me.

And in my mind I also saw her put her hand to her chest as the pains started when I told her she could no longer tag along after me. I would always take care of her, but from now on I had to lead my own life without anyone mixing in. Mama cried and fell to the floor. I had killed her with my ingratitude.

All the fantasies stayed fantasies. I didn't have the guts to settle things with Mama.

Then Joyce showed up.

I think the first time I realized that I was in love with Joyce was the first night she saw the show at the Royal Palm. Afterward, she asked if I could get her into the chorus there. "That way we'd sort of be working together."

Without thinking about it, I said, "I'd rather not have you in the show line. I don't want a lot of strange guys looking you up and down."

Joyce looked puzzled. "But that's what they were doing, I guess, when I was in the Jolson show."

"That's different," I said.

"What do you mean? What's the difference?"

My throat used to get all tight when it came to the special words. Now, I just blurted out "Because I love you, and I'm not serving you up for a lot of slobs to drool at."

Joyce's eyes got shiny, and the tears started. "You've never said that before."

I made helpless gestures while Joyce waited for me to say something more. But I couldn't. So I kissed her. "I love you too," she said.

The wedding talk started soon after. I met her father, and I thought he was a great guy. He and I played golf together. Beyond that, he knew as much show business as I knew stocks and bonds, but we got along well together. I don't know what Joyce was telling him, but I got the feeling he was treating me like his new son-in-law. Her mother, whom I also met and liked, also gave me the same feeling.

But not my mother. Maybe she was a little more careful about how she talked about Joyce, but she hit the same old notes, dragged out the same old clichés. "Sure, she's a lovely person, but what do you need with marriage now? And she has a career too. How often will you two be together? Why not enjoy what you've got when you're together? Why tie yourselves up when who knows where you'll both be next week? Look what this business did to your papa and me."

"Don't give me that, Mama. You didn't always have to be with me. You wanted to."

Mama smiled sadly. "The children always think they know everything about what a parent does and what a parent wants to do. A lot you know."

There was the old sting of guilt. I reacted with anger, and the more anger I felt, the worse things I said, and it all ended again with me hugging Mama and telling her that I didn't mean any of the things I said and how much I loved her. And, once again, we both felt better and nothing had been settled.

If Mama didn't like what was going on, Joyce never knew it. She was too busy dropping hints whenever we were alone. "I like that tie, but I wouldn't choose it for you." "What do you like for breakfast? Tell me. I ought to know."

I knew what Joyce was saying, but I pretended I didn't. I wanted her, I wanted her to be with me, but I still didn't want to face marriage. I guess it meant standing up to Mama, and I still wasn't ready for it.

Sometimes when we would say good night, Joyce would look sad. It was the end of another evening between us with nothing settled. "I always hate to say good night," Joyce once said. "It means being away from you. I don't like that, do you?"

Another hint. I laughed it off. "Come on, Joyce, we'll be together again tomorrow."

"I know," she said, "but it's not the same thing as *always* being together."

I kissed her so that she couldn't talk, and pushed her inside.

That was the thing that was hard to realize about Joyce. No matter what idea you might get about her, seeing her on stage in a skimpy costume, there was a sort of old-fashioned streak to her. Love in her mind meant one man, and one man meant marriage. That's the way she thought, and it was what she expected to happen when she loved.

I knew we couldn't go on the way we were much longer in this crazy lopsided triangle of Joyce, Mama, and me, but I kept putting off facing the situation, hoping that something would happen to straighten it all out without anyone being hurt.

Usually, that never happens, but this time I got a reprieve. First it was a radio show, *Three Ring Time*, sponsored by Ballantine Beer, to be broadcast from California. It was to go over the Mutual Network with me, Shirley Ross handling the vocals, Bob Crosby and his Bobcats as the band, and Charles Laughton, of all people, doing comedy with me. He did, for a very short time, until he decided that playing for laughs with Berle wasn't his favorite ego massage.

Then it was an offer to return to pictures. It came from 20th Century–Fox to appear in *Tall, Dark and Handsome*, with Cesar Romero, Virginia Gilmore, and Charlotte Greenwood.

Joyce returned to New York and went into a new show called *High Kickers*, starring George Jessel and Sophie Tucker. Our romance continued by telephone, which suited me better than it did Joyce. I had had years more experience at loving and stalling than Joyce had had.

Maybe it was the new nose or maybe it was the right picture, but this time around I seemed to be getting somewhere in pictures. Twentieth liked me in *Tall, Dark and Handsome*, and I had barely gotten off that picture when I went to work in *Sun Valley Serenade*, with Sonja Henie, John Payne, and Glenn Miller and his band. After that it was *Rise and Shine*. I still wasn't getting star billing, but I thought I was getting closer. I told the papers that this was the first picture in which I was in a love scene. I stood next to George Murphy while he kissed Linda Darnell.

I was still single, and while I cared about Joyce more than any other woman I had ever known, I still wanted to go out nights and get around Hollywood. I could always take Mama, but that newspaper shot of me and

Mama talking to Mickey Rooney and Ava Gardner in the middle of a nightclub dance floor pleased Mama more than it did me. I loved my mother, but not the way Mickey loved Ava. I wanted something more. It led to dating Mary Beth Hughes.

On screen, Mary Beth looked tall, seductive, and a little dangerous. Off screen she was tall, lovely to look at, and a regular gal. She was the kind of rare woman who could have just as much fun eating hot dogs at a ball game as sipping champagne at Ciro's. We had a lot in common—Mary Beth's mother tried to stay as close to her as mine did to me. I saw a lot of Mary Beth, but, surprisingly, Mama didn't seem to mind. I think —and maybe it had to do with Mary Beth's mother—Mama didn't see in her the threat she saw in Joyce.

If you ran around Hollywood, you heard gossip. That's how I first heard that things weren't so hot anymore between Jed and Linda. There was also talk that Linda was drinking too much and her studio was unhappy with her. About the baby—Larry was already a little boy, but I still thought of him as a baby, yawning, the way he was in the newspaper picture—there was nothing. Jimmy Fidler and Harrison Carroll weren't interested in kids unless they appeared in pictures.

I called Jed's house a couple of times. I planned to say I knew them both the last time around, so I was just calling to renew acquaintances, but each time I got a maid who said that both Mr. and Mrs. Weston were out for the evening. I left my number, but no one ever called back. I figured Linda got the messages and kept them from Jed.

But *I* got the message. Linda didn't want me anywhere near my son, and after the first hurt passed, I sort of saw her point. I didn't like it, but I saw it.

Mama and I were living in a house I had rented on Palm Drive. I had an early call at the studio the next day, so for once I was staying home in the evening. Mama was standing by a mirror in the front hall, fussing with her hair, while she waited for a friend to come by to pick her up for a card game. "Did you see in the paper today about your friend Joyce's roommate?"

"Huh? What?"

"It said that Bonnie Edwards is leaving *High Kickers* to marry Tommy Manville. All that money. Not bad, huh?"

"What's good about it? How many wives has he had already?"

Mama shrugged. "It says she's his fifth. So maybe this one will stick. And if not, she'll come out all right."

A car stopped outside, and Mama stuck her head out the door to answer the honk. "That's my ride," she said.

I got up to give Mama a peck on the cheek before she left. As she was going out the door, Mama said, "Too bad that Tommy Manville didn't see Joyce first. She could have done well by herself."

The anger started in the middle of my chest, like heartburn. But Mama was already on the way to her car.

I closed the door. It was eight o'clock. I thought about calling Joyce in New York, but it was five o'clock there. Who knew where she'd be at that hour? It wasn't a matinee day. Joyce could still be wandering around the department stores. Joyce was the only woman I ever knew who could walk into Tiffany's with a shopping list.

I settled down to a cigar and the radio in the living room. There were no sounds from the rest of the house. The cook we employed had already left. I was alone.

Maybe it was five minutes after Mama left that I heard a car pull into our driveway. People never dropped in in Beverly Hills without calling first, so I figured it was Mama coming back for something she forgot. Then the door chimes sounded. I got up. Mama must have forgotten her keys.

I opened the door, and there was Linda, a silver fox jacket hanging over her shoulders. She was leaning against the door frame, and even though she smelled like a brewery, she looked pretty good. "I'm returning your phone call," she said, and giggled. "Well, don't look that way, Milton. Nobody's home. I've been sitting in my car for almost an hour waiting for your mother to leave."

I stepped aside, and she came in. She swayed by me, and I smelled that perfume of hers again. All it made me feel was sad. I don't like drunks of either sex, but to me, a female lush is worse.

It had been three years since I had seen Linda. She was still in her twenties, but the booze was aging her fast. There was a slight puffiness to her face, and a sick glow to her skin. Her bones were so good that she'd probably always have some beauty to her, but the wrinkles were going to set in fast.

I closed the door behind her, and she moved into the living room. I didn't say a word. She had caught me so off guard that I didn't know what to say.

Linda turned on me. "Well, surprise! Surprise! Aren't you glad to see me?"

"Sure. Why don't you sit down?"

"Why don't you offer me a drink?"

"I think you've had enough. You don't want to pass out here."

Linda snorted at that. "I don't pass out anywhere, maybe that's my trouble. And I can hold a lot more than this, so just fix me a little bourbon and water. Just a teentsy."

I got her the drink. I sat down across from her, though she had patted the seat beside her. "What do you want, Linda?"

"Rude," she said. "I just wanted to see you. No crime in that, wanting to see somebody. Sometimes I don't see anybody for days. A maid and a cook and a gardener, even a baby, that's not seeing anybody. It'd be nice once in a while to see somebody you're married to, and if that doesn't happen too much, then it's even nice to see somebody you're not married to. What do you think, Milton, my old Tijuana buddy?"

"I think if Jed's not coming home nights, there's probably a goddamn good reason."

Linda laughed. "I hope we're not talking about another woman! Jed? He can't even make it with this one anymore! If Jed's fucking anything these days, it's got to be the studio, and he's too much of a boy scout even to do that."

"I don't want to know about you and Jed," I said. "That's your business, and I don't give a good goddamn about it. You got what you wanted, and if it isn't working, that's tough as far as I'm concerned. I only want to know about my baby."

"My, my," Linda said. "Everybody's a boy scout these days."

"The baby!"

"The baby," Linda said, "is a baby. Dark hair, blue eyes, sort of like you only without funny teeth. What else can I tell you? Babies are babies. He walks and talks and craps like all babies. And he says 'daddy' plain as can be for Jed, and maybe if I saw enough of him he'd get the hang of 'mama' too. So much for baby."

"Show me a picture of him."

Linda smiled and shook her head. "Oh, no. I thought of that before I came here. No pictures on me. You can search. Didn't think it would be a good idea if you got hold of a picture of our baby. People might wonder, and that would be bad. Bad for me, and bad for little Larry Weston. Jed's got a lot of money settled on the kid, and nothing's going to get in the way of that. Now, what'll we talk about?"

"I want to see him."

Linda's glass was empty. She held it out to me, but I ignored her. She pulled herself to her feet and walked over to the bar and made her own. "Not a chance, even if I wanted to, which I don't. Little Larry has an English governess in charge of him night and day—did you know that with the war in England, this country's infested with English governesses? I don't think there's one left over there. And she has full instructions from Jed about little Larry, and when Mommy 'smells funny'—isn't that cute? That's what we say around our house when Mommy is tying one on— she can't even see little Larry." Linda's face started puckering up like an old peach. "Oh Christ, Milton . . ."

She was crying. I felt a tug for her, but I made myself ignore it. "I want to see him, Linda. I've got to. She must take him out somewhere, sometime."

Linda brushed the hair back that had fallen over her face. "In Beverly fuckin' Hills? Christ, there aren't even sidewalks for walking. He goes out on the back lawn. That's all! And with that damn Limey broad. Give it up, Milton."

"Just once." I said it more to myself than to Linda. She didn't hear me. She was too busy trying to stop her tears.

The room grew still except for the sounds of Linda's sniffling. We sat across from each other for a long time and didn't speak. I kept thinking about how I could get to my child, and asking myself why he mattered so much to me, more than maybe anyone else in the whole world.

Linda had her head back against the couch, staring straight up at the ceiling. I didn't know until she spoke whether she was awake or asleep. When she did, her voice sounded far away, as if she were talking to herself. "Isn't it funny about us, Milton? You didn't get what you wanted, and I did, and neither one of us is happy. Only Jed. He has a son and a studio, and maybe that's enough for him. I should have married you, Milton, but who knew then?"

I must have grunted or something, because Linda went on. "You know what, Milton? I'm going down the drain, and I don't even care. I got all the way to the top, just where I wanted to be, and now I'm on the big slide downhill, and I don't give a single, solitary shit. I got everything, things my mother never even heard of back in Nebraska, I got it all, and I wish I never did. I wish I could have spent my whole life wanting, because wanting turned out to be better than getting. I built my whole life on wanting things, and it got kicked right out from under me. So I decided to make the return trip down from up there, and I got lots of friends in bottles to help me. Old Granddad. My best friend. The only one who knows me and who doesn't want something from me. He puts his picture on every bottle to tell me he's thinking of me, and he keeps me warm at night, and he takes away the headaches in the morning, and he bucks me up on the set. Oh, the things he does for me. Sometimes I rub his bottle against my breasts and he makes me feel good. And once I took the bottle and I stuck it—"

"Linda, for Chrissake, shut up."

The room was silent again. I closed my eyes, and I saw Linda the way she was when I first met her at the Beverly Hills Hotel, and the first night we were together. And then her face slipped away and there was the yawning baby. I tried to picture him with dark hair and blue eyes, walking and laughing and in my arms saying "daddy" to me.

Suddenly, I felt a hand crawling up the inside of my thigh. I opened my eyes. Linda was on the floor in front of my chair. I pushed her hand away. She smiled. "Just for old times' sake, Milton."

"I'm in love with someone else," I said.

She snorted. "Come on, Milton. This is Linda you're talking to. Don't give me that love crap. People like us, we don't love. We make love, but we don't love. You got to put your guard down for that, and we never do. Either you want to make it with me or you don't, but don't tell me about love, okay?"

She put her hand back on my leg. I stood up to shake it off. "I don't. Come on, you're going home."

I yanked her to her feet. She fell against me. "I can't go home. Drunk."

"I'll drive you."

That jerked her to her senses for a moment. "No. Jed! I think he watches me."

And then she folded up. I caught her before she hit the floor. "Linda? Linda?" I put her on the couch and slapped her face a couple of times. She moaned once, but that was all. She was out for the night.

I went through her purse and found her car keys. Then I picked her up in my arms with the fur jacket over her face in case anyone should see her, and carried her out to her car, in the driveway. I arranged her in the front passenger seat and folded the jacket high around her neck and shoulders to partially hide her face.

The Weston house, a long Mediterranean stucco job that took up over half a block of Beverly Hills property, was only a couple of blocks away.

There were lights on in the house. I drove around the block while I tried to figure out what to do. I thought of parking the car a couple of houses down the way, but that was no good. The Beverly Hills police circled all night. With no parking along the street, they were sure to spot the car and investigate. Linda would make the morning editions of all the local papers, and her face would be on the wire services across the country by midday. Linda had to go home.

I pulled into her driveway, shut off the motor, and hopped out. I ran around to Linda's side, praying that Jed didn't have prowl dogs, and opened the door. Linda fell toward me. I caught her before she came out of the car. I grabbed a shoulder with one hand and shoved the other one under her fanny and gave one swift push so that she went over to the driver's seat. I looked toward the house. Nothing had changed. I took Linda's head and put it down on the steering wheel so that her forehead rested on the horn button. Dogs started barking all over the neighborhood as the horn went off. I slammed the door and ran.

I was about a block away when a patrol car swung its light on me. "Stop right there, buddy!"

I froze and waited. A policeman came over, his hand on his hip. I turned so he could see my face. He relaxed. "Oh, Mr. Berle! You gave us a start for a minute. What are you doing out here?"

I laughed. "Just down the block, playing a little poker with some friends. I thought I'd run home. Actors don't get much exercise, you know."

The cop smiled. "Sorry, you'll have to do it in your bedroom. You know the law in Beverly Hills. Hop in. We'll drive you home."

Thank God. I don't think I could have run another block.

My problems with Joyce were settled in November, 1941. I had been depressed since Linda's visit. All of it hurt, but her crack about my being unable to really love someone hit deepest, I think because it had a ring of truth to it for me. I started thinking of all the women who had passed through my life. What did I really feel for them? How much? There were even some whose names I could no longer remember.

Then the telephone rang. It was Joyce from New York. "I didn't think I'd catch you at home," she said.

"Don't believe everything you read in the columns," I said.

"I don't, but I do believe the pictures. I've seen you with those other women." Her voice changed. "I can't take it anymore, Milton. You've got to make up your mind, and now. Either you want to be with me or you want to be with them."

"Ah, Joyce."

"I mean it, Milton. It's no good this way for me. Tell me. Me or them."

Everything Linda had got me thinking about went straight out of my head at that moment. "You, Joyce. I want you." I had said it at last, and I meant it.

We were laughing and crying together across the country. And we talked about our wedding. I promised to call her as soon as I could clear with the studio about some time off for our wedding and honeymoon.

When I hung up, I felt more alive than I had in years. It was as if some brick wall that I didn't know was inside of me had been knocked down.

Now, all I had to do was tell Mama.

❧ 18 ❧

Of course, Mama threw a scene when I told her. You could accuse my mother of a lot of things, but being a typical Jewish mother wasn't one of them. There I was, thirty-two years old, with my mother shouting at me, "What do you need marriage for?" You understand, it wasn't Joyce that Mama was against. It would have been any woman. They were all threats to what Mama saw as her partnership with me.

I'll give her credit, though. Wrong as she was to try to hang on to me, she never revealed her thoughts and feelings to anyone but me. "Go ahead, sleep with her, but why tie yourself down with marriage?" Mama shouted at me. But a day later, she told Bill Wickersham of the *Los Angeles Examiner*, " 'For the first time there'll be a beauty in the Berle family, and Joyce is as sweet as she is lovely.' " I'll bet that statement made Rosalind and my brothers' wives feel warm inside!

According to Wickersham, it was Mama who went to the airport to meet Joyce when she arrived at the end of November, 1941, because I was tied up on the set of *A Gentleman at Heart*, with Cesar Romero and Carole Landis. But on the same day that Mr. Wickersham had Joyce getting off the plane at Los Angeles, the wire services had a picture of Joyce sitting on her suitcase in the middle of the railroad tracks at Pasedena and waiting for me to pick her up. In other words, the coming marriage got plenty of publicity.

We originally planned to be married on November 27, 1941, but I couldn't get time off from the picture. All I could manage was to skip a lunch break so that Joyce and I could get down to City Hall for our license.

The wedding finally took place on December 4, with Judge Edward Brant performing the ceremony in the living room on Palm Drive in front of thirty of our closest relatives and friends.

Maybe I was the last man in America to find out that marriage is a two-person arrangement, but now I can look back on my wedding day and see that I hadn't really thought too much about *being* married. I had it mixed up with *getting* married. If I thought about it at all, I guess I just decided it meant one woman instead of a herd of them. So all I had to do was get through the ceremony, and then the party would be on again. I never let it sink in that the wedding day was Joyce's day too. Things like consideration for Joyce's feelings, and sharing plans, and tenderness just didn't cross my mind. I had something to celebrate, and that was something I knew how to do.

I took most of the wedding party to the Florentine Gardens, where N.T.G. (Nils T. Granlund) was opening his big revue, *Stars Over Hollywood*, with Paul Whiteman and his band. In our party were Mama, Phil, Frank, Jack, and Rosalind, Lou Jackson, and a whole pack of my friends. The only person Joyce had was her mother, Mrs. Gladys Mathews.

We got a big ovation when we came in. The whole town knew about the wedding that afternoon. N.T.G. made a big fuss over greeting us, and he did all the usual newlywed jokes. "There's Milton and Joyce. What are *they* doing here tonight? Well, that's four hours shot to hell!" And I tossed back some of my own, including a reference to Paul Whiteman's new shape as his "design for Livingston," a reference to his wife, Margaret Livingston.

It was a great party, as I remember it. I was successful, I was married to a very beautiful woman, I was getting laughs and lots of attention. It didn't mean anything to me that Joyce was very quiet. That was just Joyce. I was having a great time, so she was having a great time. But years later, I read a quote of Joyce's: "I just remember *that* was my wedding night. In a nightclub. I didn't cry at the table when they made jokes about us. I just kept telling myself things will be different. You live with this thing about we'll just float away to this white cottage and be alone, and hold hands the rest of our lives. Right? Well, now I know better. When you marry a man, you're going to live just the way he is. And he's going to marry you the way you are."

Maybe it was because the women in my past wanted to be seen out with me to help their own careers—I don't know—but, looking back, I can't even explain to myself what the hell I was thinking of then. Joyce and I didn't have our honeymoon alone. The night after the Florentine Gardens, I had to report for one day's work on *A Gentleman at Heart* before I was free for a honeymoon. We went on Saturday, December 6, 1941, to the Arrowhead Springs Hotel at Lake Arrowhead. It was Joyce and me—and Mama and my brother Frank and his wife. My good friend, Jimmy Ritz, and his then-wife Ruth were also up there. To be fair to everyone, especially Mama, it was my idea to take the crowd along. I don't know where my head was at the time, but I have a pretty good idea.

What is there about making it, for some of us, that requires a mob around all the time? I think it's a way of convincing ourselves that we're important. We look around at all the people we schlepp along and pick up the tabs for and then say, as if we didn't know why all those people were there, well, we must really be something or all these people wouldn't want to be around us.

It wasn't much of a honeymoon, but I can't take all the blame. The day after we got to Arrowhead, Joyce and I were sitting around the lawn with Jimmy and Ruthie Ritz, just soaking up the sun and talking. The portable radio I had brought along was on the grass beside me. Suddenly, the music stopped and we got the announcement of the Japanese attack on Pearl Harbor.

The next day, I had to leave to get back to the studio. There was a rush on to finish pictures in production. No one knew what the war was going to do to Hollywood, what materials would be available, who would still be in civilian clothes. I left my bride behind at Arrowhead with Mama and Frank's wife.

It was a couple of days before I could get back to Joyce at Arrowhead for the last few days of what we still called a honeymoon. I asked Joyce what she had done while I was away, and she shrugged sort of sadly. "What do you do on a honeymoon without your husband? We talked and ate and swam, you know, and I played cards with your mother. She taught me."

"If Mama taught you to play cards, you don't know nothin' about cards," I told her. "Any trouble?"

"No, why should there be? Your mother is very nice to me."

And when I asked Mama about Joyce, she said, "She's a nice girl. Very pretty. I don't know if I'd call her a wife. She's still a child."

"She'll grow older, Mama, I promise you."

Mama shook her head with the wisdom of the ages. "For your sake, I hope so." But she didn't sound optimistic.

That night, when Joyce and I were alone, I told her, "I've got a surprise for you when we get back to Hollywood."

"What?" Joyce was more woman than my mother ever knew, but she could be a kid about a surprise. "What? Tell me, please."

"You wait and see, but you're going to love it." And I added, in case she was wondering, "This surprise is just for you and me, and for nobody else."

Joyce beamed. "I love it already."

I had leased a house for us at 914 North Roxbury Drive. It wasn't too far away from the Tom Mix house on Palm Drive that I had shared with Mama, but it was away from Mama. It was a huge place, done in extreme modern for its time, and set way back from the street. It had four bedrooms, plus a den that could serve as a fifth, which added up to four more bedrooms than we needed, but what the hell? I was feeling like a big shot and showing off for Joyce. Naturally, there was a swimming pool behind the house. Your own pool was a big status symbol in those days. Another sign of how important you were was that you were never caught swimming in the pool, which cost plenty in upkeep.

I think at the beginning Joyce wanted very much to be all the things the ladies' magazines said a wife was supposed to be. But I'm afraid that all she got the chance to be was pretty. Even if she had known how to cook, she wouldn't have had a chance. We had a cook for what few evenings we stayed home, and she was always on duty for the Sunday cookouts around the pool. And there was a maid for the other household duties. Between them, they took care of everything. I was at the studio every day. In 1942 and '43 I was in three pictures, *Over My Dead Body*, *Whispering Ghosts*, and, the best one of all, Otto Preminger's production of *Margin for Error*, Clare Booth Luce's comedy. If I wasn't at the studio, I was doing War Bond rallies or taking entertainment units to military bases in California. When I got home at the end of a day, I wanted to unwind, loosen up, and there was nothing in my background that had taught me you did that at home. Where I unwound was out in public where people gawked at you, or interrupted your dinner for autographs, and masters of ceremonies turned the spotlight on you.

And there was still Mama. She quickly found reasons why the house on Palm Drive wasn't for her. I had stood up to her only once, when I married Joyce. I couldn't seem to do it again. I gave in, and I got her a house in the 700 block on Roxbury, only two blocks away from us. I tried to convince myself that if it wasn't for me, who else would Mama have, but I knew that was crap. Frank was in New York and Rosalind was in Florida, but Phil and Jack had also settled in Los Angeles. Sure, Mama saw them, but it was me she wanted the most from. I was still her passport to the places she wanted to go, the people she wanted to mingle with.

I talked a lot about our house on Roxbury as home, my home, but I don't think it ever felt that way to Joyce, who had grown up with more of an idea of what home really meant. What I had called home could have been any one of the hotel rooms I used to stay at. It was still a place where I went to change clothes, to sleep, to make love to a woman; the only difference now was that the woman was my wife.

I remember once being aware of the sadness I saw growing in Joyce's eyes. There had been too many nights in a row going from club to club with a mob of friends and hangers-on, with Joyce just there at my side, smiling but silent. So I planned an evening for just the two of us. Out, of course, because I wasn't thinking that clearly yet. About a half-hour before we were set to go, the doorbell rang, and there was Mama, in a long dress and her fur jacket.

I exploded. "Mama, we want to be alone for once!"

Mama stepped past me into the house as if I had given her a welcoming kiss. She turned around so I could see her. "What's the matter? I'm not dressed well enough?"

I knew I was lost, and Joyce knew it too. I heard a door slam upstairs. I went up to her. Joyce was sitting at her dressing table, the tears running down her face. I tried to turn her around to me, but she shook me off. "Please, Joyce, please, baby. Try to understand. I'll work this out. I swear."

Joyce nodded, but she couldn't stop the tears. I took her in my arms. "Please don't cry. You know I love you, only . . ."

Joyce shook her head. "Oh, Milton, it's not just your mother. It's everybody. We're with the whole world every night. We're never alone. I don't feel important to you, and I want to. Sometimes I feel like I'm not there at all. Or I'm just another person at your table. I want to be important to you."

I held her close, and I could feel her tears soaking into my jacket. "Joyce, you are, you are. I'm sorry, I'm just doing it all wrong, I guess."

Mama called up the stairs, "Hey, up there! Enough in the bedroom. There's a lady down here starving to death!"

"We'll be right down, Queenie!" I shouted. "What do you want me to do, Joyce? Tell me, and I'll do it. You want me to tell her to go home?"

Joyce shook her head. "No, it's your mother. You can't." She took a look at her face in the mirror. "I'm a mess."

"Not to me. You're gorgeous."

"With these eyes? Red like a rabbit. Look, I don't feel hungry anyway. Why don't you take your mother out to dinner. Just the two of you. I'll find something in the refrigerator. Tell her I don't feel well."

"You sure?"

Joyce smiled for the first time. "Sure."

I gave her a peck on the cheek. "Okay, and I'll come straight home after. You be wearing something gorgeous—but not too much, huh? And we'll have the rest of the evening, just the two of us."

Joyce threw herself into my arms and gave me a long kiss.

Only it didn't work out as planned. Mama didn't want just dinner. She was dressed for a night on the town, so it was one of the big clubs. I figured we'd eat and catch the ten-o'clock show, and then I'd drop Mama and beat it home to Joyce. But have you ever been to a nightclub where the floor show went on on time? At 10:00, they were still squeezing in the tables. It was 10:30 before the show began. For once in my life, I was hoping that I wouldn't be introduced from the floor, but the m.c. spotted me, and there was applause and the lights hit me, and that was it. I was off and running, everything but the laughs and the applause driven out of my mind. And then there were people at the table, slapping me on the back, saying, "Remember me?", ordering drinks on my bill. The party was on again.

I didn't get home until one in the morning. There was a light on in the bedroom. I went up, and there was Joyce, looking absolutely sensational in a lacy negligee, sound asleep on the bed. I didn't have the heart to wake her. She stirred in her sleep and mumbled my name when I pulled the covers over her, but she was out for the night.

Considering so much of our courtship had taken place at night, after her show, between my shows and after, it came as a surprise to me after we were married to find out that Joyce wasn't a night person. If she could stay awake long enough, until she got her second wind, Joyce could make a night of it, but it didn't come naturally to her. Given her choice, she'd prefer going to bed early. Either way, unless she was completely knocked out from the night before, Joyce was an early riser. When it was morning she was up and cheerful, and when it grew dark outside she was ready for bed. I got better as the day rolled on, and at night I was at my best. Even with my trouble sleeping, forget me in the morning. It's the worst part of my day.

When did we start thinking that our marriage was in trouble? I can't tell you, because I don't think either of us knew. There were just things that were wrong, but there were things wrong with every couple, with every marriage. I know I wasn't easy to live with. When I wasn't working on a picture, I was doing radio broadcasts for overseas troops or taking a unit to a camp somewhere. And there were always the scratch sheets, and the bookies, and the track, and the phone calls that went with the betting. And there were the meetings with agents and producers and writers about future projects. And at night there were the clubs you went to because a friend was opening, the previews that the studio requested your presence at, the parties you went to because they were important. And, of course, there was always Mama.

I expected Joyce to be part of everything. She had been in the business. She was supposed to understand. And I guess she expected me to understand that it was all rough on her, that she had been somebody in her own right before she married me and I had reduced her to being nothing more than the prettiest member of a mob scene. She talked about going back to work again, and I objected. She tried to tell me that meeting the girls for lunch didn't make for the most exciting life, but I was still against her going to work. So we talked about having a baby, but it didn't happen for us. According to the doctors we consulted, there was no reason why we couldn't have a baby, but we didn't.

Mama, of course, was against the idea of a baby when I mentioned it to her. "Do you have time for a baby? Does Joyce? Both of you rush here, rush there. You can't do that with a baby. A baby is a taker. It takes everything from the parents. Pleasure is all it can give. It needs time, and care, and a home. It needs a father at home, and it needs a mother with it, not a shopper!"

Mama knew where to plant the needles when she wanted to. And she knew that Joyce's passion for shopping was driving me crazy. She tossed money around as if it were confetti. I was making big money, but between me and my horses and Joyce and her shopping sprees, I was always in hock.

But most of the time, at the beginning, I kept quiet about her spending. I felt the acids churning inside of me, but I didn't say anything because I felt guilty. At least she had something to show for the money she tossed away most of the time, while all I had was IOUs and slips of paper from the bookies. And I kept quiet because I had the idea that Joyce would simmer down when we were happier, and that would come if I could ever straighten things out about Mama being with us so much.

I thought we were out of the woods when I got the offer I had dreamed of since the 1930s. The Shuberts wanted me for a new edition of the *Ziegfeld Follies* they were going to put on in the spring of 1943.

I had just finished *Margin for Error*, and there was nothing holding me in Hollywood. I talked it over with Joyce, and the idea of getting back to New York, the theater, and her friends made her face light up. The army was no problem to me. I had taken a physical and been turned down. The doctors took one look at my crazy feet, asked how much I paid for shoes that allowed me to walk comfortably with toes wrapped over one another like strands of spaghetti, gulped at the price, and said that I could do more by entertaining the troops than I could as a soldier.

We both thought New York would mean Joyce and me alone, but we guessed wrong. When I told Mama about the *Follies*, she said she'd be right there cheering me on as usual. "It's time we went back to work," she said.

"What are you talking about? I've got to go to New York. Your home is out here now, Mama." Don't worry, I knew what she was talking about, but I was hoping to head her off.

Mama laughed. "So? Your home is out here, and you're going to New York to work. What's the difference? Our home is where we work. It always was, it always will be."

"Mama! For Chrissake, I'm married now!"

"Don't raise the voice to me, Milton. I'm still your mother. And don't tell me that you're married. I know. I know. I meet the lady every now and then when she finishes buying out the department stores—"

"Lay off, Mama."

"And don't tell me about you're married when we are talking about doing a show. You're not married on the stage, are you? It's not going to say the *Ziegfeld Follies* starring Milton Berle who is married, is it? Your career is you and me. That you're married is a different problem."

So we moved back to New York. Joyce and I took a large apartment at 875 Fifth Avenue, and Mama moved into the Essex House on Central Park South.

The Essex House was the scene of a story about my mother that got wide circulation. It was passed around as a gag, but it actually happened.

First, I have to tell you that I spoke with my mother every day of her life. Either I saw her or I'd telephone her, no matter where I was. That became so well known that it even made Ripley once. "Believe it or not, Milton Berle has called his mother every day for the last twenty years."

So one day I called her at the Essex House, and Miss Finnegan, the operator, said that Mama had left word that she was on her way down to the lobby if I called. Miss Finnegan said to hold on while she paged Mama. I don't know what it's like now, but at the time of this story, the house phones at the Essex House were in open booths right out in the middle of the lobby. After maybe a minute's wait, I heard the lobby phone pick up. Mama said, "Hello?"

I said hello back, and I heard Mama say in a loud voice so that the whole lobby could hear, "Is this my son, Milton Berle?"

That was Queenie, a star anyway she could make it.

There were almost as many producers as there were principals involved in the *Ziegfeld Follies of 1943*. The show was put on by the brothers Shubert in association with Alfred Bloomingdale and Lou Walters, and, of course, with the permission of Billie Burke, who was the widow of Florenz Ziegfeld, Jr. I was the first performer ever to get his name starred over the title, breaking a longtime tradition of the *Follies*. But then, this was *a* Ziegfeld Follies, without Ziegfeld himself in charge. Other top performers were Ilona Massey, Arthur Treacher, Jack Cole, Sue Ryan, Dean Murphy, Imogene Carpenter, Bill and Cora Baird with their puppets. Also featured was a very sexy lady named Christine Ayres, who was better known in burlesque circles as Charmaine. Our director was one of the greats, John Murray Anderson.

There's an old saying among businessmen that when the business is good, the partnership is fine no matter what happens, but everything is wrong between the partners when the business is no good. I think you could say that about a marriage, too. There was the continuous triangle of Mama, Joyce, and me that I wasn't strong enough to break; there was the unhappiness between Joyce and me over the baby we wanted but couldn't seem to have; and there was the whole crazy life that we were leading. It all added up to stresses and strains between us, my yelling and Joyce crying, and then the making up, which was always sweet and warm and full of love. And afterward we'd look at each other and wonder what the hell the fight was all about, and we'd swear not to do that to each other ever again—until the next time. We were in trouble, and we didn't even know it yet.

Whatever we did to each other, whatever hell one of us put the other through, we trusted each other. I think that's why one scene stands out in my mind—not because it was such a big fight, because it wasn't, but because it said something new and bad was eating into our marriage.

As part of its pre-Broadway shakedown, the *Ziegfeld Follies* played Boston. Elliot Norton, Boston's leading critic, gave us a good review, and while that didn't guarantee a hit when we came into New York, it gave us reason to hope. On top of that, the show that was set to open on Broadway the night before us was supposed to be a dog, which might make us look better. Its producers, the Theatre Guild, had already changed its name from *Away We Go* to *Oklahoma!*, and the story had gone around about Lawrence Langner of the Guild inviting Mike Todd and Billy Rose up to see the new musical and give their opinion. Both of them told Langner that *Oklahoma!* didn't stand a chance.

Anyway, one day during a rehearsal, Joyce came to the theater and saw me with my arm around the shoulder of Lucy Cochrane, one of the girls in the show. I didn't think anything about it, because I wasn't up to anything. I was just talking to Lucy about some bit of business in the show. But when I got back to the Ritz, where Joyce and I were staying, Joyce started in accusing me of carrying on with Lucy. It was crazy. In a business where everybody kisses on the lips when they say hello, and where you even call strangers "darling," what the hell does putting an arm around a girl's shoulder in front of a whole cast mean? Joyce, who had certainly been with enough shows, knew that, but I guess she wasn't in any shape to understand. And with the tensions I had with a new show coming to Broadway, I wasn't in much of a mood to be patient and understanding. So we screamed at each other and said terrible things. Joyce got so angry she yanked off her wedding ring and threw it down the toilet. Thank God, she wasn't sore enough to flush the toilet. Later, when we had both calmed down and admitted how crazy we had been, I went into the toilet bowl up to the elbow and fished out the ring.

But only later could I see that that silly fight marked the first time distrust had ever shown up in our marriage.

Opening nights are always hell, but April 1, 1943, the night the *Ziegfeld Follies of 1943* opened at the Winter Garden in New York, was the worst because of what had happened the night before. That dog the Theatre Guild was stuck with, *Oklahoma!*, turned out to be the smash hit of the century, with the critics screaming that it marked a change in the look of musical comedy.

Oklahoma! was cheered because it got rid of the standard chorus line, because it integrated ballet with the story line, because it got rid of the standard opening production number, and God knows what else. And there we were opening the next night with chorus girls hoofing their brains out and big production numbers. The artiest material we had in the *Follies* dealt with black marketeers and zoot suiters.

Just before the opening of the *Follies*, Harry Kaufman, who was the guiding genius of the Shubert organization in those days, came back to see me. "How long is your opening monologue, Milton?"

I said, "About eleven minutes."

Harry said, "I want you to cut it down to five tonight."

"Why?"

"It's a very sharp crowd out front there. We've got to grab them and hold them. Cut all of the standard jokes. I want you to sort of give a new flavor to the opening."

The opening number had all the chorus boys on stage in top hats and tails. I was in the back row. There were specialties with a boy stepping out of the line to do his bit. When it came my turn, I moved forward, tripped, and fell on my face, at which point the audience recognized me.

"Cut! Everybody get off the stage!" was my first line. From that point on, I was thinking as I worked, doing the monologue. "See what happens when the Shuberts put on a *Follies?* This couldn't have happened if Ziggy was around today."

The crack got a big laugh, telling me that the audience was very theater-wise. They knew what the name Ziegfeld stood for with a show, and they knew all about the Shubert reputation for saving a buck. I knew which way to go—hip and inside. "How do you like the costumes, folks? They're left over from *Blossom Time* and *The Student Prince.*" The more I worked with inside material, the more the audience liked it.

The notices the next day started the lines at the box office. Not that the critics liked everything about the show. Most of them took swipes at the sketches for not being terribly funny and the music for not being very memorable. My notices were great, but the praise centered on material I had been doing for years all over the vaudeville circuit and nightclubs.

Ward Morehouse, in the New York *Sun*, summed up what turned out to be wartime New York's attitude toward our big girlie revue: "But it's my prediction that this first *Follies* in seven years is going to have a wallop at the box office. As one veteran first-nighter remarked last evening, it's something for which the tired welder has been waiting."

On the night of the second performance, Harry Kaufman came back to my dressing room again, grinning from ear to ear. "We're in, Milton. Tonight, I don't care how long the opening runs. Throw the whole book at them if you want."

The trick with a long-running show is to keep it as fresh as it was on opening night and like it was on opening night. But about seven months after we opened, on a cold night in November, something happened that changed the look of the *Follies*. My dressing room didn't have a bathroom, so I had to use the one across the stage. As usual, I showed up at the theater about ten minutes before the overture and raced into my tails for the opening. This night I also had to make a stop at the john. It was bitter cold and sleeting outside, and the john window was slightly open. With my nervousness about catching colds, I immediately tried to close the window. It stuck. I slammed down on the top of the frame with my palm, and my hand went right through the window. The first thing I was aware of was the murmur of an audience in its seats, and the sound of the orchestra tuning up, which meant curtain time. Then the pain started growing in my right hand. There was an ugly gash from the top of my thumb right down through the center of my palm.

They had to hold the show up for about forty minutes while the management rushed in a doctor to stitch up my hand. When the curtain went up, I entered with a big bandage on my hand and a giant lump of bandage where my thumb was. It looked ridiculous—I had asked the doctor to exaggerate the bandage on the thumb—but because of the long delay on the opening curtain, the audience didn't know whether to laugh or not. I had to do something to get them into the *Follies* mood.

"You must think I got into trouble, right? Wrong. I'll tell you why I got this on. You see, this show's been running for seven months. Now, at the beginning, everybody likes each other, but actors will be actors, and they start trying to steal scenes from each other. Well, you've got to protect yourself, so that's why I'm wearing this white thing. So any time you see me do this"—I held up the bandaged hand and wiggled it with the thumb sticking straight up—"you'll know it's me."

The audience laughed and relaxed, and I turned the thumb, which was killing me, into a running gag. In the first sketch, which was about meat rationing, I always made my first appearance coming up from behind a butcher's counter. This time I sent the thumb up first and wiggled it, for another laugh. I used that thumb right through the show and even into my final curtain call.

That bandage became such a terrific piece of business that I kept it in the show even after the cut had healed. And it led to a great final laugh on the show. As the star of the *Ziegfeld Follies*, I came on for last bow with the entire cast on stage. They were all standing there with their hands behind their backs. I gave the audience the high sign with my bandaged thumb. The audience laughed. Then, as I went into my bow, the entire cast brought their hands out from behind their backs, and every one of them held up a bandaged thumb. It brought the house down.

I suppose if I had ever gone to a shrink, I could have uncovered and gotten rid of the drive that made me keep pushing myself on and on. Once again, I was on top of the heap and it wasn't enough. I had my name up in lights over one of the most prestigious names in show business, Ziegfeld, and I couldn't let myself stop to enjoy it. Somewhere inside, I guess, I was still hearing the hungry cries of the Berlingers—Milton, bring home money; Milton, keep the food coming; more, Milton, more. So I took on a column in *Variety*, which I called "The Berle-ing Point." It was a collection of whatever I heard around town, plus every gag I ever knew, plus every switch on every gag I ever knew.

I co-produced a farce called *Same Time Next Week*, which starred the dancers Paul and Grace Hartman as a famous radio team. When the show opened in Boston, Elliot Norton called it "an inept comedy, inexpertly written, poorly directed and badly acted." It died a quick death. At least that was some money of mine that the bookies didn't get.

Then there was radio, first with Ballantine Beer sponsoring *The Milton Berle Show*, then with Eversharp for a program called *Let Yourself Go*. It might have been a great show for television, but we only had radio then. The idea was that listeners wrote in describing their suppressed desires, and the writers selected got a chance to act them out on the show. Each week we had a guest star. Zasu Pitts was on the opening show. Her secret desire was to knock off a top hat with snowballs. I wore the hat. Later on in the run of the show, we had Grace Moore, with her dress secured in place, singing "One Night of Love" while standing on her head. The studio audience had a good time every week, but what the radio listeners across country got out of it, I'll never know. (The best part of the show, for my money, were the special comedy parodies written by a young man named Alan Jay Lerner who was destined to write bigger things—namely *My Fair Lady*.)

The show went on on Tuesday nights from 7 to 7:30. From there, I went over to the Winter Garden to do the *Follies*, and then back to the radio studio to do the repeat broadcast for the West Coast.

Whenever I could I did benefits for all sorts of charities, and every possible soldier show. I personally paid the bill one Sunday to take the entire cast of the *Follies* to Camp Upton to do the whole show for the soldiers there.

Anyway, as busy as I was back in 1944 with the *Ziegfeld Follies*, my radio show, soldier shows, and benefits, I always found time to lose money on the horses. I made lots of audiences laugh, but no one enjoyed me more than the bookmakers.

Hell, I was getting laughs all over the place, except at home. Joyce and I loved each other, but we weren't the happiest of couples.

❧ 19 ❧

Joyce never swore. Maybe if she had, that would have been an outlet when things got too much for her. But she didn't, so when it really got bad, she threw whatever her hand touched first. Once she was by the telephone when we were arguing about something. Before I knew it, I got clipped on the head by the telephone receiver. Most of the time it was something little, like an ashtray, that flew across the room. And, thank God, Joyce never aimed.

That may not sound like we were in love, but we were. It's just that there was so much wrong with us. There was Mama, of course, who was always polite to Joyce, but who was always with us, just as if I had never gotten married, or even grown up. There were the career demands on my time, and the mob of hangers-on that was always around, so that Joyce and I were never alone too much. There was my gambling, and Joyce's wild shopping sprees. Between the two, the money ran with the speed of Niagara. There were my desires to unwind nights after the *Follies* at Lindy's and other night spots, and there was Joyce's claim that she wasn't a night person. There was Joyce's desire to go back to work, and some male stubbornness in me that didn't want her to. There was the baby we both wanted and couldn't seem to have. We could always find something to argue about. The only good that came out of the arguments was the making up.

One problem settled itself when Joyce and I finally decided to adopt a child. Joyce said that if we had a choice she wanted a girl, and that was okay by me. We made applications with every good adoption agency we heard about, filled out stacks of forms, went through interviews—and then waited.

One morning, I was having a meeting in our living room with writers on the radio show. The room was gray with cigar smoke, ashtrays were jammed with butts, and dirty coffee cups were everywhere. All the guys had their collars open and their ties hanging loose. The place looked like an all-night poker session had taken place. The doorbell rang, and Joyce came out of the bedroom and worked her away across the living room like Eliza crossing the ice, jumping from clear space to clear space over the papers that were everywhere.

She came back with a neatly dressed older woman. Joyce looked like she was in pain. "Milton, this is Mrs. Anderson from the adoption people."

I jumped up, spilling cigar ashes down my shirt. I got all confused between trying to get rid of my cigar, shake Mrs. Anderson's hand, and fix my tie, all at the same time. And I started trying to explain what was going on. Joyce, meanwhile, was opening windows and trying to fan the smoke out with her hands.

We were in luck. Mrs. Anderson turned out to be a fan of mine— even asked for my autograph—and didn't see anything that suggested we would be unfit parents. So we went back to waiting and hoping.

Meanwhile, Joyce was after me to let her go back to work. Not that I was the kind of husband that gave orders and expected them to be obeyed. I guess I was a little old-fashioned, but not *that* old-fashioned. I think I didn't want Joyce to go back to work because somehow it meant that I wasn't enough for her. When I said it to her, she looked at me as if I were crazy. "You, of all people, Milton, shouldn't be saying that. Frankly, I don't know if you *are* enough for me, because I've never had all of you to myself, except when you're asleep. The rest of the time there's always other people around. You want me, and you want every comedy writer you're working with, and every bright young comic you discover, and your mother. You want the whole world at your table, but that's no good for me. Don't you understand, darling?"

I did. And I didn't want to. "Joyce, you knew me before we got married. You know this business. There are always people—"

"Because you *want* the people!"

"Not always. Be with me every night, Joyce, after the show, like I ask you. You know you come first with me." I was shifting the argument to

Joyce's ground, my anger with her over the excuses she made when she didn't come around to the Winter Garden after the show.

Joyce started pacing, frustration building to anger. "You just won't understand that everybody isn't made like you. I'm not a night person. No matter what time of night I get to bed, I wake up early. I can't help it, that's me. And I get tired early at night. I can't run around half the night the way you do!"

"Bull! You worry more about your looks than you do about being with me. That's why you go to sleep early."

"That's not true!"

"The hell it isn't. I catch you staring at yourself in the mirror all the time. And I hear you introducing yourself to people. It's 'Joyce Mathews Berle'! Why isn't 'Joyce Berle' enough for you?"

Joyce whirled on me. "Because I was Joyce Mathews a lot longer than I've been Joyce Berle! Maybe I wasn't as big a star as you, but I've worked in the profession, and people know me as Mathews. That's my stage name, and the people we see are in the same business I was in. They know me, or they recognize me, as Joyce Mathews, so I keep the name. That's all there is to it!"

"I don't buy that! Not for a minute. Being my wife is just a sideline for you! You never quit show business. You've still got the big career drive!"

Joyce burst into tears. "That shows how little you know me, Milton. Be with me, come home nights to me, and I never want to set foot on another stage! But I've got to feel important to someone. I don't feel important to you, and I'm getting so I don't feel important to myself anymore. That's why I want to go back to work."

I said, "To make you feel important, *I'd* have to stop working."

That argument ended that night when Joyce came around backstage at the *Follies.* Later on, when we were finally alone, we went through the routines of I-didn't-mean-what-I-said, and you-know-I-love-you-and-it-kills-me-when-I-hurt-you, the words we were beginning to say more and more to each other. Anyway, Joyce went to work.

But it didn't last for very long. She opened on November 24, 1943, in *Get Away, Old Man* by William Saroyan, and she was out of work thirteen performances later.

Her next show didn't do much better. It was a musical called *Allah Be Praised*, and Alfred Bloomingdale, of the department-store family, produced it. The show was in such trouble out of town that he called in

Cy Howard to doctor it. Howard watched the show twice, and then went to Bloomingdale, who asked his opinion. Cy told him, "If I were you, I'd close the show and keep the store open nights." That one opened on April 20, 1944, and ran for twenty performances.

Neither show did much for Joyce's career. I got more out of her shows than she did. When she was in rehearsal and performing, she didn't have time for shopping, and that meant a lot of money saved around our house.

The way I saw it, Joyce approached money the way a child did. It was meant to provide pleasure, but where it came from, how hard it was to get, and what could happen if it ran out didn't seem to cross her mind. Money just seemed to be made to be spent. And Joyce was as generous to herself as she was to whatever girlfriend was along shopping with her that day. It could be a lipstick or it could be an expensive dress, and Joyce would spot it in the store and say, "Oh, look at that! Isn't it darling? It would look just perfect on you. Try it on. Please."

And when whatever it was that was tried on turned out to look great, Joyce just had to give it to her friend. If a husband could stand that sort of thing—and I don't know one who could—he might be able to step back and think that there was something sweet and warm in Joyce's gestures. I didn't, but when I really hit the roof, Joyce's comeback about the money I threw away on horses from which you got absolutely nothing back made me twice as angry.

If Joyce and I were to end up with any money, the only solution was that my income not come straight to me. It went instead to Irving R. Kaufman, the lawyer who handled my money. Joyce and I got weekly allowances. I got $125 a week and Joyce got $150, which isn't bad pin money, because all the bills for rent and food and other necessary expenditures were paid by the lawyer. But the allowance system didn't work for either one of us. The bookies were always happy to take my IOUs, and the stores just thought it was great to let Mrs. Milton Berle say, "Charge it." Even so, I could almost count on it that, come Monday, Joyce would laugh and say, "Darling, I need fifty dollars." And lots of times it was "Can you spare a hundred until the end of the week?"

I was asleep one morning and I kept being disturbed by little rustling sounds, like paper crackling. I opened one eye, and there was Joyce with her hand in my pants pocket. I shook my head, "Uh uh." Joyce put the pants back over the chair, and I went back to sleep. Maybe she did this at other times that way, but I don't know. Because, with the gambling action I was getting, and the nighttime tabs I was picking up, I never knew for sure how much money—ten bucks or ten thousand—I was carrying from one day to the next.

But one day Joyce's system of self-service went too far. Back when I was in Hollywood, one of the people I got to know fairly well was Benny Siegel—no one ever called him Bugsy to his face! Every now and then I'd get together with him and some of his boys during the evening. One of Benny's favorite late-night hangouts was downstairs at the Trocadero, Billy Wilkerson's nightclub. It was like a wine cellar, and it had a piano. Benny and his boys used to take their dates down there. Even in the cellar, Benny always sat with his back against the wall, with at least one of his henchmen on either side.

The night I'm talking about, Benny was with some twenty-year-old blond. He said to me, "Get up on the floor, Milton, and give her one of your high-powered nightclub intros. She's a singer."

"Come on, Benny," I said. "There's nobody here except your table."

"Do it for me," Benny said.

So I got up on the floor, and just as if I was working a packed room upstairs at the Troc, I gave Miss Clydespeck, or whatever the hell her name was, the big buildup, to one table of eight people. "Now, ladies and gentlemen, it is my extreme pleasure to introduce a very, very darling young lady who's a popular singer of songs. I know you're going to enjoy her . . ." etc., etc.

I sat down, and Miss Clydespeck went over to the pianist and told him what she was going to sing. And she sang it, and she was pretty lousy. When she had finished and sat down with us again, Benny Siegel took off the pinky ring he wore and handed it to me. It had an eight-carat diamond in it. "This is for you," he said.

"What for?"

"Because I like you, that's why. Don't you remember the other day you were admiring it? So I want you to have it."

"I can't take it from you, Benny . . ."

Now, Benny Siegel was a handsome guy, but when he got mad he was scary. He would just glare at you, and you'd swear there was fire coming out of his eyes. "I said take it."

I took it. It was a flashy ring, and not my style at all, but I was impressed by it, just figuring out how many thousands it must have cost. And I wore it now and again, but I never said who gave it to me.

Whenever I wore it around Joyce, she always said something about it being too showy, and about how it would really look a lot better if she

did something with it for herself. I never offered it to her. It may sound
crazy if you didn't know Benny Siegel, but the ring had a sentimental
value for me.

Joyce and I went out one night while I was in the *Ziegfeld Follies*,
and I wore the ring. When I got undressed for bed that night, I emptied
my pockets on the table by the bed, and I thought I put the ring there
too.

I woke up the next morning around ten. Joyce's side of the bed was
empty. I called her name once or twice. No answer. So I figured she had
gone out. I got up, and when I started to dress I put on my wedding ring
and my wristwatch. It was then that I realized the diamond ring wasn't
there. I started searching the room, all the tables, then down on the floor,
looking under all the furniture. Could it have fallen off my finger when
I was hanging up my coat? I searched the front closet. Did I leave it in
the living room? Another search.

I kept thinking about that ring and the huge diamond all day. Joyce
came in around 5:30, as usual with some store-wrapped packages. I went
straight to her. "Joyce, I'm a wreck."

"What's the matter, dear?"

"My diamond ring. I can't find it anywhere."

Joyce opened the closet and hung up her coat. Over her shoulder she
said casually, as if she were reporting on the weather, "Oh, I took it."

It was like she had punched me in the stomach. "Whaaa?"

Joyce smiled. "I took it to Tiffany's. I thought you wouldn't mind if
I had it broken up and made into earrings."

I hit the roof. "Wouldn't mind! That's my ring. Did you even ask?"

Joyce seemed confused by my anger. "Well, I always told you that I
didn't like it on you, and I could really do something swell with it—"

"If I were going to give it to you, I'd give it to you. And anyway, you
should have asked me before you just took it. Now, I'll tell you what you're
going to do. You're going to get up early tomorrow and go straight to
Tiffany's. You be there the minute they open the doors, and you get that
ring back before they break up the stone."

She got it back—they hadn't started to work on the stone yet—but
if there was any lesson to be learned, Joyce didn't get it. Maybe a week
later, I woke up to find Joyce all dressed to go out for a day of shopping
with one of her girlfriends. I got that bright, innocent smile that was part
of Joyce. "Can you spare me two hundred, Milton?" We were back to
normal for us.

It was impossible to keep Joyce's spending hidden from Mama. If the bills could be kept away from her, the daily delivery of packages couldn't. "Milton, why don't you just make an offer to Saks Fifth Avenue to buy the place outright? It'll be cheaper than doing it a little at a time."

"Lay off, Mama."

"Listen, I've got a right to say what I'm thinking. We worked long and hard to get where we are. Are you just going to let Joyce throw it away?"

"Mama, you live at the Essex House, and those aren't rhinestones around your neck. And I gamble. If you want to complain about spending, complain about all of us. Why do you just pick on Joyce?"

Mama's hand went to her breast. "You and I worked for it, we got a right to a little foolishness—"

I cut her short. "And Joyce is my wife, Mama!"

"All right, but don't say I didn't warn you," she said, and marched out of the room.

I was still defending Joyce to Mama, and Mama to Joyce. Instead of taking any real stand, I was standing still and hoping that if I shouted enough and bluffed enough, everything would straighten out. Of course, it didn't.

One of my favorite late-night spots after Lindy's quieted down was La Martinique, the nightclub at Sixth Avenue and 57th Street. I made it a regular weeknight hangout after the first time I saw a young comic there named Jan Murray. I thought he was bright and fast and was going places, and it didn't hurt our growing friendship when he told me that I was his idol when he was first starting out.

Back in the wartime '40s, the nightclubs ran three shows a night, with the last one going on at 2:30 in the morning. Most of the time, that show played to half-filled rooms, but the word got around town that I was showing up almost every night for the late show and ad libbing with Jan Murray. The show sold out, and our friendship grew.

It led to a weekend when we were both free, which must have been in August of 1944 after the *Ziegfeld Follies* had closed. Joyce and I were going to Laurel in the Pines, in Lakewood, for a weekend, and I invited him to come along. When we got there, Joyce wanted to rest, so Jan and I agreed, after unpacking, to meet down in the recreation room for a game of pool.

I was in the middle of a shot when I glanced up from the table and saw Jan scratching at his crotch. At first I didn't say anything, but when he continued scratching, I said, "What's the matter with you? You got crabs?"

Jan's face turned red. "That's a terrible thing to say. I've never had anything like that."

"It's no crime, you know. Anybody can get them. It's not like a venereal disease."

"Please," Jan said, "drop it. Let's play pool."

But a few minutes later, without even being aware of it, he was scratching again. "There you go again," I said. "I'll bet you got crabs. And they don't go away by themselves."

"I don't want to talk about it."

"Look, Jan, let's find out. If you got them, we'll take a hop down to a drugstore and get some stuff that will get rid of them."

"Milton, please forget it."

But when it happened a third time, I insisted that Jan come to the men's room with me. When we got there I took him into one of the booths. I sat down on the seat cover, and Jan stood in front of me. With two of us in there, we couldn't close the door. I told Jan to drop his pants and shorts, and I started examining him. "You got them all right," I said, "but don't worry. We'll get some blue ointment and get rid of them easy."

At that moment, a man entered the room. He took one look at me seated in front of Jan Murray with his pants down and he froze. Jan looked over his shoulder and smiled at the guy. Jan pointed to me. He mouthed the words, "This is Milton Berle. He loves me."

The guy turned and ran.

The *Follies* closed on July 22, 1944, after 553 performances, the longest run of any *Ziegfeld Follies*.

It was back to radio and the nightclubs again. The radio shows came and went. As I've said before, radio was for the ear, and I was a visual comedian, so, as much as I wanted a big radio success, I really can't say I ever did better than okay. After *Let Yourself Go*, there was a show called *Kiss and Make Up*, in which I did a comedy version of John J. Anthony's *Court of Human Relations*. The audiences preferred Mr. Anthony's milking the misery to my mugging it.

The important addition to my nightclub work between 1944 and 1945 was Leonard Sues, who had been an MGM kid in movies like *Babes in Arms* and others, and had grown up to become a top conductor and trumpeter. I met him through his brother, who worked under the name of Jack Melvin as a Hollywood press agent. I hired Jack to do work for me when I was on the Coast in 1942. One day he asked me if I would hear his brother, Leonard. I did, and liked him. From that time on, whenever I took out a nightclub revue I would get Leonard Sues, if he was available, to conduct the band behind me, do some schticks with me, and his own trumpet solos.

We became friends, as did his mother, CeeCee Sues, who traveled with him, and mine. One night Leonard and I got to talking. I was feeling way down. I think there had been another argument between Joyce and myself, or I had lost my temper with someone in the show over one of the many details I can't seem not to worry about. And after blowing up, as usual I felt guilty and upset that someone might be sore at me. We were in my dressing room backstage at some club. "What's the matter with me, Leonard?" I said. "There's a packed club out front just waiting to see me, maybe jealous of the great life I'm supposed to be leading. I've got a gorgeous wife, I make good money. Hell, I've got everything, so why ain't I happy?"

It was then that Leonard Sues started telling me about himself and Christian Science, and what it had done for him. He took out his copy of *Science and Health*, by Mary Baker Eddy, and read passages to me. I liked what I heard, but I was doubtful. "I'm a Jew, Leonard. Maybe not devout, I wasn't raised that way, but I'm a Jew."

And Leonard said, "There are many Jews who participate in Christian Science. It is not a religion, but a scientific statement of being."

"I don't follow that."

So we talked some more, and as we moved from club to club we kept talking, and I felt myself getting more and more interested. One Sunday morning in Boston, Leonard asked me to come to a service with him at the Mother Church. I felt uncomfortable walking into a church, but as the service progressed I felt myself relaxing, the tension in my body easing up. It was peaceful, I guess, and I started attending on Sundays and going to Wednesday-night testimonials whenever I could. And through Christian Science I met several wonderful people who seemed to have found the peace within themselves that I wanted so badly. I remember a lovely lady named May Mehlinger at the church at 63rd Street and Park Avenue. She was a Christian Science Practitioner and gave many hours of her time to teaching me and helping me to understand.

I'm not a Christian Scientist today, though I was for about twenty years. I think now the reason for my leaving was part of the agonies that still torture me. I said I was a perfectionist, and that can be a terrible thing if you can't ever accept that there is no such thing as perfection. It's just a mark to shoot for, but one you really can't reach. I think my turning away from Christian Science happened because I expected to find perfection in it and through it. It has always been a failing of mine that I become completely open and naive when I finally trust. I expected to find every Christian Scientist I met absolutely honest, without greed or jealousy, and filled with love. And when a few of the men and women I met in church on Sunday turned out, on weekdays, to be just like everybody else in the world, I turned away from Christian Science, instead of turning away from them, once again disappointed by the imperfect.

Now I can see that *I* wasn't always the man I was on Sunday mornings and at Wednesday-night testimonials. But when I quit Christian Science I wasn't thinking about me and asking questions. I was judging others and using them for my personal out. As long as no one else was perfect, I didn't have to ask myself if I was.

20

Nineteen forty-five. Good news, great news, and, oh boy, bad news.

The good news was one of the most satisfying things I've ever done in my life. Together with Horace MacMahon, who was a well-known tough guy of both movies and stage, Danny Rogers, a young comic, and Lorraine Vernon, a juggler, I made a tour of 387 military hospitals in the United States. My brother Frank took charge of moving us from place to place. I don't think I ever worked so hard before as when our USO unit moved down the entire Atlantic seaboard—at the hospital at Valley Forge, I threw my back out of whack and missed a performance for the first time in my life. I can't remember her name, but there was a girl singer whom I always had to send out of the hospital wards. She'd start singing, "Candy, I call my sugar Candy," and the tears would begin running down her face as she looked at the men injured and crippled by the war, and I'd have to cut her short and send her outside.

The great news, of course, was the end of World War II. The Japanese surrendered on September 2, 1945. But that was only great news for the entire world. What was even greater news that day was the birth of Victoria Melanie Berle, whom Joyce and I got through private adoption. We named her Victoria in honor of the day, and the M in Melanie stood for the first initial of my father's name, Moses. We saw her for the first time shortly after she was born. It was love at first sight. "Look," I said to Joyce, "she's smiling at us."

Joyce shook her head. "I don't think babies smile right away. I think it's gas."

"Well, then she's burping at us. It's a sign."

Joyce and I looked at each other. We both had tears in our eyes.

When Joyce brought Vicki (who shortened her name almost as soon as she could talk) home to our new place, the top two floors of a townhouse in the east Eighties, I was deep in rehearsal for a new musical. And that's the bad news.

The Shuberts and Monte Proser had wanted me for another musical since the success of the *Ziegfeld Follies*. The one they came up with was called *Spring in Brazil*. The book was written by Philip Rapp, who had written for Eddie Cantor. The music and lyrics were by Robert Wright and George Forrest, who had had a smash hit when they'd worked with Grieg's music and come up with *Song of Norway*. Harry Kaufman, who was the genius of the Shubert office, was supposed to take charge of the show, but unfortunately he died. We were promised big names for the show. The Shuberts were going to get Carmen Miranda and Xavier Cugat and his whole orchestra, names that would really cash in on the South American craze that was sweeping the country. And we'd have Robert Alton do the dances. They didn't get any of them. The biggest name they signed was Rose Marie, who was as South American as I was. And we didn't get Robert Alton as choreographer. We got his ex-wife, Margery Fielding.

It was to be a plot show, with me playing a mousy assistant librarian in an explorer's club who winds up deep in the jungles of Brazil, where his father disappeared. Rose Marie played my girlfriend, a stewardess on the Pan-American *Clipper*, and Bernice Parks—another Latin American star!—played a South American bombshell who also wanted me.

One day, when I had some time off from rehearsals, I dropped up to Lee Shubert's office over the Shubert Theatre. Lee was a little guy with skin that looked like leather from years of sun-lamp treatments. He was hunched behind his desk when I bounded in. With great enthusiasm, I said, "Mr. Shubert, I am one of the happiest men in the world."

"That's nice," he said in his dry way.

"Let me show you why," I said, and whipped out a little leather case and opened it to show him three pictures of Vicki. "This is the baby that Joyce and I have adopted," I said proudly.

Lee Shubert just glanced at the pictures. "What are you so thrilled about?" he said. "It's not actually yours."

I don't think I've ever been so hurt in my life. It was as if he'd thrown a bucket of ice water over me. I didn't say a word to him. I just turned and walked out.

Spring in Brazil opened at the Shubert Theatre in Boston on October 2, 1945, to standing-room only. It was the last packed house it ever played to. The next day, the kindest of the critics thought there might possibly be something to the show if a lot of work was done. Elliot Norton, who had loved me in the *Follies*, wrote: "The new Berle, as presented at last night's premiere in the Shubert Theatre, is not a comedian, as was the old one. The new one is an 'actor,' a fat, middle-aged, giddy goon. In 'Spring in Brazil,' two girls want him. They can have him!"

And *Variety* reported: " 'Spring' took pride in having a book, and what a book! It flew apart like a 30-year-old flivver. . . ."

As soon as the notices came out, the meetings started on how to save the show. I suggested scrapping the book of the show, saving only the songs and sketches that were highlights, adding new material, and turning it into a revue called *Brazilian Nights*. Phil Rapp refused to have his book tampered with, Wright and Forrest objected to having any other music with theirs, and Lee Shubert was certain the show could be saved. In other words, we were on a sinking ship and all hands aboard were busy polishing the fixtures.

I blew up a couple of nights later. There was a tender moment in the show when Walter, the mousy hero, boards the *Clipper* for Brazil. He says good-bye to his girlfriend, Katie, which leads into her ballad, "I'm Gonna Miss Him So." I made my exit up the ramp to the plane, and the next thing I heard was Rose Marie, as Katie, start the ballad, then stop in the middle and say, "Yes, I'm going to miss him. I miss everybody when they leave," and suddenly she was doing her imitation of Jimmy Durante singing, "Who Will Be with You When I'm Far Away."

I grabbed Rosie as soon as the final curtain came down. "What the hell was that with the Durante?"

Rose Marie shook her head. "Don't blame me, Milton. I don't think it fits either, but that's what I was told to do."

Jesus Christ, they were ruining a bad show. I went wild backstage, exhausted from weeks of work, making changes day after day, learning new lines, new bits of business, putting material in one night, yanking it out the next. I shouted at anybody who came near me. "This is crazy! The show stunk and it's getting worse! Did you hear that Durante?"

And there was Lee Shubert in his topcoat and bowler hat like an old brown monkey. "Hold it down, Berle. Hold it down."

"Hold nothing down!" I shouted at him. "How dare you do this? Did you see the show tonight? You're breaking whatever continuity this lousy show has. That Durante imitation doesn't fit."

Shubert just stared at me. "I'll decide what fits and what doesn't. It's my money in this show."

With that, he turned to walk away. I followed him. "Yeah, it's your money, and I made a pile of it for you with the *Follies,* so at least please listen to me for a change—"

To my amazement, Lee Shubert, who was seventy-two in 1945, gave me a hard shove that caught me off balance. I stumbled backward before I caught myself. Shubert just glared at me. My fists automatically came up before I caught myself. I couldn't hit an old man. In my frustration, I spit on the floor in front of him and walked away.

The decision was made to keep *Spring in Brazil* on the road while it was shaped into a hit. We moved from Boston to New Haven to Philadelphia to Pittsburgh. New songs went in that turned out to be no better than what they replaced. New scenes laid the same eggs that the old scenes laid. Rose Marie was replaced by Mary Healy, who, thank God, couldn't do a Durante imitation. Bernice Parks gave way to Marian Colby. Christine Ayres, our jungle queen, turned her beads and feathers over to Dorothy De Winter. By the time *Spring in Brazil* limped into the Nixon Theatre in Pittsburgh—a turkey nobody needed that Thanksgiving week—I was one of the few original cast members still with it. The creative people on the show were still trying to shake some life into it, and John Murray Anderson, our director, was still trying to hide the fact that it was dead.

The morning after our opening in Pittsburgh, the reviews and a blizzard came at the same time. Both were bad. If that wasn't enough, there was an item in one of the gossip columns that deepened my depression:

HOLLYWOOD—*Linda Smith has asked for and been granted release from her contract with_____ where she was set for the female lead in the new Technicolor big-budget_____. The reason given was ill health, but the word around Celluloid City is there's more to it than that. According to a studio release, Linda is going to take a long-needed rest before she makes any future decisions. When this column contacted Linda's husband, movie biggie Jed Weston, he refused to say where Linda is taking that rest. Obviously her rest doesn't include husband Jed or six-year-old son, Larry. They stayed home.*

I made a couple of calls to friends at Linda's studio, and I got the true story. Her contract had been canceled because of her drinking. According to my friends, Linda had become a full-time alcoholic. Jed had sent her to a sanitarium, and two days after he had checked her in, she had skipped out and disappeared.

I no longer cared about Linda, and while it always hurt, I had pretty much given up the idea of ever seeing my son. But the wish died hard. Through contacts I hired a detective agency to try to find Linda. I didn't want her. I just didn't want her to disappear into some bottle no one would ever find. As long as Linda existed, there was the hope that some-day my son would know me. She was my only link to him.

The snow set in heavy, to the point where you could have taken bets at the Nixon Theatre that night on whether there were more people on stage or in the audience.

Irving Gray, my business manager, came backstage after the final curtain, and we walked silently through the snowdrifts back to the hotel. There were Thanksgiving decorations on restaurant windows, and they made me feel twice as miserable. Thanksgiving was a family holiday, and I was alone in Pittsburgh in a snowstorm. As soon as we got to my room, I put in a call to Joyce. We talked about how the show was going and about what Joyce was doing, and mostly about what Vicki was doing. Then there was a squeaking sound on the phone. "That was your daughter saying hello," Joyce said. "I tickled her."

"God, I miss you both," I said, and plunged in to why I had really called. "Joyce, how about coming down here to spend Thanksgiving with me?"

"Oh, Milton," Joyce said, "we already talked about that. You're doing two shows that day. What sense would it make? And what about Vicki? You want me to take her out in a blizzard? She's only two and a half months old—"

I cut in. "Come on, Joyce. You're using Vicki as an excuse. We've got a nurse for her."

"Yes, but she did say that she wanted to go to her family on Thanksgiving."

"Yeah, and what about our housekeeper? Is Svea going back to Sweden for Thanksgiving?"

Joyce gave a tired sigh. "Milton, please. What'll happen if I come down? I'll sit through the matinee, then I'll hang around backstage while you tear up the place and have meetings with everybody within two miles of the show. And then I'll sit through the evening show, and we'll go out and unwind with a mob. No, Milton. Please, no."

"Look," I said, and I felt as if I were pleading for my life, "I spoke with Mama and she said she might catch a train down here. You could catch the same train with her and . . ." I stopped. I had made a bad mistake.

"You see," Joyce said, "you won't be alone on Thanksgiving."

"I guess you're right. Well . . ."

"I love you, Milton."

"And I love you, Joyce." And the line went dead.

What happened right after that sounds like a bad burlesque blackout, but I swear it happened. When I hung up the phone, I felt worse than before I called. Suddenly, all the weeks of work and discouraging reviews, the news of Linda, the bad call to Joyce, all crashed in on me. I was sitting on the bed, and I started sobbing uncontrollably.

Irving Gray got up from his chair. "Milton? You all right, Milton?"

"What the hell is it all about, Irving? Why do I put myself through all of this? One minute you're a big success on Broadway, the next you're a bum that can't fill a house in Pittsburgh. I'm killing myself, and nobody cares. Not even my own family. I honest-to-Christ wish I was dead."

As if I were walking in my sleep, I started for the hotel window. Irving grabbed me when he realized where I was heading. "Milton. Please, Milton, come sit down!"

"Let me go, Irving. I'm sick of everything."

"Milton!" He screamed it at me so I was forced to hear, grabbed me, and wrestled me to a chair.

I doubled up. "I don't care anymore. I just don't care."

Irving sat on the window ledge to block it from me, and picked up the phone. "Room service." He said to me, "I'm gonna order us some dinner. You'll feel better after, you'll see."

"I don't want any dinner. I don't want anything."

"Sure, sure. Just leave it to me."

The tears were running down my face. "I tell you, Irving, I can't take it anymore. I don't care. It's too much, it's too much . . . see how their roast beef is."

Irving did a double take. That's when I heard what I had just said to him. With the tears of self-pity still on my face, I broke myself up laughing, until I was so weak I collapsed on the bed and fell a-sleep.

The next morning it was back to *Spring in Brazil.*

On the night of January 12, 1946, sixteen weeks after we had opened in Boston, *Spring in Brazil* finally gave up the ghost at the Great Northern Theatre in Chicago. Peter Lind Hayes had come into town to see the show, and Mary Healy. I got together with him in my dressing room before the show and worked out a closing gag.

After I had taken my final bow, I held up my hand to quiet the audience. "Well, ladies and gentlemen, I hope you liked the show, and if you want to see the scenery you can go over to Cain's Warehouse later this week."

At that point, Peter Lind Hayes, who could do a great drunk, stood up in the stage-left box and shouted, "Author! Author!", only he slurred it as if he were plastered.

"You want the author?" I called up to him. I went off stage to where Joe Burns, who played a gorilla named Lana in the show, was waiting in his costume, and I brought him on. "Okay, Mac, you want the author? Here's the author."

Peter took a gun filled with blanks he had hidden in the box and shot the gorilla. Joe dropped to the stage floor, and I said, "That's it, folks." I paused, then said quietly, "Berle owes you one."

If I needed to feel worse after sixteen weeks on the road trying to bring a dead turkey to life, I got it when I went through the mail that was waiting for me in New York. The detective agency I had hired to find Linda had bombed out. A woman who might have been Linda had been seen at the bus depot in San Francisco, but identification wasn't positive. But what bus if any she took, no one knew. A check with what family she had left in Nebraska had come up with nothing. They hadn't heard from her, and didn't expect to.

I told the agency to keep looking for her, but I didn't have much hope. If they hadn't found her right away, the chances of catching up with her as time passed would grow slimmer. Every city, big and small, in the United States has its slum and its skid row. She could have disappeared into any one of them.

My one big happiness at the beginning of 1946 was to stand by Vicki's crib and watch her. She could move a finger, or burp, or kick a leg, and my eyes would fill up with love. If no one was around, I'd make crazy noises and say love words to her. But if Joyce, or the nurse, or Svea Johnson, our housekeeper, was around, I would just watch her quietly. I guess that's part of me too. I find it very hard to express love openly. But I could do it when I was alone with our baby.

Her nursery was still the bar room we had brought her home to. The room was decorated with framed celebrity pictures on the wall behind a curved black bar. Vicki was supposed to be in there only temporarily, but somehow Joyce never got around to setting up a real baby's room. To tell the truth, Joyce was only the most beautiful housewife, not the best. She was not equipped to give the orders that got things done. She could never fire anyone—I think it had something to do with her wanting to be liked. After enough bad meals had shown up and after I had complained enough about the cook, for example, Joyce would give me the treatment—lots of helpless looks and batting eyelashes—and I'd end up playing the heavy and firing the cook.

Nicky Blair's 1,000-seater, the Carnival, was New York's newest nightclub, the place to go in 1946. It was located on Eighth Avenue at 51st Street in the Capitol Hotel. Toots Shor, who was Nicky's backer, wanted me to follow Martha Raye into the club, and invited me over to take a look. I went to see, and what I saw was Martha Raye doing my act.

One of my biggest laugh-getters in the *Follies* was the act I worked out with Ben Yost's Vikings. The Vikings were dressed in guardsmen uniforms with swords and shakos, singing big virile stuff like "Stout-Hearted Men." I came out in the same costume, my hair parted down the middle and a couple of front teeth blacked out. I tried to work with them, and everything went wrong, including continually stabbing myself in the groin with my sword. The act went over so big that I had set it for my own nightclub act. And there was Martha Raye at the Carnival, teeth blacked out and hoking it up with her own singers.

I was sore all right, but the record-breaking salary Blair agreed to pay me to play the Carnival helped me to feel better. I got a $10,000-a-week guarantee plus a percentage. Business was so good, I stayed for one week shy of a full year, and my take-home each week was around $12,000 to $14,000. What's more, I kept the act with the Vikings in. Thank God, Broadway had seen me do it in the *Follies* or I would have been accused of stealing it from Martha Raye.

The only good I got from *Spring in Brazil* was some material for my nightclub act, lines like: "We should have opened in Brazil and closed in Boston"; "Business was so big, we sent the whole audience home in a taxi"; "They arrested the doorman for loitering."

So I was a hit again, and making more money than any nightclub entertainer working a place that didn't have gambling had ever been paid before. And knowing that I'd be living in one place for some time gave me hope for my future with Joyce. (We still had our arguments—her shopping now included outfits for Vicki, costing as much as $150, that the baby would outgrow in a couple of months—but we still loved each other.) Maybe I had to work nights, but I'd have the days to be with Joyce, so we could build a life like other couples'. Only our time schedule would be different.

I suggested that with summer coming on, maybe it would be a good idea if we got a place outside of New York. It would be good for us, and great for Vicki. Joyce went along with me, and we sent out the word that we were looking.

Even Mama liked that idea, but anything that had to do with Vicki's happiness pleased her. Mama and Vicki were crazy about each other. And coming over to see Vicki also gave Mama the excuse—not that she needed one—to see me and keep up with what was happening in the business she refused to be retired from.

Not that Mama didn't have her own life now, away from Joyce and me. At the age of sixty-nine, she still had the drive and sparkle to attract friends half her age. Her card-playing lady friends liked her for herself, not because she was easy to beat. Mama broke up a table of women in their thirties one night by saying, "I'm not feeling so good. Do any of you girls have a Tampax?"

She had other friends, too, but I didn't ask too many questions about them. I knew that Mama was friendly enough with Bugsy Siegel for him to invite her to the opening of the Flamingo in Las Vegas, the year before, and fly her out there. Sometimes I wondered about Mama's friends and connections through the years.

As I said, if you worked the clubs you got to know the top men in the underworld. And if I had met them through the years, so had Mama. And some of them had become her friends. Once or twice, I had been tempted to ask Mama if she had ever used her pull with the big boys to get me favorable bookings, to square beefs, or for any one of a hundred favors a friend in the right place could perform. But I always backed off. I didn't want to know. I had even once been told that Mama had the clout to arrange for a hit. I refused to believe that, but I didn't want to check it out with Mama.

While I was at the Carnival, I played as many benefits as I could squeeze in. One show I did turned into a pretty sour evening, but it was also more important to me than I knew at the time.

The occasion was a dinner and show AFRA (American Federation of Radio Artists) was putting on. Henry Morgan was the master of ceremonies. When it came my turn to go on, Henry didn't say any of the gracious things one usually does when a busy performer takes time from his own show to do one for free. It was just "And now I'd like to introduce a member of AFRA who's appearing at the Carnival . . ."

So I went on and did my nightclub act. I remember noticing Henry's table, which was down front, and the woman sitting there with the empty chair beside her. She was a cute girl with dark hair, and that was about all I had time to notice.

When I finished my act, I left straight through the audience, to save time getting back to the Carnival. Morgan was at the mike again as my applause was dying down. I was at the doors when I heard him say to the audience, "That's all right if you like that nightclub crap!"

I threw my coat in a corner and ran back to the stage. "Okay, pal," I said to Henry Morgan, "grab yourself a funny mike!"

He turned pale. "I'm sorry. I lost my head."

"That's okay," I snapped, "you got another one."

I went on from there to take Henry Morgan apart in front of an all-show-biz crowd completely on my side. That is, all except his date that evening, a lady named Ruth Cosgrove, whom you are going to hear plenty about later on. She didn't like me much that night.

Business continued to boom at the Carnival. Night after night, week after week, the place was packed. The weather started to turn warm, but we continued to sell out for every show. It made Joyce and me talk more and more about getting a house somewhere out of New York. We agreed that it would be healthy for Vicki, and I think we both thought it would be better for both of us. We'd be alone together more, and maybe a lot of the pressures that were on us in the city would go away.

We found a house on Church Avenue in Lawrence, Long Island. It had trees and a yard and fresh air, and it was only about an hour's drive from the Carnival. Only we didn't move in when we'd planned to. Instead, in the late spring of 1947, Joyce went into a Broadway show. We fought like hell over that. What about the house? What about Vicki, who wasn't even two years old? What about everything we had planned for being together more? Mama had some comments, too, but she made them when Joyce wasn't around.

But Joyce was determined. The show was a comedy called *Open House*, starring Mary Boland. It opened at the Cort Theatre on June 3, 1947, and closed, seven performances later, on June 7. *Then* we moved to our house.

It was great for Vicki, but Joyce and I brought our troubles with us. Most of our arguments centered around my wanting Joyce to be with me nights. "Look, you don't have to sit through my show. Come on in. I'll get you a ticket for any show in town, and then come over to the Carnival. When I finish, we'll go anywhere you want—to Lindy's, Toots Shor's, El Morocco, you name it. Only for an hour, and then we can drive home together."

But Joyce rarely wanted to. "I don't like leaving Vicki alone."

"What alone? We've got Svea. We've got a nurse. She won't be alone." I didn't mention *Open House*—she had had to leave Vicki to do that—because the show was still a sore point between us.

"Oh, Milton, we've gone over this a hundred times. You know how I get late at night. Why don't you just come straight home after your show?"

I had done that a couple of times. But Joyce was never waiting up for me. She was always in bed, sound asleep.

It burned me. "I can't change my hours for you. My work is done at night. And when I'm through, I want to unwind a little. Christ, you knew all this about me before we got married. What if I was a taxi driver and I had to work all night? Wouldn't you change your hours for me? Millions of wives change their pattern of living to fit the hours their husbands have to work to make a living. Why can't you?"

So she'd try it for a night here and there, but it never lasted. And I'd be back to grabbing a late bite with other entertainers and their wives, and then making the lonely drive back to the house in Lawrence, where only a light in the hall was waiting up for me.

One night, around three or four in the morning, I was driving back by myself, feeling very, very tired. The road was a mess because of the building that was going on for what was going to be Idlewild Airport. I fell asleep at the wheel—luckily, I wasn't going very fast—and went off the road and into a tree. I wasn't hurt, but it deepened my anger at Joyce.

The house in the country didn't bring us any happiness, or bring us any closer together, and we gave it up at the end of the summer. We moved to a large apartment at 40 East 88th Street, and I sank a fortune into having it decorated.

Mama's comment when we came back to New York was "Well, it's nearer to the stores."

I was unhappy with Joyce, but how unhappy she was with me was something I wasn't too aware of until one afternoon when I came home from a meeting about a radio show. I remember that I had told Joyce before I went out that I'd be back around 5:30.

Svea met me at the door, and she was very upset. "Please, Mr. Berle, come quick. Something's wrong with the madam. I can't wake her up."

I threw off my coat and ran into the bedroom. Joyce was sprawled out on the bed. There was an empty pill bottle on the night table. I grabbed her and shook her. She moaned, but she didn't wake up. In the nursery, I could hear Vicki playing in her crib, so I knew she was all right.

I slapped Joyce a couple of times. Then I ran into the bathroom and got some water and threw it in her face. She didn't open her eyes.

I grabbed the phone and called a doctor who was a close friend. I told him about Joyce and read him the label on the pill bottle. They were sleeping pills, but I had no idea of how many she had taken. Until that moment I didn't know that Joyce had any sleeping pills.

The doctor said he'd be right over.

Svea filled me in on what little she knew. She had last seen Joyce sometime after four, when she went in to Vicki's room. Then Joyce told Svea that she was going to take a short nap. She also told Svea to wake her before I came home. Svea went in about five minutes before I came home and found Joyce.

The doctor showed up, and right in the bedroom he pumped Joyce out and gave her a shot of something. He brought her to, but she was sick as a dog. After he had her cleaned up and out of danger, he came out to me. "What happened?"

I told him what I knew, and he said, "I don't think it was a serious attempt. Not when she knew the time you'd be coming home. If she really wanted to kill herself, she could have taken the pills right after you left for the Carnival for the night. That would have given her plenty of time. You probably wouldn't have known what she had done until morning when it was too late. My guess is that she wanted you to find her, and in time. As to why she did it, you'd know that better than I would."

"I don't know."

The doctor looked at me sadly. "Then you'd better find out, Milton."

I helped him on with his coat. He did me the favor of a lifetime by not reporting what had happened in the bedroom. Not a line about it appeared in any newspaper.

The next day, when I asked Joyce about the suicide attempt, I got nothing out of her except some kisses and nervous giggles. "Please, please forget it, darling. I don't know why I did it. It was stupid and dramatic. Please, let's forget it."

About the pills I found out even less. Where Joyce got them, how long she had had them, if she was taking them regularly—"Well, sometimes, if I'm out with you for the night, and I don't want to wake up early, the way I always do, I take one."

"They're dangerous, Joyce."

"One or two aren't, and that way I can sleep late. Otherwise, no matter what time we come home, I'm up with the dawn."

Naturally, I didn't tell Mama what had happened.

Business was tremendous at the Carnival when I called it quits. I had worked there for fifty-one weeks, and that was more than enough. I was a comedian, not an institution. The incident of the pills made me nervous about leaving Joyce alone too much.

In 1947, I had another radio show—for a guy who never made it big in radio, I was always on. This one was the *Philip Morris Playhouse*, and, like the more famous *Lux Radio Theatre*, we did one-hour versions of famous movie and Broadway comedies. I played every week with a different guest star. It was an okay show, and I was anxious to be renewed for 1948, and it wasn't just for the work. I wanted to be able to stay home with Vicki and Joyce. There were enough stresses and strains between

Joyce and myself without adding to them by weeks of separation when I played out-of-town clubs.

Maybe it was because I had been around when the so-called brains of vaudeville were laughing at silent movies as just a fad that the public would soon tire of, or maybe it was because I saw that television could give a visual entertainer the exposure he could never get from radio. Whatever it was about television, it appealed to me. And in 1947 it seemed to be showing big signs of life. People were starting to talk about the free plays you could get right in your living room from the *Kraft Theatre*, and there was *Howdy Doody* for the kids. The wrestling matches packed the local bars that had a set.

But more people talked about television than actually saw it, because most people wanted to wait and see before they shelled out money for a set. But the big stars, and the big guns along Madison Avenue just dismissed television as a no-threat gimmick.

I wanted Philip Morris to renew me on radio for 1948. I would have settled for that, but I also wanted to tell them about me for television. When the time came to talk 1948 business, Harry Ommerle of the William Morris office, which was still representing me, made an appointment for me to get together with Milton Biow, who headed the Biow Agency, which handled the Philip Morris account. Working with Milton Biow, we planned the pitch for television I would make to Alfred Lyon, the president of Philip Morris, and his top men. My pitch stressed the importance of television as the coming medium, while showing them there would be no conflict by continuing me on radio.

Biow brought me over to Philip Morris's boardroom, and I made the big pitch for picking up my option for twenty-six more weeks on radio while also going into television, since I felt I was a natural for it. When I finished the pitch, Milton Biow gave me the big "okay" sign. "Great job," he whispered. "You're in."

In what? Philip Morris didn't pick up my option for radio, and they didn't want to go into television with me. A while later, I found out that Milton Biow himself had made the decision that Philip Morris should drop my radio show, one month before he got together with me to prepare my pitch for the sponsor!

As it turned out, Philip Morris wasn't the only one to drop me in 1947.

I can't remember the evening exactly, except that it was one of the best Joyce and I had ever spent together. For once, there were no arguments, no stresses at all. And it ended beautifully in bed. I can remember the next morning, however, very clearly. The telephone woke me up. I remember looking at the clock and seeing it was only about 9:30. And I looked over my shoulder to Joyce's side of the bed. She was sound asleep. That bothered me. Since the afternoon when Joyce had taken the pills, I worried when she slept late in the morning.

The telephone rang again, and I picked it up. I was still half asleep, and I didn't get the man's name or that of the firm he was with. I had to ask him to repeat it. I got the part where he said, "Our firm is representing Mrs. Joyce Berle."

"What is this?"

"I called because I didn't want the news to come as too much of a surprise to you."

Now I was waking up. "What's this about?"

The man said, "You're going to be served with papers, Mr. Berle. Your wife is divorcing you."

And he hung up. I turned in bed to look at Joyce. She was still asleep. I put my hand on her shoulder, and she stirred. "Joyce," I said.

"Mmmm?"

"Joyce, your lawyer just called. He said you're going to divorce me. Is that true?"

She didn't even open her eyes. "Mmm hmm," she said, and pushed deeper into the covers.

1940-1950

Joyce Mathews arrives in Pasadena, California, in 1941 to marry Milton. (UPI)

Milton's first present to Joyce Mathews was a portable radio. (MODERN SCREEN)

Milton and Joyce after their wedding on Dec. 4, 1941. (MODERN SCREEN)

The Berles with Laird Cregar at a Hollywood premiere in 1942. (MODERN SCREEN)

Nose to nose with Jimmy Durante, 1941.

A scene from Whispering Ghosts, 20th Century-Fox, 1942.

A *scene from* Gentlemen at Heart, *with Cesar Romero, 20th Century-Fox, 1942*.

A *scene from* Margin for Error *with Otto Preminger and Joan Bennett, 20th Century-Fox, 1942*.

Hoofing with Dean Martin, Eddie Cantor, and Jerry Lewis on the 1949 Damon Runyon Memorial Fund telethon, the first in TV history.

Milton with Arnold Stang on The Milton Berle Show *sponsored by Texaco, 1948.*

Milton and Joyce remarried, with adopted daughter Vicki in 1949.

Opera star Grace Moore on Berle's radio program, Let Yourself Go, *in 1944.* (UPI)

Newsweek

MAY 16, 1949 20c

Milton Berle: Television's Whirling Dervish

Milton on the cover of Newsweek, *May 16, 1949.* (NEWSWEEK, © *1949*)

❧ 21 ❧

I talked ("Joyce, do you know what you're doing? Do you know what a big step you're taking?"); I argued ("Goddammit, even if you don't love me anymore, there's still Vicki to think of!"); and once I even pleaded ("You know you still love me, and I still love you. Why are you doing this to us?"). But Joyce stuck to her guns. "Milton, I am thinking of you and me, and especially of Vicki. For every good day we have, we follow it with a bad day. You don't belong to me. The whole world is your audience, and you belong to them—and to your mother."

Joyce got her divorce in Reno on October 23, 1947. The grounds we had agreed to were mental cruelty. According to the New York *Daily News*, we "became incompatible when she wanted to continue her theatrical career and he insisted on being the only star in the family." (A couple of years ago, when an interviewer asked Joyce if she had ever had a big career drive, she said, "Oh, no. Never in my life. I worked, but I never had a big drive.")

The divorce didn't make anybody happy, not even Mama. "It's a shame, it's a shame," she kept saying.

"What's a shame?" I snapped at her. "You didn't like Joyce, admit it. So now it's over, so where's the shame?"

"The divorce, that's the shame," Mama said. "And don't say I didn't like her. Joyce for Joyce is fine. I just didn't think she was right for you, but that doesn't mean I want to see a divorce. And what's going to become of poor Vicki?"

"Mama, nobody divorced Vicki. She's with Joyce, and I'll see her plenty." I wouldn't admit anything to Mama, not even that I worried for Vicki. Not that I didn't trust Joyce. She was a good mother, and she loved Vicki as much as I did, but we both knew that two parents were better than one.

When Joyce and Vicki came back from Reno, I moved into a hotel. I called almost every day to ask about Vicki. At first when I called, Joyce and I were stiff with each other on the telephone. We'd say nothing much more than "Hello" and "How are you?" and then I'd ask Joyce to put Vicki on the phone. I didn't understand half her babytalk but I'd say anything to keep her talking.

I also saw her every weekend unless I was out of town playing a club. Joyce always answered the door, and we'd talk a minute or two before I asked if Vicki was ready to come out with me.

In time, things loosened up between us. We even went out to dinner a couple of times. And I'd come home, thinking to myself that I had more fun being with Joyce than with anybody else, so why the hell did we get a divorce? But then I'd remember the fights, the silences, the unhappiness we caused each other, and I knew we had done the right thing by calling it quits. But it killed me when I read in the columns that Joyce was seen around town with Mike Todd. It was as if I had come home and caught my wife cheating on me. I wanted to call up Joyce and tell her that I forbade her to see Todd. Then it hit me that I was jealous, but I didn't let myself think about why I was jealous of any other man but me being near Joyce.

And anyway, what right did I have to tell Joyce who she could see? I wasn't staying home nights with a good book. I was seen around with Jennie Lewis, who was going to be very famous in a few years as Dagmar on late-night television; Jane Morgan, the singer; Evelyn Knight— remember her recording of "Dance with a Dolly with a Hole in Her Stocking"?—for whom I wrote "Lucky, Lucky Me"; and, most of all, Junior Standish. For my money, she was the most beautiful of all of New York's Latin Quarter girls. Junior was tall, blond, and stately, and, if that wasn't enough, an awfully nice person.

I used to wonder if Joyce read the items about me and Junior in the columns. Did it bother her the way Mike Todd bothered me? I hoped so, but I wasn't ready to face the fact that I was still in love with her.

It was typical of me that I faced only what could be handled with my fists, or by shouting, or by laughter. The rest I ran from. Mama had taught me everything about the world, except how to trust, how to open up and reveal my true self. That was the only thing I found dangerous in my world.

So, as usual, I buried myself in my work. There were nightclubs that wanted me, charities that said they needed me at their benefits, and horses that never ran as fast as my money did.

When I played Los Angeles, I naturally asked around about Linda Smith. My search for her had turned up nothing more than an occasional rumor of some woman in some town who looked something like her. But it never proved to be Linda. No one in Hollywood had seen her, either. And Jed Weston was in Europe—a vacation with a little business mixed in—and had taken his son with him. So that was that.

Now, I can see that there was a pattern—maybe—to the women whom I was attracted to at the time. Most of them were slender blonds and gorgeous—just like Joyce. When I met and dated Adele Jergens, she was starring in a B picture over at Columbia called *Ladies of the Chorus*. I dropped over one afternoon to visit her set, and I spotted another blond who had something about her, besides great beauty, that made you stare at her openly. When Harry Romm, who was producing the picture, stopped to talk to me, I asked who the girl was. She had her back to us, so I pointed to her.

Harry said, "Oh, her. She plays Adele's daughter."

"You're crazy," I said. "Adele can't be more than a couple of years older than she is."

Harry shrugged. "What can I tell you? It's a story about a mother and daughter in the chorus line. The mother can't be an old bag, can she? Wait till you see Adele. We put some gray in her hair. She looks great."

"So who's the daughter?" I asked.

He called her over. "I want you to meet Milton Berle. This is Marilyn Monroe."

She actually blushed when we shook hands. It added to that special wide-eyed quality she already had. We talked for a few minutes, and I asked her if she would have dinner with me. She said yes.

So I began taking her out, and usually to the big night spots. Sure, there were women who were so sensational-looking you wanted to be seen with them, but that wasn't the reason I took Marilyn to the splashy places. It was because I got such a kick out of showing them to her. It was like taking a hungry kid into a bakery. Marilyn didn't put on phony airs. She didn't pretend that she was used to this world. She'd just sit at the table, wide-eyed, looking everywhere. And she'd ask question after question, and she'd almost always follow it with "Oh, I didn't know that!" or "Oh, really?"

Sometimes she'd talk about herself and her ambitions. She wanted very much to be a star, but not in the way that Linda had wanted it. Marilyn wanted to be somebody, but it was somebody to herself. Somehow, she thought that if she became a star it would fill in that "empty feeling"—that's how she described it—she had had as a kid, when she was going from one foster home to the next.

Marilyn was on the climb in Hollywood, but there was nothing cheap about her. She wasn't one of the starlets around town that you put one meal into and then threw in the sack. Maybe she didn't know exactly who she was, but she knew she was worth something. She had respect for herself. Marilyn was a lady.

She wasn't out to please me because I might be able to help her. She made it clear that what happened between us happened because she liked me.

And I liked her. We didn't pretend that our affair was a big thing. It was just part of something nice between us. And after a while it was over. I had finished my nightclub appearance and was overdue getting back east, and I think there was pressure on Marilyn from Johnny Hyde, who was vice-president of the William Morris Agency and in love with her, to break it off with me.

The next time I saw Marilyn, she was already a star. It was just after Elizabeth Taylor and Eddie Fisher were married. I was in Las Vegas getting set for my opening at the Flamingo. Eddie was at the Desert Inn, and Elizabeth had come down to be with him. Frank Sinatra was also appearing in Vegas, at the Sands, and his guest was Marilyn. When it came time for Eddie and Frank to go and do their shows, they both asked me to escort their ladies. You can imagine what it was like when I entered with Elizabeth Taylor on one arm and Marilyn Monroe on the other. The place went wild when I shouted out, "Who says nobody knows me?"

The last I saw of Marilyn was in late 1959, when I appeared with her and Yves Montand in *Let's Make Love* at 20th Century–Fox. I didn't see much of her during the making of the picture, but neither did anyone else. She spent most of her time in her trailer. George Cukor had a rough time directing her, and Jack Cole went crazy working with her on the "My Heart Belongs to Daddy" number. She could do only four bars at a time.

The wide-eyed, naive Marilyn Monroe I had first known was gone. This Marilyn was more beautiful than ever, but she seemed like someone lost in her own thoughts most of the time. The biggest conversation we had during the shooting of the picture was about the cigars I smoked. She liked the aroma. I told her I thought they would be better for her than cigarettes, and I bought her a box of small cigars I thought she would like. If she ever smoked any of them, I don't know. She took the box into her trailer, and that was the last I ever saw of them.

As for the relationship we had had when she was in *Ladies of the Chorus*, she never said one word to indicate she remembered it. Whatever Marilyn had become by the time of *Let's Make Love*, it wasn't a phony. She wouldn't pretend to draw a blank on something in her earlier life because it might be embarrassing for her to remember when she was at the top. I think she actually could not remember that she and I had been together for a while eleven years before.

When I came back to New York from California early in 1948, one of the first people I heard from was Myron Kirk, the Madison Avenue man who had put me on *Gillette Original Community Sing* back in 1936. He was now with the Kudner Agency, and he thought I was the man for the new radio show he and his boss, Jim Ellis, were lining up for their client, the Texas Company. Was I interested?

I wanted the radio show, but I made a pitch to Mike Kirk for television. Hadn't anybody heard about it besides me? Mike had heard about it, and Texaco *was* interested, but their first interest was radio. That was the big time. Television could wait.

Maybe nobody today remembers the *Texaco Star Theatre* on radio, but it was the best radio show I ever did. It went on on Wednesday nights from 9 to 10 over the ABC network. The genius behind the show was its head writer, Nat Hiken, not to mention Aaron Rubin and two bright young brothers, Danny and Neil Simon. Working with me were seasoned pros like Pert Kelton, Arnold Stang, Charles Irving, Kay Armen, Frank Gallop, and Al Kelly, the master of doubletalk. It was a hell of a funny variety show. Its weekly highlight was "The Berles at Home," a family situation-comedy.

Now, with the radio show launched and running well, Mike Kirk said Texaco wanted to talk television. They had decided that they wanted to be the first big show on the new medium in the fall of 1948. But before they went on, they wanted to try a couple of test shows in the summer. Did I have anything in mind for myself?

I thought about it, and decided to take the advice I had given to so many others when their big break came. Don't go looking for something new. Do what you have done best, what got you to your big break. So I suggested to the powers at Texaco a show in which I would serve as host, do some of my routines and introduce guest stars, who would do their specialties, and then I would mix it up with them for some comedy—in other words, what I had been doing for years in vaudeville and nightclubs.

I was told that I was one of three stars they were talking to about doing a test show in the summer. I won't mention the other two's names, but they did their shows, and I did mine in June of 1948, and Texaco decided on me. That was when I got nervous about television. Would it mean giving up the radio show? I didn't want that. As much as I thought my kind of comedy was right for television, it was still an unknown medium. Radio was here to stay, but was television?

Texaco felt the same way, so I was renewed for the fall of 1948 for Wednesday nights on radio, with Tuesday nights at 8 scheduled for the *Texaco Star Theatre* on television. In 1948–49, I did thirty-nine radio shows for Texaco on ABC and thirty-nine television shows for Texaco on NBC—seventy-eight live shows in one season!

ᵉ22ᵉ

Oh, we're the men of Texaco.
We work from Maine to Mexico.
There's nothing like this Texaco of ours.
Our show tonight is powerful.
We'll wow you with an hour-ful
Of howls from a showerful of stars.
We're the merry Texaco men.
Tonight we may be show men,
Tomorrow we'll be servicing your cars.

FIRST MAN: *I wipe the pipe, I pump the gas,*
I rub the hub, I scrub the glass.

SECOND MAN: *I touch the clutch, I poke the choke.*

THIRD MAN: *I clear the gear, I block the knock,*
I jack the back, I set the clock.

FOURTH MAN: *So join the ranks of those who know,*
And fill your tanks with Texaco.

ALL: *Sky Chief—fill up with Sky Chief,*
And you will smile at the pile of
new miles you will add.
Fire Chief—fill up with Fire Chief.
You'll find that Texaco's the finest
friend your car has ever had!

That opening song was written by Buddy Arnold and Woody Kling. The music, in part, came from Liszt's *Hungarian Rhapsody.* Texaco loved this opening, performed by four singers in Texaco-station coveralls. It so tied the sponsor to the show that audiences didn't think of one without the other. From the viewpoint of Buddy and Woody, the song was a big mistake. Not that the song wasn't good, but because nobody knew how good it was.

Texaco had total identification, through title, through the opening number, and through the comedy commercial done by Sid Stone every week in the middle of the show as a sidewalk pitchman working out of a suitcase., (Today, the individual sponsor is gone, replaced by advertisers who buy time on a show. Even the regular watchers of a show can't tell you who the sponsor is.)

The trouble with television when I went into it was that nobody knew what the hell they were doing or what anything was worth. Today, Buddy Arnold and Woody Kling could have retired on the money the Texaco song would have earned them if they had hung on to it. But who knew? They sold it outright to the Texas Company for $375 apiece.

The first *Texaco Star Theatre* television broadcast of the series went on on September 21, 1948, from Studio 6B of the RCA building in Rockefeller Center, New York. The acts on the first show were the Four Carters, Evelyn Knight, Phil Silvers, Park and Clifford, Stan Fisher, and Smith and Dale. Studio 6B had been a radio studio. It had a raised stage, and parallels (platforms) in front of it. We put the TV cameras on them. Since there were no monitors on which the audience could watch the show, they had to do as well as they could by looking around the cameras, which blocked their view of the stage. I learned quickly that I couldn't do anything small, because the studio audience couldn't see it, and if the studio audience didn't laugh, chances were the home audience wouldn't either.

This was the time of blue shirts, because white bounced the light; of no jewelry that would flash; of last-minute hysterical sewing of gauze patches on the front of a star's dress that was cut too low. Our sets were usually just painted drops (called rollerdrops) that were rolled up and down. Camera work was crude to the point where even the home audience was aware when the picture cut from one camera to another, and sometimes even when the picture went out of focus as a lens adjustment was made. Microphones hung from booms (long poles) over the performer's head, and were often visible to the home audience.

The budget for the first year of the Texaco show was only $15,000 per show—and that meant for everything: me, the guests, the writers, the band, everything. Today you can't get a star to sing eight bars of a song for that amount. Luckily, when my show became hot everyone wanted to be on it, and was willing to work for peanuts for the chance of television exposure. (No unions then!)

For my first three shows, I didn't even have a writer. I did have Hal Collins, a very fine comedy writer, helping me, but not in the creative capacity he would serve later on. What Hal did was help me dig up routines and bits I had done throughout my career, and organize them into what we thought would make a television show. But that system only lasted a few weeks, and then we had to have writers to create material specifically for television, and we all learned as we went along.

Whatever we were doing, it turned out right. Less than two months after *Texaco* began on television, the show was so popular that it was the only program not canceled on Tuesday, November 2, 1948, for the election returns of the Truman-Dewey contest. Our show had an 80.7 Hooper rating, which was a fat 28.9 points ahead of the next most popular show.

Crazy things started happening all over the country. In Detroit, an investigation took place when the water levels took a drastic drop in the reservoirs on Tuesday nights between 9 and 9:05 P.M. It turned out that everyone waited until the end of the *Texaco Star Theatre* before going to the bathroom. In New York, Mrs. Adella Meadows, who ran a residential hotel on Eighth Street, reported showing a suite on a Sunday to a man whose long marriage was breaking up. He wanted to move out as quickly as possible. Mrs. Meadows said the suite would be ready for him on Monday morning. The man said that was too soon. He would take it on Wednesday, as his wife was retaining custody of their television set and he didn't want to miss Milton Berle. Buddy Hackett remembers that the nightclub he was appearing in, which, like most clubs, closed on Monday nights, changed its closing to Tuesday nights because of *Texaco*. Restaurants stayed empty during the Tuesday dinner hours. A theater manager in Ohio sent me the poster he had put up in his lobby: "Closed Tuesday. I want to see Berle, too." A laundromat at Brighton Beach installed a TV set and advertised "Watch Berle while your clothes whirl."

By the end of 1948, Texaco and I agreed to drop the radio show and concentrate on television. It meant a loss of a large salary for a small one, by comparison—my salary for television that first year came to $1,500 a week—but it meant more time to work on the television program, and doing a one-hour *live* show every week was a killing grind. (This was back when "live" meant exactly that. You got what you saw; you saw what you got. It was nothing like today's "live on tape," where mistakes can be corrected. In *Texaco*'s time, what went wrong went wrong right on camera, with the whole country watching.)

The week went like this:

Wednesday: The first meeting for the next week's show took place at nine in the morning in the office I had at 51st Street and Broadway. It was a very small room with a couch, a desk, and a lot of chairs around a table. At the meeting would be the five writers; my brother Frank, who was my manager; Irving Gray, my aide; my secretary, Sandy, who became Irving's wife; and the booker for the acts we would use—that would be either Harry Kalcheim or Ben Griefer of the William Morris office. (There was only one window in that room, and because I have this crazy thing about drafts, it was always closed, no matter how hot or smoky the room got. The night our show won its Emmy awards, I remember standing out in front of Toots Shor's with Hal Collins, Irving Gray, Jay Burton, and a couple of the other writers. We were all in black tie and trying to decide what to do and where to go to celebrate. One of the comedy writers said, "I know what. Let's go up to the office and open the window!")

The Wednesday problems were to work out tentative ideas for the next week's sketches. For example, if the Kefauver committee was currently in the news, how about a sketch on that? And who could we get to play Kefauver? Another problem area was the big finale (Buddy Arnold and Woody Kling wrote them)—what would be the theme? How could we work everybody into it? What other acts were available who fit the finale theme—like apache dancers if we were doing a Paris-nights finale? The Wednesday meetings ran all day long. I had to leave halfway through because of the *Texaco* show on radio that night.

Thursday was spent in booking the acts, writing those parts of the show that hinged on me alone, like the opening monologue. Based on what we knew of the sketches, Hal Collins would meet with Arthur Knorr, who did our sets, and make rough plans. Then Hal would rejoin the other writers, who were working at his apartment. We could have had office space for the writers at NBC, but I didn't trust that setup. Bob Hope had once had his whole opening monologue, which he was going to do that night, delivered on a kiddie show the same afternoon by another guy whose writer had gotten it from an NBC secretary he was friendly with. And back in my radio days, I remember dinner at a writer's house, and being taken back to his work room and seeing stacks of other writers' scripts for upcoming shows. *Texaco* meant too much to me to run the risk of the NBC mimeograph room or a secretary who was being romanced by a hungry writer. So we had our own mimeograph machine in Hal's apartment, and we kept every gag—even the ones we threw out— a secret.

The other big secret was the opening costume I'd wear for each week's show. I worked that out with my sister, Rosalind, who costumed the show, and her assistant, a bright young guy named Sal Anthony, who is a very top man in the industry today. Every week I'd come out in some crazy costume that tied in with the opening setup of my monologue. If I had just come back from Florida, where the weather had been cold, I showed up as an Eskimo on a dog sled. For Thanksgiving I was a pilgrim. The costume could be drag or straight, but always crazy, and always a surprise for the audience. Aside from designing and making the costume—with next to no budget for costumes—Roz's other problem was to make it a breakaway, a costume I could get out of easily on stage and wear over a suit.

By Friday, we had most of the people set who would be on the show. More often than not, someone we had wanted and had built a sketch around turned out to be unavailable. That meant coming up with ideas and material to fit the performers we could get—another all-day meeting.

By Saturday, we had the show set in rough form. I'd start going through the jokes, picking maybe three from every twenty that each writer came up with. Saturday night, a secretary, either at my office or at Hal's apartment, would type the show script directly onto the mimeograph stencil, so there would be no rough copy that could get into outside hands. Hal would run off the scripts half the night on the machine in his apartment.

Rehearsals started on Sunday at 9 in the morning at the Nola Studios on Broadway, and over in the ballroom of the Henry Hudson Hotel, on 57th Street near Ninth Avenue. Rehearsals went from Sunday to Monday, and then we went into dress rehearsal Tuesday morning in Studio 6B. You could almost count on it that we wouldn't finish the dress rehearsal before we had to break to get ready for the live show Tuesday night.

At the first blocking rehearsals, we usually split up the material between the rehearsal spots. The musical stuff, the singing acts, the musical portions of the finales were usually rehearsed at the Henry Hudson, where

Alan Roth had room enough for the band. Hal Collins usually stood in for me over there, while I worked on the sketches and the opening monologue at the Nola Studios.

Add to all of that the nights when I'd run to a nightclub, maybe in New York, maybe in Philadelphia or Boston, to catch an act that we hoped would bring something new and different to the show, plus the hell of the people running back and forth between the Nola Studios and the Henry Hudson to take costume measurements, check a prop, straighten out any one of a thousand problems that came up every week, and you had a continuous nightmare, a rat race not even rats would enter.

I'd like to think it was the breakneck pace of the work that made me too exhausted to spot a great business opportunity. During a busy rehearsal a little guy named Irving Kahn came to see me. He wanted to sell me a piece of his invention which would enable a performer to see his lines so he wouldn't have to worry about drying up in front of the cameras. I tried it out for one show, but I didn't think Mr. Kahn's moving cue sheet was the answer, so I turned down the chance to buy 25 per cent of Teleprompter for $2500.

My working clothes, aside from slacks, almost always were a leather jacket, a hat of some sort, a towel around my neck, and a whistle hanging from a chain. The jacket and the hat had to do with my crazy fear of drafts. The towel was for that too, and also because I always sweat when I work. I used the whistle to stop whatever was going on in a rehearsal in order to give a direction or a correction.

That whistle got me bad publicity in the columns and throughout the business. The word that went around was that Berle had no respect for other performers, he treated them like circus animals with himself as the trainer who told them when to stop and start by blowing his whistle.

That's a lot of crap! I used that whistle for one, and only one, very good reason: to save my voice. No matter what happened from Wednesday to Tuesday, come Tuesday night at 8, I had to appear on camera and talk and clown and sing, and it was *live*. That whistle saved me a week of needless shouting, "Cut!", "Stop!", "Hold it!" or whatever. But nobody ever thought of that, or even bothered to ask me why. I was a superstar, at forty a thirty-five-year overnight sensation, and as much as everybody in this country likes to get on the bandwagon of the current sensation, that's how much they like to see that person destroyed.

Everybody loves to root for the guy on the way up, but watch out when he gets there. That's when the mob turns. That's when you start hearing that he's a drunk, he's a fag, he's cheap, he gets his kicks in weird ways —you name it, somebody knows about it for sure. That that somebody has never met the man he has the facts on, and doesn't even know anybody who knows the man, has nothing to do with what he knows for sure. And everybody believes the bad news and passes it on.

This is not to say I was a saint during the *Texaco* days. I was rough, and I have lots of regrets about things I did and said, for the way I pushed and shoved and bullied during those hysterical years. My only defense, which is no defense, is the pressure I worked under, and the person I was raised to be. You take a kid at the age of five and make him the star of the family, and then take that same kid out into the world and make him a star with everybody catering to him as if he were something more than another perishable human being, and it's a miracle if that kid doesn't grow up to be a man who believes he's Casanova and Einstein and Jesus Christ all rolled into one.

I guess that was me, and I was a perfectionist besides. I would try to pass out authority, but I couldn't leave anything alone, couldn't let myself trust anyone completely to get something done exactly the way I wanted it. So I ran like a maniac all week, directing when we had a director, getting into the dance blocking when we had a dance director, setting shots for the camera men, giving readings to actors, demanding costume changes, light changes—hell, I got into everything. As much as I talked about wanting peace and hating the tensions that were always part of our rehearsals, that's how much I know now that I was one of the creators of the tensions and the fights.

Because I wasn't good at delegating authority, I set people against each other. My brother Frank worked around the show supposedly to clear all sorts of problems out of my way. But too often, when Frank felt I should turn something over to him—and maybe he was right—I would call for Irving Gray. (Almost everybody connected with *Texaco Star Theatre* recalls, whenever we meet, the day I blew up about something and shouted, "Jesus, Mary, and—*Irving!*") There was bad feeling between the two men, but instead of straightening it out, I didn't want to hear about it. I just didn't have time for their bitching and backbiting.

But it reached a head one day, and I saw red. Without even thinking, I turned and swung. I knocked my brother, Frank, to the floor. To make things worse, somebody tipped the story to Earl Wilson, and "BERLE

FLATTENS BROTHER" made all the papers. Frank and I patched it up a couple of days later, but I've never forgiven myself for hitting him. Frank worked hard for me—he deserved better.

One day I discovered that a weekly event on the show was the pool on how many times Berle would stop the dress rehearsal with his whistle. Somebody would put the numbers in a hat, from 60 to 150, and everybody would chip in a quarter and draw a number. People who drew low numbers usually just forgot the whole thing. They knew they didn't stand a chance.

The week after I found out about the pool, I demanded to get in on it. I tried not to think about the number I drew, which was on the low side, but I think it affected me that day. I didn't win, but there were fewer whistle blasts than ever before (I think the winner was 87), and it was one of the worst shows we ever did.

No matter how busy the show kept me, I still called Mama every day —that is, unless she came to the rehearsal—and, of course, I saw her every Tuesday night at the show. Mama was leading the laughter for television, just the way she had done for radio, and nightclubs, and vaudeville. And I called Vicki, and I made a point of seeing her every week no matter how busy I was.

It would bother Joyce when I told her to get Vicki dressed up because I wanted to take her down to the studio or to a rehearsal. "I wish you wouldn't," Joyce said. "That's no fun for a child. I don't think it's a good atmosphere for her, either."

But I insisted. "I want to show her off, what's wrong with that? Other fathers take their kids down to the office. Why shouldn't I? I'm proud of my daughter. I want people to see her."

I think Vicki liked it. I know I did. What else did I have to give my child then? Joyce bought her everything she could possibly want or need. I could only give her television. It was my only world then.

There were occasional women—some things you make time for no matter how busy you are—but only one of them was really memorable during the early days of the *Texaco* show, and she was memorable not because we were such a big romance, but because of the craziness of the whole thing.

I met Kitty Grant in New York, at some party I can no longer remember, but I had promised whoever was giving it that I'd stop by. So I did, and I was dead tired after a long day on the show. Maybe I worked my way once around the room, talking to a couple of people here and there, and then I was ready to call it quits. I went over to the host to say good-bye. He said, "Did you meet Kitty Grant?"

The name didn't ring a bell. "Who's that?"

He pointed to a tall brunette across the room. She was a good-looking young woman with a great-looking body. "You got to meet her, Milton."

"Why?"

The guy just laughed and took me by the arm and started steering me over to her. "You'll find out."

So I met Kitty Grant, and we went through the how-do-you-do's, and the I-like-your-show routine. Just as I was wondering how I could get away and what the hell was so special about her, this very well-mannered lady said, "I hear you're lots of fun in bed."

It had been so long since anything had shocked me that I had forgotten what it felt like. "I beg your pardon?" was my sharp comeback.

Anyway, Kitty Grant and I went to bed together, and it was wild. Kitty went about sex the way a man did. She liked it, she wanted it, and she went after it.

She wasn't a pro. In fact, from nine to five Kitty was a top secretary on Madison Avenue. What she did after five was just about anything anybody could think of. You could say to Kitty, "Now what I want you to do is hang by your heels from the chandelier wearing only a football helmet and holding a bottle of Cel-Ray Tonic in your left hand and a copy of the *Wall Street Journal* in your right while I make love to you." Kitty wouldn't even blink. She'd just smile and say, "Let's try it."

And that's how Kitty Grant became Dr. Grant. I bought her a complete nurse's uniform—hat, cape, white stockings, the whole thing—and a black medical bag, which we filled with all sorts of half-empty prescription bottles and junk from our medicine cabinets. Kitty kept the outfit and bag at her office.

It might happen during a rough day of putting together a sketch, or in the middle of an especially bad rehearsal, when I was filled with tension. I wanted to relax. I'd suddenly think of Kitty. I'd start moaning, or coughing, or showing pain, until somebody would ask me what was wrong.

I'd say I wasn't feeling too good, and could they call for my doctor, Dr. Grant, the phone number was in my book. I'd go to my dressing room and say that I wanted to be alone to rest. In about twenty minutes, looking very crisp and efficient in her white uniform and blue cape, there was Dr. Grant. "Now, what seems to be the trouble, Mr. Berle?" she'd say as she closed the door behind us.

And I'd say, "It hurts down here, Doctor."

When Dr. Grant left to go back to her office and change into her secretarial clothes, it didn't hurt down there anymore.

Television was booming. In 1947, according to *Life* magazine, there were 17 stations throughout the country broadcasting to 136,000 sets, but by the end of 1948 there were "more than 50 stations, 700,000 sets and a potential audience of almost four million." For once I had really hit it right. I was being called "Mr. Television," and it looked like the title might be worth having. (I loved Joe E. Lewis's line: "Berle is responsible for more television sets being sold than anyone else. I sold mine, my father sold his . . .") Of course, you wouldn't have known television was going anywhere if you checked the Hollywood brain trust. Even as television was killing off box-office business at movie houses across the country, the Hollywood studios were showing no interest in being part of the medium, and most Hollywood stars avoided appearing. But one step in the right direction was that my agents, the William Morris office, acknowledged that all the business my show was giving them warranted a department to handle it. So William Morris, using the name of Stellar Attractions, which I suggested to them, went into television.

As the show rolled along, week after week, growing bigger and bigger, I kept worrying about the fact that all our work was going to waste. The only record of it was on kinescope, which I knew wouldn't be good enough for the future. Kinescope was a picture of the picture on the television screen. It was gray and grainy in comparison to what could be gotten on film. But there was no interest in putting television shows on film in 1948–49. The Hollywood money men were watching and waiting.

On April 9, 1949, I ran the first telethon. I did it, with Walter Winchell and Leonard Lyons, to raise money for the Damon Runyon Cancer Fund, but I'll admit that it crossed my mind that a show with all the advance excitement that the publicity for the telethon was creating might make the film magnates reconsider the power of television. It didn't, but I had the satisfaction of raising pledges of $1,250,000 in twenty-two hours for the Fund.

One of the big reasons I wanted to go on film was to eliminate the mistakes that went out over the tube. With film, the show we had planned and rehearsed could be the show the viewers would see, not the epic fluffs and the embarrassing mistakes, the terrible accidents that got big laughs but threw the show so off schedule that too often I had to stop an act in the middle and kill a sketch before we got to the punch line, because it was time for the sign-off.

The stories of what went wrong on camera during the early years of the *Texaco Star Theatre* run into the millions. I'll only give you a few thousand.

One time, I was dressed in drag as a bride, playing opposite Fatso Marco as my groom. Fatso came out in front of the rollerdrop walking at the slow, measured step of a man going down the aisle to get married. Then there was the announcement, "And here he is, America's number one June bride, Milton Berle!" and I started out across the stage in a crazy white gown with a long train. As I hit center stage, the rollerdrop started rolling up to reveal the chapel setting. The drop caught the long train of my dress, and the next thing I knew, I was hanging in mid-air. When I didn't turn up at Fatso's side, he got nervous and started looking around, shouting off stage, "Where is he? Where is he?" while I was hanging in mid-air over him. The audience thought it was planned, and went crazy laughing while I was ad libbing gags in mid-air but scared stiff. We ran seven minutes over that night. No finish again.

Then there was the night I was doing a scene with Red Buttons that I had done many times in the past without any mishaps. It was called "Confidential Auto Loan." Sometimes I played the straight man and sometimes the comic. The night of this story, Red played the comic, the guy who goes to a finance company wanting to borrow five hundred dollars. The high point of the sketch is where he is told to take off his clothes for the physical examination. My sister, Roz, made a breakaway suit for Red that worked fine right through the dress rehearsal, when I yanked it off him, revealing Red in his undershirt and big, baggy comedy drawers.

Center stage, in front of the cameras, we came to the moment where I shouted at Red, "Take off your clothes! Take off your clothes!"

Red just looked confused and embarrassed, as he was supposed to. I reached out and grabbed at his shirt and jacket, but the suit didn't break off the way it should have. So I really grabbed and yanked. Only I grabbed too much, and suddenly there was Red looking very red and giving America a quick look at more than his buttons before the camera cut away.

Carmen Miranda, the Brazilian Bombshell, ran into Red's kind of trouble on the show the night she made a quick change between her solo number and the dance she did with Cesar Romero. In the dance, she went into a spin that raised her skirt. She had forgotten to put on her panties, and gave the country an idea of what was happening south of the border.

Ted Lewis made his first television appearance on *Texaco*, and at his wife Ada's insistence bought a toupee for the occasion. Naturally, he did his famous number, "When My Baby Smiles at Me." At the close, he did his line, "Yes sir, is everybody happy?" and bent his head so that his top hat would drop off and roll down his arm, the way he had done it for decades. The hat came off on cue, and the toupee lifted from the back and fell over his face. It was awful for Ted.

Sharkey, a trained seal, had a great act. He could balance anything. One of the things he balanced was a potty. Only nobody told Sharkey that NBC had cut the potty bit—too offensive in those days—from his act. Everything went great in Sharkey's act until it was time for him to balance the potty on the tip of his nose. No potty. The poor seal kept wandering around the stage looking for his potty. He wouldn't get off. The audience howled, and the show ran overtime again.

One of the sad moments was the week we booked Tallulah Bankhead on the show. Not that the audience knew what the rest of us were feeling. They laughed and found Tallulah as outrageous as ever. Only they didn't know that she wasn't getting the laughs she had rehearsed, or that even she didn't know some of what she was doing on camera. All through the dress rehearsal, she had been drinking spirits of ammonia in water. By show time she had reached the foggy state that I guess she wanted or needed to be in.

The night that Grady Sutton came on the show, he broke it up completely. Remember him? The tall fat guy with the face of a baby? Because I was, as usual, involving myself in every phase of the show, I asked Hal Collins to fill in for me in the sketch I was going to do with Grady. Grady was playing one of his fuss-budget store-manager types, and I was to play the delivery boy.

Grady never saw me until the night of the show. Having worked with Hal Collins all week, he assumed Hal was the actor he would appear with on the show. On the night, Grady went into the sketch and made the telephone call: "Would you send a boy right up to deliver a package?"

There was a knock on the set door, and I came in in a comedy outfit and yellow shoes, with my front teeth blacked out. Grady stared at me and said, "What happened to the little fat man?" I cracked up.

Nobody ever had it worse on the show than Basil Rathbone—or at least, that's what he thought at the time. In fairness to him, it must have been rough for a man of Basil's dignity to find himself in front of the camera with Martha Raye and me. Both of us can go pretty wild in the low-comedy department when we forget our lines. Which is exactly what happened in some sort of Sherlock Holmes takeoff that was dreamed up for Basil's guest shot. We just ran wild around him, pushing, shoving, ad libbing, mugging, swinging burlesque bladders. Mr. Rathbone looked stunned throughout the whole thing. As soon as he got off stage, he said to the first person he met, "Nevah again will I work with those two fucking people! Nevah!"

He was on the show three weeks later, after everyone he knew had congratulated him on how marvelous he looked and on what a great flair for comedy he had displayed.

Bruce Cabot appeared on *Texaco* and was never introduced, thanks to Fatso Marco. Half of the reason why Fatso was so funny on a stage was the confusion that was always part of him. There was always something punchy about him. Besides that, Fatso couldn't read or write, and he was terrible at learning lines.

We were doing a Cleopatra sketch, with me playing Cleopatra to Bruce Cabot's Julius Caesar. Fatso's big line was "And here he is now, Julius Caesar." Fatso had the line worked out fine, until at the dress rehearsal it was decided that it would be funnier if Fatso said "Sid Caesar" instead. The last-minute switch threw Fatso, and I think he got Sid and Irving Caesar mixed up in his mind. On camera, the sketch was running long and in trouble before we got to Fatso's line, because my falsies kept slipping out of place. And then we got to Fatso and he proudly announced, "And here he is now, Irving Sussman!", whoever the hell that was. Bruce Cabot came on in his toga and wreath, looking about as Jewish as Gary Cooper, and found himself lost in a sketch that had gone Yiddish on him. And worse, it ran so long that I never got the chance to introduce him to the audience on the closing, because we got cut off.

The credit for what was probably the most screwed-up sketch we ever did on television has to go to Edward Arnold. Off stage, he was a delightful, witty man; on stage, a polished performer. He was going to play in a sketch with me and Mary Beth Hughes called "The King Of Mars." I was to be a newspaper reporter from the *Daily Rabbit* sent up to Mars to find out if there was life there and bring back a story. Eddie was the king of Mars, and Mary Beth his daughter.

What I didn't know was the advice friends of Eddie's had given him before he flew east. "Watch out for Berle. He'll ad lib you right off the stage. He doesn't always stick to the script."

Okay, we're on live, and Eddie makes his entrance in his fancy cloak and a hat that made him look like a bishop. I started to interview him for the *Rabbit* about life on Mars. "How long have you been here?" I asked.

It was a line we had rehearsed, but I think Eddie forgot it and decided I was ad libbing. He answered, "I just flew in from California," and he added, "I heard about you."

I didn't know what was going on. How could the king of Mars have heard about me when I just came up from Earth? I went on with the script. "Do you like it here?" I meant Mars.

Eddie said, "Oh, yes, I haven't been in New York for a long time."

I saw Mary Beth standing out of camera range, waiting to come on and looking very confused. I decided that Edward Arnold was having television's first live nervous breakdown. Maybe if I could get Mary Beth Hughes out on stage, we could still salvage something of the sketch. "Are you here alone?" I said heavily, trying to remind him about Mary Beth.

Eddie grinned. "No, I brought my wife along."

I gave up. "Mary Beth Hughes, get out here, please!"

Eddie did that famous belly laugh of his. "Some ad libbing, eh, Milton?"

Sometimes what got the big laughs from the audience were no laughs at all to the performers. One week we rented a very funny sketch called "Full Fathom Five" that Sid Caesar had done in the Broadway revue *Make Mine Manhattan*. It had to do with a guy testing a fountain pen to see if it really did write under water. It meant that the guy ended up at the bottom of a transparent glass tank filled with water, testing the pen.

The only source of water that we had around Studio 6B was the sink in my bathroom, so they had to get a hose and pipe it from there. What with my fear of drafts and with the way I sweat before I go on, and how much I sweated under the hot television lights, I insisted over and over again that the guys in charge make sure the water in the tank was lukewarm. When I went into the water in front of the audience, it was freezing cold. I could barely say my lines. I was sneezing before the sketch was over, and I was out of the show for two weeks afterward.

Almost as bad was what happened when Lauritz Melchior and James Barton were guests. Melchior did a solo number, after which, for an encore, he announced that he had a request to do "Figaro" from *The*

Barber of Seville. The set was a barber shop, with Melchior as the barber and me as his customer. He was supposed to lather me and shave me while he did the song. At the finish he would take the whole bucket of lather and dump it over my head. I had requested and been promised a plastic bucket for the lather. And that's what Melchior thought he had when he threw the bucket over my head. It turned out to be tin, and it gashed my nose—my nice straight plastic-surgery nose!—right across the bridge. I was bleeding like a stuck pig when I came off camera.

If that wasn't bad enough, in the next number I had to be in blackface (it was still allowed then) to do a double act with James Barton. We used Band-Aids on top of Band-Aids to absorb the blood, and put the cork on over that. Luckily, this was before color television, because by the end of the number the blood that was soaking through the Band-Aids and cork was running down my face.

I raced straight from the show to the nearest hospital, and thanks to some medical genius whose name I never knew, the bleeding was stopped and I didn't have any stitches taken.

But of everything that ever went wrong on *Texaco Star Theatre*, the worst of all was the appearance of Ella the Elephant, and Company, a three-elephant act that must have been fed only on beans. I was in front of the rollerdrop doing my opening monologue while the elephant act was being set up behind. No one could miss the sounds of the elephants breaking wind behind the drop. And it didn't stop. The sounds exploded throughout my entire monologue. I pounded on the drop once and yelled out Fred Allen's line, which he once said to a hawk that relieved itself on his show: "Stop ad libbing!" It didn't help. The audience was in hysterics, I was breaking up, and even the cameras were shaking.

I was both laughing and furious when I got to the end of my monologue and introduced the act, while the terrible sounds were being picked up by the boom mike. "And now I would like to introduce an act that is dying to get on, and when they get on, they'll die. Ladies and gentlemen, Ella the Elephant, and Company!"

Alan Roth led the band into the circus-music intro, and the drop rose, and there were the elephants, one large and two small—and a very unhappy trainer. There were unmistakable piles of elephant shit all over the stage floor. The act was a disaster, because you could hear the elephants' music over Alan Roth's. Worse still, you couldn't really appreciate the animals' tricks, because the cameras had to shoot high so that the viewers didn't see what else the elephants were doing on stage.

But the worst was still to come. Because this was live television, you couldn't stop the show to clean up the stage before the next act. And the next act was the very classy Jack Cole and his dancers, the Kraft Sisters. It was just terrible to watch Jack and his troupe trying to do their exotic Indian routines while slipping and sliding all over the stage.

But not everything that went wrong on the show turned out for the worst. If it weren't for a mistake, I'd never have been "Uncle Miltie."

When the show hit and people started stopping me in the streets, very often I'd get a woman saying to me that she had trouble getting her children to go to sleep at the right time on Tuesdays. Couldn't I please say something to them over television about going to bed when they were supposed to? I always explained that I wasn't allowed to. The sponsor wouldn't like it, and there was an FCC ruling against personal messages, that sort of thing.

When we began the 1949 season, and the sponsor was putting more money into the show, we hired a script girl with a stopwatch to time the dress rehearsal and give us an idea of how much time we should allow for the laughs. Assuming nothing went wrong on the show, we still knew that all she could give us, based on our stop-and-start dress rehearsals, was an educated guess.

That night, on the opening show of the season, I came out to sing the sign-off, "Near You," and do the closing spiel. Ralph Nelson, a great director today but a floor man on our show then, held up seven fingers to me. It caught me by surprise. "We have seven more minutes to go?" I said over the air. "Okay, somebody bring out a chair."

I started ad libbing, digging out anything I could think of. Then I said to Nelson, "How are we doing?" It felt like I had used up fifteen minutes.

He held up five fingers.

That's when I remembered those requests from mothers. Since I was running out of things to say, I went into a spiel off the top of my head. "Since this is the beginning of a new season, I want to say something to any of you kiddies who should be in bed, getting a good night's rest before school tomorrow. Listen to your Uncle Miltie, and kiss Mommy and Daddy good night and go straight upstairs like good little boys and girls . . ."

Finally I got the sign-off signal, and maybe two minutes after the show was over I forgot that I had used the name "Uncle Miltie." It was just an ad-lib time-filler, a name I had made up on the spur of the moment.

I didn't remember it until the next day in Boston. I had promised to make an appearance there for the Catholic Youth Organization. They brought me into town from the airport in an open car. At one point the motorcade passed a gang with picks and shovels working in the street, and one of the guys yelled out, "Hey, Uncle Miltie!" That's when I first knew that I had found a tag that stuck with people.

I got the idea confirmed when I was back at the airport and a man with a little boy pointed to me and said, "Look, there's Uncle Miltie."

You can work for years and never come up with a line, a word, a gesture that catches on and becomes identified with you, and without thinking I had lucked into one. When I got back to New York, I told the writers what had happened, and on next week's show, when it came sign-off time, I said, "Good night to all you boys and girls, my nephews and nieces, this is your Uncle Miltie saying good night."

I started getting letters addressed to Uncle Miltie, USA, and I knew the handle had taken. So I started writing safety songs and all kinds of poetic advice for the sign-off. I even wrote and published a song, "Uncle Miltie," which somehow didn't replace "The Star-Spangled Banner."

If people shouting "Uncle Miltie" when I walked down the street once told me how popular the *Texaco* show was, the same phrase today tells me that time has moved on. Several times, I've had a man or a woman in his or her thirties or forties come up to me with a child and say to it, "Say hello to Uncle Miltie," and the kid has said, "I don't have an Uncle Miltie."

But of all the memories I have of that name, my favorite goes back to the time when Bishop Fulton J. Sheen had his program on the Dumont channel at the same time as mine on NBC-TV. One night he began his program by saying, "Good evening, this is Uncle Fultie."

❧ 23 ❧

Joyce opened on Broadway on January 11, 1949, in the Jackie Gleason–Nancy Walker revue, *Along Fifth Avenue*. On June 16, 1949, two days before the show closed, we got married again.

Why? Because we loved each other. Maybe we would never have found it out, but little Vicki kept us in touch. And the more Joyce and I talked, the easier it became for us to talk, and then I started picking her up after her show went dark for the night, and we'd go somewhere for a late supper or she'd come along with me when I did a benefit. During that time, I think we both worked harder at being the person the other one wanted than we did when we were married.

It was hard with me having the top television show in the country to plan quiet evenings for two without a mob of hangers-on, but for our late suppers I usually took her to places off the standard late-night run of the Broadway crowd. And if Joyce was tired, she did her best to hide it from me.

What brought things to a head, I think, was the agreement with Warner Brothers for me to make the picture *Always Leave Them Laughing* during my summer layoff. Suddenly I faced two months without seeing Vicki and Joyce, and the time seemed like years to me. I called Joyce to tell her about the picture and that I'd be gone all of July and August. Joyce just said, "Oh," and it sounded sad.

"Is that all you can say?" I asked.

"Vicki's going to miss you."

"Is anybody else going to miss me?"

There was a long silence—I couldn't breathe while I waited—and then Joyce said, "I'll miss you very much, Milton."

"And I'll miss you."

Another silence. I broke this one. "Joyce, what are we going to do about it?"

And suddenly we decided.

I told Mama the same afternoon. "I suppose you know what you're doing?" she said. But Mama made it sound as if I didn't.

I felt that old tension starting in me that always came when I didn't want to face my relationship with Mama. That it was too strong, that it was too close. "Mama, Joyce and I have a little girl now. I love Vicki, and I can't stand being separated from her so much. I want her with me all the time." So I built my explanation—even while I hated myself for feeling the need to explain—around Vicki, not around my love for Joyce.

"Then you shouldn't have gotten a divorce in the first place," Mama said.

"We all make mistakes."

Mama nodded, and the discussion was over.

That it ended so easily made me take a good look at Mama. She had always been there. I never noticed the changes through the years. Mama just *was.* But suddenly I saw the little pause before she picked up something from the table, the slight shuffle to her walk. Mama didn't look it —she was seventy-two—but she was getting old.

I felt a tremendous rush of love for her. I went to her and hugged her against me. "It's going to be all right," I said. "It's going to be just great."

So Joyce and I got married, at the home of Surrogate William T. Collins, and we celebrated with lunch at "21." We toasted each other with champagne, and made incredible promises for our new future together.

Then we took off for Hollywood, the three of us—Joyce, Vicki, and me—and checked into the Beverly Hills Hotel. It was a happy time, a sort of work-honeymoon. During the day I was on the set of *Always Leave Them Laughing,* with a first-rate cast—Virginia Mayo, Ruth Roman, Bert Lahr—and even if the picture was being rushed to cash in on my *Texaco* popularity, it was still being given the A-picture polish. By nights, Joyce and I were out on the town having a great time together, but calling it an evening early because I had to work the next day and because we really wanted to get back to our bungalow at the Beverly Hills Hotel to be alone. It was like the best days of our first marriage, only better, we thought, because we knew what had gone wrong the first time and could protect ourselves from its happening again.

And then it all fell apart. We had been in California only two weeks when Mama showed up.

That sounds terrible, so I've got to explain. I owe that to Mama's memory. She didn't come out to destroy my marriage, or even to interfere in it. That wasn't Mama's way. She knew enough of life to have learned acceptance a long time before. Mama fought a situation only when there was a chance of winning. She never wasted her strength on a fight that was already lost. Mama came to Hollywood because that's where I was working. It was as simple as that to her. She came the same way a man will fight his way across a desert to get to water. It means life. Just as I knew no other life but show business, neither did Mama. And just because I appeared on stage while she sat in the audience, it didn't make my career any less hers.

I say all that because I understand it now. But I didn't really understand it then. Only partially. The rest of me was torn apart between anger and guilt. And in a different way, so was Joyce. On the one hand, a mother was a sacred thing to her, and on the other, a marriage meant only two people. The marriage could expand to three and more if it meant the children of the two, but the only adults in a marriage were one man and one woman.

Much as I was pleased to see Mama blooming because she was back in the middle of show biz again, she brought tensions with her for Joyce and me. The promises we had made to each other before being married the second time didn't seem to hold anymore. Joyce had explained to me that she wanted to work and I had to understand, and I said I would. But suddenly now, if I had a day off from the picture and I woke up to find Joyce's side of the bed empty, I was angry. And when she showed up and said something like, "I heard there might be something over at MGM for me so I thought I'd check it out," I started boiling.

It was as if we had gone straight from the altar onto the rocks.

When we returned to New York, it felt good moving back into the apartment I had left when Joyce and I had divorced the first time. And I thought it would make it a little easier on me when Texaco decided to drop the radio show and concentrate just on television for 1949–50. It didn't. It just gave me a little more time to drive myself and everyone around me that much harder to make the *Texaco Star Theatre* better.

That was about all the good news that fall. Things did not pick up for Joyce and me when we got back to New York. I'm sure I was tough enough to live with, what with all the pressures I brought with me every day from the show and rehearsals. Our marriage didn't need outside help, and that's what Joyce was getting from the friends she was spending her time with. Her friends were Beverly Whelan; Kay Buckley; a gorgeous showgirl named Rose Teed; Carrie Denny; and Jacqueline Susann, then an actress.

If they were Joyce's good friends, I didn't think of them as mine, but the fault was Joyce's. Joyce, instead of working out her own problems, was a great one for asking advice, and whoever got in the last word, that was whom Joyce listened to. Joyce and I might have had a minor blowup at breakfast. By lunchtime she had just about forgotten it, unless she happened to mention it to one of the girls, who said to Joyce, "What do you mean you're going to forget about it? I wouldn't take that from him!" Joyce came home all steamed up again.

One of our lesser fights occurred because of a mistake a friend of mine, Harry Collins (Hal's father), made. He was around the Nola Studios one day during a rehearsal. There was a singer I was supposed to hear later in the week. I remember her first name was Gloria. I was busy, so I gave Harry the number. "Dial this number for me, and ask for Gloria. Say Milton Berle's calling."

So Harry went to the phone. He was half watching the rehearsal while he dialed, which probably explains why, without thinking, he dialed my home. And when he heard a woman's voice, he said, "Gloria? Milton Berle calling."

The voice at the other end sounded hard. "This isn't Gloria. It's Joyce!"

Harry hung up, shaking.

That night when I got home, an ashtray and a paperweight went flying around the room. Joyce never believed the true story. I heard about Gloria for weeks afterward.

The big blowup came at the beginning of December, 1949, when neither of us was expecting it. We had planned to go to Miami for two weeks around the holidays. I had been working hard, and Joyce was finishing up a stock engagement of the Maugham play *Theatre*, with Jessie Royce Landis, over in New Jersey. We both were looking forward to Miami and getting off by ourselves, maybe getting the marriage back on the track it had been on six months before.

The night it happened, I had arranged to meet Joyce at the Copacabana right after her show. We figured she could get back to New York by 12:30. I got to the Copa Lounge around 12:15. It was a rainy night, so the place was half empty. While I waited for Joyce, I chewed the fat with Jack Eigen, who broadcast from the Lounge.

Twelve thirty came and went, and no Joyce. The later it got, the angrier I got. It was after two when Joyce showed up with her girlfriend, Kay Buckley. Joyce was wearing a raincoat and a bandanna over her hair. She didn't seem the least upset about keeping me waiting. "Where the hell have you been?" I asked.

Joyce just smiled. "We got mixed up. We were waiting for you over at La Martinique."

"You know I told you the Copa."

Joyce shrugged her shoulders as if it were nothing. "Well, I'm here now."

It was the smart answer that did it. I grabbed her by the scarf that was around her neck and hair, and I started shaking her. Joyce started screaming, "You're killing me! You're hurting me!"

She dug her nails into my hand to free herself. Then, screaming and sobbing, she ran for the ladies' room.

Kay Buckley glared at me. "Why did you do that? You want to kill her?"

"You stay out of it!" I snapped at her.

Kay followed Joyce to the powder room.

The fight made all the columns and added fuel to the fire. Then came the Miami trip. I went alone, and Joyce went to her lawyers.

This time she went to the Virgin Islands for the divorce.

I came back from Miami in time for the loneliest New Year's Eve of my life. And the most ironic.

Billy Rose and his wife, Eleanor Holm, threw a New Year's Eve party in the big rehearsal hall on the eighth floor of the Ziegfeld Theatre, which he owned. Every top name in show business was invited. Billy made an announcement at the beginning of the evening that this was a party for all his friends, and none of them was expected to entertain. You might as well tell ice not to melt. I grabbed a mike and emceed a show that no producer could afford. Mary Martin and Ethel Merman were only two of the names who performed for free.

And then it was midnight, and everybody was kissing everybody. I felt so alone I wanted to die. I grabbed the hatcheck girl and kissed her, but all I could think about was Joyce.

That's when Billy Rose came over to me. He didn't know Joyce at that point. He shook my hand for the New Year and said, "If you want a happy New Year, Milton, just keep it in mind that blonds like Joyce are a dime a dozen."

I suppose he meant well, but at the time his remark hurt deep. Only a little later on, it became one of the saddest, funniest lines I ever heard. He still had his two marriages to Joyce ahead of him.

On January 27, 1950, the National Academy of Television Arts and Sciences presented its second annual Emmy awards. I won for "Most Outstanding Kinescoped Personality," and the *Texaco Star Theatre* won for "Best Kinescope Show."

The show and other performers on it received nominations in later years, but aside from being asked to appear at the awards celebration of Emmy's tenth year in 1959, I have never been asked to present an award, take a bow, or even attend. But then, they've never shown their appreciation to Ed Sullivan or Jackie Gleason either. No comment.

Joyce's divorce from me became official on March 30, 1950. The combined alimony and support figure came to $30,000 a year. We shared custody of Vicki, with the agreement that Joyce would not take her out of the country. Beyond that, Joyce and I agreed that Vicki would be raised as a Christian Scientist, and we promised each other that neither of us would ever say anything against the other in front of Vicki.

So I was free again. Free—what a lousy word when you're still hurting inside. I did what I always did: I worked harder, played every benefit that wanted me, spent more time losing money at the track and with the bookmakers, and took out—or tried to—every beautiful woman I met.

And I still saw Joyce. With two divorces behind us, we still occasionally went out together. I don't think either one of us knew what the hell we were doing. The columns started hinting that we might marry for a third time, but we never mentioned it to each other.

Meanwhile, the *Texaco Star Theatre* continued to skyrocket. The first reading from the new Nielsen ratings gave me the number-one spot on television: We pulled down a 79.9, a mile ahead of *Arthur Godfrey and His Friends,* in second spot with 55.2.

In the summer of 1950, I went out to Hollywood determined that what I was doing on television wasn't going down the drain. I wanted the shows on film. So I made an appointment to see Louis B. Mayer at MGM, and made my pitch.

He listened to me, but he seemed puzzled. "MGM-TV. What would that be?"

I explained how MGM could take one of their sound stages and transform it into a television studio, and—but Mayer cut me short. He stood up to show me to the door and said, "Mr. Berle, MGM is in the motion-picture business, not the television business."

From Mayer, I went to Darryl Zanuck at 20th Century–Fox, and from him to Harry Cohn at Columbia. They turned me down too. Television was already crippling the motion-picture industry, but the big three were still not facing the facts.

Naturally, whenever I got to the Coast I would ask around about Linda and Jed Weston. There was absolutely no word on her—some people thought she was dead, others guessed she was in retirement, and nobody really cared. Jed, I heard, had suffered a stroke and was seeing no one. I was told that his boy, Larry, was staying with Jed's parents—but no one knew for certain where they lived—while Jed was recovering.

The only fun I had that summer were my dates with Ann Sheridan. In a town like Hollywood, where everyone took themselves very seriously, Annie never did. She liked being a star, but she couldn't be bothered believing all the garbage that went with it. I remember one night when we were at the Trocadero together and Annie spotted Florabelle Muir, one of the top syndicated gossip columnists, eyeing us from a nearby table. "Watch this," Annie said and got up.

She went over to Florabelle's table. She said something to her, and Florabelle took one pop-eyed look at me and began making frantic notes on a pad. Annie came back with a big grin on her face. "What the hell did you tell her?" I asked.

Annie looked very satisfied with herself. "I just asked her if she had heard the news about you and me?"

"What news?"

"That we're getting married in two weeks."

Ann Sheridan and I both broke up. But Florabelle didn't. She printed her big exclusive across the country.

When I read it, I remember that the first thing I thought of was, what will Joyce think when she reads it?

Aside from Ann Sheridan, I also had some dates with Linda Darnell, Audrey Meadows, Myrna Dell, and Veronica Lake while I was in California. The papers picked those stories up too, and again I thought about Joyce. Today, I think about that summer of 1950 and I wonder if I wasn't deliberately going out after the biggest names, the most beautiful women, like some kid saying, "I'll show you!"

I went into the 1950–51 television season with the top-rated show on every rating system—Hooper, Nielsen, Trendex. My salary was now up to $11,500 a week, but I still wasn't happy. Week after week, the work was going down the drain on kinescope. If the shows were as good as they were supposed to be, why the hell wouldn't NBC do something about preserving them so that there would be a chance of reruns and residuals in the '60s and '70s, when it was all over? Film was the coming thing for shows, film was the answer. NBC just listened and said, "We'll see. We're thinking about it."

Another thing that was a constant anger to me was that I didn't have approval on the acts and performers I wanted on the show. I remember clashing with the sponsor and the advertising agency over my signing the four Step Brothers for an appearance on the show. The only thing I could figure out was that there was an objection to black performers on the show, but I couldn't even find out who was objecting. "We just don't like them," I was told, but who the hell was "we"?

Because I was riding high in 1950, I sent out the word: "If they don't go on, I don't go on." At ten minutes of eight—ten minutes before show time—I got permission for the Step Brothers to appear. If I broke the color-line policy or not, I don't know, but later on I had no trouble booking Bill Robinson or Lena Horne.

In June of 1950, the first issue of *Red Channels*, with its so-called facts on performers' political affiliations, appeared, and clearance for performers became really difficult. I screamed and pleaded, but I could never get my good friend John Garfield on the show. And I couldn't even get an explanation of why I couldn't have Gertrude Berg on, even though she had her own television success with *The Goldbergs* at the time.

Later on in the '50s, however, she was booked and there was no problem. I realize now that at the time I wanted her, she was fighting the witch-hunters, who demanded she get rid of Philip Loeb, who played Jake to her Molly. Those "super-patriots" had enough juice to hurt Mrs. Berg in every way to force her to do what they wanted. In time, in order to save the show and the jobs of everyone connected with it, she was forced to let Loeb go. Philip Loeb, a lovable man, saw his whole career shrivel to nothing, and the son he supported in a private mental hospital was transferred to a state institution. Philip Loeb committed suicide in a hotel room.

I was still on top in 1950–51, my third year on television, but around Christmastime, something very important happened. Unfortunately, everybody connected with the show—myself included—missed it. I took two weeks off for a rest, and our rating dropped. It took about three weeks after I returned to bring the rating back up. That should have been a warning, but instead I took it as a compliment to me.

It's one thing to believe in yourself, but maybe I was beginning to believe too much. There were Uncle Miltie comic books, Uncle Miltie chewing gum, tee-shirts with my name on them, wind-up Uncle Miltie cars, a backlist in the hundreds of thousands of requests for tickets to the show, top acts willing to work for peanuts to get on the show, offers for guest appearances at fat figures (I had appeared for 11 minutes on the *Elgin-American Thanksgiving Show* for $1,000 a minute!), mob scenes wherever I went. I think in the back of my mind some part of me forgot all the years of up and down, and I was starting to believe that this would last forever.

I didn't see that there were shifts in the show that were beginning to hurt it. I started allowing too much time for the big finales, because I felt they were a little more sophisticated than the rest of the show, and I wanted some of that gloss to rub off on me. Sure, I liked the fact that the *Star Theatre* had a big appeal for kids, but I also wanted to make it with the sharper adults. So, to accommodate the finales, I was cutting short or cutting out the sketches, often substituting duller stand-up bits with guest stars, because they took up less time. A little of the craziness was draining out of the show, and while it hadn't shown up yet on the ratings, it was there like an undiscovered cancer, eating away.

If my ego needed any more boosting, I got it on May 3, 1951, when NBC sat down at the conference table with me and my lawyers to sign what was called a lifetime contract. This was NBC's answer to my badgering about going on film. They were offering me a future instead of future residuals. And from their point of view, they were solving the problem of the guest appearances I had been making on other networks.

The lifetime contract was for 30 years. It gave NBC-TV exclusive use of my television services through August 31, 1981. In return, I was to be paid $200,000 a year for each of those 30 years. It seemed more fantastic at the time than it turned out to be. Because what it meant was that if the day came when NBC-TV didn't have anything for me to do, I couldn't work anywhere else on television.

That sort of deal would probably be fine for most people. But for me, life is work, and relaxation is just a word in the dictionary. Money—having it or not having it—is not frightening to me. I've lived both ways. Money never produced ulcers for me. But not working eats me up inside. And without thinking about it, that's what I signed up for when I signed that contract.

⪻ 24 ⪼

The summer of 1951 was one I won't ever forget. It began with the musical *Seventeen*, based on the Booth Tarkington novel. I was one of the producers, and this time out I was sure I had a hit, which would make it the first one I ever produced. It wasn't. *Seventeen* opened on June 21 and struggled to stay alive for 180 performances. It was too ice cream and cake for New York audiences, which were more accustomed to the caviar of *South Pacific* and *Kiss Me Kate*.

I was still not recovered from Joyce, and I didn't like the rumors I was hearing around town that Joyce was seeing Billy Rose, who was supposedly happily married to Eleanor Holm. I decided I wanted to get away. I flew to London and from there to Paris, and spent most of my time scouting acts that might work on the television show.

I flew back on July 14, and I was swamped with reporters at the airport. I came off the plane smiling and doing bits, thinking they were there because of my television fame. The first question I got stopped me cold. "What do you think about the William and Joyce Rosenberg thing, Mr. Berle?"

"I don't know what you're talking about."

The reporters gave me a quick synopsis. All I could say was that Joyce was no longer my wife and what she did was her concern. Then I cut out quickly and ducked into my car. The minute I got back to the apartment, I sent out for all of the papers, and there it was, the story of how Billy Rose and Joyce Mathews Berle, traveling under the name of Mr. and Mrs.

William Rosenberg—his real name—had flown up to Montreal together. It was one of the dumbest stunts I had ever heard about. How did they think they could get away with it? They were both pretty well-known faces —Joyce had become hostess of a television show for Ansonia shoes, and had done some commercials for Tintair and the Vim stores, and who hadn't seen pictures of Billy with his wife, Eleanor Holm? Joyce and Billy had barely gotten to Montreal before they were told that the New York papers had gotten wind of the trip, so they turned right around and came back. Joyce told the press that she was in conference with Billy about some television work, and she had flown along with him so they could wind up the talks. You needed assumed names for *that?*

I grabbed the phone and called Joyce. "Are you out of your mind?" I shouted at her.

"Please, please," Joyce said. "It was crazy, I know."

"Look," I said, "I don't give a damn what you do. That's your business. But it's my business when it involves Vicki's mother. Do you know I could have you declared unfit and take Vicki away?"

I heard Joyce catch her breath. "You wouldn't! Please, Milton, you wouldn't!"

"I didn't say I would. I'm just warning you, Joyce, that I could."

And that ended the conversation. It completely ended any romantic hangover I still had about Joyce.

I thought Joyce and Billy—if she was still seeing him after Eleanor got through tearing him apart over the Montreal trip—would keep whatever they were up to way underground in the future.

The Montreal trip was nothing compared to what happened next. I spent the weekend with Vicki. I took her to Atlantic City. That's where I got the call on Sunday, July 15, that Joyce had tried to commit suicide in Billy Rose's apartment in the Ziegfeld Theater. (Ironically, the show at the Ziegfeld was *Gentlemen Prefer Blondes.*) I grabbed the next train for New York.

When I got into New York, and left Vicki with my close friends, Ken and Norma Roberts, the early editions of Monday's *News* and *Mirror* were already on the stands. The story was incredible. Joyce and Billy had quarreled about something in his seventh-floor apartment, and Joyce ran into the bathroom and locked the door behind her. Billy started pounding on the door, and then hacking at it with a jade letter opener. In desperation, he called the police, who had to get axes to break through the heavy door, where they found Joyce. She had slashed both wrists with a double-edged razor blade. With blood running all over the place, she was on the window ledge when they grabbed her and took her to Roosevelt Hospital with both wrists in tourniquets made from ripped towels.

As my cab raced across town to the hospital, I read the papers. She had handled the press pretty well as she was taken from the Ziegfeld to the ambulance outside. Her only two statements—she made one to the *News* and one to the *Mirror*—as to why she had cut her wrists were, "I happen to like razor blades" and "I was shaving my wrists and the blade slipped."

Billy was quoted as saying to everyone, "No publicity, please. No publicity," and then, "This is the time a man needs his wife." He sent for Eleanor, who shot down from their home in Mt. Kisco, embraced him in front of the press, and then raced off in a car with him.

I got into the hospital through a side entrance to avoid the newspapermen out front. I was braced for another mob upstairs, but there was only Saul Richman, who was Joyce's press agent, and two orderlies on guard in front of her door.

I expected to see Joyce white and weak, maybe not even conscious, from the loss of blood. Instead, she looked as beautiful as ever, and she was sitting up in bed smoking a cigarette. I looked at her wrists. There was only a small bandage on one, but nothing on the other.

Her story, which I had to believe because of the evidence of her wrists, was nothing like what the newspapers carried. "After you called, Milton, I was very upset. I kept thinking about what you said, and about the whole Rosenberg mess, and about Vicki. And my mother got all upset and kept saying you were going to take Vicki away from me. How there was that thing about moral turpitude in our divorce settlement. Finally I couldn't stand it anymore, and I had to talk to someone, so I called Billy, and he told me to come over to the Ziegfeld."

And Joyce said she poured out the whole thing to Billy, maybe hoping that he'd say he would divorce Eleanor and marry her, and that would make everything look better and I wouldn't take Vicki away from her. But Billy didn't say anything, until Joyce repeated, "I'm going to lose my child."

And Billy said, "Don't worry, I'll make it good. What can I give you?"

That's when Joyce got hysterical. "Give me? Give me?" she screamed and ran for the bathroom. "I wanted to do something big and dramatic so that Billy would help me. I never really planned to commit suicide! My God. All I thought was that I had to make Billy realize . . ."

So Joyce took a razor blade out of the medicine cabinet and put it to her wrist. She made one little nick, expecting that at any moment Billy would break down the door—"Isn't that what people are supposed to do?" —and see her with the razor, and that would change everything.

Only Joyce hadn't known how thick and strong the doors were that Flo Ziegfeld had put up. And she didn't count on her own reaction when the nick turned red and a drop of blood welled up. "I just looked, and then I fainted dead away on the bathroom floor. I didn't come to until the police burst in and were standing over me. That was when I really wanted to die. The police, and all those people downstairs when they took me out to the ambulance . . ."

I thought of Joyce the afternoon when she took the sleeping pills in our apartment. This was it all over again—the big dramatic gesture, right out of some bad movie, that was supposed to straighten everything out.

"I suppose it's in all the papers, huh?" Joyce asked.

"What did you expect?" I said.

"Oh, if only Billy hadn't called the police. He shouldn't have done that."

"What else could he do? For all he knew, you were dying in there."

Joyce nodded. "You took a chance coming to see me, don't think I don't know that, Milton. This could hurt your television show."

"Forget it," I said, "I can take care of myself. But you and Billy are in for it now."

Joyce shook her head. "I never want to see him again."

Then she started to cry. "I'm so worried about Vicki. Do you think Vicki will find out?"

"I don't know. Let's hope not."

"Milton," she said, and she hesitated. "I've been stupid, and a lot of other things, but you know I'm not an unfit mother. You know how much I love Vicki. Please don't take her away from me."

"I told you I wouldn't when I called you the other day. Why didn't you believe me then?"

"I was so worried, and so ashamed. Just don't take her away from me, Milton. Please! Please!"

"I won't. So long as I know you're taking good care of Vicki, I'll never do that to you."

Joyce and Billy must have prayed for a war or at least an earthquake or a train wreck that summer of 1951 to take them off the front pages, but nothing seemed to happen anywhere in the world. And they stayed in the headlines, with the papers making up what they couldn't find out, right through the divorce trial—which the papers christened "The War of the Roses"—with Joyce named as corespondent by Eleanor. Joyce spent the whole time indoors, hiding out from the newsmen.

But during that time, she had very little to come out for. Her television show for Ansonia shoes was immediately canceled. Any interest that Tintair or the Vim stores had in her for future commercials was forgotten. Even her agents forgot that she was a client.

It was a bad time for Joyce. Eventually, as everybody knows, Joyce married Billy Rose twice, just as she had done with me. They had been divorced—for the second time—when Billy Rose died, but he left her comfortably provided for.

Joyce, today, is as beautiful as ever, but, to give her great credit, she has changed her life style completely. She's leading the quiet life and working hard as a travel agent in southern California.

Except for my worry about Joyce—in terms of Vicki—August was one hell of a month for me. I played the Roxy Theatre in New York with a guaranteed salary of $35,000 a week. Because I played to packed houses for my entire run, my salary came to more than that, but between what the government was taking and what I was pouring into *Seventeen* to keep it open until the public could find out—which they didn't—what a great show it was, I wasn't wearing holes in my pants pockets.

September. New York began revving up for fall. I started getting back into the *Texaco* grind, not knowing it was going to be my last year of the show the way it had been. And not knowing that I was about to meet the most important woman in my life.

1950-1960

Marilyn Monroe was one of the women in Milton's life between his marriages to Joyce. (MILTON H. GREENE)

Rehearsing with Martha Raye for the Texaco Star Theatre.
(THE FRIARS CLUB)

As Cinderella on the Texaco show. (NATIONAL BROADCASTING COMPANY, INC.)

Milton used a runway with his studio audiences on TV just as he had in vaudeville. (NATIONAL BROADCASTING COMPANY, INC.)

The Texaco Men. (TEXACO, INC.)

At left, *backstage on the Texaco* Star Theatre. *Below, with ventrilo-quist Jimmy Nelson and puppets Danny O'Day and Farfel, the dog.* (PHOTOS COURTESY OF THE NATIONAL BROADCASTING COMPANY, INC.)

The Texaco show *became the* Buick-Berle Show *in 1953. At right, Milton with Frank Sinatra (far left) and Tallulah Bankhead. Below, Milton directing a rehearsal in 1954.*

Milton married Ruth Cosgrove in 1953. (WIDE WORLD PHOTOS)

Milton is flanked by Mama and Ruth with daughter Vicki in front. Ruth's parents, Mike and Sophie Rosenthal, are at right.

A portrait of Mama was presented to Milton on a This Is Your Life show on June 6, 1956. To his right are Jan Murray, Jerrey Lewis, and Phil Silvers.

The Milton Berle of television had many faces.

At right, Berle as a hillbilly in his act at the Sands, Las Vegas, in 1952. (RAY FISHER)

Below, with pitchman Sid Stone on The Mike Douglas Show.

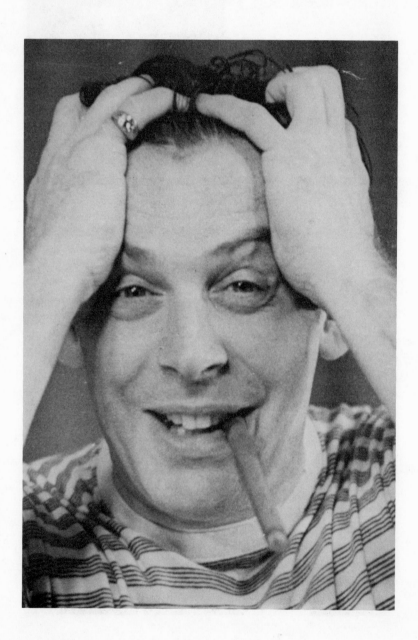

1960-1974

At the dinner given for him by the Friars Club on the occasion of his 60th anniversary in show business at the Beverly Hills Hotel on October 13, 1973. He jokes with Carroll O'Connor as Sammy Davis, Jr., looks on at left.

Milton receiving a Friars Club award from Joe E. Lewis. George Jessel is second from right. (THE FRIARS CLUB)

With the late President Lyndon Johnson at the White House in 1964.

With Frank Sinatra and the late President John F. Kennedy at the Inauguration banquet in 1960.

From the television special "Doyle Against the House." Milton was nominated for an Emmy for this performance. (WIDE WORLD PHOTOS)

Ruth Berle with Vicki and Billy, the son Ruth and Milton adopted in 1962.
(PATRICK CURTIS)

Backstage with Ruth in 1968 when he starred in Herb Gardner's The Goodbye
People. *His 75-year-old makeup by Dick Smith aged him fifteen years for the part.*
(WIDE WORLD PHOTOS)

Milton with his son, Billy. (WIDE WORLD PHOTOS)

Ruth and Milton Berle at a New York premiere.

The Berles at home. (MARTIN MILLS)

✦ 25 ✦

In the late summer and early fall of 1951 I dated Fran Keegan, who had been in *Gentlemen Prefer Blondes*. Fran was always telling me great stories about her roommate, an attractive girl named Ruth Cosgrove, who did publicity for Sam Goldwyn's pictures.

In September I got busy with the first shows for the fourth year of *Texaco Star Theatre*. Fran told me that she and Ruth Cosgrove were going to Las Vegas to vacation for a week or two. That was okay by me, because I was working night and day on the show.

Television was expanding. The medium was developing its own writers, and stars who had refused to appear at the very beginning were more than anxious to get on. New shows were cropping up, and the fight to stay on top was tougher than ever. Competition was heavy against the *Star Theatre*. There was *Your Show of Shows*, with Sid Caesar and Imogene Coca, the *Philco Television Playhouse*, *Arthur Godfrey and His Friends*, Red Skelton, and Lucille Ball and Desi Arnaz with a situation comedy called *I Love Lucy*. None of these shows, which built enormous popularity, was put on in the same time slot as *Texaco*, which was still regarded as murder to buck, but in their own time slots they were racking up high ratings and getting higher.

But after three solid years of doing a live revue each week, I was feeling tired. I insisted on and got the right to take every fourth week off. And that was a big mistake!

The first week of October, I got a call. "This is Ruth Cosgrove. I'm calling for Fran Keegan."

"Oh, hello!"

"I just left Fran in Las Vegas, and she asked me to let you know that she was going to stay on another week or so."

We talked for another minute or so, and I said, "I've heard so much about you, Ruth, I'd like to meet you. How about coming down to see my show this Tuesday night, and we'll have dinner together afterward?"

There was a pause, and then Ruth said, "Well, I really don't want to stay out late. I've got a rough week at the office. Goldwyn's coming out with a big picture soon, *Hans Christian Andersen*, and it's keeping us all pretty busy."

"So we won't make it late," I said. "Come on. I want to meet you."

"Well, all right."

"Great," I said. "I'll have a ticket waiting in your name."

Mama still made Tuesday night at the show a regular thing, and she was always out front—once or twice I had even brought her on camera —to lead the laughter. Almost always Mama planned on being with me after the show.

This time I didn't want her, not on a first date. My brother Jack was working around the show now, and I spoke with him and told him that he had to help me out. He had to take Mama out for dinner afterward, anywhere she wanted, but just see to it that she wasn't with me.

I liked Ruth Cosgrove on sight. She was a cute brunette with short curly hair and a good figure. She was both warm and feminine, and also brutally honest. "What did you think of the show?" I asked when we got away from the studio.

"I liked it," she said. "I mean, there were a couple of things here and there I could have done without."

That annoyed me. "What do you mean by that?"

Ruth looked me straight in the eye. "You asked me what I thought, so I'm telling you. If you don't really want to know, you shouldn't ask."

That was Ruth, a very different woman from Joyce, who knew all the feminine games. Ruth probably knew them too, but she just couldn't be bothered playing them.

All through dinner, I found myself staring at her with more and more respect. There was a strength about her—and I don't mean that in any way that took away from her femininity—that I found myself admiring. I didn't think that Ruth was at all impressed by being out with Milton

Berle. I had the feeling she could take me or leave me, depending on how she felt about me. And that she didn't particularly want anything from me. Ruth could take care of herself.

She talked honestly about herself. Her maiden name was Ruth Rosenthal. She had twice been married briefly. Ruth became a WAC in World War II. She served for four and a half years, working her way up through the ranks and coming out as a captain.

It had been raining hard when we went to dinner. When we left the restaurant it had stopped, so we decided to walk. By this time I really liked her. And I wanted her. Only for once I wasn't sure of my approach, because I wasn't sure of Ruth. She was a brand-new kind of woman to me. So, of all the dumb things, I said, "Say, would you like to see my office? I just had it redecorated."

Ruth looked at me a little funny. "Where is it?"

"Sixteen fifty Broadway."

"What time is it?"

I glanced at my wristwatch. "It's only two o'clock."

Now Ruth really looked at me. "Two o'clock in the morning you want to show me your office? Why?"

I don't think I was that clumsy, even back in the *Florodora* days. "Because . . . well. Because it's decorated."

Why Ruth didn't crack up, I don't know. She was very polite about it. "No thanks. I've seen decor before. But I want you to know I think you're very charming and nice. And some afternoon I'd be very happy to see your office."

So I took Ruth Cosgrove home to her apartment and I left her at the door. And I've never forgotten the night of October 7, 1951, since.

I started seeing Ruth exclusively. I can't say Mama liked her right away, but I think she respected her. As Mama was a woman who did not allow herself to be pushed around, she respected the same thing in Ruth. Even when it interfered with Mama's plans. Fairly soon after Ruth and I started going together, she said to me, "Look, I understand that it's meaningful for your mother to come out with us, but not all the time, Milton. Now, if Tuesday after the show is a big night for her, just let me know. As much as I like being with you, tell me if you feel she should be with you that night. That's one night I can skip, because I have to be up by seven every workday anyway."

Ruth took care of another situation easily, too. The way other people say, "Let's have lunch," or "Give me a call and let's get together," whether they mean it or not, that's how I used to invite women to come around to the dress rehearsals of the show.

And I invited Ruth, too. When she came over, there were four or five other women sitting around, watching. Ruth went over to each one of them and said, "Hi, my name's Ruth. Did Milton ask you to come over?"

The answer was yes. Ruth shook her head. "Just who the hell does he think he is, some kind of sultan and us his harem? You know what we should do? Let's teach him a lesson. Let's all get up and walk out on him."

And that's what they all did, with Ruth leading the way. About fifteen minutes later, Ruth came back alone.

And that's why I was falling in love with Ruth. She wasn't one of the people who go through life sitting back and wringing their hands about what hadn't happened and what the world owed them—I had enough people like that in my life already. Ruth did something about her life. She went after what she wanted, got rid of what she didn't want, and, win or lose, she went on. I admired her enormously.

Today, if a television show is in the top thirty, the sponsor is happy. But back at the beginning, the sponsor was nervous if you weren't in the top five, and if you fell below ten you were dead.

Whenever I took my week off in the 1951–52 season, the show took a nose dive. There were now enough shows on television for the viewer to shop around. And when I came back after a week off, I had to work twice as hard to pull the show back up.

In September of 1951, Nielsen rated our show number one with 56.2. But the climb of *I Love Lucy*, Red Skelton, and other top talent, plus my appearing only three weeks out of four, cost us plenty. According to *Newsweek* magazine, "Berle's Nielsen rating slid from No. 1 to No. 20 between January and June" (September 29, 1952).

And after four years the press, which had helped put me on top, started turning against me. Suddenly, everything they originally liked about me, they didn't like anymore.

Because they had liked me—and let's face it, I also liked the publicity they gave me—rehearsals for the show were always open to guys like Jack Gould, Jack O'Brian, Ben Gross, Bob Williams, and John Crosby. So one day, one of the columnists dropped in. I was working with Dinah Shore. The band played her intro and she came out, and I said, "Applause, applause, applause, go ahead, Dinah." We did our stand-up together, and then she did her specialty. When she finished, I came back out and said, "Wonderful, wonderful, applause, applause, applause."

I found myself attacked in print for wanting applause, for planning applause. I couldn't believe it. The guy who wrote that had been around television and radio long enough to know that a show is timed, that in rehearsal you had to plan on how much time was going to get eaten up by applause and laughter. I was backtiming the show, in the same way that every other show with a live audience was doing it.

The only thing I could do was have NBC install an electric applause sign with a blinker—a first for television—as a way of solving part of the problem.

I was also attacked for horning in on every act, which was part of my style of work from way back to my early days as an m.c. At first, when I was the darling of the television critics, they wrote that I joined in on the fun with the guest stars. But now, doing the same thing, I was a ham and a hog, and I was horning in. Again, the writers had to know that everything that happened on the show was planned. When I came out in drag as Carmen Miranda's sister and took a banana from her head-dress and ate it, that was planned. Rather than horning in, it kept the guest on camera longer than if he or she did a solo and left the stage.

I never worked my way into anybody's act without their permission. The only acts that groused about my hogging were the acts that were sore because they were never asked to appear on the show. None of this is any big secret revealed. All of the columnists knew how I worked. They had been to rehearsals, and had seen these spots planned and worked out.

But suddenly it was "get Berle time," and they went out to get me. The industry knew the truth, but the public had nothing to believe but what they read.

The only public attack I got any pleasure from was the one dreamed up by Hy Kraft and Johnny Mercer, and starring Phil Silvers. It was a big Broadway musical called *Top Banana*, in which Phil played an egomaniac named Jerry Biffle who had a top-rated television show and who directed his rehearsals with a whistle. It was a vicious and funny swipe at me, and I loved it so much, I offered to sue Hy Kraft for the publicity value. Anything to help. After all, I had put some money into the show.

What with the sag in the ratings and the attacks in the press, the Texas Company started to worry, and that meant pressure from the Kudner Agency. They wanted a change.

I admitted that there were repetitions in the show. Sure, the audience knew the minute they saw Sid Stone open his sidewalk suitcase that they were in for a commercial. But what Texaco and the Kudner Agency no longer wanted to accept was that repetition, the crazy costumes, the slapstick bits—all of it was what had put the show on top in the first place.

The panic was on. Rather than a fight to build back the ratings, the network, the agency, and the sponsor wanted a change, wanted me to become something I wasn't. To this day, I'm sorry I went along with them and abandoned the vaudeville format of the show.

To give Myron Kirk credit, he lined up top talent to create the new Berle. Kirk brought in Goodman Ace, considered the best comedy writer in radio. The writers that Ace brought with him were Selma Diamond, George Foster, Mort Greene, and Jay Burton—all great. Our choreographer was a young dancer from the ballet world named Herbert Ross. I heard of a young guy just in from Chicago, Greg Garrison, and our show made him the hot new director.

What they came up with was very clever. I played a character named Berle who was caught up weekly in the trials and tribulations of putting on a television show. The people around me were Ruth Gilbert, who played my love-struck secretary, Max; Fred Clark, as my agent; and Arnold Stang. The only trouble was that I was not the Milton Berle of the crazy costumes and all the zany schticks my audiences had come to expect. I was everybody's straight man.

While to this day I have the greatest respect for Goody Ace as a comedy writer, he was not a writer for the sort of comedy that the character "Milton Berle" made people think of. Goody Ace was more suited to the humor of a Fred Allen, or the acid of a Tallulah Bankhead, for whom he had written *The Big Show* on radio for two years.

That, I think, was my big worry about Goody Ace. He was a radio writer, and this was television. Whatever the *Star Theatre* had or had not been before, it was visual. But when Goodman Ace came to revamp the show, he had never written for television before. It would drive me crazy when I'd go up into the control room to check on how a dress rehearsal was going and find Goody sitting with his back to the television monitors. He was listening to the show as if it were on radio, when he should have been watching it. (Of course, I drove him crazy, too, by always telling him he had to make the jokes more "lappy." In time, he came to me and confessed he didn't know what the hell I was talking about, and I explained that I meant the jokes had to be laid right in the audience's lap.)

But the truth was that while the show he and his colleagues were writing certainly had jokes and funny situations, you could listen to it without looking—like too much of today's television—and get most of everything that was going on.

On September 16, 1952, the show moved to the Center Theater on Sixth Avenue just off Rockefeller Center, and the ratings did come up during the season of 1952–53. The critics were happy with the revamped show (Jack Gould wrote in *The New York Times*, "It is not every player who will try to mend his ways in Macy's window"), but I wasn't completely comfortable working with a Milton Berle I didn't know.

Mama was seventy-four, almost seventy-five. She wouldn't admit she was slowing down, but she was. She no longer came to every show, and Rosalind took over her laugh in the audience. She was starting to have trouble with her eyes. Cataracts were forming. But these were things you could find out for yourself only if you knew her well. Mama wasn't a complainer. She was still too busy living—but it was on a slower pace.

For the hell of it, just because it would please her, Ruth and I told her to pack her best stuff, and we took her with us for a weekend down to Miami Beach, where we planned to catch Billy Daniels's opening at the Casablanca Hotel.

Mama spent all day Saturday at the beauty parlor getting the works: a blue-gray rinse, manicure, pedicure. That night, Queenie was riding high, making her big entrance into the club with her sable coat and all her best jewelry. And when Billy Daniels introduced her—"And now, ladies and gentlemen, I want you to meet one of the greatest ladies in show business"—Mama got up looking younger than she had in years. She loved taking bows, and it was as if Billy had given her a transfusion.

When she sat down, Billy said, "I would like to dedicate my final song to you, Mrs. Berle."

The lights dimmed, and he started singing "My Yiddishe Momme." Mama put up with the syrupy lyrics until Billy got to:

> *How few were her pleasures.*
> *She never cared for fashion's style.*
> *Her jewels and treasures,*
> *She found them in her baby's smile.*

That's when she leaned over to me and whispered, "I wonder who the hell he's singing about."

Comedians don't make great audiences. We're too busy listening to how a joke is told, how it can be improved on. But Ruth had a sharp sense of humor, and she could break me up. I think that was another reason I was falling deeply in love with her. I once took her to a baseball game, got seats right down front behind home plate. Ruth had her team picked out, and, as with everything she did, she was passionately involved in cheering them on to victory.

It was the ninth inning, and her team had the bases loaded. There were two men out. The tension was fierce. The next man at bat popped up. The ball came back toward the screen right in front of us. The catcher threw himself against the screen to catch the ball. He missed it, and as the ball fell to the ground, Ruth jumped to her feet, screaming, "Oh, beautiful!"

And there she was, almost eyeball to eyeball, only the screen separating them, with the catcher, a huge man who was glaring at her. Without a pause, Ruth started singing, "Oh, beautiful for spacious skies . . ."

Another Ruth story: We were at a party for Jan Murray. After dinner, a bunch of us guys got to talking about the war years, 1943, '44, '45, and reminiscing about where we were. I said I had been in the *Ziegfeld Follies*. Jan talked about La Martinique. Jerry Lewis had been doing a record act at the Havana Madrid. Danny Thomas recalled coming to New York from the 5100 Club in Chicago. Ruth was silent through the whole thing. Finally, she said one sentence: "I'm the only one here who was in the service."

But falling in love with Ruth wasn't all fun. There were hate letters that I received: "You're making a great mistake. You should never have left Joyce." "If you marry Ruth Cosgrove, it'll never last." The letters were never signed. I guessed the writers were some of Joyce's friends, but I could never pin them down. To this day, I don't know if Ruth ever received any letters. I once asked her, but all I got was a funny smile.

Our other problem was Vicki. When she came to spend weekends with me, she resented having Ruth around. Vicki was only seven, and neither of us blamed her for seeing Ruth as a threat to her security. Ruth worked hard at establishing a friendship with Vicki, but Vicki sulked and fought it. To give Ruth great credit, she never lost her patience with Vicki. It really did hurt Ruth more than Vicki when Ruth had to spank her. Joyce had told Ruth that if Vicki was naughty she should be punished. And so Vicki got it once. It didn't make her like Ruth more.

I tried to talk to Vicki, but it didn't really work. How much could she understand at seven? When I finished talking about boyfriends and girlfriends, hoping I had gotten through, Vicki said, "Yes, but why does she have to be here?"

Poor Vicki was having a rough time at both ends of her world. If she came to me, there was Ruth. With Joyce, there was Billy Rose.

Texaco ended its sponsorship in June of 1953, and Buick took it over for the '53–'54 season. It would be the show that Goody Ace had created the previous season.

I played Las Vegas that summer and then went on to fill some engagements in San Francisco and Los Angeles. I was out there when I heard about Mama. She had gone up to the Concord in the Catskills, and because of her cataracts she had missed a step and fallen, chipping a bone in her ankle. I would have canceled everything and flown back to be with her if I had been told about it right away. Maybe that's why the news was kept from me.

By the time I got back to New York, Mama was back in the Essex House, but holding her card games from a wheel chair. Mama patted the arm of the chair. "Don't even look at this, Milton. It's only temporary."

"Sure, Queenie. If the Shuberts couldn't stop you, it'll take more than an ankle."

Mama took my hand. "That's what I want to talk to you about, Milton. The years are flying. I'm no spring chicken anymore."

I put my hand on her mouth. "I don't want to talk about such things."

Mama brushed my hand away. "We've got to talk. Things have to be said. One day there won't be any more time to talk. I can't last forever, Milton. Nobody can."

"You're just feeling sorry for yourself because of your ankle. But the doctor says . . ."

Mama smiled. "When did you ever know me to feel sorry for myself, Milton? Why should I? I've had the best. You gave it to me. But we've got to talk about the family, Milton, and what's to come."

I got out a cigar and took a lot of time unwrapping it and clipping the end. I couldn't look at Mama.

"I look back on all those years with you, Milton, and I wonder how it could have been different. How I could have stretched myself more so that your brothers and sister could have had more mother in their lives. But even today I don't see how. What was had to be. Maybe I have regrets today for the hurt I done them, but yesterday—right or wrong—is over."

"Mama, you know we all love you. They understand."

"I hope. But I want you to promise me, Milton, that you'll take care of your brothers and sister. You're the youngest boy, but still you're the head of the family. You have to be."

"Sure, Mama. You know I will."

"Promise me, Milton. Promise. I have to know."

"I promise."

Mama gave a big smile, and did a couple of tap steps with her fingers on the arms of her wheelchair. "See? I feel better already."

I didn't. I knew Mama was speaking the truth about what was ahead for her. But she had planted new guilt within me toward my brothers and sister, guilt which was to eat at me for the rest of my life.

Jed Weston died in the fall of 1953. I hadn't known Jed well enough to feel deeply about his death, but I read every paper I could get my hands on for anything about my son. There was nothing in them I didn't know. The boy was fourteen; his mother was Linda Smith Weston, the actress. A couple of days later, one of the papers had a picture of Larry at the funeral, but his head was down. He looked sort of skinny and tall, and he had dark hair. There was no mention of Linda turning up for the funeral.

With Jed dead, and Linda missing and maybe dead, I knew Larry was a closed chapter in my life.

The *Buick-Berle Show* was Nielsen-rated a very healthy 52.7 in October 1953. Even so, we were in the fifth spot in nationwide popularity, behind *Lucy*, leading the pack with 65.9, and followed by *Dragnet*, the *Colgate Comedy Hour*, and *Racket Squad*. Bucking me in my time slot was Gene Autry for the first half-hour, and Red Skelton for the second.

By December, we had moved up to number three. Television was becoming really big time now, and the soft spots—those nothing shows that channels used to put on to fill out an evening—were disappearing. Tension around the show grew even more fierce.

Ruth and I decided to get married. We set the day for December 9, 1953, a Wednesday, the day after my television show. The first person I told was Mama. She was no longer in the wheelchair, but she was thinner than I had ever seen her before. When I told her, she said, "I was expecting it."

"Ruth's a great girl, Mama. She makes me very happy."

I could see Mama's confusion in her eyes. She knew the years had caught up with her. She wasn't part of "our act," as she thought of it, anymore. The time had come to let go, but Mama didn't know how. It was the one thing she hadn't learned through all the wild and wonderful years we had spent together—how to lose.

I think Mama liked Ruth as much as she could like any woman who would take her son, and the limelight he carried with him that Mama loved so much, away from her. But she also knew that all of the old ammunition she once could have fought with was gone. She kissed me. "Just be happy," she said.

It was harder to tell Vicki. It must have seemed to her that her world was falling apart around her. The Mommy and Daddy she saw every day suddenly were in two different places, and she could see only one at a time. And Vicki didn't know why she wasn't enough for either one of them. Mommy was all caught up with Billy Rose and hoping he would marry her. And now I had to tell her that her other rock had found someone he needed. It was an awful lot for a seven-year-old to understand.

I tried my best to explain to her about love and marriage, but Vicki kept interrupting. "But why, Daddy? I could take care of you, honest." "But you wouldn't be lonely. I come to see you all the time."

I ended up weakly, just telling her that there would come a time when she would be grown up and understand, and that I didn't love her less because I loved Ruth, and how much it would mean to me if she could learn to like Ruth, because Ruth liked her and really wanted to be her friend.

I got a teary kiss and a hug, and a promise that Vicki would try.

Two nights before the wedding, the Friars Club of New York—the theatrical club I had served as Abbot—gave me a bachelor dinner I'll never forget. It was the dirtiest, filthiest, funniest evening of my life. The only really embarrassing parts of the whole thing were the references to the coming wedding night, because I had brought Mike Rosenthal, Ruth's father, to the stag as my guest.

When it was over, Mike and I, along with Goody Ace, who was also there, went to meet Ruth and her mother, Sophie, over at Lindy's. When we came in, Goody's first words to Ruth were "Hello, Ruth. We were just talking about you." Mike and I couldn't stop laughing, and we refused to explain.

Ruth and I were married at City Hall by Judge Moe Eder. Vicki was our flower girl, and she pretended through the whole thing that our wedding was one of her dreams come true. Our reception at the Plaza, when we first had decided on it, had been planned for about sixty people. By the time the day came, we had thrown away the guest list and just told the Plaza to keep the champagne coming. Everybody, from mobsters to stars, including my favorite waiters from Lindy's, showed up. We didn't know it at the time, but this was Mama's last big party—and I will always love Ruth for refusing to name the day until Mama's ankle was healed —but with the mobs of friends around her, the champagne, and the music, Mama carried on as if it were her first.

From the reception, Ruth and I flew to Miami for a week's honeymoon. Then it was back to New York—a five-room apartment on the East Side—and work.

As the movies had done several decades before, television was starting to move west. The networks were building "television cities" around Los Angeles, and the movie studios were becoming television studios. It was decided that the last six shows of the *Buick-Berle Show* season would be telecast from California, from the studio I had designed for NBC in Burbank. Ruth and I moved into the Beverly Hills Hotel. I did four of the shows, and was into the rehearsals for the fifth show when the phone call came. To this day, I can't remember who called. I kept saying, "No. No. No." over and over again. And then I just sat there with the telephone receiver in my hand, staring at nothing. Ruth came over and took it away from me, and said, "Hello." She listened and then hung up the phone.

Mama was dead.

On the evening of May 31, 1954, Mama had called her best friend and card-playing buddy, Len DeGoff, from her apartment at the Essex House. "Get dressed up, Len. Eddie Fisher is doing a concert at Carnegie Hall, and we're going."

When Len came over, Mama was ready and waiting, her blue-rinsed hair freshly set, the diamonds in place, and a fur stole on the table by the door. Only Mama was sitting down, and there was pain on her face.

"Are you all right, Sandra?" Len asked.

Mama said, "A headache."

"Is it bad?"

"I think the blood pressure is up. Anyway, I took something."

Len said, "Look, Sandra, this isn't the only time Eddie Fisher will ever sing. I don't think we should go."

No one ever told Mama "don't." She stood up. "Eddie's a darling boy. I don't want to disappoint him."

So they went to the Eddie Fisher concert. And the headache didn't go away. Mama came home to the Essex House and died of a cerebral hemorrhage.

Just as if he had nothing else to do in the world, no other demands on his time, Bob Hope was there to take over the show for me. Tony Martin, Red Skelton, and Ray Bolger also pitched in. Ruth, Rosalind, and I flew east.

I took charge of the funeral arrangements for Wednesday, June 2, at the Riverside, on Amsterdam Avenue at 76th Street. I went through the whole thing numb, knowing what I was doing, yet not facing it, a part of me pretending this was a show I was staging.

I broke down only once. That was when Roz and I went to Mama's apartment, so that Roz could get the dress Mama was to be buried in. She had once told Roz that when she died, she wanted Roz to see that she was buried in her blue lace dress and with a strand of pearls. It was when Roz went out of the bedroom to pack the dress and pearls that I suddenly started crying. I was surrounded by Mama. The closets were full of her. Her extra pair of glasses were still on her night table. I even thought I could smell the cologne she liked in the air. I pressed my face against the wall behind the bedroom door and cried without control.

I was in control again by the funeral. I was able to help my brothers and sister through it, while keeping myself back in that protective fog I had created. The service seemed like a show I had staged for Mama to star in, and all the people there were her fans.

She was buried at Mount Eden in Westchester, next to my father. I had to smile when we brought Mama there, because I looked over at my father's headstone, and thought, "Look who's back, Pa." At last, Mama and Pa had time to spend together.

After the funeral, we all went back to my apartment, and Ruth's father, Mike, who was more religious than any of us Berles, said we should say *kaddish*, the prayer for the dead. The trouble was that when he had passed out the prayer books—I had to read the English from the right side —we realized that there were only nine men present, and the Jewish religion required ten for a *minyan*. Just then my uncle Mickey Cohen— the man who had introduced me to the pleasure of losing on the ponies —came in. Only, he wasn't wearing a hat, and the religion requires that the head be covered during prayer. I ran to the hall closet and grabbed my hat, a 7⅜ and gave it to my uncle, a short man only about five feet four. He put the hat on, and Mike began the *kaddish*.

I happened to look up during the reading, and there was Uncle Mickey with no eyes. The hat was down over them, resting on the bridge of his nose. I started to laugh, and I got a dirty look from Mike Rosenthal, and I got a shove from my brother, Phil, who was standing in front of Uncle Mickey. I nudged Phil to turn around and look at him. Phil started laughing too.

When *kaddish* was over, Mike came over to me. "You ought to be ashamed of yourself. It's disrespectful to be laughing."

"Wait a minute, Mike," I said, "I want to show you something."

I got hold of Uncle Mickey and had him put the hat on again. Of course, Mike laughed. We all did, and I said, "If Mama was here—and she is here—she would have laughed harder than all of us."

Ruth and I went to Europe at the end of June. We were in Paris, and some friends were going to take us nightclubbing. That's how I ended up shopping with Ruth. She needed an evening bag. Why she needed me along, I don't know, but I went.

Ruth stopped short in her tracks in front of a little store window. "That's what I've always wanted," she said, and pointed to some bags that didn't look so special to me.

"What's so great about them?" I asked.

"That's petit point," Ruth said. "All those little stitches are done by hand."

We went in, and Ruth looked at all the bags before she chose one. I figured that was it, when Ruth said, "Milton, give me one of your cigars."

I didn't know what the hell she was up to, but I handed her one. Ruth took it, opened the bag, and put the cigar in. The bag wouldn't close. Ruth said, "I'm afraid it won't do." She tried the cigar in several of the other petit-point bags. They were all too small. She ended up choosing a black silk bag that fit my cigar.

That night, when we were getting dressed, Ruth took the cigars out of my dinner jacket pocket and put them in her purse. "Now you won't look so lumpy when we go out." I've called her my "humidorable" ever since.

It's crazy that a little thing like that should mean so much to me. I had to leave her and go into the bathroom to wipe away the tears in my eyes. I think that for the first time in my life I really knew what love was about. For the first time, there was someone in my life I didn't find myself looking at and wondering, "Is it me or is it Milton Berle? What if it all ended tomorrow and I was just Milton Berlinger?"

Maybe that's why I decided to buy Ruth the goddamnedest present she'd ever gotten.

I hit all the top jewelers in Paris looking for something really sensational for Ruth. Finally, I found it at Van Cleef and Arpels: a tiara—hell, it was almost a crown—that was wall-to-wall diamonds, with a couple of rubies and emeralds tossed in to dress it up a little. I was told that, though it really wasn't certain, it was believed that this tiara had once belonged to a Romanov.

It cost a fortune, but wasn't Ruth worth it? I bought it.

When Ruth opened the velvet box, she said, "Oh my God!" which could have meant anything.

I said, "You like it?"

And Ruth, who doesn't know how to lie, said, "Milton, darling, it's fantastic, but what am I going to do with it? Where would I ever wear a thing like that?"

I hadn't thought about that. But I did think of what I had gone through at the store until I found the tiara. "Look," I said, "I'm not going back there to return it. Not in a million years."

"Don't worry," Ruth said. "I'll take care of it."

The next morning it was raining hard, but that didn't stop Ruth. In her slicker, with a scarf over her hair, she didn't look very much like Mrs. Milton Berle or a lady with a Romanov tiara. The clerk refused to unlock the front door for her. He motioned her to the back entrance.

The clerk was most apologetic when she identified herself. She handed him the tiara. "Surely, Mrs. Berle, there can't be anything wrong with this fabulous piece. Have you noticed how carefully the stones have been matched for color and brilliance?"

Ruth said, "I agree. It's stunning, but I just can't use it."

He said, "But why?"

And Ruth said, "I already have one just like it at home."

While we were in Europe, we decided to go over to Italy. Because I can't go anywhere without a cigar in my hand, I put all the cigars I had brought to Paris with me in a suitcase. I think I took about five hundred with us. But the inspector at Customs coming into Rome said I was allowed to bring in only one hundred cigars. The rest would have to be confiscated.

God bless Ruth. Like a shot, she took one of my cigars out of her purse, stripped off the cellophane, and asked for a light.

That got me an extra one hundred cigars into Italy. But they confiscated all of Ruth's cigarettes.

We got back to New York in the middle of August, 1954. There was just enough time to unpack before Ruth and I headed up to Saratoga for the races.

Even though I had figured out that through the years I had lost at least three million dollars on the horses, I still wasn't cured.

On Saturday, August 28, we went to the running of the Hopeful Stakes. Like a maniac, I bet $20,000 on Nashua, the favorite, to win. He went off at 11 to 20. My heart started pounding when the horses came out of the starting gate. By the time Nashua came into the home stretch, neck and neck with Summer Tan, the pounding of my heart was all I could hear. When they announced Nashua as the winner, I collapsed.

When I came to, I was certain I had had a heart attack, but it was just the tension that had gotten to me. For my $20,000, I got back $11,000 plus my original wager. It wasn't worth it, emotionally, and finally I took the pledge. I haven't bet on a horse since.

Just before the fall 1954 television season began, Phil Silvers came to town, and Ruth and I had dinner with him. "What are you doing now?" I asked.

"I'm going back into television with a situation comedy."

I said, "So I heard. What's it about?"

"It's called *You'll Never Get Rich*. I play an Army sergeant named Bilko. Nat Hiken created it."

"Nat's a genius. I worked with him on radio years ago. You got a time slot yet?"

Phil looked uncomfortable. "Uh huh. Tuesday nights at eight thirty on CBS."

"Oh, Jesus, Phil. Why did you let them do that to you?"

Well, Phil didn't do it to me, at least not at first. At the beginning, his show died during my second half-hour. It wasn't until November that Phil's show started to cut in, and cut in deep. Then CBS switched him to eight o'clock. Between Phil Silvers on CBS and Bishop Fulton J. Sheen on the Dumont network, the *Buick-Berle Show* was getting attacked from both sides.

On top of that, there were "new" comedy faces making an impact on television. Jackie Gleason was rising fast in the ratings game. Jackie and I had had our beefs in the past, and with variety shows on television fighting for acts, we were still having them. Yet of all the many things that have been written or said about me throughout my career, it was Jackie Gleason, in an interview with Louis Sobol, who touched me most deeply:

I turned the conversation to his then current hassle with Milton Berle, observing that Berle's rating was dropping while Phil Silvers' was going up. "He's fading. The champ's ready for the towel," jeered a denigrator at our table.

Gleason turned serious. "Don't say that," he snapped. "This guy Berle was up there for seven long years, the Number One man. Seven years! That's a couple of lifetimes in this teevee racket. How many guys you think there are now—name any of them—me, too—who will be up there, blasting away with the funny stuff and holding on to the top like Berle did? I'm not in love with the guy, but he's got it, and he's still Mr. Big in my book.

"Tell you something else. Wasn't for Berle, a lot of us wouldn't have got a break either. When he became Mister Television, those network guys began saying: 'We gotta get comics. They want funny stuff. Let's get funnymen.' Whatever else you say about Berle, don't forget that. And don't count him out, don't ever count him out. He'll be in there pitching for a long time."*

*Louis Sobol, *The Longest Street* (Crown, 1968), p. 289.

I went into the 1954–55 season feeling good. Maybe there were newer faces than mine coming up on television, but I had a twenty-six-week vote of confidence in my pocket from Buick. The Nielsen ratings for the end of September put us in second spot with 50.1, just behind the leader, *Dragnet,* with 51.2

Fall had just set in. I was walking over to the Center Theater to begin the day's rehearsals for the fourth show of the season. I stopped at a corner newsstand and picked up one of the trade papers, and there it was: "BUICK SIGNS GLEASON."

I had been axed. The man swinging it was Myron Kirk, good old Mike Kirk, who had "discovered" me for Gillette in 1936, and "discovered" me for television in 1948.

It's one thing to fail, but not before you take the test. And what hurt most of all was that Myron Kirk didn't even have the decency to tell me to my face. I had to buy a paper to find out that I was going off television for Buick at the end of the year.

How the hell do you get through the rest of the your season knowing that? The answer is, you do.

The last show took place on June 14, 1955—even the Center Theater was scheduled to come down after we vacated—and while I felt depressed, at least the edge was off it. I had already signed with RCA Whirlpool and Sunbeam to do the first color series from California over the cable for the 1955–56 season.

Ruth and I decided that we would move to California. It was where so many of our friends had gone; it was where television was going.

I suppose it was a new beginning—a new *Milton Berle Show,* California, color—but it didn't feel that way to me. For me, what had begun in 1948 with Texaco was ending in 1955 with Buick. Whatever instinct there was in me that made me want television when other entertainers avoided it now gave me the feeling of the end of something. The hour variety show with star names was getting tougher and tougher to do. The unions were in, costs were mounting, star acts had learned the value of television and were demanding more. But most of all, I worried about myself.

I had violated one of my basic rules of work. For years I had told new young comics that they had to decide on their own personal image before they worked, and that they must never violate that image in the public's mind. A Jack Benny, a George Burns, or a Lucille Ball could roar with laughter at a joke and then refuse to use it because it didn't fit the image.

But when I had cooperated with Goodman Ace and the men of Madison Avenue and turned the aggressive, pushy "Milton Berle" into a passive straight man for the "Buick" format, I had broken my image and hurt myself, even when the ratings went up.

I had to go back to the "Milton Berle" I had always played, the one I was comfortable with, but I knew it was not going to go over with the impact it once had had. It would take time for the original "Berle" to regain credibility.

What I got in California was a good season, a class show, but that was about it. There were other television shows after that. I did the *Kraft Music Hall* (1958–59) and then a half-hour game show called *Jackpot Bowling* (1960–61). And then there was nothing for me in television.

26

Don't get me wrong. I wasn't hurting. Financially, I was as sound as the mint. And as far as work goes, I had plenty of it. I played Las Vegas every year. I did other nightclubs, made *Let's Make Love*, with Marilyn Monroe and Yves Montand, and I had television offers. But just offers. Because I couldn't accept them. I had a thirty-year exclusive contract with NBC. I either worked for them on television or for nobody.

On December 27, 1961, while I was appearing at the Flamingo in Las Vegas, Ruth got a telephone call. It was from a nurse at the hospital where the child we were to adopt was going to be born. It was a boy, and he was ours.

Ruth flew back to Los Angeles, and with our good friend Bobby Van, went to bring our son home. We had decided on his name before I left for Las Vegas. It would be William Michael Berle—William for our friend, director Billy Wilder, who would be our son's godfather, and Michael for Ruth's father, who had passed away. It was on December 31 that the hospital said Billy could come home. However, when Ruth showed up with Bobby Van, the nurse said she couldn't have him. "I don't think it's right. Both parents should be here."

Ruth explained that I was away working. The nurse still didn't want to release Billy.

And that did it for Ruth, who had seen Billy and was already in love with him. People didn't horse around with ex-Captain Cosgrove. Ruth went wild. She grabbed the nurse by the neck and slammed her against the wall. "You give me my baby, or I'll kill you!"

Why Ruth became a mother that day instead of a convict, I'll never know, but she got Billy.

Bobby Van drove them home to Beverly Hills. As they went along the Sunset Strip, Ruth spotted a large sign over the street. "Please stop a minute," she said.

Bobby pulled over to the curb and Ruth got out. The sign said, "Now Appearing At The Flamingo—Milton Berle," and there was a huge picture of me. Ruth held the baby up toward the sign. "Look, Billy, that's your daddy!"

I flew in on New Year's Day to meet my son, and I've been in love with him ever since.

But why is it that so many of the happy moments in life are tied to pain? On the night of January 13, 1962, when I was back in Beverly Hills, Audrey and Billy Wilder gave Ruth a shower in honor of the arrival of Billy, their godson. Among the guests were Ernie Kovacs and his wife, Edie Adams. They came in separate cars, because Ernie was working late that night on a television pilot.

It was after one in the morning when the party broke up. Ernie told Edie he would drive home in the station wagon, a car he wasn't too familiar with. Shortly before two in the morning, he smashed into a power pole on Santa Monica Boulevard near the Beverly Hilton Hotel. Ernie was killed instantly. When they found him, there was an unlit cigar in his hand. The guess was that he was fumbling around in the strange car to find the lighter, and he lost control of the wheel on the wet road.

Ruth and I were at the airport in San Francisco. The limousine that we had ordered in advance wasn't there. I went over to the Avis counter to find out where the car was. The girl said to me, "Aren't you Phil Silvers?"

I glared at her and said, "That's why you're number two."

Ruth and I laughed about it at the time, but the story lost its humor the more I thought about it. How quickly the public forgets.

Not that I wasn't working. The years couldn't have been busier. I was appearing in Vegas and doing summer packages of my nightclub show across the country. I introduced theater to Las Vegas with *Never Too*

Late. I made *It's a Mad, Mad, Mad, Mad World* for Stanley Kramer. I had gotten an Emmy nomination for my performance in *Doyle Against the House* on the Dick Powell television show.

But for every television appearance I made, there were two that I was offered that I had to turn down because of the NBC exclusivity contract. On May 21, 1965, I signed an agreement with NBC, taking a 40 per cent cut—to $120,000 a year—for the freedom to appear on any network I wanted to.

The next year I did *The Milton Berle Show.* With a format that was a forerunner of the *Laugh-In* show. It was not a roaring success on ABC (and, as I later told a friend, "The way to end the Vietnam war is to put it on ABC—it'll be over in thirteen weeks!"), and after that *The Hollywood Palace.*

A slew of movies—*The Oscar, The Loved One, The Happening, Who's Minding the Mint?* I toured with plays—*The Impossible Years, The Last of the Red Hot Lovers,* and *Norman, Is That You?*—and I showed up briefly on Broadway in Herb Gardner's play, *The Goodbye People.*

I've done guest appearances on almost every comedy and dramatic show on television. The years have been good to me.

Yet I remember the night of July 12, 1968. There had been a party that Ruth gave for my sixtieth birthday. But now it was late at night. Ruth was getting ready for bed, and I was alone in our living room having a last cigar.

Sixty is a time to think about it. You don't pass that one lightly. The first thought that crossed my mind was the time someone said something to George Burns about retiring, and he answered, "Retire to what?"

I knew what he meant. I looked at myself and realized that maybe I was the American Dream and Horatio Alger rolled into one. Poor kid works his way up to rich man. Happy ending.

Only I wasn't happy. And I wondered if I had ever been happy. What was I missing? I couldn't figure it out.

With Ruth I had found love to last a lifetime. Vicki had become Mrs. James Nokes, and she was happy. (She's made me a proud grandfather twice.) Billy was a joy to me. I was still working, still wanted. Name it and I had it.

Except that whatever it is that makes a man happy was missing in me. Or maybe I should say, in all of us Berlingers, with the exception of Mama who relished every minute of her life. The circumstances under which

Moe and Sarah's kids grew up left me racked with guilt, and I think left my brothers and sister frustrated, and maybe feeling cheated because of Mama's concentration on me. But I can only guess about that, because they all keep their hurts to themselves. I can only hope it wasn't the way I think it was for them. I especially hope so for my brother Frank who died in May of 1973. He had been both my friend and my brother all of my life. He deserved happiness.

I'm still searching for an answer, still running to the next show, still coming alive under the lights, still making love to an audience that I know will go home to make love to one another and leave me alone again. When I am on the road I think of Billy and Ruth, and I want to be with them so badly that I hurt inside. Yet, when I am home for more than a week, I pace the room like a trapped animal, worrying about when I go to work again.

I realize now that I spent my whole life working for the jackpot, only to find out when I won that there was no payoff for me. I had paid too much along the way for the prize to have any meaning to me.

I guess I've made all the dreams that Mama and I had come true, but I spent so many years chasing those dreams that I don't know how to stop running.

And if I did stop, what would I stop for? Retire to what? As a kid, I loved reading, but too many years have passed since then. I've lost the pleasure and the patience for it. I'm a rotten spectator at a play or a movie, because I can't turn off my performer's critical eye. I play a little golf, but I don't really have the patience for it. All sports, to me, are something you do for relaxation when you're not working. But if I'm not working, how can I relax? And as for people, I'm shy of them, unless they are old friends in the business. People with homes and regulated lives make me nervous, because I don't know what to say to them, what to talk about. I don't understand their lives, because I've never had what they've got. The idea of approaching tomorrow with peace because you know it will be like today is something I've never known. I guess it must be great, but I wouldn't know.

There's one more story. Every year in May, the big charity event in the Los Angeles area is the SHARE show. It's held at the Santa Monica Civic Auditorium. The women of Beverly Hills rehearse for months for this $100-a-plate evening which benefits retarded children. Everybody turns out in western costumes for the night.

Whenever I'm in town in May, I always go, because Ruth works so hard on the evening. This one particular year—it was in the '70s—I was wandering from table to table after the show, talking with friends, like Walter and Carol Matthau, Roz Russell and Freddie Brisson, John Wayne, Felicia and Jack Lemmon. I forget whom I was with, but we were deep into something when this tall, thin young man—he looked about twenty-eight or thirty to me—joined our group. There was so much noise that I didn't catch his name, but I didn't get the impression that anybody in our crowd knew him too well.

Anyway, my feet hurt, and I was tired, and I felt the beginning of a headache, and I wanted to get home. Maybe that explains why I sort of ignored the kid. And when he started talking business to me, I was really annoyed. He said, "It's funny meeting you this way, Mr. Berle. I mean, we've been talking about you a great deal for this television series we're readying for a pilot . . ."

Everybody in California has a pilot they are "readying" for television, so I wasn't overly impressed. "Sure, sure," I said, "but I've got lots of commitments for my time. Anyway, you don't want to talk to me, young man. Get in touch with Danny Welkes, who handles my work."

I turned away from him. I guess he sensed my annoyance, because when I turned back a minute later, he was gone.

As we were leaving the auditorium, I said to Ruth, "The nerve of that kid. I'll bet he doesn't even have the facilities to make a pilot. Probably an office boy . . ."

Someone in our crowd said, "You've got to be kidding."

"Why? I didn't even catch his name."

He told me the name of the kid's company. They already had one series on television that was doing very well. "I thought you knew who he was. Remember Jed Weston, who used to be very big out here in the thirties and forties? That's his son, Larry."

I stopped short. Ruth grabbed my arm. "What's the matter? Are you all right, darling? Is something wrong?"

I nodded that I was okay. But I couldn't speak.

I hung around the house for almost a whole week after that, hoping that it would be my son every time the phone rang.

Then I started bugging my manager to call and set up an appointment for me with Larry Weston about the pilot. Whatever the series he had in mind, I would do it. But the word came back that Mr. Weston had signed someone else, and he was no longer interested in me.

*   *   *

On the night of October 13, 1973, the Friars Club of California honored me with a banquet for my sixtieth year in show business. Of all the great names that showed up and said kind things to me, it was Archbishop Fulton J. Sheen who moved me most, when he said:

> . . . *I think that anyone who is full of life loves repetition. For example, a child. A child is full of life. You put a child on your knee and tell the child a story, the child will say, "Do it again." You blow smoke through your nose or through your ears, and the child will say, "Do it again." And God is full of life, and every morning He says to the sun, "Do it again," and every evening He says to the moon and stars, "Do it again," and every time a child is born into the world, He asks for a divine encore and says, "Do it again." And, Milton, for sixty years you've entertained us, and you've made us laugh, and we say to you, "Milton, do it again."*

I want to.

But the next time, I want to laugh, too.

INDEX